The Political History of Modern Japan

Spanning the 130-year period between the end of the Tokugawa Era and the end of the Cold War, this book introduces readers to the formation, collapse, and rebirth of the modern Japanese state. It demonstrates how, faced with foreign threats, Japan developed a new governing structure to deal with these challenges and in turn gradually shaped its international environment. Had Japan been a self-sufficient power, like the United States, it is unlikely that external relations would have exercised such great control over the nation. And, if it were a smaller country, it may have been completely pressured from the outside and could not have influenced the global stage on its own. For better or worse therefore, this book argues, Japan was neither too large nor too small.

Covering the major events, actors, and institutions of Japan's modern history, the key themes discussed include:

- Building the Meiji state and Constitution.
- The establishment of Parliament.
- The First Sino-Japanese and Russo-Japanese Wars.
- Party Politics and International Cooperation.
- The Pacific War.
- Development of LDP politics.
- Changes in the international order and the end of the Cold War.

This book, written by one of Japan's leading experts on Japan's political history, will be an essential resource for students of Japanese modern history and politics.

Kitaoka Shinichi is President of Japan International Cooperation Agency and Professor Emeritus of the University of Tokyo and Rikkyo University, Japan.

The Political History
of Modern Japan

Foreign Relations and Domestic Politics

Kitaoka Shinichi
Translated by Robert D. Eldridge
with Graham Leonard

Routledge
Taylor & Francis Group

LONDON AND NEW YORK

JPIC

JAPAN LIBRARY

First published 2018
by Routledge
2 Park Square, Milton Park, Abingdon, Oxon OX14 4RN

and by Routledge
711 Third Avenue, New York, NY 10017

Routledge is an imprint of the Taylor & Francis Group, an informa business

© 2018 Kitaoka Shinichi

'Nihon seijishi: gaikō to kenryoku, zōhoban' by Kitaoka Shinichi

Copyright © Kitaoka Shinichi, 2011, 2017

Originally published in Japan by Yuhikaku Publishing Co., Ltd., Tokyo, in
2011 and 2017

English translation arranged with Yuhikaku Publishing Co., Ltd., through
Japan Publishing Industry Foundation for Culture (JPIC)

English translation copyright © Robert D. Eldridge with Graham Leonard, 2018

British Library Cataloguing-in-Publication Data
A catalogue record for this book is available from the British Library

Library of Congress Cataloging-in-Publication Data
A catalog record has been requested for this book

ISBN: 978-1-138-33765-7 (hbk)
ISBN: 978-1-138-33767-1 (pbk)
ISBN: 978-0-429-44223-0 (ebk)

Typeset in Times New Roman
by Apex CoVantage, LLC

Front cover photograph: The Former Prime Minister's Office. It was built
in 1929, at the peak of prewar party politics, but became the target of the
February 26th Coup D'état in 1936. This building had been the center of
Japanese politics until 2002 when the New Office was completed. It is still
used as the Prime Minister's Official Residence.

Cover image: © jiji

Contents

Key individuals

Kawaji Toshiakira (Chapter 2)
Fukuzawa Yukichi (Chapter 3)
Ōkubo Toshimichi (Chapter 4)
Itō Hirobumi (Chapter 5)
Yamagata Aritomo and the House of Peers and Privy Council (Chapter 6)
Mutsu Munemitsu (Chapter 7)
Gotō Shimpei (Chapter 8)
Hara Takashi (Chapter 9)
Shidehara diplomacy and Tanaka diplomacy (Chapter 10)
Ugaki Kazushige (Chapter 11)
Kiyosawa Kiyoshi (Chapter 12)
Yoshida Shigeru (Chapter 13)
Kishi Nobusuke (Chapter 14)

Figures

Tables

Notes on Japanese names and dates

Japanese names in this book are written following Japanese custom, that is, sur-
name followed by personal name. Years are in principle written using the Western
calendar, and dates are in principle based on Japanese time except for events that
happened in the United States, such as the signing of the Portsmouth Treaty and
the attacks on Pearl Harbor.

Preface to the English edition

This book is the English version to my *Nihon Seijishi: Gaikō to Kenryoku* [Political History of Modern Japan: Foreign Relations and Domestic Politics]. It was originally published in 2011, but I subsequently expanded it in 2017 to include a supplemental chapter on Japan's colonies and their fate after the Second World War. This English version includes the additional chapter.

The additional chapter was added based particularly on some scholarly experiences I had over the past decade and a half. For example, I participated in a Japan–South Korea joint historical research project, financially supported by the governments of both countries, beginning in 2002 for two years. And for three years beginning in 2006, I participated in a similar joint research project with China, supported by the Japanese and Chinese governments as the chairperson of the Japanese team. I was able to learn quite a deal and felt that it was the participants' dialogue on history rather than any particular book or research that was the most meaningful. Furthermore, in 2015, I served as the deputy chair of the Advisory Panel on the History of the 20th Century and on Japan's Role and World Order in the 21st Century (*20 Seiki o Furikaeri 21 Seiki no Sekai Chitsujo to Nihon no Yakuwari o Kōsō Tame no Yūshikisha Kondankai*), otherwise known as the Commission on a Framework for the 21st Century (*21 Seiki Kōsō Kondankai*), whose recommendations Prime Minister Abe Shinzō (1954–; in office 2006–2007, 2012–) referred to as he prepared his statement on the 70th anniversary of the end of the Second World War.[1]

This book was originally written for a Japanese audience. Thus, for the benefit of readers of the English language edition, published thanks to Routledge, I have decided to include additional notes and explanations to assist those who may not be aware of some of the historical information and personalities with which Japanese readers would naturally be familiar.

However, other than these modest additions, I have done nothing to change the original meaning of the text. This is because I have sought to eliminate, where unnecessary, cultural explanations and to focus on universal aspects in order to explain Japanese politics and diplomacy within this book. I have tried not to hide behind phrases like "Japanese style" or "typically Japanese."

Many of the events described in the book are already well-known. However, I believe I have presented some new interpretations amid the historical and geographic context of the time. With regard to these and other explanations, I have provided footnotes where interpretations differ, in cases where it is my own idea or that from another scholarly work. Sections where there is no serious academic disagreement I have left unfootnoted.

The path Japan has walked for the past 160 years has had a continuous and important impact on the world. Moreover, Japan's experiences have been rather unique and interesting. If the reader becomes more interested in modern Japan as a result of this book, I would have fulfilled my mission.

Kitaoka Shinichi
Tokyo, Japan

Note

1 Prime Minister Abe's statement was released on August 14, 2015, and is available in Japanese, English, Chinese, and Korean (http://japan.kantei.go.jp/97_abe/statement/201508/0814statement.html). The video of the prime minister's statement in Japanese is subtitled in Chinese as well.

Preface

The Political History of Modern Japan is both an historical analysis of modern Japanese political power and a history of modern times centered on this political power. Its focus is neither Japanese politics from ancient times nor an overview of the modern period. Moreover, it does not examine politics at the local or regional levels but instead addresses the questions of politics and political power at the central level. This originates, in my view, because modern nations possess the following certain characteristics.

First, modern states hold overwhelming power over the members of those states. In the middle of the seventeenth century, Hobbes described the absolutist state that was emerging as the Leviathan, the monster of the Bible. Today, it is even worse. The authority of the state reaches to every corner of people's lives, and the United States and Soviet Union during the Cold War each possessed the capability of destroying humanity with their nuclear weapons many times over. In no such period in the past has such power existed.

However, on the other hand, the authority of modern states cannot exist without the broad support of the people. With the political principle of power residing with the people that emerged toward the end of the eighteenth century, it has become necessary to involve the public proactively for the development of the nation, even in countries that do not accept that principle. In the modern states of today where the equal political participation of all citizens is guaranteed as a right and mass media has greatly developed, it is difficult to adopt policies that go against the public will.

Moreover, in modern nations, the difference between political pros and amateurs has become clear. As the work of the government dramatically increases, it is near impossible to handle the issues halfheartedly, and thus a lot of people have to be devoted full-time to politics. As a result, there is a professional group involved in politics made up of politicians and bureaucrats and an amateur group made up of the public that is responsible for monitoring their work.

One more characteristic was the close connection between foreign relations and domestic politics. For example, the Tang Dynasty (618–907) in China and the Roman Empire did not possess important diplomatic relations with one another, but with the Industrial Revolution and the development of trade, transportation, and communications technology, international relations have become very much intertwined. Today, no country can make important decisions exclusively on its own. No country can separate its domestic affairs from foreign affairs when considering matters, and, similarly, no country can make decisions about other countries without considering their internal dynamics. Modern nations not only exercise a lot of influence on other countries but are also affected by them as well.

This strength and concurrent weakness are connected with the formation and development of political power in modern nations. Clarifying this is one of the basic challenges of political history, within the field of political science. This is the reason that political history examines modern politics and political power at the central level.

Political history, interestingly, has not been a popular subject in the field of history until recently. As seen in the examples of Herodotus and Thucydides, historical studies began as political history. However, the field of political history, which focused on persons in authority, increasingly began to be criticized as behind the times. For example, history, the argument goes, is decided principally by economic power (according to Marxism, by production capability and production relations). From a long-term perspective, this may be correct. However, economic reasons alone cannot explain certain phenomena like the outbreak of war, for example. These short-term problems are what are most decisive in the contemporary age. Economic history itself is important, and it is a necessary to consider it in political history, but one cannot simply interchange political history for economic history. Major political decisions must be seen against the backdrop of important political dynamics. The same could be said for economic history and social history as well.

Other views place emphasis on the role of the people rather than on the power of a particular authority figure who wields the power. However, simply examining people's movements will not give you the full story when looking at significant political decisions, such as Japan's decision to go to war with the United States in 1941. Of course, it is important to highlight how difficult and often tragic people's lives are during war, but it is probably more important to understand how a war happened in the first place. Thus, a people's history cannot replace a political history.

In other words, while political history may seem to be old-fashioned or overly specialized, it is meaningful to recognize that the field of history began with political history. Since politics have an enormous impact on people's lives today, political history is even more important now.

The formation of the modern state in Japan begins with its encounter with the West in the Bakumatsu period. This book covers the 130-plus-year period between the end of the Tokugawa Era and the end of the Cold War and has as its subtitle, "Foreign Relations and Domestic Politics" because it examines the response of Japanese authorities to external problems. Faced with foreign threats in the mid-1850s, Japan developed a new governing structure to deal with them, and, in turn, this power ended up gradually influencing the international environment. The mutual effect on changes to the international environment and the restructuring of domestic political structures is a constant theme throughout modern Japanese political history and is something that continues to this day. If Japan were a major power that was self-sufficient like the United States, Japan would likely have not been influenced by its external relations as it in fact was. And, if it were a smaller country, it would have been completely pressured from outside and could not have, on its own, influenced things externally. For better or worse, Japan was neither too large nor too small.

It is difficult to avoid certain dangers on facts and interpretations for much more recent periods, such as the 1970s and 1980s. Nevertheless, by covering the years from Bakumatsu until the end of the Cold War as one overall period can possibly help readers to understand that they are involved in making contemporary history themselves. In addition, it might grow the ability of the reader to evaluate the politicians of today. This book was written with these intentions in an attempt to cover 130-plus years in a limited number of pages.

This book was published in 1989 with the same title as a textbook for the University of the Air, now known as Open University of Japan, a lifelong and distance education center that had begun accepting students in 1985.

There are probably two ways to go about writing a textbook. The first is to do so when one is young, relentlessly going about it unafraid, almost in one sitting. The other is to write it slowly, after many years of experience. With the former, it is written based on one's own judgment, and thus it might contain mistakes but be forceful. The latter might be somewhat profound, but it also could be banal at the same time. The book, as it was published in 1989, was of the former style, and I basically wrote it in one sitting.

Fortunately, the reviews were highly favorable, and the book was used not only in many universities as a textbook but also in some preparatory schools as well. Because it was a textbook for the University of the Air at the time, when I discontinued being a lecturer there, the book went out of print.

Afterward, I was asked many times by readers and editors to produce a revised edition. However, I was involved at this point with developing my own lectures and begged off, saying that I was making a more detailed textbook. However, after turning 50, I began to feel that it would be difficult to do. The more I studied, the more I felt I did not understand things. I increasingly lost confidence in the ability to judge events with conviction and came to think that an update of the textbook was difficult to produce.

What I thus decided to do was to do both. In other words, I greatly revised the earlier textbook, adding columns, charts, and other materials, while not changing the youthful style of writing. In addition, I committed to writing a longer textbook as well.

This approach was born through discussions with Mr. Seikai Yasushi, a veteran editor of Yūhikaku Publishing. I am deeply grateful for his patience in waiting for my ideas to be formulated, and I learned much from his comments. If there are any errors in the book, they rest with me as author.

As introduced in the preface to the original version, I was strongly influenced as a student and researcher by classes and seminars on Japanese political history. While the notes from these classes and discussions did not come from a particular book and am thus unable to introduce them in the bibliography, I wish to express my appreciation once again to the late Professor Satō Seizaburō and Professor Mitani Taiichirō who led those sessions.

Kitaoka Shinichi
Tokyo, Japan

About the author

Kitaoka Shinichi was born in Nara Prefecture in 1948. He graduated in 1971 from the Law Faculty of the University of Tokyo. He completed his doctoral course at the Graduate School of Law and Politics, University of Tokyo, in 1976, earning his PhD. He has been a professor at the College of Law and Politics, Rikkyo University, the Graduate School of Law and Politics, University of Tokyo, and the National Graduate Institute for Policy Studies, in addition to serving as the president of the International University of Japan before becoming the president of the Japan International Cooperation Agency in 2015. Between 2004 and 2006, he was the Ambassador Extraordinary and Plenipotentiary, Deputy Permanent Representative of Japan to the United Nations. In addition to being a professor emeritus of the University of Tokyo and Rikkyo University, he is also a recipient of the Japanese government's Medal with Purple Ribbons honoring his contributions to academia. His books include *Nihon Rikugun to Tairiku Seisaku, 1906–1918* Nen (The Japanese Army and Continental Policy, 1906–1918) (Tokyo: University of Tokyo Press, 1978); *Kiyosawa Kiyoshi* (Biography of Kiyoshi Kiyosawa) (Tokyo: Chūō Kōron-sha, 1987; Expanded Edition, Tokyo: Chūō Kōron Shinsha, 2004, winner of the Suntory Prize for Liberal Arts); *Nichibei Kankei no Riarizumu* (Realism in Japan–U.S. Relations) (Tokyo: Chūō Kōron-sha, 1991, winner of the Yomiuri Prize for the Opinion Leader of the Year, 1992); *Jimintō* (The Liberal Democratic Party of Japan: The 38 Years in Power) (Tokyo: The Yomiuri Shimbun, 1995; Tokyo: Chūō Kōron Shinsha, 2008, winner of the 1995 Yoshino Sakuzō Prize); *Dokuritsu Jison* (Independence and Self-Respect: Challenge by Yūkichi Fukuzawa) (Tokyo: Kodansha, 2002; Chūō Kōron Shinsha, 2011); *Kanryōsei to Shite no Nihon Rikugun* (The Japanese Army as Bureaucracy) (Tokyo: Chikuma Shobō, 2012); *Monko Kaihō Seisaku to Nihon* (The Open Door Policy and Japan) (Tokyo: University of Tokyo Press, 2015), and many others.

About the translators

Robert D. Eldridge is an award-winning author, editor, or translator of and contributor to approximately 70 books about U.S.–Japan relations, Japanese political and diplomatic history, Okinawa, and military basing issues. Among his translations are Miyazawa Kiichi's *Secret Talks between Tokyo and Washington* (Lexington, 2007), Iokibe Makoto's *The Diplomatic History of Postwar Japan* (Routledge, 2010), Watanabe Tsuneo's *Japan's Backroom Politics: Factions in a Multiparty Age* (Lexington, 2013), and Watanabe Akio's *The Prime Ministers of Postwar Japan: Their Lives and Times* (Lexington, 2016), among many others. Recent books include *The Origins of U.S. Policy in the East China Sea Islands Dispute: Okinawa's Reversion and the Senkaku Islands* (Routledge, 2014) and *The Japanese Ground Self-Defense Force: Search for Legitimacy* (Palgrave Macmillan, 2017, coedited with Paul Midford). He earned his doctorate at Kobe University and was a tenured associate professor at Osaka University. Currently he is affiliated with several universities, think tanks, and foundations in Japan.

Graham Leonard is an independent translator and researcher in the Seattle, Washington, area. He holds a MA in Japanese studies from the University of Washington and received a doctorate from Osaka University's School of International Public Policy as a Monbukagakusho Scholar. His primary research interests include the history of U.S.-Japan relations and modern Japanese history, especially as related to defense and alliance issues. He is currently researching the Fukuryū Maru Incident, and his publications include *Changing Security Policies in Postwar Japan: The Political Biography of Sakata Michita* (Lexington, 2017, cotranslated with Robert D. Eldridge) and "The 1954 Shunkotsu Maru Expedition and American Atomic Secrecy," *International Public Policy Studies*, Vol. 15, No. 2 (March 2011).

1 The political characteristics of the Tokugawa political system[1]

Comparisons of the West and the Tokugawa Japan

Sixteenth-century Japan and the West

Japan and the West have encountered each other twice through the course of history, first in the sixteenth century and again in the nineteenth. The impact of their first meeting was no less significant than that of their second: the introduction of firearms completely transformed the nature of contemporary Japanese warfare and played a decisive role in the country's unification. Christianity also began to spread rapidly throughout Japan; within 50 years of its introduction in 1549, there were more than 700,000 Japanese Christians (or more than 5% of the total population), while the current Christian population is under 1 million (or approximately 0.8% of the total population). The Shimabara Rebellion (1637–1638) was the final barrier to the Tokugawa's unification of Japan. Christians were the final obstacle to be overcome.

This Western influence was still limited enough to be controllable, however, as can be seen from Japan's ability to successfully implement its policy of *sakoku* (isolation).[2]

The nineteenth-century encounter, in which the West sought to bring Japan into international society, was different, however. The West was prepared to use force to achieve its goal, and Japan did not have the means to resist. There had evidently been major changes between their encounters in the intervening period. What were they?

To begin with, it has only been in the past few centuries that the West has become an advanced part of the world in various ways. Prior to this period, the Islamic world had been more advanced than Europe. The forces of Islam invaded the Iberian Peninsula in the eighth century and were only driven out in 1492. Moreover, the Ottoman Empire that lay to Europe's east only reached its peak under Sultan Süleyman I (1494–1566, reigned 1520–1566) and would continue to expand territorially until the 1680s.

And while the roots of Western society lie in Greek civilization and Christianity, both of these originated outside of Western Europe. The Renaissance – the starting point of the modern West – provided an opportunity for the European

Figure 1.1 Nagasakikō Fukan Saimitsu Ga (Depiction of Nagasaki Harbor). Dejima is in the center. (Circa 1818–1830. From the collection of the Nagasaki Museum of History and Culture.)

rediscovery of Greek civilization, but it had been the Islamic world, not the West, that had preserved this knowledge. Even as the West began to expand eastward; it was not carving out utterly new paths for itself as it did so. Rather, it was merely seeking new ways to the East as worsened relations with Islamic countries severed its existing routes.

This would serve as the prelude to Western global supremacy, however. The West would come to dominate the East for 400 years, beginning with the 1498 arrival of Vasco da Gama (c. 1469–1524) in Calicut. What the West sought at this time, however, was luxury goods like spices, not conquest. Trade took the form of monopolies held by the crown or trading companies (such as the British East India Company founded in 1600 and the Dutch East India Company founded in 1602). Expansion was thus abandoned fairly readily when they encountered strong local resistance or when trade profits were only meager. It was during this period that the first meeting between Japan and the West occurred.

Trade ceased to revolve around luxuries with the coming of the Industrial Revolution, however. Instead, it was believed that if China's massive population of four hundred million could be persuaded to purchase British textiles to even just a limited extent, it would be sufficient to guarantee eternal prosperity for the industry. This sort of "myth of the China market" spurred on new Western inroads into China. As monopolies had come to be regarded as little more than hindrances by this point, the British East India Company's monopolization of Indian trade was abolished in 1813 (followed shortly thereafter by the loss of its Chinese trade monopoly in 1833). And so the West came seeking to open Asian markets to Western goods, and it was prepared to use force if necessary, as was seen in the First Opium War (1840–1842). To Japan's great fortune, it was merely considered a small country on the periphery of China.

Western pluralism

Now, as previously mentioned, Western civilization was neither remarkably old nor remarkably original. It was instead its pluralistic nature, the way it incorporated diverse elements despite the tensions that might lie among them, that was its most distinctive feature. It was this diversity that allowed the West to achieve such rapid development over the course of the sixteenth to nineteenth centuries.

In the first place, Europe, an area roughly equivalent in size to China, has long been divided geographically into a number of countries such as England, France, Spain, Germany, and Italy. It's actually a bit strange, when you think about it, that, despite the many years that this situation has persisted, Europe has never been completely unified, nor has it become extremely fragmented.

This European pluralism extended from geography to its political structures as well. Feudal assemblies based on the estates of the realm existed in medieval Europe that limited the authority of the monarch. England's Magna Carta (1215) is a prominent example of such a limit. And although royal authority would later expand, especially beginning in the seventeenth century, strong resistance from the nobility remained. Before long, these feudal assemblies developed into modern legislatures. Institutions equivalent to these assemblies were a rarity in other world civilizations. The concept of the right of resistance, one of the major characteristics of Western civilization, originated with these bodies.

Another example of this pluralism was the relationship between religious and temporal authority. While it was common in most civilizations for one of these to absorb the other, the tense relationship between the authority of the Pope and that of kings served as a major characteristic of the West.

Yet another example would be the strained relationship between Christianity and Greek civilization. Despite being seemingly fundamentally incompatible with one another, neither was able to completely overcome the other; both played major roles in the formation of the Western world.

Simply put, this pluralism became the driving force behind the Western world's remarkably dynamic character. And this character is responsible in turn for the aggressive nature of Western civilization, the way it seeks to reshape the rest of the world in its own image.

The centralism of the Tokugawa political system

How did the characteristics of the Japanese society of the Edo period (1603–1868) differ from this? At first glance, Tokugawa society would seem to possess a number of qualities reminiscent of the feudal system of medieval Europe. Certainly, many foreigners thought so at the time. But despite these seeming similarities, the concept of feudalism doesn't particularly suit Edo Japan well in a number of ways.

Under feudalism, a lord provides a reward, such as territory, to his vassals in exchange for their loyalty. The relationship, in other words, is a mutual one under which both parties are obligated to carry out contractual duties. A vassal has no obligation to obey a lord who fails to reward his loyalty. Because of this nature, vassals are independent; the instruments of a vassal's power, such as his weapons, belong to and are paid for by him. These characteristics, while quite applicable to the Kamakura period (1185–1333), do not suit the Edo period. The lord–vassal relationship needs to be distinguished from the control structure known as patrimonialism, a system under which an entire country is controlled as if it were a single family. Under that system, the lord–vassal relationship is absolute; the lord is not bound by anything resembling a contract, and vassals are dependent. Patrimonialism is a generally an older system than feudalism and was commonly seen in ancient empires and the like. The modern bureaucracies found under absolute monarchies do have characteristics reminiscent of patrimonialism, however, in that the bureaucrats are absolutely subordinate to their monarch and do not possess the means of their own control. Although the Tokugawa political system, or *bakuhan* system, contained elements of both feudalism and patrimonialism, it was clearly closer to the latter.

The defining characteristic of the *bakuhan* system, when simply contrasted with the West, was its remarkable concentration of power. The long existing regional powers had been swept away, as had any local warrior clans who could potentially resist the authority of the *daimyō,* or regional landholding feudal lords. The samurai (*bushi*) class was reorganized into patrimonial bureaucratic vassal bands (*kashindan*), completely severed from any ties to the land, and required to live in the vicinity of their lord's castle. This practice is the reason why, when the modern municipal system was established in the Meiji period (1868–1912), most of the newly created cities were former castle towns.

The shogunate-*daimyō* relationship was another characteristic of the system. Because Tokugawa Ieyasu (1542–1616), the first shogun, had, like other *daimyō,* once been a vassal of the Oda and Toyotomi clans theoretically, the shogunate-*daimyō* relationship was almost one of "first among equals" when the shogunate was first established. An overwhelming gulf soon formed between the two positions, however.

A third characteristic was the relationship between the shogunate and religion. Although Kamakura Buddhism had once served as a source for the creative energies of the masses, most of these sects had become largely powerless by the end of the Sengoku (Warring States) period (c. 1467–c. 1603).[3] The only sect to maintain its strength, the Ikkō-shū, had been the greatest obstacle to Oda Nobunaga's

(1534–1582) national conquest. Christianity was also powerful but was restricted by the new shogunate's isolationist policies as the Sengoku period ended and the Edo period began. Other religions were placed under the strict control of the temple and shrine commissioners (*jisha-bugyō*) through mechanisms such as the temple registration system (*terauke*) and religious census registers (*shūmon ninbetsu chō*).

Finally, the imperial court and nobility, which had frequently served as a nucleus for power struggles in the past, was strictly controlled by the Regulations for the Court and Nobility (*Kinchū Narabi ni Kuge Shohatto*) of 1615. Their power was drastically reduced, and they also became greatly impoverished.

The Tokugawa political system was thus a centralized one in which domestic forces potentially capable of acting independently of the authority of the shogun and shogunate were minimized to the greatest extent possible.

The shogunate also lacked any external threats. Japanese relations with China had become tense after the Ming dynasty fell and the Qing came to power in 1644; control of the great Chinese empire by a non-Han ethnic group caused fear in Japan that something like the Mongol invasions (1274, 1281) would occur. But while the Qing were initially expansionistic and would ultimately build themselves an empire that could rival the Yuan's as the greatest in Chinese history, their relations with Japan soon became stable. Japanese relations with Korea, which had been poor after the invasions of Korea (1592–1593, 1597–1598) by Toyotomi Hideyoshi (1537–1598), became calm as well. As relations with the West were tightly controlled through the shogunate's policy of isolation, the Tokugawa political system was thus essentially free from foreign threats.

As a result of the absence of internal and external threats, the factors that drove Japan to continue to increase its strength disappeared. In the West, the continued development of firearms brought about changes in military tactics and required the maintenance of great standing armies. These armies in turn brought about the large bureaucratic and financial systems necessary to support them. Similar changes had initially occurred in Japan as well, but they came to a halt following the Summer Siege of Ōsaka (1615). Japan had been one of the world's greatest military superpowers at the end of the Sengoku period and had possessed more firearms than any other country. But by the time of the final years of the Tokugawa shogunate, known as the Bakumatsu (1853–1868), the foundations of the shogunate's power, despite appearing overwhelming at first glance, had actually become extremely obsolete and fragile. The weapons that were carried by some of the vassals of the shogunate in the campaign against Chōshū in 1864 were not much different from those that were used 250 years before that. The Bakufu's military supremacy went to nil when new military technology was introduced from the West. In the early seventeenth century, the Tokugawa military government had the power to stop all domestic challenges, but paradoxically this led to the failure in ability to reform themselves from within.

The issue of legitimacy

But authority cannot be measured solely in terms of force. Another aspect, legitimacy, is also important. Legitimacy, simply put, is the moral justification for rule. Rulers will always be greatly outnumbered by those they rule; their rule will therefore not be long-lived if a large number of the ruled come to believe the ruler to be unjust. It will be unstable unless a large number of the ruled accept, either actively or passively, that it has a legitimate basis. So how did the *bakuhan* system justify its rule?

First, there were significant differences between the *hanshu* (lords of the domain) of the Edo period and the medieval lords who preceded them. The latter had ruled over territory on the basis of their personal power. But outside of a few domains (*han*), such as Satsuma and Chōshū, that had existed since the medieval period, many of the Edo period *hanshu* had the mindset of patrimonial bureaucrats appointed by the shogunate. There was a sense that their domain didn't actually belong to them; rather, it belonged to the shogunate. This lack of ownership is apparent in other aspects of the system as well, such as the right of the shogunate to control successions. Had the domains been independent political units, the questions of how the *hanshu* was determined and who the successor would be would have been left to them. Also, when a *hanshu* was dismissed from his position or transferred to a different domain, he left behind his arms. Leaving behind the most central instruments a *hanshu* had for wielding power symbolizes just how weak their sense of ruling on the basis of their own strength was. In short, the basis for a *hanshu*'s rule was that he had been entrusted with it by the shogun. (See Figure 1.2.)

The basis for the shogun's rule, however, took the form of the title *seii taishōgun* (Great General to Subjugate the Barbarians), an honor that had been granted to him by the imperial court that stretched back to antiquity. He also received the court ranks of junior first rank (*jūichii*) or senior second rank (*shōnii*) from the court. In a sense, receiving these ranks meant that the position of the shogun was

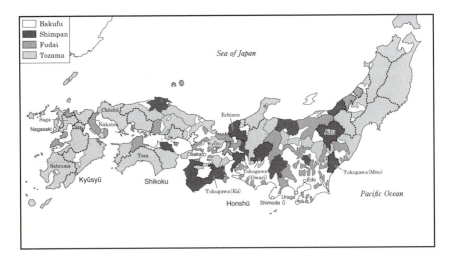

Figure 1.2 Major *daimyō* domains (1664).

not absolute in relation to the other *daimyō*, as they received court ranks as well. Prominent intellectuals of the shogunate such as Arai Hakuseki (1657–1725) and Ogyū Sorai (1666–1728) believed that it was necessary for the shogunate to establish an independent framework for its legitimacy.

Easy collapse, easy unification

As previously mentioned, the Tokugawa political system was surprisingly fragile in terms of both actual power and legitimacy. The conditions that would later be responsible for the system's unexpected collapse and the rapid reunification of the country afterward can be seen in how the system was realized and stabilized.

The weakness of each domain's independence contributed to making unification easier. By way of comparison, the extremely strong sense of independence of the German states made German unification very difficult; it would only be during the Nazi regime that Germany managed to achieve a level of unification comparable to that of the Meiji government.

The lack of strong religious authorities made it possible for social problems to be viewed from a secular viewpoint rather than a religious one. As Max Weber (1864–1920) made clear in *The Protestant Ethic and the Spirit of Capitalism*, a certain type of religion could serve as a major force in the development of capitalism. But at the same time, because religion views the world through the lens of a particular, intense doctrine, it can often impede a realistic perception of matters. Unhindered by religion, Japan was able to react flexibly to external stimuli.

Legacies of the Tokugawa Japan

The peace dividend

The *bakuhan* political system provided a lengthy period of peace, which in turn furnished important basic conditions for Japan's unification and modernization.

The population of Japan in 1600 is estimated at 12 million and rose 258 percent to 31 million by 1721. Meanwhile, the population had already reached 5 million by the year 800, which means 800 years was needed for the population to become 12 million (a growth by 240%). In other words, while it took 900 years for the population to not quite double between the Nara and Edo periods, it more than doubled in just a little over a century in the first half of the Edo period.[4] While the population would stagnate in the late Edo period (especially in eastern Japan, which suffered a stretch of poor weather), it reached a size in the first half of the period the likes of which were rarely seen in the early modern world. The impression many have of the Edo period as some kind of dark age is a mistake derived from focusing on the state of eastern Japan in the late Edo period and from trying to directly compare their living standards with those we enjoy today.

How was this population growth achieved? First, the size of the area under cultivation was greatly expanded. Plains were opened up for farming as controlling the flow of large rivers became technologically possible and each domain made efforts toward developing its land, whereas agricultural land in ancient times had been centered on basins such as the Yamato Basin. The wide dissemination of steel farm tools, made possible by the end of warfare and the drastically reduced demand for weapons, was also a technologically significant development as it made it easier for farmers to cultivate deeply. Steel tools are considered one of the three great agricultural innovations in Japanese history, along with the introduction of rice in antiquity and of chemical fertilizers following the Second World War.

In terms of commercial development, the establishment of a national market due to the development of coastal routes can also be mentioned. Rice and other goods from around the country were sent to Osaka to be converted to money or to Edo; this was only possible due to these routes. Incidentally, the establishment of this great national market is one reason why the arrival of Commodore Matthew C. Perry (1794–1858) and his black ships was considered a crisis that affected not just the shogunate but the country as a whole. The black ships, which could appear without warning, were a threat to these coastal routes and thus a danger to the entire national economy.

Even more important was the spread of education. While it couldn't be assumed during the early Edo period that any given member of the samurai warrior class was literate, by the end of the period an illiterate samurai would be exceptional. The Japanese literacy rate is estimated to have reached 40–60 percent for adult males and 10–20 percent for adult females by the Bakumatsu, an extraordinarily high level for a preindustrial society; there are a number of countries in the world today that have not yet achieved it. The spread of education had numerous effects on the country. One was that it made document-based administration possible as it becomes possible to effectively communicate complicated instructions via documents once the literacy rate surpasses 10 percent.[5]

The samurai ethos

Another important change brought about by the protracted period of peace was in the mindset of the leadership class, something that plays an extremely important role in politics. Humans interpret their environment through the filter of their perceptions and then project this understanding into the political process.

The leaders of Japan at this time were, of course, the samurai. The ethos of samurai, known as *bushidō*, originally linked the ambition of a warrior with his loyalty to his lord. The premise of *bushidō* was that a samurai would be diligent in his devotion to his lord, earn glory on the battlefield, be rewarded, and thus be even more devoted to his lord. The problem was that the opportunity for a warrior to show his devotion to his lord had been lost with the end of warfare.

Many samurai lived in peace with this development and enjoyed their privileges. But there were also those who sought to reexamine what, exactly, it meant to be a samurai. What did it mean to be a warrior who received his lord's favor one-sidedly, in the absence of any battlefield on which it could be repaid? Wasn't such a relationship contradictory to his very existence? These warriors' perception of the one-sided nature of these rewards led to an increased emphasis on one-sided loyalty. The mutual, contractual lord–vassal relationship was transformed into a one-way, unconditional one.

So what exactly should a samurai do? What were a warrior's responsibilities and obligations during peace? It was Confucianism, and Neo-Confucianism in particular, that provided the answer to this dilemma: a ruler must be virtuous and guide the ruled. It was a philosophy under which it was a ruler's duty to achieve "benevolent rule and a tranquil people (*jinsei anmin*)."

This change also brought about a shift in the nature of a samurai's loyalty. While loyalty had originally been directed at an individual, the samurai's lord, loyalty to the house (*o-ie*) now became dominant. The practice of *junshi* (suicide following the death of one's lord), something that had once been considered a virtue, was now prohibited because having a capable vassal die with his lord endangered the security of the house. With this change, the samurai's loyalty became directed toward an abstract principle. While that may have reduced the strength of the loyalty, it also increased the possibility of a warrior independently choosing what to be loyal to. It was this shift in the nature of loyalty that made it possible for samurai to rapidly change their loyalty from their domain to the emperor or to the state as the Bakumatsu gave way to the Meiji period.

But even with this change, the samurai were still samurai. They didn't lose all their warrior qualities. The most basic rule of war is to accurately perceive the current situation and gauge the capabilities of one's friends and enemies ("If you know the enemy and know yourself, you need not fear the result of a hundred battles"). It is the actions taken themselves that are important in war, not theory or the significance assigned to them ("Speed is the essence of war"). Because of this realistic and action-centered philosophy, the samurai interpreted the arrival of the black ships first and foremost in military terms and responded rapidly.

In comparison, no ethos of actively taking on the crisis arose among the non-samurai classes. Unlike the Western bourgeoisie, the Japanese merchant class had never been able to transcend their parasitic/passive state despite dwarfing the samurai in terms of power. Conversely, many nonsamurai strove to be faithful to the ideals of *bushidō* (literally, way of the warrior), often compared to Western ideas of chivalry. Shibusawa Eiichi (1840–1931) is a representative example. A farmer, he left home to participate in the movement against the shogunate but ended becoming an aide to Tokugawa Yoshinobu (1837–1913), who later became the final shogun. After serving as a government official in the Meiji period, he became a leader of the financial world. It is stated in *Bushido*, written by Nitobe Inazō (1862–1933), that *bushidō* originated with the samurai but then spread out to the other classes. In that sense, it's symbolic that in the Meiji Constitution the people were referred to as *shinmin*. The people were thus vassals of the emperor as well. In other words, a goal of the Meiji government was to instill the samurai ethos in the general public.

Notes

1 Here I use the phrase "Tokugawa political system" to describe what is known in Japan as the *Bakuhan Taisei*, which combines the words *bakufu* (feudal military government, exercised through the *shōgun*) and *han* (domains, of which there were 280–290 during the Edo period). This system was in place from 1192 until 1867. Some scholars call the *bakuhan* system as "centralized feudalism" because bakufu was stronger than the central governments in other feudal systems. The *han* were led by a *daimyō*). There were three kinds of such feudal lords. The first was *fudai*, who had been the vassals of Tokugawa since before the Battle of Sekigahara in 1600 when Tokugawa established their rule over Japan. The fudai were relatively small and located near Edo or other strategically important places to defend Edo because they were believed to be more loyal to Tokugawa than other *daimyō*. The second group was *tozama* who accepted the rule of Tokugawa after Sekigahara but were considered outsiders. They were relatively big and located far away from Edo. The third was *Shimpan* who were relatives of the Tokugawa family. The most important of these were *Kii*, *Owari*, and *Mito*. Shimpan were large and located in strategically important places.

2 Varying theories about the concept of *sakoku* have been raised in recent years. What is referred to here as *sakoku* is the shogunate's policy of maintaining strict control over external relations, not some complete closure of the country. It goes without saying that trade continued with foreign countries such as Korea, the Qing Dynasty in China, and Holland even while this system of control was in force.

3 Kamakura Buddhism refers to those sects that originated during the Kamakura period, including Sōtō and Rinzai Zen, Pure Land (Jōdo-shū) and True Pure Land (Jōdo Shinshū) Buddhism, and Nichiren Buddhism (Hokke-shū).

4 Although there are several important works, I based my description on Kitō Hiroshi, *Jinkō de Yomu Nihon no Rekishi* (Understanding Japanese History Through Its Population) (Tokyo: Kōdansha Gakujutsu Bunko, 1990).

5 Ronald P. Dore, *Education in Tokugawa Japan* (Berkeley: University of California Press, 1972); Ronald P. Dore, *The Diploma Disease*: *Education, Qualification and Development* (Berkeley: University of California Press, 1976); and Herbert Passin, *Society and Education in Japan* (Tokyo: Kōdansha Gakujutsu Bunko International, 1983). However, Richard Rubinger, *Popular Literacy in Early Modern Japan* (Honolulu: University of Hawaii Press, 2007) estimates the literacy of Japan to be much lower than both Dore's and Passin's figures, particularly among the girls and women and local rural areas. The main reason for those differences is that, while Dore and Passin estimate from the number of temple schools (*terakoya*) in the Edo period, Rubinger tries to discover the actual literacy from the data in the Meiji period.

2 Responding to the West

Open the country or keep it closed?

Japanese perception of the outside world

While Japan was not the only East Asian country to be confronted by the West at this time, its response to the challenge was remarkably different from that of China and Korea. The primary reason for this was the difference in how the Japanese perceived the outside world.

The first distinctive characteristic of this perception was the deep-rooted Japanese awareness that they were a smaller and more peripheral country than China. The Japanese had thus long recognized their position relative to others and felt no difficulty in acknowledging the existence of something superior.

But to the Chinese, China was the center of the world. *Zhonghua* (a Chinese word that means "central glory") was the flower of civilization that bloomed in the center of the world. The more removed a country was from China, the more barbarous it was. The existence of a civilization superior to that of China was unthinkable.

Second, while the Japanese were located on the periphery of Chinese civilization, they were not completely overwhelmed by it. Indeed, they rebelled against its influence and had an intellectual tradition of searching for their own uniqueness. This backlash was especially strong during the Edo period in which Confucianism served as the regime's legitimizing ideology, as was the pursuit of a uniquely Japanese identity. The continuity of the imperial bloodline and a tradition of being undefeated thus came to be emphasized. The former made the rapid spread of the *sonnō* (reverence for the emperor) ideology possible, and the latter became a way of stoking the pride of the samurai.

In the case of Korea, which was also in the Chinese cultural sphere, the influence of Chinese civilization was more unrelenting. The attitude developed in Korea, where acceptance of Confucianism had long permeated society, that Korea was second only to the Ming dynasty and that they, rather than the non-Chinese Qing dynasty, were the legitimate successor to Confucian civilization. This sort of "miniature" Chinese ideology made Korea respond to the West in much the same way as China.

Figure 2.1 Landing of Commodore Perry, officers and men of the Squadron, to meet the Imperial Commissioners at Yokohama, Japan, March 8th, 1854 by Wilhelm (William) Heine. (From the collection of the Yokohama Archives of History.)

Third, the framework of the Japanese view of the outside world strongly emphasized military aspects. It was thus possible for them to gauge the outsiders using the universal yardstick of military power. Indeed, many among the shogunal bureaucrats who met Perry and Yevfimiy V. Putyatin (1803–1883) felt that the foreigners, while enemies, were still admirable for their mastery of warfare. But in the cases of China and Korea, these outsiders were, above all else, cultural barbarians. When barbarians wished to visit China, they were expected to follow the appropriate procedure; it was unethical to accept them otherwise. Procedure – the *sangui-jiukou* ritual (repeatedly kneeling three times and kowtowing nine times altogether) performed when entering the presence of the emperor, for example – was thus not something that was open to compromise. It took two wars – the First and Second Opium Wars (1856–1860) – and having its capital sacked before China finally opened its doors to the West.

In the case of Japan, *sakoku*, the policy of closing the doors of the nation to the rest of the world, had been intended as a system to prevent external danger. It was therefore meaningless to continue the policy after acknowledging the black ships as a major military threat if doing so actually increased that danger. Even so, there were naturally strong cultural, racial, and visceral responses to any change. Isolation had been in place for centuries and was one of the fundamental laws that the

Tokugawa political system had been built upon. The shogunate placed great emphasis on tradition, and the policy was not something that could be easily revised. The shogunate thus had no choice but to attempt a compromise policy under which war was avoided, but this policy of self-imposed isolation remained in place.

Western ships had begun to visit Japan in the late eighteenth century seeking to return Japanese castaways or to open trade with the country. Adam K. Laksman (1766–c. 1806) came to Nemuro in Hokkaido from Russia in 1792, and Nikolai P. Rezanov (1764–1807) visited Nagasaki in 1804 seeking to open trade. The British frigate HMS *Phaeton* came to Nagasaki in 1808 for the purpose of capturing Dutch ships. In response to these incidents, the shogunate issued the Edict to Repel Foreign Vessels (*Muninen Uchiharai Rei*) in 1825. When the *Morrison*, an American merchant ship, appeared in Uraga Bay and Satsuma in 1837, it was fired upon. Criticism of the repulsion edict heightened when it was learned that the *Morrison* had been attempting to return Japanese castaways. When Japan learned of the Chinese defeat in the First Opium War, it repealed the edict and replaced it with the Edict to Supply Fuel and Water (*Shinsui Kyūyo Rei*), adopting a policy of responding to emergency requests.

Commodore James Biddle (1783–1848), commander of the American East India Squadron, sailed into Uraga Bay in 1846 but was ordered to go to Nagasaki, and his requests for trade and diplomatic relations between America and Japan were ultimately rejected. In July 1853, seven years later, Commodore Perry, who had studied Biddle's failure, came to Uraga to negotiate directly with the shogunate. He returned in February of the following year and concluded the Treaty of Kanagawa (Convention of Peace and Amity), successfully opening the two ports of Shimoda and Hakodate. Despite this, it was still possible to view this treaty as merely stipulating exceptions to the closed-door policy rather than directly contradicting it.

However, this was followed by the arrival of Townsend Harris (1804–1878), who emphatically sought to conclude a treaty of amity and commerce, to serve as U.S. consul general in 1856. The Second Opium War had broken out in China by this time, making the international environment even more turbulent. The issue of this treaty became a serious problem for the shogunate as it became pressed to choose either to open up the country (*kaikoku*) or to keep it closed off.

Expectations placed on the shogunal leadership

Perry's visit was followed by the rapid spread of a sense of crisis throughout Japan. This was by no means a self-evident phenomenon, however. There are always those in many societies who welcome the arrival of external enemies because it may cause difficulties for those in power; indeed, imperialism has frequently made use of this response by those who oppose central government. It is therefore rather worthwhile to focus on the rise of this sense of national crisis in Bakumatsu Japan.

The ripening of a sense of national unity provided the historical and cultural conditions for the sense of crisis. And because of the establishment of a national market through the development of coastal routes, the arrival of the black ships immediately meant danger for the entire country.

A great majority of the domains were suffering financial collapse, however, and had lost the ability to cope with this danger. There were therefore heightened national expectations toward the response of the powerful shogunate. The arrival of the black ships did not immediately lower the shogunate's credibility; rather, it strengthened expectations of shogunal leadership. It was only when those expectations weren't met that the shogunate's prestige crashed.

It was self-evident to the shogunate that drastic reforms were unavoidable if the danger was to be addressed. More specifically, reforms in the following three areas became political issues.

First was administrative-level reform of the military and foreign affairs. On the initiative of *rōjū* (senior councilor) Abe Masahiro (1819–1857), the position of coastal defense officer (*kaibō-goyōgakari*) was established in 1845. Many talented individuals would be appointed to this office in the coming years, including Tsutsui Masanori (1778–1859), Kawaji Toshiakira (1801–1868), and Iwase Tadanari (1818–1861).

Kawaji Toshiakira (1801–1868)

Kawaji Toshiakira was born the eldest son of Naitō Kichibei, a low-ranking official in the magistrate's office (*daikansho*) of Hita, Bungo Province, Kyūshū. Kichibei had wandered the country as a *ronin* (masterless samurai) from the Takeda clan prior to serving at the office, but he had a strong desire to serve the shogunate and traveled to Edo in 1808, where he received the rank of *gokenin* (low-level vassal) and joined a unit of foot soldiers (*kachigumi*). Toshiakira was adopted into the Kawaji family in 1812 and in 1817 passed the arithmetic examination (*hissan ginmi*) to become a low-ranking official in the financial commissioners' office (*kanjō-bugyosho*). As a result of actively seeking to make connections wherever possible, he was promoted to managing accounting officer (*shihai kanjō shutsuyaku*) in 1818. The recruitment system of Edo Japan was surprisingly flexible and made use of adoption, examinations, and the sale of the rank of *gokenin*.

Kawaji advanced exceptionally quickly due to his talents and diligence and was appointed financial surveillance officer (*kanjō ginmiyaku*) in 1835. It was around this time that he began to associate with Watanabe Kazan, Egawa Hidetatsu, and Mamiya Rinzō. Because of these connections and through his work, he came to have an interest in the West. He only narrowly avoided falling victim to the "purge of barbarian scholars" (*bansha no goku*) in 1839 that targeted Watanabe and others. He was appointed commissioner of Sado (*Sado bugyō*) in 1840 and returned to Edo in 1841 to serve as commissioner of lesser public works (*kobushin bugyō*) and later commissioner of public works (*fushin bugyō*). He was appointed commissioner of Nara (*Nara bugyō*) in 1846 and eastern commissioner of Osaka (*ōsaka Higashimachi bugyō*) in 1851. These experiences serving as a commissioner stationed away from the capital (*ongoku bugyō*) fostered an awareness of the responsibilities of governing that surpassed that of a bureaucrat. He had been exposed to the narrow-minded views of the local people while living away from Edo and had come to realize that Japan's views might be similarly narrow-minded within the world.

He received the important position of commissioner of finance (*kanjō bugyō*) in 1852, simultaneously serving as coastal defense officer (*kaibō gakari*) as increased pressure from the West became tangible. He was involved in numerous negotiations with foreign countries; he was granted full authority in dealing with Putyatin (as we will see), was the officer in charge of supervising the American consulate in Shimoda (*Shimoda torishimarigakari*), and dealt with Townsend Harris. He also successively held the positions of military reform officer (*gunsei kaikakugakari*), Military Training Institute construction officer (*Kōbusho kensetsugakari*), inland sea gun batteries repair officer (*uchiumi daiba shurigakari*), official in charge of the Investigation of the Barbarian Books (*Bansho Torishirabegakari*), coinage reminting officer (*tsūka kaichūgakari*), trade investigation officer (*boeki torishirabegakari*), and supervisor of the Naval Academy (*Gunkan Sōrenjo kantoku*). During this period, Kawaji came to feel that Perry and Putyatin, who had traveled to Japan from so far away, were true warriors worthy of admiration despite being enemies.

Kawaji hurried to Kyoto with Hotta Masayoshi in 1858 to receive imperial sanction for the treaty of amity and commerce with the United States but returned empty-handed. He was placed under arrest during the Ansei Purge and retired from the shogunal administration. He would later be appointed commissioner of foreign affairs (*gaikoku bugyō*) in 1863 but accomplished little in this position.

Kawaji was raised in extreme poverty and received an extremely strict education from his parents. His younger brother Inoue Kiyonao would also serve as commissioner of foreign affairs and commissioner of finance; the two were said to have been brought to tears by memories of the love and hardships of their parents. Kawaji remained strict and industrious even after he had been elevated to important positions; he continued to learn all he could outside of work and to train his body, making thousands of spear thrusts every day. Although a man of letters, Kawaji was quite fixated on military affairs. He was also extremely loyal to the Tokugawa clan because of his extraordinary rise in its service and took Ieyasu as the focus for that loyalty. He committed suicide the day after he learned of the surrender of Edo Castle.

As a Bakumatsu administrative officer of the enlightenment faction (*kaimei-ha*), the personal history and thoughts of Kawaji are extremely interesting.

Gun batteries were constructed in Edo and Nagasaki to help defend against foreign ships, and the Naval Training Institute (*Kaigun Denshūjo*) was established in Nagasaki in 1855 for the purpose of introducing Western naval technology. The school had a Western ship that had been provided by the Dutch, as well as a Dutch instructor. Katsu Rintarō (1823–1899) (more commonly known as Kaishū), Enomoto Takeaki (1836–1908), and Godai Tomoatsu (1835–1885) were among this school's students. Turning to the army, the Military Training Institute (*Kōbusho*) was opened in 1855 and taught Western gunnery as well as traditional martial skills. The school's gunnery instructors included Egawa Tarōzaemon (son of Hidetatsu), Takashima Shirōdayu (son of Shūhan), and Katsu Rintarō.

Collecting more information about foreign countries was urgently needed for Japan to pursue diplomacy in a broad sense. The government thus expanded the Office for the Translation of Barbarian Books (*Bansho Wage Goyō*), which had been created under the auspices of the Office of the Official Astronomer (*Tenmonkata*) in 1811. It also opened the Institute of Western Learning (*Yōgakusho*) in 1855, which was renamed the Office for the Investigation of Barbarian Books (*Bansho Shirabesho*) the following year. This office taught Dutch and English to retainers of the shogun and *daimyō*, produced translations, and conducted negotiations with foreign countries. It was accorded status equal to the shogunate's high institution of Confucian learning known as the *Shōheikō*, a school for shogunal officials in 1862, and renamed the Office for the Study of Western Books (*Yōsho Shirabesho*). It would become the *Kaiseisho* in 1863 and later form part of the University of Tokyo.

The second area of reform was the expansion of participation in the government. Participation in the shogunal administration had originally been limited to the *fudai daimyō*, those who had been Tokugawa hereditary vassals before the Tokugawa established its hold on power in 1600. Abe Masahiro, however, now put forward a plan arguing that, given the national crisis caused by Perry's arrival, the opinion of all the domains should be sought, that powerful *daimyō* such as Tokugawa Nariaki (1800–1860) of Mito, Matsudaira Yoshinaga (1828–1890) of

Echizen, and Shimazu Nariakira (1809–1858) of Satsuma should be allowed to participate in the government. Abe's plan was an attempt to achieve national unity and to justify changing the *Sohō* (ancestral laws) through *Kōgi* (public debate). Loosening the requirements of *sankin kōtai*, the policy requiring *daimyō* to alternate their residences between Edo and their domains as a way to monitor them and ensure their loyalty, was also considered. This alternate attendance system was designed to make them waste their resources by traveling and living in two places. The wives and heirs of the daimyo had to live in Edo as hostages of a sort. While the policy had its disadvantages, it did contribute to the development of a communication and transportation network and to the dissemination of Edo culture across the nation.

The third target of reforms was the need to put forward a powerful shogun. The twelfth shogun, Ieyoshi (1793–1853) had died in the midst of Perry's visit in 1853, and his successor Iesada (1824–1858) was extremely sickly. It was therefore necessary to determine who would be his heir. The two candidates were Tokugawa Yoshitomi (1846–1866, who later ruled as Iemochi as the fourteenth shogun) of Kii and Hitotsubashi Yoshinobu (1837–1913, the son of Tokugawa Nariakira). Yoshitomi had the better claim of the two in terms of lineage but was only eleven years old in 1857. In comparison, Yoshinobu was twenty and known to be genius of rarely seen caliber. Those who supported Yoshinobu (the Hitotsubashi faction) expanded their efforts against the faction of Nanki (another name for the Kii region) that backed their relative and lord, Yoshitomi.

All of these changes met strong resistance. The administrative reforms naturally meant individuals would be recruited on the basis of ability rather than social standing and met opposition for that reason. And allowing the powerful domains to participate in the government was strongly opposed by many of the *fudai daimyō*. It was especially hard for the shogunate to enact changes to the sankin kōtai policy as it was both a symbol of the shogunate's authority over the *daimyō* and a long-standing tradition. There was hostility from those who emphasized the importance of tradition in the succession dispute as well. Reform was no easy task for a political system like the shogunate, which had placed such emphasis on the authority of tradition.

The confrontation between the so-called enlightenment (*kaimei-ha*) and conservative (*hoshu-ha*) factions is apparent in all of these issues. Of the two groups, the enlightenment faction headed by Abe Masahiro and his successor Hotta Masayoshi (1810–1864) had the upper hand, but the confrontation between the two groups had not yet become fierce; that would only happen when the issue of gaining imperial sanction for a treaty with America was added to the existing issues.

The issue of imperial sanction for the treaty and the shogunal succession

Having decided to sign the Treaty of Amity and Commerce at the end of 1857, the shogunate dispatched Hotta, a *rōjū* (one of several elders in the Tokugawa government appointed from the *fudai daimyō*) to Kyoto in March 1858 to receive imperial consent for the treaty. They did not foresee any particular difficulty in obtaining this. Numerous political forces were making efforts aimed at the imperial court at the time, however. The Hitotsubashi faction was actively attempting to obtain an imperial edict that would aid Yoshinobu in being named successor, and the antitreaty faction was also active at court. As a result of these efforts as well as the antiforeign character of the imperial court itself, the court refused to give its sanction to the treaty.

The shogunate was stunned by this result. The conservative faction, to which most of the *fudai daimyō* belonged, and the Nanki faction believed that the scheming of the Hitotsubashi faction was responsible for the failure, and it stiffened their resolve to force their way through the opposition. Ii Naosuke (1815–1860) was appointed *tairō* (great elder) in June. As the Ii clan was the largest of the *fudai daimyō* and the position of great elder was appointed only during emergencies, this shows that the conservative faction was attempting to establish the strongest support structure for itself that it could. Hotta was dismissed, Yoshitomi's designation as heir was announced, and the Treaty of Amity and Commerce was signed without imperial sanction on July 29.

These moves were followed by harsh suppression of the opposing factions: many of the Hitotsubashi faction *daimyō* were forced to step down or were subjected to house arrest, and numerous shogunal vassals belonging to the enlightenment faction were demoted. A number of politically active figures such as Hashimoto Sanai (1834–1859) and Yoshida Shōin (1830–1859) were also put to death. These actions are known as the Ansei Purge (*Ansei no Taigoku*). The sudden death of Shimazu Nariakira, an influential member of the Hitotsubashi faction, also dealt a great blow to them.

This concept of emphasizing the importance of tradition in order to successfully change the traditional policy of isolation was filled with contradictions, however, and going too far trying to strengthen tradition can in fact make it easier to destroy. Additionally, the conservative faction was never actually particularly passionate about the idea of opening Japan to the outside world. This extreme suppression sparked a backlash; *rōshi* (masterless samurai) from Mito assassinated Ii Naosuke in March 1860 outside the Sakurada gate of Edo Castle in what would be known as the Sakuradamon Incident.

The unrest of the Bakumatsu

Outbreak of the "Revere the Emperor, Expel the Barbarian" movement

High shogunal officials, led by Andō Nobumasa (1819–1871) and Kuze Hirochika (1819–1864), changed course following the Sakuradamon Incident, rescinding the punishments levied during the purge and rehabilitating the honor of those who had been executed. They compromised with the imperial court and loosened the burdens of sankin kōtai of having the lords spend part of their time in Edo. These actions meant that the shogunate was acknowledging that it had made mistakes in the past; the assassination of the great elder had already greatly damaged the shogunate's authority by itself, but this change of course only exacerbated this loss.

The shogunate now poured its efforts into *kōbu gattai* (unity of the court and the shogunate), a policy designed to strengthen the shogunate by using the symbol of the emperor to its advantage and showing the country that the court stood with them. The marriage of Princess Kazu (1846–1877), the younger sister of the emperor, to the shogun was at the heart of this policy. But the shogunate encountered strong opposition to this as it had already lost the ability to ensure that its interpretations prevailed. As rumors circulated that the shogunate was going to take Princess Kazu hostage, suppress the imperial court, and then appoint the shogun's son as emperor, Andō Nobumasa was injured in an assassination attempt in February 1862, known as the Sakashitamon Incident.

For their part, the powerful domains had begun to consider a policy of "involvement in state affairs" (*kokuji shūsen*) at this time. Nagai Uta (1819–1863) of Chōshū put forward his "sea voyage policy" (*kōkai enryaku saku*) in 1861, which advocated overcoming the West by opening the country and actively expanding through trade (he was soon brought down by the antiforeign *jōi* (expel the barbarian) faction within the domain). Shimazu Hisamitsu (1817–1887), who had effectively succeeded Shimazu Nariakira after his sudden death (although Hisamitsu's son Tadayoshi [1840–1897], was the actual *hanshu*), raised troops and departed for Kyoto in 1862, where he advocated for reform of the shogunal government. The imperial court agreed, and Hisamitsu then departed for Edo accompanied by an imperial envoy.

Hisamitsu's proposals resulted in what is known as the "Yoshinobu-Yoshinaga government": the appointment of Hitotsubashi Yoshinobu as the shogun's guardian (*kōken*) and of Matsudaira Yoshinaga as *seiji sōsai* (supreme councilor) in August 1862. Although the domains' "involvement in state affairs" had been intended at least in part to bolster the strength of the shogunate, it seemed to have, objectively speaking, weakened it. The shogunate suspected the domains of acting against it, and this mutual distrust resulted in a situation where it became impossible for decisions to be made.

It was important at this time for the shogunate to do all it could to accommodate the imperial court and gain its favor; it therefore made concessions to the *jōi* position. This greatly enhanced the prestige of the court, and public opinion (*kōgi yoron*) began to greatly favor the advocates of those desiring a hard-line against the West.

But what, exactly, *jōi* meant was rather ambiguous. No one – neither the shogunate, the imperial court, nor the powerful domains – had the authority to assign it a clear definition. The situation was being propelled forward by radical factions who defined *jōi* for themselves and acted accordingly. With violent outbursts from the *sonnō jōi* movement occurring from 1860 on, the shogunate decided in December 1862 to obey an imperial order to expel the foreigners. It promised on June 6, 1863, that this would be implemented on June 25. Despite this promise, the shogunate had no actual intention of attempting to drive out the foreigners, however; it merely ordered its subordinates to defend themselves if attacked, a reiteration of the policy already been in place. Chōshū, however, used the shogunate's deadline as grounds to begin opening fire on foreign ships traversing the Shimonoseki Straits.

It was here, at the height of "revere the emperor, expel the barbarians" activity, that the movement came crashing into harsh realities. The first of these was the actual capabilities of the great Western powers. America and France immediately launched a severe retaliatory attack on Chōshū; the Shimonoseki gun emplacements were destroyed, and the town was occupied in July 1863 (Shimonoseki Incident). The Anglo-Satsuma War then broke out in August as Britain dispatched warships to Satsuma to force it to take responsibility for the 1862 Namamugi Incident in which British nationals had been attacked. Satsuma performed well and caused a fair amount of damage to the British, but this merely reflected a lack of British preparations; Satsuma came to realize that Japan could not match the strength of the Western powers.

The powerful domains were another obstacle for the movement. Shimazu Hisamitsu had many Satsuma radicals put to death in the 1862 Teradaya Incident and joined with Aizu (the domain charged with Kyoto's protection by order of the shogunate) to wipe out the city's antiforeign radicals on September 30, 1862. The powerful domains sought to increase their influence in national politics, and the radical expel the barbarian factions were a hindrance to this.

The search for and collapse of a shogunate–domain alliance framework

With the radical factions thus in retreat by late 1863 and the shogunate's policy of unity with the court compatible with the powerful domains' desire for increased involvement in national affairs, attempts began to create an alliance between the shogunate and the domains.

The establishment of a conference of councilors (*sanyo kaigi*) symbolized this effort. Created in late 1863, this body consisted of Hitotsubashi Yoshinobu (the shogun's guardian), Matsudaira Yoshinaga (supreme councilor), Yamanouchi Toyoshige (1827–1872, of Tosa), Shimazu Hisamitsu, Date Munenari (1818–1892, Uwajima in Iyo), and Matsudaira Katamori (1835–1893, Aizu, protector of Kyoto). This arrangement lasted only three months, however.

The first point of contention between the two sides was a political one. The shogunate wanted to limit the power of the powerful domains as much as possible, and the domains lashed out against this. The conflict between Yoshinobu and Hisamitsu was especially overt. Economic issues were another source of discord. The shogunate wanted to monopolize the profits from trade, while the domains wanted to make trade freer. This issue would also come to involve the foreign countries interested in trading with Japan. That is to say, Britain desired freedom of trade; having become aware of Satsuma's capabilities during the Anglo-Satsuma War, it began favoring it.

The loose cooperation between the shogunate and strong domains would still briefly continue, however. When Chōshū marched on Kyoto in August 1864 (the Kinmon Incident), Satsuma and the shogunate cooperated to drive it away; this cooperation was repeated in the First Chōshū Expedition launched the following month to force Chōshū to take responsibility for its actions. Forced into a difficult corner as Shimonoseki was also being bombarded in September by a British, American, French, and Dutch joint fleet, Chōshū had no choice but to surrender and make a number of concessions to the shogunate in December 1864.

Both the shogunate and the domains took steps to strengthen themselves following the collapse of the conference of councilors. The adoption of a pro-French policy by the shogunate at this time is an especially noteworthy development. French envoy Léon Roches (1809–1901) had, since his appointment in April 1864, actively worked to become close to the shogunate. France, under the rule of Emperor Napoléon III (1808–1873, reigned 1852–1870), was in the final stage of its industrial revolution at the time and was increasingly interested in trading with Japan. Napoléon III's policies, collectively known as Bonapartism, were characterized by the state acting as a mediator in the intensifying conflict between the bourgeoisie and the proletariat and actively pursuing foreign expansion to enhance national prestige and direct that domestic discord outward. The French intervention in Mexico (1862–1867) is an example of Bonapartist policies. Pro-French bureaucrats who responded positively to Roches's overtures became influential within the shogunate and sought to use French support to restore the shogunate's strength. Commissioner of Finance Oguri Tadamasa (1827–1868) and Commissioner of Foreign Affairs Kurimoto Kon (1822–1897), who gained power within the shogunate in late 1864, were central players in this effort.

The plans of Roches and the pro-France bureaucrats involved the following. One of their ultimate goals was the dissolution of the feudal system and the establishment of centralized government under the shogunate. They planned to restore and strengthen the system, requiring the presence of the lords in Edo as a first step toward this. The shogunate's policy had been loosened in 1862 to require the *daimyō* to reside in Edo for only one year or for one hundred days every three years; restoring the prior requirements would strengthen the shogunate's control over the *daimyō*. They also considered making the shogun the *de facto* sovereign by having him assume the title of regent (*sesshō*) or chancellor (*kanpaku*) and thereby render the imperial court powerless.

In terms of reform of the shogunate, they sought the establishment of a specialized bureaucracy and the creation of a responsible cabinet system. They envisioned reform of the ambiguous authority of the elders council of state as the first stage. They wanted to create an organization similar to a five-minister cabinet under a prime minister by making the head *rōjū* (elder) an official without portfolio and dividing responsibility for foreign affairs, domestic affairs, the army, the navy, and finance among the other elders. They also wanted to create a modern, standing army for the shogunate. To that end, the troops of the *fudai daimyō* would be gathered in Edo where they would be made direct vassals of the shogun and their training, arms, and equipment standardized.

The collapse of the shogunate

These types of proposed reforms sparked a strong backlash from the powerful domains. A Satsuma-Chōshū (Sacchō) alliance was formed in March 1866, shortly before the dispatch of the Second Chōshū Expedition. If Chōshū, one of the two strongest forces opposing the shogunate, fell, it might well serve as the trigger for reunification of the country by the shogunate. As is well-known, it was Britain who brokered the alliance between the two domains, as the rivalry between the shogunate and the two domains paralleled that between Britain, who sought open trade, and France, who sought to use the shogunate to make inroads into Japan.

The situation from 1866 on was thus a convoluted one involving three groups: the French-backed shogunate under Yoshinobu, which sought to establish itself as an absolute authority; Satsuma and Chōshū, who sought to defeat the shogunate through the use of force; and a "return the prerogative [i.e., all his power as national leader] to the throne" faction (*taisei hōkan-ha*) led by the domain of Tosa. This third group sought to eliminate the shogunate and establish a new order centered on a "domain conference" (*reppan kaigi*), in which the Tokugawa would participate with status equal to that of the other *daimyō*.

At first glance, there would appear to be little separating the latter two groups, as those who sought to defeat the shogunate didn't seek to completely eliminate the Tokugawa clan's as feudal lords, either. The problem was that if a domain conference was established, the Tokugawa clan, with its 8 million *koku* of income, Yoshinobu's capable leadership, and the support of France, would naturally assume a position of leadership.

It was for that reason that Yoshinobu decided to return power to the throne, submitting his decision to the emperor on November 9, 1867. Driven into a corner by this decision, Satsuma and Chōshū, who had been busily concentrating their troops in Kyoto at the time, proposed on January 3, 1868, that an imperial pronouncement (*daigōrei*) be issued, announcing the restoration of imperial rule and the personal rule of the emperor. Yoshinobu was ordered to return all his ranks and land to the throne at a meeting held later that day at the Kogosho, a building on the imperial palace grounds.

The two domains also sought to create a situation in which an armed confrontation with the shogunate was unavoidable through harassment techniques such as setting fires in Edo. The enraged shogunate had the Satsuma manor in Edo burned on January 19. The Battle of Toba-Fushimi that began a week later on the 27th resulted in an imperial victory, albeit one that was at least partially due to chance.

The conditions necessary for a "low-cost" revolution

What's fascinating about this battle is that the course of the war against the shogunate was decided in a single day; following the imperial victory, all of the domains outside the Hokuriku and Ōu regions in northeastern Japan rushed to join the victors. Why did this happen?

First, there was great opposition throughout the country to continuing the war. The people had become acclimated to the sustained period of peace and didn't want the disturbances of war; a long, large-scale war would cause considerable disorder. There was also strong cultural resistance to utterly destroying one's enemy. Tokugawa Iesato (1863–1940), Yoshinobu's adopted son and successor, would be active in public life for many years. Later granted the title of prince, the same rank bestowed upon the heads of the Mōri and Shimazu clans (the rulers of Chōshū and Satsuma domains), he served for many years in the House of Peers, was once asked to form a government (although he declined) and represented Japan at the Washington Naval Conference. This was an uncommon path for the loser of a revolution.

Second, there was a powerful intermediary force. Britain, with its eye on expanding trade with Japan, didn't want the war to grow larger. Due partly to a request from Katsu, British envoy Sir Harry Smith Parkes (1828–1885) strongly opposed any attack on Edo by Saigō Takamori (1827–1877). The desires of the great naval power played an important role in achieving a bloodless surrender of Edo Castle, the shogunal stronghold.

Third, there was comparatively strong leadership on both sides. Successful negotiations between Katsu and Saigō were still necessary even with Parke's intervention.

Looking at a situation that played out under other circumstances, the fighting in the Hokuriku and Tohoku regions that followed wasn't unavoidable. Aizu and the other domains weren't determined to give sustained resistance; they merely wanted to surrender on the most favorable terms possible. But there was no one to play the role of mediator. Britain considered the war already over, and it was difficult to restrain Tōhoku from Yokohama. Additionally, the imperial army's lines were overstretched, and it was under leadership that was both second-rate and hungry for fame.

Finally, the presence of a sense of national unity shouldn't be ignored. There was no small awareness that Japan might well be destroyed if the imperial court and the shogunate fought to the bitter end. This was one reason that the pro-French policy did not achieve adequate success within the shogunate.

There may be questions about how, exactly, those who had supported *sonnō jōi* rapidly moved toward opening up the country during the Meiji Restoration. But *sonnō jōi* should be understood as a slogan that incorporated two aspects of Japanese nationalism: *sonnō* stood for "a unified government" and *jōi* for "independence from outsiders." The question of exactly what kind of revolution the Meiji Restoration was is a long-standing issue. Some say that it was the establishment of absolutist government, while others point out its similarities to bourgeoisie revolutions. As the use of the *sonnō jōi* slogan shows, however, it was a nationalist revolution.

3   Building the Meiji state

Establishing a centralized government

Securing wider support

One of the largest tasks facing the new Meiji state was establishing a centralized governmental structure.

The new government had to first strive to secure the support of as many domains as possible in order to ensure its own stability, however. The basic policies of the Meiji government were made clear in the Charter Oath (*Gokajō no Goseimon*) presented by the Meiji Emperor (1852–1912, reigned 1867–1912) to the court nobility and *daimyō* on April 6, 1868. The first article welcomed the participation of the domains in the government by stating that "deliberative assemblies shall be widely established and all matters decided by open discussion." The new structure of the government was revealed in the *Seitaisho* ("Document on Governmental Structure," June 1868). Article Five of this document stated that "each *fu, han*, and *ken* shall furnish representatives [*kōshi*] to serve as delegates.[1] A deliberative body shall be created so that public opinion can be openly discussed." Seven bodies known as *kan* were created within the Dajōkan, the central government. One of these, the Giseikan, which served as the system's legislative body, was composed of the decision-making Jōkyoku (upper house) and the deliberating Gekyoku (lower house). The Gekyoku was composed of one to three representatives from each *fu, ken*, and domain.[2]

Concentrating power

But as the new government's position became increasingly secure, the policies aimed at securing popular support were deemphasized and the government instead focused on its initial goal of centralizing power. The Giseikan had ensured each domain's participation in the government; its dissolution in June 1869 immediately following the fall of the Goryōkaku in Hakodate and the end of the Boshin War (the war against the new government) symbolizes this shift in focus.

Dismantling the power of the domains was a necessary first step toward centralizing power. The *hanshu* of Satsuma, Chōshū, Tosa, and Hizen petitioned the throne to allow them to return their domains to the emperor (*hanseki hōkan*). This

Figure 3.1 The Iwakura Mission in San Francisco in January 1872. From left, Kido Takayoshi, Yamaguchi Naoyoshi, Iwakura Tomomi, Itō Hirobumi, Ōkubo Toshimichi. (From the collection of the Yamaguchi Prefectural Archives.)

decision reflected their understanding that Japan could not become a modern state without a centralized governmental structure, as can be seen in the petition's statements that "[e]very matter great and small ought to be made one. Only then will we be true to our name and capable of standing equally with foreign countries." The government accepted the petition in July and other domains followed suit afterward. Each lord was appointed governor of his former domain. The titles of the court nobility and *daimyō* were abolished and replaced with titles from a newly created peerage. And the specifics of the Dajōkan system, which had been ambiguous up to that point, were made clear in August. Looking at those appointed at the vice-ministerial level or higher within the newly created ministries, with the lone exception of Matsudaira Yoshinaga, former lord of Echizen, all were either court nobles or originated from Satsuma, Chōshū, Tosa, or Hizen.

In the next step toward centralization, 10,000 soldiers from Satsuma, Chōshū, and Tosa assembled in Edo in April 1871. This was the first military force to be directly under the control of the new government; prior to this point, all soldiers, with the exception of the roughly 500 members of the imperial guard, had belonged to various domains. The forthcoming imperial rescript on the abolishment of the domains and the establishment of prefectures (*haihan chiken*) in

August were made possible by this newly created military. Unlike in the case of *hanseki hōkan*, this abolishment of domains was carried out by a small number of Satsuma and Chōshū officials backed by the authority of the emperor. The wishes of the former *daimyō* class had not been taken into account, and even Shimazu Tadayoshi, the *hanshu* of Satsuma, his father Hisamitsu, and Tosa Councilor Itagaki Taisuke (1837–1919) were kept in the dark. The officials responsible were Ōkubo Toshimichi (1830–1878), Saigō Takamori, Kido Takayoshi (1833–1877), and a few officials from Satsuma and Chōshū.

It is truly surprising that the government had been able to move from the decentralized *daimyō-bunkoku* system to an entirely centralized system of government in a mere three and a half years from the Restoration. The foreigners who witnessed this marveled at the miracle. The reasons that this change was possible have already been repeatedly touched upon. First, the domains had already reached the point of financial collapse, and many desired to give up their responsibilities. Second, the *daimyō-bunkoku* system was weak in terms of legitimacy: many of the *hanshu* were aware that they had merely been vassal-bureaucrats of the shogunate. Finally, there was a sense of national crisis and a widespread understanding that Japan could not become a modern state without centralization. All of these factors can be given as reasons for the change.

In any case, the *hanbatsu* bureaucrats of Satsuma, Chōshū, Tosa, and Hizen embarked on the unification of state power, making use of the emperor's authority rather than that of the old domains. With the domains dismantled, the next job was naturally strengthening the new government's power.

Establishing the foundations of power: military affairs

Military strength is always central to establishing and maintaining power. The legal monopoly on the use of force is one of the greatest characteristics of the modern state.

Garrisons formed from men assembled from neighboring domains were first placed in the four cities of Tokyo, Sendai, Osaka, and Kumamoto in October 1871. These were then placed under the direct control of the emperor/the Ministry of the Military in December. A little over a year later, in January 1873, the new government made clear its policy of creating a broadly based military force assembled from the public rather than from the traditional samurai class by issuing a conscription ordinance. This policy was first initiated by Ōmura Masujirō (1824–1869) and completed by Yamagata Aritomo (1838–1922) following Ōmura's death in 1869. Both men were critical of the samurai elite; Ōmura wasn't a member of the class but a scholar and medical doctor, and Yamagata had been low ranked. They had also experienced numerous tough battles in Chōshū and other areas during the Bakumatsu and seen for themselves that nonsamurai troops could be brave and the samurai surprisingly ineffective. The Franco-Prussian War that broke out in 1870 was also a decisive influence as Prussia's total victory in the war was attributed to its force based on general conscription of the population and its large number of reserves. The Japanese army had modeled itself on the French since the time of the shogunate, but it now moved to a German-style system of conscription. Following the hiring of German Major Klemens Wilhelm Jakob Meckel (1842–1906) in 1885, the entire military system was changed to the German model.

The imperial edict (*chōhei kokuyu*) that announced the conscription policy invoked an ancient tradition of the Japanese to farm in peacetime and then become soldiers and fight during war. It also contained vehement criticism of the samurai, referring to them as "the so-called samurai with twin swords on their belt, the arrogant and idle, those who killed flagrantly yet had the authorities treat it as if it were not a crime." With the Restoration only a mere five years gone, this was the kind of harsh language it took to deny the importance of the samurai.

With a universal conscription system in place, the continued existence of the samurai was now only harmful to the new nation. They were expensive (more than 30 percent of government expenditures at the time went toward stipends to the class), inconsistent with the implementation of conscription, and dangerous; the government could not just ignore them. It thus embarked on the elimination of the class itself. In 1876, it issued the Sword Prohibition Edict (*Haitōrei*), distributed severance bonds (*kinroku kōsai*) to the samurai, and eliminated their stipends (*chitsuroku shobun*). The progress of inflation (currency expansion) soon made these bonds worthless. The Meiji Restoration, which had been driven forward by low-ranked samurai, had thus brought the unexpected result of abolishing the class.

Establishing the foundations of power: finances

A second power base to establish was a financial one. Public finances are, along with military strength, one of the most important aspects of power. For that reason, land tax reform regulations establishing a land tax of 3 percent of the land price were distributed in July 1873. The government's efforts focused on a land tax because other revenue streams were impossible. A modern income tax was naturally out of the question, as the state was still no way near capable of determining the income of the people. Customs duties, which frequently play a role in the finances of late developing countries (see Chapter 5) were kept low and could not be easily increased as Japan did not have the right to set its own tariffs. Japan was not well trusted, making foreign loans difficult to obtain; even if loans had been available, they would have likely carried high rates of interest. The government also feared that taking on foreign loans could lead to Japan's colonization. The Suez Canal had opened in 1869, and memories of the shogunate's loans from France were still fresh. When former American President Ulysses Simpson Grant (1822–1885, in office 1869–1877) visited Japan and met with the Meiji Emperor in 1879, the danger of foreign loans was the subject he placed the most emphasis on.

To summarize all this, at the time Japan had no method available to it other than levying taxes on agricultural income. The government decided to determine land value based on productivity and take 3 percent as a land tax (it would take seven years, until 1880, for land values to be completely determined). Annual revenue had been unstable under the *nengu* method that had been used previously, as it was based on paying a proportion of crop yield. Introducing a land tax meant that tax revenues would become stable, and being able to calculate tax revenue is a necessity for compiling a modern budget.

Another key element of this policy was that the taxes were applied to landowners. The *bakuhan* system had, in principle, worked on the theory that the taxpayer, cultivator, and landowner were all one and the same individual; tenant farming was not officially condoned. But the government now acknowledged the fact that absentee landlords had become increasingly common during the Bakumatsu and attempted to stabilize its tax revenue by extracting taxes from the actual landowner (it also repealed the shogunate's Prohibition on the Sale of the Farmland [*Denpata Eitai Baibai Kinrei*] in 1872).

This reform of the land tax also had the following secondary effects: first, through its confirmation of landownership, the government gained a complete understanding of the state of the farming class down to the lowest levels; second, since the land tax was quite high, a number of people gave up their land due to the burden. The land tax reform thus promoted an increase in absentee landlords and the commercialization of land. The tenant farmer class expanded as a result, creating a surplus of labor. This meant lower wages, which in turn supported the international competitiveness of Japanese products.

Creating "citizens"

Creating a national foundation: introducing Western civilization

This centralization of power was only one aspect of political modernization; power alone was not enough for the government to create a modern state. There also needed to be an abundance of "citizens" in the modern sense, people who equated the state's fate with their own and acted accordingly. It was thus necessary to draw out the energies of the public while providing them with direction.

The direction the government chose was *bunmei kaika* (civilization and enlightenment), the introduction of Western civilization.

The introduction of Western civilization proceeded rapidly during the early Meiji period. A telegraph line was laid between Tokyo and Yokohama in January 1870 and then between Kyoto and Osaka in 1872. Railroad tracks were laid between Shimbashi, Tokyo, and Yokohama in 1872. The creation of communication and transportation networks facilitated the government's control of the country and also promoted the coordination of domestic markets. The government-controlled Tomioka Silk Mill began operations in 1872.

The passion of the new government for introducing Western civilization is best shown by the dispatch of the Iwakura Mission. This large delegation of more than a hundred members including Iwakura Tomomi (1825–1883), Ōkubo, and Kido left for America and Europe in November 1871 (a mere three months after the dissolution of the domains) and spent twenty-two months abroad. It went totally against common sense for the nucleus of a revolutionary administration to head abroad for such a long time so soon after the revolution and immediately after the implementation of a major reform like the establishment of the modern prefectures. Although there were many reasons for the dispatch of the mission, the greatest was that they were eager to find the direction that Japan should pursue in the future. The scale of the mission shows just how acute this desire for direction was.

The mission's delegates observed the West's various strengths during the trip and became painfully aware of Japan's backwardness, feeling an intense sense of shame. Ruth Fulton Benedict (1887–1948) famously described Japanese culture as a "shame culture" in her classic study *The Chrysanthemum and the Sword*. These men truly acknowledged that they were embarrassed by the disparity between Japan and the West. They were seized by a burning desire to somehow overcome this gap.

The fruit of the Iwakura Mission was the government's new industrial promotion (*shokusan kōgyō*) policy. The government's initial industrial policy, already in place before this, had been led by the Ministry of Industry and was intended to promote political and economic unification through the construction of infrastructure such as railroads and mines. Full-blown promotion of industry only began after the Iwakura Mission returned, and it was the Home Ministry (created in 1873) under Ōkubo that headed this effort.

A strong army needed a rich nation to support it, and Ōkubo understood that doing that would require building an industrial base first. The state would thus bear the initial risk (the creator's cost). Examples of this policy in the field of agriculture include the creation of Shimousa Farm as a government-managed model farm, Komaba Agricultural School as a government-managed agricultural school, and drainage operations in Fukushima's Asaka region. Ōkubo also used his own money to purchase seeds and seedlings to create a privately run model farm. Although the government had already made some efforts in manufacturing prior to the Iwakura Mission, it now increased them, constructing a number of government-managed model factories.

Because shipping and trade were largely controlled by foreign merchants at the time, the government promoted and guided the direct export of tea and raw silk and protected Mitsubishi's shipping business. As a result, Mitsubishi soon dislodged foreign shippers from Japan's coastal routes and then expanded into East Asia.

These efforts make the intense sense of mission felt by Ōkubo clear. Strongly protectionist policies were adopted under his leadership, and, apart from those in the field of agriculture, the government's industries were soon cheaply sold off to the private sector. The government's industrial promotion policy, including its support of Mitsubishi's shipping concerns, was thus extremely unfair in that sense.

Regardless of the question of fairness, it was an extremely effective policy in terms of macroeconomics. Industrialization requires an initial supply of capital, at least during the early stages, and that means the gap between rich and poor inevitably increases. "Don't lament poverty, lament inequality" ("*mazushiki o ureezu, hitoshikarazaru o ureu*") may be a Confucian ideal but it's not a very practical approach to industrialization. One way to rapidly concentrate capital in a late developing state is for the government to make itself the initial nucleus of indus-trialization, as in socialist countries. As it is now clear that doing so ultimately destroys private corporate interest, governments normally support private capi-tal formation instead. This in turn promotes the emergence of *zaibatsu* (financial combines or conglomerates) and collusion between private industry and the state. As this is, to an extent, unavoidable when promoting industrialization in a late developing country, the question is how to control it.

The government hired a number of foreign scholars as specialists when imple-menting this policy. Its basic plan was to gather talented personnel by paying generous salaries and then to change over to Japanese who had studied with them as quickly as possible. The government naturally promoted studying overseas as well.

Mobilizing human energy

Now, in addition to industrial promotion, the state also intended to mobilize the energy of the people and took steps in that direction.

First, it abolished various legal restrictions on the public. The government granted people the freedom to choose their own occupation and made the four social classes of the Edo period equal, for example. While these might seem like natural rights to us today, this was a watershed change at the time.

Second, special mention needs to be made of the educational system. The gov-ernment created its school system in 1872 and made clear that it was intended to educate all citizens. The 1879 Education Law (*Kyōikurei*) made at least sixteen months of regular education in four years compulsory. Educational systems nor-mally are established in higher education first and often involve class differences. Its emphasis on compulsory education from the beginning and the creation of a uniform national school system that applied to all classes were distinguishing characteristics of the Japanese approach. The education system as a whole was quite expensive as it placed heavy burdens on localities and prevented children from working. Schools spread rapidly despite this, however.

This was a legacy of the spread of education during the Edo period. Although the quantitative factor of the large number of *terakoya* (temple schools) located throughout the country can be raised, equally important was the qualitative fac-tor that the idea had taken hold among the public that learning was essential to becoming a good person. As can be seen from the numerous examples of devel-oping nations following the Second World War, if the people don't hold this kind of perception of the value of an education, educational efforts often fail, even if schools are constructed and the utility of education to later life is publicized.

Education for adults was also necessary, and the government invested efforts in fostering newspapers and magazines to that end. Many former shogunal vas-sals became newspapermen as they knew more about the West than those in the antishogunate factions. They wanted to contribute to the modernization of Japan but were either too proud to enter the government or unable to. Journalism was an attractive job to people like this because it allowed them to play a role in bunmei kaika. Incidentally, this is one of the origins of Japanese journalism's oppositional character regarding the government.

The adoption of conscription also played a significant role as another method of adult education: after entering the military, youths from farming villages wore Western clothes and slept in beds for the first time. Gathering soldiers from all across the country also contributed to the spread of a common vocabulary.

Fukuzawa Yukichi (1835–1901)

Fukuzawa Yukichi, the child of a low-ranking samurai from the domain of Nakatsu in Buzen Province (part of today's Oita Prefecture), was born at the domain's storehouse (*kurayashiki*) in Osaka. He was ordered to Edo by the domain in 1858 after studying at Ogata Kōan's private school Tekijuku for three and a half years. Visiting Yokohama shortly after the port was opened to foreigners, he was shocked to learn that he couldn't communicate with them in Dutch. He started studying English and departed for America in 1860 on the *Kanrin Maru*. He traveled to Europe in 1862 as a member of the shogunate's embassy to Europe and visited America for a second time in 1867.

Very few men could travel abroad three times during the Bakumatsu, and he wrote the widely read *Seiyō Jijō* (Western Things, published 1866–1870) based on his observations. While appointed as a translator by the shogunate, he came to feel that it was necessary for an absolutist government based on the shogunate to be created and for Japan to open up to the world. He strongly supported the Second Chōshū Expedition.

Worried that the new government led by the Satsuma and Chōshū domains supported a continued isolationist policy, Fukuzawa withdrew from society following the Meiji Restoration. He gathered his friends and danced for joy when he learned that the new government would in fact pursue a progressive open door policy and stated that he wouldn't regret dying now that he had seen something so wonderful. He was especially pleased when the policy to dissolve the domains and establish the prefectures was implemented.

He wrote the first volume of *Gakumon no Susume* (An Encouragement of Learning, 1872) while in the midst of this euphoria. It became a bestseller. Fukuzawa would continue writing the series until the final seventeenth volume in 1876. He also published *Bunmeiron no Gairyaku* (An Outline of a Theory of Civilization), a more theoretical work in 1875. Although these two works published in the period between dissolution of the domains in 1871 and the Satsuma Rebellion in 1878 promoted the modernization of Japan via the introduction of Western civilization, they by no means held that the West was unequivocally correct. Although Fukuzawa argued that national prosperity was more important for modernization than a powerful military and that an independent spirit was the foundation that modernization would rest on, he missed the spirit of resistance that had been found within *bushidō* (even as he despised the samurai for having lost their spirit).

Following the Satsuma Rebellion, Fukuzawa called for the establishment of a legislature and joined with Ōkuma Shigenobu to advocate for the rapid introduction of a constitution. He became an advocate for the opposition following the dismissal of Ōkuma in the 1881 Political Crisis (see Chapter 4) and established the *Jiji Shimpō* newspaper in 1882. This campaign of words and his educational work at Keiō Gijuku became his primary work. Fukuzawa took on a rather more realist approach after cutting his ties to the government. He began to advocate for increased state power through *kanmin chōwa* (armony between the government and the people).

Fukuzawa's Asian policy was his most divisive. His essay "*Datsuaron*" ("On Leaving Asia"), written in 1885, is often spoken about as if it had advocated an ideology that promoted the invasion of Asia, but this interpretation is incorrect. The essay's origins lie in the contemporary collapse of the Korean reform faction that Fukuzawa had held high hopes for. His argument was that diplomacy toward Asia undertaken with special emotional attachments did more harm than good.

The issue that Fukuzawa addressed in his works was whether or not modernization was possible outside the West. As this was a question grounded in world history, so was the answer he gave. Those who take Fukuzawa for a superficial believer in enlightenment or ignore the historical context of his work overlook this point. Toyabe Shuntei, a well-known Meiji period biographer and critic, wrote that the influence of Fukuzawa was at the very least comparable to that of the three so-called Heroes of the Restoration (Saigō, Kido, and Ōkubo) and was far above that of Itō Hirobumi, Yamagata Aritomo, and Kuroda Kiyotaka.

These policies for mobilizing the energies of the public were a great success, and a strong passion for self-advancement was created among the people. The government's policies were a revelation for skilled youths who had been cut off by class walls before this point.

There were also areas where the government's coercive policies led to opposition, however. Supporters of traditional Japanese culture fought against the sudden introduction of Western civilization, and there who those who opposed the state's industrial promotion policy as well, especially its collusion with the *zaibatsu*. Even if the land tax reform didn't, on the whole, actually increase the burden on farmers, it still naturally caused friction and produced a backlash at first. Because local areas had to pay education costs, it placed a heavy financial burden on them. And the imposition of conscription was, of course, unwelcome.

Furthermore, there was opposition by those excluded from the centralization of power. There was especially strong dissatisfaction among the samurai class, now stripped of its economic and social privileges and its honor.

Finally, the newly created newspapers and magazines had an antigovernment quality to them from the very beginning. Even though these had been launched with governmental support as "enlightened" (*keimō*) publications, their content soon shifted to focus on political discourse.

These oppositional trends culminated in the eruption of an antigovernment movement.

Notes

1 The areas that had been under the direct control of *bakufu* were made fu; the domains that had opposed to the new government after Edo had surrendered were made *ken*; other domains remained as *han* as they had been. It is almost impossible to give the exact number of *fu*, *ken*, and *han* because of so many change in a short period of time, but there were roughly 9 *fu*, 50 *ken*, and *260 han*. In the July 1871 reorganization(*haihan chiken*) when domains were to be dissolved and prefectures established, they were reorganized to 3 *fu*, 40 *ken*, and 261 *han*.
2 In addition to the 273 domains, the territory that had formerly been under the direct control of the shogunate had been divided into 9 *fu* and 21 *ken*.

4 Rise of opposition

Establishing foreign relations and the samurai revolt

The international order and modernity

In its efforts to become a modern state, Japan had to develop its foreign relations as it established its domestic structure. The first problem it faced in doing so was the remarkable difference between the traditional East Asian international order and the modern one it sought to enter.

Modern international relations take the sovereign state as their fundamental structural unit. Sovereign states have absolute authority over and responsibility for affairs within their borders or relating to their people, and all these states are theoretically equal within the order. Those countries that are not sovereign states are colonies governed by them. Accordingly, the concepts of territory and citizenship rigidly demanded that the world's lands and inhabitants could each be subject to only a single country. As such, not belonging to any country or belonging to multiple countries was, in principle, impossible.

Judging from world history, this was not an obvious principle. The concept of territory has frequently been vague, for example; it wasn't rare for a piece of land to belong to multiple countries or to no country at all. Rather, it was more natural for states to have little interest in land that was worth little economically. The Japanese of the Edo period thus had little interest in their northern borders prior to the arrival of the Russians.

An equal relationship between states is another historically unusual approach; systems based around a single powerful country were more common. The order that developed in East Asia was a hierarchical one centered on China: the countries surrounding China were ranked in a hierarchy according to their relationship with it. Under this system, peripheral countries acknowledged Chinese superiority and swore to obey it. In turn, China acted as a generous protector. Surrounding countries sent tribute to China, which would be returned with gifts worth several times more than the initial tribute (*chōkō*). This Sinocentric, asymmetrical relationship merging politics and economics is known as the tributary system.

That Korea, the country located closest to Japan, considered China to be its suzerain posed a problem for Korean-Japanese relations. Japan entering into an

Figure 4.1 Saigō Takamori, by Higo Naokuma. (From the collection of Reimeikan, Kagoshima Prefectural Museum of Culture.)

equal relationship with Korea while the latter remained in a suzerain relationship with China would mean placing Japan in a subordinate position as well. To secure equal status with China, it was necessary for Japan either to treat Korea as an independent state, rejecting its subordinate relationship, or to assume a superior position over Korea in the same manner as China.

The Ryūkyū Kingdom presented another problem. The *Ryūkyū Ōchō* had effectively been under the control of Satsuma since the seventeenth century, but because its tributary relationship with China had been beneficial for Satsuma, it had pub-licly treated it as a tributary state independent from Japan. Japan needed to reshape these two relationships into ones suitable to modern international relations.

Seikanron

The first of these to become a major issue was Korea.

Korea had had relations with Japan during the Edo period using the Tsushima domain as an intermediary. The country had adopted an antiforeign stance at about the time of the Restoration, however, and was critical of the Japanese decision to open itself to the West. When Japan notified Korea of the Meiji Restoration, the lat-ter refused to acknowledge the change in government as the Japanese documents used terms such as "emperor" and "imperial edict" in reference to the Japanese emperor; the Korean position was that such terms could be used only in reference to the Chinese emperor. Since Korea would not recognize any method of contact between the two countries other than through Tsushima, relations were effectively severed once the domain was abolished under the new government's policy to establish modern prefectures. This included those activities undertaken through the Sōryō Wakan, the Japanese trading post established by Tsushima on the south-ern part of the Korean Peninsula in Busan. The view spread within the Japanese government and the public that Korea's actions were an extreme "insult" and that Japan should take a hard-line stance on the issue and be prepared to use force. This position was known as *seikanron* (literally, advocacy of an expedition to Korea).

Predecessors of this argument had been put forward during the Bakumatsu for a variety of motives. While these included a simple desire for territorial expansion, there were also those who believed that Japan should work together with Korea to resist the West, using force should Korea refuse to cooperate. There was another type of argument that a foreign crisis would strengthen domestic unity, too.

The question of whether or not to export Japan's revolution arose following the Restoration. The export of revolutionary ideologies following a successful revo-lution is a common phenomenon and can be easily linked with a desire to aggra-vate foreign tensions for the purpose of suppressing postrevolutionary domestic unrest. The discontent of the former samurai class was an especially important factor behind the support for a military expedition to Korea in the Meiji period. The samurai harbored deep dissatisfaction over being stripped of their long held pride in their status and economic privileges. Another important factor in the argu-ment was the assertion that it was necessary to strengthen Japan's foothold in Korea in preparation of a Russian expansion eastward.

In any case, it was decided in August 1873 to dispatch Saigō Takamori as an envoy and to pressure Korea to open. There was no clear agreement within the government as to whether Saigō's primary goal was to open the country or to justify an armed invasion. There was no small probability that his dispatch would result in a military clash, and for this reason, Iwakura Tomomi, Ōkubo Toshimichi, and Kido Takayoshi opposed it. Having just returned home from the Iwakura Mission and shocked by the great disparity between Japan and the West, they worked to reverse the government's decision, believing that domestic construction should be given priority and dangerous policies of this type avoided. On October 24, they managed to have the dispatch canceled. The councilors who had supported the policy of dispatching a special envoy to Korea all resigned in protest in what is known as the Political Crisis of 1873 (*Meiji Roku-nen Seihen*). With the resignation of Saigō, Itagaki Taisuke, Etō Shimpei (1834–1874), Soejima Taneomi (1828–1905), and Gotō Shōjirō (1838–1897), there were only four councilors remaining: Ōkubo, Kido, Ōkuma Shigenobu (1838–1922), and Ōki Takatō (1832–1899).

Although there had been widespread opposition to and dissatisfaction with the new government from early on in the Meiji period, this opposition had needed a nucleus around which to rally in order to become a political force; the failure of *seikanron* would now serve as that rallying point.

Rise of the antigovernment groups

A strong opposition to the government was thus born, presided over by figures who had prior to that point been central figures in the new government. This opposition consisted of at least two groups, the first of which was the *minken-ha* (people's rights faction) led by Itagaki. The other – even if not necessarily as clearly self-defined – was the *shizoku*, or samurai, faction that rallied to Saigō. These two groups attacked the government, which was now under the leadership of Ōkubo.

Of the two groups, it was the people's rights faction that rapidly organized and made their movement's rationale and goals clear. They formed the Public Party of Patriots (*Aikoku Kōtō*) and submitted a "Petition to Establish a Popularly Elected Assembly" (*Minsen Giin Setsuritsu Kenpakusho*) to the government in January 1874. The signatories of the petition included four of the councilors who had resigned in October (Itagaki, Gotō, Soejima, and Etō); Furusawa Shigeru (1847–1911), Okamoto Kenzaburō (1842–1885), and Komuro Shinobu (1839–1899, born in Tango province and a former samurai of Tokushima) of Tosa; and Yuri Kimimasa (1829–1909) of Echizen. The petition criticized the current state of the government, arguing that power lay in the hands of officials rather than in those of the emperor or the people. It referred to this as "tyranny by those in office" (*yūshi sensei*) and called for public opinion (*kōgi yoron*) to be taken seriously. This same phrase had been used in the past to mean the opinions of the powerful domains. It had then evolved to refer to the opinions of all of the domains and now, ultimately, came to mean broad popular opinion.

Despite these progressive symbols, the people's rights faction was tightly connected to the samurai faction, a link symbolized by the participation of Etō Shimpei. A member of the Public Party of Patriots and a signatory of the faction's petition, Etō would also be the leader of the later Saga Rebellion (*Saga no Ran*) in February–March 1874.

Appeasement and its limits

It was Ōkubo who became the central figure of the new government and went to work against this eruption of antigovernmental forces. His strong leadership would continue until his assassination in May 1878. He first adopted a policy of appeasement toward the factions. He worked to prevent them from expanding and coordinating their activities, and he suppressed individual factions when they split off and radicalized, but he otherwise continued to pursue his policy of *fukoku kyōhei* (rich nation, strong military), which emphasized strengthening the economy through industrial promotion and carefully managed foreign relations.

Ōkubo Toshimichi (1830–1878)

Born the child of a low-ranking Satsuma samurai, Ōkubo received the patronage of Shimazu Nariakira and later that of Hisamitsu. He accompanied Hisamitsu to Kyoto in 1862 and was deeply involved in Satsuma's diplomatic efforts from that time on. He took the lead in pushing forward the policy of defeating the shogunate through force during the final stage of the Bakumatsu and played a decisive role in the restoration of imperial rule and the decision at the Kogosho to order Shogun Yoshinobu to resign and return his lands to the throne.

Following the Restoration, Ōkubo advocated for the country's capital to be relocated to Osaka and served as a councilor and finance minister. He observed Europe and America as a deputy head of the Iwakura Mission in 1871 and used his leading position in the government to oppose and overturn the advocates of a hardline on Korea following his return home. In 1873, he created the Home Ministry (*Naimushō*) and became the first Lord of Home Affairs, effectively the prime minister. He directed the government's policy of achieving a "rich nation, strong military" through industrial promotion and invested his own funds in this effort as its head. When the Saga Rebellion broke out in February 1874, he headed to the scene with full authority from the government, immediately crushed the revolt, and executed Etō Shimpei. He pushed through the Taiwan Expedition in May of the same year and afterward headed to Beijing for the peace negotiations. He wrote in his diary after the successful negotiations that it had been "a truly unprecedented thing, the like of which I will never see again."

Ōkubo headed to Kyoto and took command during the Satsuma Rebellion, which pitted him against Saigō Takamori, his closest friend since his youth. He did not allow the National Industrial Exposition (*Naikoku Kangyō Hakurankai*) to be canceled because of the rebellion, however.

Ōkubo truly was the cornerstone of the Meiji government from the time of the *seikanron* debate on, personally taking on and resolving every difficult problem the government faced. His authority was such that it cleared the area around him; it is said that, when he entered the Home Ministry, the building fell utterly silent apart from the sound of his footsteps. Even among the quick-tempered politicians of the Restoration, there were supposedly few who could speak frankly to him.

On a morning in May 1878, Ōkubo told a guest that the first ten years since the Restoration had been for establishing the foundation of the country and that the next ten would be for building. He said that he hoped to retire and pass on the reins to the next generation once that time of building had passed. He then departed for work and was assassinated *en route*. He left no savings behind following his death, only debts.

The Taiwan Expedition of 1874, while concerned with the issue of the status of Taiwan and Ryūkyū, also involved an element of appeasement toward the advocates of punishing Korea. Japan and the Qing Dynasty had signed the Sino-Japanese Friendship and Trade Treaty in 1871, nominally establishing modern, equal diplomatic relations between each other, but the treaty was less than comprehensive and a number of points of ambiguity remained. In November of that same year, fifty-four Ryukyu Islanders washed ashore on Taiwan and were massacred by the local inhabitants. When Japan protested, China took the position that, although Taiwan was Chinese territory, it was beyond the influence of the emperor, and it would not take responsibility for anything that happened there. It also stated that, as the Ryūkyū Kingdom was a Chinese tributary state rather than Japanese territory, there was no reason to debate the subject with Japan. The argument that Japan should send troops to force the Chinese to take responsibility had been ongoing since the time of the debate over Korea, the government only finally making the decision to do so in February 1874.

It appears contradictory that Ōkubo, who had opposed dispatching an envoy to Korea a mere four months earlier on the grounds that Japan needed to concentrate on internal development, embarked on this path. And in fact, Kido opposed this action on those same grounds and resigned as councilor. But there were important differences between the two cases: there was less risk that dispatching troops to Taiwan would result in a military conflict, and the need to appease the samurai had increased. The decision to approve the expedition was made immediately after news of the Saga Rebellion had reached the government and was made in an attempt to prevent that conflict from spreading to Kagoshima Prefecture (Satsuma); Saigō Tsugumichi (1843–1902), Takamori's younger brother, was appointed as head of the expedition, and a large number of the force's troops were recruited from Kagoshima.

The force departed in May, and Japan achieved its punitive goals. Ōkubo began difficult negotiations with the Chinese in Beijing and made the Qing authorities acknowledge that the Japanese action had been "a noble undertaking" and to pay a solatium in October. This was a better result than the Western powers had expected and was a victory for Japan that showed it had successfully learned and then made use of modern international law.

The Ryūkyū Islands had been made part of Kagoshima Prefecture during the dissolution of the domains in 1871 and was designated the Ryūkyū Domain in 1872. But as the Ryūkyūan king Shō Tai (1843–1901) continued to be a tributary vassal of China even following the Taiwan Expedition and still hoped to be saved by the Chinese, Japan hastened its unification of the islands with the mainland, dispatching troops and creating Okinawa Prefecture in 1879. Shō Tai was granted the title of marquis and forced to live in Tokyo. This is known as the Ryūkyū Disposition (*Ryūkyū Shobun*).

The government also needed to do something about the unresolved Korean issue. In September 1875, it dispatched a warship to the southwest coast of the Korean Peninsula in a challenge to the Korean government, resulting in a military clash (known as the Ganghwa Island Incident) when the Koreans opened fire on the ship. Japan then used the incident as the excuse needed to conclude the Japan-Korea Treaty of Amity in February 1876, thereby successfully forcing through a Western-style unequal treaty via gunboat diplomacy in imitation of the Western powers. In an attempt to disavow Korea's status as a tributary vassal of the Qing Dynasty, the first article of the new treaty stated that "Korea is an independent state." As Korea's agreement to the treaty was done at least partially in response to a Chinese recommendation that it do so, however, Korea's dependence on China had not completely disappeared.

Although unrelated to Japan's appeasement policy toward the samurai, the demarcation of the country's national borders was also proceeding at this time. Japan signed the Treaty of St. Petersburg (Treaty Exchanging Karafuto and Chishima) with Russia in May 1875, under which it received all of the Chishima (Kuril) Islands in exchange for giving up its rights to Karafuto (Sakhalin), which had had the unusual status of being shared between the two countries at that point. Although the exchange may seem a poor one for Japan in terms of area, it was an unavoidable step as Japan's power over Karafuto had been significantly inferior to that of Russia.

Japan also solidified its control over the Ogasawara Islands in October 1876. Britain and America had previously desired the islands, but Japan at last made its control definitive. And, as previously mentioned, Japan dispatched warships to Okinawa in April 1879 to establish the new prefecture. Relations with China meant that it was necessary for Japan to quickly resolve the Okinawan issue, but strong local resistance had delayed action before this.

Of course, the advocates of a hardline stance on Korea weren't the only group that the government needed to appease. It held the Osaka Conference (*Ōsaka Kaigi*) in February 1875 in an attempt to placate the people's rights faction. With the Taiwan issue largely resolved, Ōkubo hoped to have Kido and Itagaki return to the government and thus met with them in Osaka. The two rejoined the government as a result of the conference, on the basis of a number of conditions.

First, the government would adopt a policy of gradually establishing a constitutional system of government. Second, it would create a number of new bodies: the Chihōkan Kaigi, an assembly of prefectural governors; Genrōin, a legislature; and the Daishinin, a supreme court. Finally, in order to ensure that responsibility within the government was clear, councilors would not be allowed to serve as ministers (*kyō*). An imperial rescript was issued in April making the government's policy of gradually moving toward a constitutional system clear.

The Satsuma Rebellion

These efforts at appeasement were not necessarily successful, however. There were those who criticized that the government had not gone far enough during the Ganghwa Island Incident and that it had shown too much weakness in its negotiation of the Treaty of St. Petersburg. The appeasement of the people's rights faction was similarly insufficient; the policy of moving toward a constitutional system actually gave newspapers and magazines extra momentum and Itagaki, who had returned to serving as a councilor, soon resigned due to differences over the government's reform policies. In 1876, most importantly, there were a steady series of samurai revolts as the government continued to remove their privileges. The government was forced to lower the land tax from 3 to 2.5 percent in early 1877, a measure considered unavoidable due to extreme concern on the part of the leadership that any revolt by farmers could potentially join forces with the rebelling samurai.

The Satsuma Rebellion began in February 1877. In a Japan where power was steadily being centralized, Satsuma was the area where remnants of feudalism remained most strongly. Saigō's private school (*shigakkō*) was closely connected to the prefecture's administrative and educational organizations, and even the policies of the central government went unimplemented unless they had the school's agreement. Satsuma Prefecture was almost a *de facto* independent state, and this was a situation the central government absolutely needed to address in order to further the country's unification and modernization. But those around Saigō interpreted the government's attempt to do so as the beginning of a crackdown by Ōkubo and revolted. The Satsuma samurai were ultimately defeated in a little over six months, however. The government's army of conscripts, whose capabilities had been in doubt up to that point, proved itself, showing the entire country that the age of the samurai was over.

It would be incorrect, however, to interpret the Satsuma Rebellion as a purely reactionary event. This is because Saigō's private school, largely composed of lower-ranked samurai, was clearly different from Shimazu Hisamitsu's force of high-ranked samurai. The samurai rebellions and those in favor of a hard-line stance on Korea thus partly involved the expansion of rights, just as the people's rights faction had quite nationalistic aspects to it. This is why there was empathy between the two groups. In fact, the *Risshisha*, a people's rights group in Tosa, rose up in response to Saigō's actions and was defeated.

Kido Takayoshi died of illness as the Satsuma Rebellion was ongoing, and Saigō committed suicide at its conclusion. With the assassination of Ōkubo in

May of the following year, all three of the so-called Heroes of the Restoration were gone.

The freedom and people's rights movement

Development of the people's freedom and rights movement

With the defeat of the Satsuma samurai, the strongest group in the country, armed rebellion against the government came to be regarded as impossible. Antigovernment energies were thus solely focused on the people's rights movement.

Itagaki went to work reviving the Patriotic Society (*Aikokusha*) in April 1878 and completed this in September. The goal of the movement soon centered on the creation of a national legislature; this reached its apex in 1880. A petition for such a legislature presented by the League for the Establishment of a National Assembly (*Kokkai Kisei Dōmei*) in April of that year had 100,000 signatories, and the movement itself was said to have 240,000 members. Numerous other petitions were also being worked on.

The samurai made up the movement's primary base, as their antigovernment energy fed into the people's rights movement following the Satsuma Rebellion. This was first and foremost because they possessed the ability to understand the movement and its ideology. But given the size of the movement, it's clear that its participants included more than just the samurai; it reached the wealthy farmer (*gōnō*) class as well. This participation by farmers was groundbreaking as, in a sense, the political conflicts within Japan from the Bakumatsu on had been nothing more than struggles within the samurai class.

The participation of the wealthy farmers was promoted by the establishment of metropolitan and prefectural assemblies (*fukenkai*) beginning in 1878. These had been given recognition from the government for the purpose of stabilizing local governance and gaining the active political support of the wealthy farmers for the government. Contrary to the desires of the government, however, the wealthy farmers, who had been expected to be conservative, became politicized as well over local issues such as road construction. The *Sekiyōsha* and *Sanshisha* formed by Kōno Hironaka (1849–1923) in Fukushima are representative examples of these local political groups.

The influence of journalism on this process can't be ignored, either. The political fever of Tokyo was spread throughout the country via journalism. There were also a number of children of local elites who, returning home after studying in Tokyo, brought the political debates of the capital with them.

The antigovernment movement, who had previously been divided between the shizoku and the people's rights faction, thus became united within the latter group; the differences between the samurai and farmers disappeared, and the influence of journalism reduced the importance of local differences. The division within the government as to how to handle the people's right movement led to the 1881 Political Crisis.

The 1881 Political Crisis

Since Ōkubo's assassination in 1878, the government had been led by the trio of Ōkuma Shigenobu, Itō Hirobumi (1841–1909), and Inoue Kaoru (1835–1915), with Ōkuma holding the dominant position. As the central figure at the finance ministry since 1869, he had controlled the country's finances and developed a close relationship with Mitsubishi. He was also close to Fukuzawa Yukichi (1835–1901), which gave him access to capable young officials that made up Fukuzawa's followers. Ōkuma was able to use these advantages to create a gap between himself and the other two leaders of the government; there was thus an unstable situation where, despite personnel from Satsuma and Chōshū being dominant in the government as a whole, Ōkuma, the outsider, was in a superior position at the top level of the government.

The government issued the Assembly Ordinance (*Shūkai Jōrei*) in April 1880 in response to the rise of the people's rights movement. This regulated gatherings debating political issues, severely restricting them. But the government also actively attempted to show off the plans it had for the establishment of a national legislature in response to the public pressure. Since the government had already made clear that it was moving to a constitutional system, it was necessary for it to give specifics. It thus sought the opinion of each councilor.

Ōkuma outmaneuvered the other councilors by presenting a quite radical proposal in March 1881 that included the establishment of a national legislation in two years as well as a parliamentary cabinet system. It is believed that Ōkuma's intention was to use Fukuzawa journalists and create a political party built around Fukuzawa officials that would serve as the base of his power. Thus even though he spoke of implementing a cabinet system, he had no plans to relinquish power to the people's rights movement. Even so, the plan was shocking to his colleagues, and Itō and Inoue were outraged.

The sale of the assets of the Hokkaidō Development Office (*Kaitakushi*) provided another source of political disorder. Fourteen million yen had been invested in the office since 1872, and it was approaching the end of its ten-year plan in 1881. Despite being believed to be worth more than 30 million yen, its assets were sold to Kansai Bōeki Shōkai, a company operated by Satsuma and Chōshū figures, for only 380,000 yen (to be paid in interest-free installments over a period of thirty years). As the head of the office was Kuroda Kiyotaka (1840–1900) of Satsuma, the apparent collusion became the subject of severe criticism.

Fukuzawa journalists led the way on the criticism of the sale, and Satsuma saw the controversy as a conspiracy by Ōkuma, Fukuzawa, and Mitsubishi (a rival of Kansai Bōeki Shōkai) to bring down Satsuma and Chōshū. Although Itō and Inoue did not necessarily share that opinion, they were forced into a position where they had to choose between backing Satsuma and Ōkuma. They chose the former and agreed to oust Ōkuma from the government in October 1881. At the same time, the government also made clear that the national legislature would be established in 1890.

It was thus the 1881 Political Crisis that provided answers to the questions prompted by the people's rights movement: what goals would the new system be built on, and what groups would be taking the lead? The Political Crisis reconfirmed the supremacy of the Satsuma and Chōshū *hanbatsu* (domain cliques). Itō, Inoue, and Yamagata of Chōshū and Kuroda and Matsukata Masayoshi (1835–1924, Ōkuma's replacement as head of finances) of Satsuma became the leaders of the government. Ōkuma's pro-British direction was also discarded in favor of a pro-Prussian stance.

The peak and decline of the people's rights movement

The people's rights movement began its transformation into full-fledged political parties following the 1881 Political Crisis as the Liberal Party (*Jiyūtō*) and Progressive Party (*Kaishintō*) were formed.

The Liberal Party was the first to be formed, in October 1881. It was initially based on the Risshisha of Tosa, but the relative importance of members from Kantō would increase over time (although the leadership would continue to be dominated by Tosa). It had about a hundred members at the time of its formation. By the time of its dissolution in 1884, that number had grown to about 2,500. There were a much larger number of peripheral participants in the party, of course. There were urban professionals such as lawyers and journalists among the party's members, as well as the usual members of the wealthy farmer class. Hoshi Tōru (1850–1901), Ōi Kentarō (1843–1922), Baba Tatsui (1850–1888), and Ōishi Masami (1855–1935) are examples of this group. Their activities made the spread of the party across the country possible.

Meanwhile, the Progressive Party was formed in April 1882 and was based on Ōkuma and the former officials affiliated with him. The rest of the party's core was made up of urban professional such as lawyers and journalists. While the Liberal Party was oriented such that its primary base was outside the capital, the opposite was true for the Progressive Party. But the Progressive Party worked hard to establish its influence in the metropolitan and prefectural assemblies. By 1883, it had outmatched the Liberal Party and possessed outright majorities in five prefectures, held 30 percent or more of seats in another three, and had party members serving as speaker or deputy speaker in seven (most of the membership of these assemblies were unaffiliated with any party). It also held social gatherings in Tokyo for local assembly members as part of an effort to spread "enlightenment" out from the capital.

This peak of the people's rights movement did not last long, however, as the central government engaged in skillful persuasion and heavy suppression. Examples of the latter include the revision of the Assembly Ordinance in 1882 and of the Newspaper Ordinance (*Shimbunshi Jōrei*) in 1883. The government also misrepresented the source of funds for a trip by Itagaki to the West in late 1882 in order to diminish the Liberal Party's influence. The two parties fought each other viciously over these issues, weakening themselves. The government also embarked on policies, such as providing subsidies for public works, designed to cause local elites to break away from the parties. As many of these elites were only participating in politics only with the hope of benefiting their regions, these policies were effective to a certain extent.

The largest blow to the parties was provided by the so-called Matsukata Deflation. Matsukata, who had been placed in charge of finances in late 1881 following Ōkuma's departure from the government, implemented a policy of fiscal austerity to eliminate the inflation caused by government spending during the Satsuma Rebellion. These policies included such elements as currency adjustments and tax increases and caused serious deflation; the price of rice was halved from 1880 to 1885. Since the land tax was unchanged, this stuck a heavy blow to the wealthy farmer class, who withdrew from the people's rights movement and caused it to stagnate.

The movement increasingly radicalized as it stopped making progress; at each stage, moderates were pushed away, and the remaining radicals became more extreme. This phenomenon is shown by the extremist incidents that occurred around the time of the Liberal Party's dissolution in 1884. These included the Mt. Kaba Incident (*Kabasan Jiken*, an attempt to assassinate members of the government), the Chichibu Incident (*Chichibu Jiken*, a peasant revolt), and the Iida Incident (*Iida Jiken*, a coup plot). These all occurred in 1884 and were defeated by the government, meeting the same fate as the samurai revolts of 1873 to 1877. The Progressive Party also effectively disbanded later in 1884 when Ōkuma and other members left the party (although it would subsequently resume its activities).

5 Creation of the Meiji constitutional structure

Enactment of the Meiji Constitution

The road to constitutional enactment

Japan was substantially the first non-Western country to adopt a modern constitution (the Ottoman Empire enacted a constitution in 1876, but it was abrogated two years later). The course it followed in doing so was remarkably different from that of the West, however. In the West, constitutions were generally created as the result of revolutions or clashes between monarchs and their feudal legislatures. These constitutions thus contained stipulations pertaining to restrictions on royal authority and delineating the forms that the exercise of royal authority could take. While, as already mentioned, demands from below played a significant role in the enactment of a constitution in Japan as well, they were clearly of relatively less importance. Rather, the government largely took the lead in the creation of Japan's constitution.

There were a number of reasons for the government's proactive stance toward a constitution. First was a reason that was "from abroad" rather than "from below." Aside from Britain, which did not have a written constitution, all of the advanced Western nations had constitutions. It was thus felt that such a constitution was a self-evident necessity for a "rich country, strong military." A constitution was also a symbol of civilization. The great powers took the stance that they could not sign an equal treaty with a country that did not even have a constitution and that did not protect the rights of its citizens.

Second, there was a reason "from above." There was an understanding within the government that it was necessary to grant the people a suitable status in order to draw out their energy. In a November 1873 opinion paper, Ōkubo Toshimichi divided forms of government into constitutional and nonconstitutional systems. He then further divided constitutional systems between those where the king and people shared power and those in which the people basically ruled alone. Of the two, he believed that the latter was ideal. However, external security and a certain degree of maturity in the people's knowledge were necessary prerequisites for such a system; as Japan lacked both, he felt that it should go forward with the former type of constitutional system for the time being and aim at eventually

Figure 5.1 Kenpō Happushiki no Zu (Ceremony for the Promulgation of the Constitution) by Inoue Tankei. (February 11, 1889. From the collection of the University of Tokyo Graduate Schools for Laws and Politics' Center for Modern Japanese Legal and Political Documents.)

changing to the latter. That such thoughts were held by the leader of the so-called Ōkubo dictatorship shows how fervently the Meiji government wanted to mobilize the energy of the public.

Third was a reason that can be deemed as coming "from within" the government-led enactment of a constitution. The leadership of the Meiji government was extremely disunited. It usually requires a capable ruler or a great leader to accomplish great feats while leading a disunited government and state. But such a strong leader did not well suit the Japanese political climate, and Japan possessed neither a strong leader like Otto Fürst von Bismarck (1815–1898) nor the extraordinary power of the Prussia that had supported him. Capable rulers and outstanding leaders are both products of fate; a political system capable of proceeding in the absence of a "great king" or "wise prime minister" was ideal. Creating a framework in which the exercise of power was institutionalized and a variety of forces could cooperate was one method of achieving this, and this was another reason for the government to actively take on constitutional enactment.

The path to constitutional enactment had many parallels to the expansion of participation in the government and the efforts the government made to prepare rules for such. Ōkubo sought to have Kido and Itagaki return to their positions as councilors in the government during the Osaka Conference of 1875 that was discussed previously (see Chapter 4). As conditions for their return, he promised to gradually move toward a constitutional system of government, create a Chihōkan Kaigi (prefectural governors conference), Genrōin (senate), and Daishinin (Supreme Court), as well as to divide the councilors and the ministers. All of these were attempts to reverse the concentration of power within the government and to apply rules for its use. Decentralization through rules was necessary to operate the Meiji government, which was composed of diverse groups.

A Prussian-style constitution

Although efforts by the government to create a constitution had begun by around 1871, it was ultimately only following the 1881 Political Crisis (see Chapter 4) that they took on definite shape. That crisis determined the approximate direction that constitutional enactment would take and who would be in charge. Until that point, a British-style constitution had been the primary candidate under consideration by the leadership. This was true even of Itō Hirobumi and Inoue Kaoru. But now, with Ōkuma's plan for a parliamentary cabinet system rejected, a direction toward a Prussian-style constitution surfaced. Inoue Kowashi (1844–1895) was responsible for this change. Inoue, a native of Kumamoto who had studied in France in his youth, had long studied the Prussian constitution and had produced a translation of it in 1875. He had also researched the nature of the Japanese legal system from antiquity on and was passionately inclined toward rejecting a British-style parliamentary cabinet system. He had actively worked against Ōkuma's proposal when he learned of it and had pushed Itō and Inoue Kaoru to do the same.

Itō Hirobumi (1841–1909)

Itō Hirobumi was born the son of a commoner in Chōshū but became a lowly foot soldier (*ashigaru*) after his father was adopted into an ashigaru family himself. He studied at Yoshida Shōin's Shōkasonjuku and was active as a loyal follower in the "revere the Emperor, expel the barbarian" movement under Kido Takayoshi (see Chapter 2). He studied abroad in Britain with Inoue Kaoru and three others in 1863 but hurriedly returned to Japan upon learning of the bombardment of Shimonoseki by the allied fleets (British, American, French, and Dutch). There he tried to avoid war and to convince Chōshū that it should abandon its efforts to expel the foreigners and also sought to promote cooperation between Chōshū and Satsuma, the two most powerful domains to fight against the Tokugawa government.

He made use of his command of English following the Restoration, serving as head of the government's Foreign Affairs Bureau (*Gaikoku Jimukyoku*), as governor of Hyōgo Prefecture, and as the first minister of industry. He also participated in the Iwakura Mission as a deputy head. Although originally a subordinate of Kido, he gradually became close to Ōkubo Toshimichi; after returning from the Iwakura

Mission, he supported Ōkubo's emphasis on domestic development *(naichi yōsen)* and helped mediate the Osaka Conference
in 1875.

He became a leader of the government with Ōkuma Shigenobu and
Inoue Kaoru following Ōkubo's assassination but drove Ōkuma out in the
1881 Political Crisis and gained control of the government. He departed
for Europe in 1882 to study constitutions and afterward played a central
role in the creation of the Meiji constitutional system.

In addition to becoming the first prime minister in 1885, he held
the office again from 1892, during which time he guided the nation
through the First Sino-Japanese War and led the revision of the unequal treaties. His failure to achieve any major accomplishments during
this third government in 1898 made him resolve to form a political
party, and this led to the creation of the Seiyūkai (Friends of Constitutional Government) in 1900. He soon resigned, however, feeling that
being a *genrō* (founding father) was incompatible with being the leader
of a political party. [1]

He became president of the Privy Council and served as the first resi-
dent general of Korea following the Russo-Japanese War. After resigning
from that office, he was assassinated in Harbin in 1909 while heading
to Russia.

Itō was a man of great brilliance and rich ideas. He had extraordinary
energy and frequently displayed his capabilities as a consensus builder.
His mentor, Yoshida Shōin, had acknowledged these skills, referring to
him as a mediator *(shūsenka)*. But Itō did not merely engage in building
agreement; his mediation was backed by a deep understanding of the
world and history. That was his strength.

Itō could be overconfident in his own abilities and was not notably
enthusiastic about building his connections into an organization. He was
frequently caught off guard by Yamagata Aritomo from the time of the
Russo-Japanese War on for that reason. But the Meiji Emperor's trust in
Itō was solid, and he never lost his influence as the head of the *genrō*.
He continued to emphasize international cooperation and to feel uneasy
about the out-of-control military until the end of his life.

Itō headed to Europe shortly after the 1881 Political Crisis, where he studied
constitutions from March 1882 to August 1883. His studies under Rudolf von
Gneist (1816–1895) in Germany and Lorenz von Stein (1815–1890) in Austria, two world-renowned constitutional scholars of the day, were of particular

importance, and von Stein had an especially strong influence on his thinking. This was partly because both men supported constitutions with strong administrative powers, but that wasn't the only reason. Von Gneist and von Stein were leading figures in the fields of comparative law and the history of law. They were scholars who considered the nature of law and the state in areas with different cultures and traditions from a historical, comparative, and functional perspective rather than beginning their arguments with the question of what the law and state should be. The scholarship of von Gneist and von Stein could offer many suggestions on how to introduce a Western system into an area remarkably different from the West.

Ancillary systems for the constitution

Having returned from Europe, Itō created the Institutional Research Bureau (*Seido Torishirabekyoku*) within the imperial court in March 1884. This would be the body to draft the constitution, and he would serve as its head. He began his work by promoting the introduction of various institutions that would serve as prerequisites for a constitution.

Two of these were the imperial household (*kōshitsu*) and peerage (*kazoku*) systems. As imperial household minister, Itō strengthened the foundations for the household by enacting the Imperial Household Law (*Kōshitsu Tenpan*) and setting out the nature of the imperial household's property. These actions were intended to render the imperial household immune from the influence of the new legislature. He also created a new nobility in addition to the existing peers by allowing titles (prince, marquis, count, viscount, and baron) to be bestowed upon distinguished samurai and commoners through the Peerage Law (*Kazokurei*), enacted in July 1884. The peerage was to serve as a bulwark protecting the imperial household (even being called the *Kōshitsu no Kanpei*) and was expected to form the basis for the upper house of the new legislature. While upper houses were created in Europe due to the presence of the nobility, in Japan it was the nobility who were created for the sake of an upper house.

The bureaucracy was also strengthened further. The most important change was the creation of a cabinet system in December 1885. The Dajōkan system in place until that point had had three tiers: the three ministerial (*daijin*) posts of prime minister (*dajō daijin*), minister of the left (*sa-daijin*), and minister of the right (*u-daijin*) were at the top; below them were the councilors (*sangi*); finally, there were the ministers (*kyō*) who served as the heads of the ministries. It had been Iwakura Tomomi, the minister of the right and a man of rare ability for a member of the nobility, who had enabled this system to function; it thus became dysfunctional following his death in 1883. If effective governance was to be restored, either capable *hanbatsu* politicians would have to be appointed to the three ministerial posts or a new system would have to be created. The creation of the cabinet system, a more functional and rational system than the *daijin-sangi-kyō* hierarchy, was the result of this dilemma. It was Itō Hirobumi who served as the first prime minister of this cabinet. The elite of the Tokugawa shogunate had held power only during the Edo period, but now Itō, who came from lowly foot soldier stock, held the highest position in the government, second only to the emperor. The Meiji Restoration was thus also revolutionary in terms of the selection of personnel for office.

Additionally, the Higher Examination for Civil Officials (*Bunkan Kōtō Shiken*) was implemented in 1887, solidifying examination results and qualifications as the basis for appointment to the bureaucracy. The police and military were also further developed during this same period. These were all measures taken to prevent the beginning of Diet politics from disturbing the bureaucracy.

Characteristics of the Meiji Constitution

With these changes in place, work on a constitutional draft had begun by about late 1886, and a final draft was put together in April 1888. This was then examined by the Privy Council (*Sūmitsuin*) for a little over half a year from June before being confirmed with amendments and promulgated on February 11, 1889.

The most significant characteristic of the Constitution of the Empire of Japan (the Meiji Constitution) was the massive amount of power invested in the emperor. The emperor personally possessed total authority: he controlled and exercised the rights of sovereignty (*tōchiken*), passed legislation with the "consent" of the Diet, gave sanction to laws, appointed and dismissed civil and military officials, determined the organization of the army and navy, had supreme command (*tōsuiken*) over them, could declare war, make peace and conclude treaties, declare martial law, confer titles of nobility, orders, and other honors, and grant amnesty and pardons.

Meanwhile, the protections granted for civil rights were weak. In Europe, such rights of the people were described as being inalienable to either the people or nobility, but the theoretical framework for these rights in Japan was that they were being conferred upon the people by the constitution. These rights also had the reservation attached to them that they were applicable only within the limits of the law. And the traditional affection for the people by the imperial ancestors was given as the basis for this conferral.

For this reason, the powers of the House of Representatives, nominally intended to reflect the opinions of the public, were also limited. Not only was a coequal House of Peers created, but the authority of the Diet was merely to "consent." Ministers of state were responsible not to the Diet but to the emperor. Also, the most important power granted to the Diet, the right to oversee the budget, did not extend to "already fixed expenditures" based on the constitution (Article 67). And in the case of a failure by the Diet to pass a budget, the government could carry out that of the previous year (Article 71). The authority of the Diet also failed to extend to items related to the emperor, and it had no diplomatic powers such as treaty ratification.

The limitations on the Diet seen as the most problematic were those related to the military. Matters having to do with the administration of the military, that is, those related to its organization, were conducted through advice given by the war and naval ministers to the emperor. Matters having to do with military orders (commands) – those related to the operational command of the military, in other words – were under the immediate control of the emperor. Accordingly, although the authority of the prime minister extended to matters of military administration to a certain degree, he had no power over military orders, and the Diet was even more powerless. This state of affairs is famously known as the independence of the supreme command (*tōsuiken no dokuritsu*). Systems that would later develop to further guarantee this independence included the right of direct access to the throne (*iaku jōsō*), the ability to report to the emperor without going through the prime minister, military ordinances (*gunrei*), a form of providing commands to the military that did not pass through the cabinet or Diet (established in Military Ordinance No. 1 in 1907), and the requirement that only active duty high-ranking generals and admirals could be appointed to serve as military ministers (*gunbu daijin geneki bukan-sei*).

This massive concentration of power in the emperor – and the comparative lack of civil rights – had the following origin. In Western constitutional systems, state sovereignty originally took the shape of a division of authority between the sovereign and legislature. In other words, the existence of absolute sovereignty was a prerequisite for the creation of a constitutional system. But that concept didn't exist in Japan yet; it therefore had to be created first before transition to a constitutional system would be possible. A theoretical framework was thus adopted under which the existence of absolute imperial authority was first assumed and limitations were placed on that authority by the will of the emperor himself (Article 4, "The Emperor is the head of the Empire, combining in Himself the rights of sovereignty, and exercises them, according to the provisions of the present Constitution").

Accordingly, even though the great authority of the emperor was laid out in the constitution, in reality, all of his powers were exercised in a limited fashion in accordance with advice provided by the organs of the state. In that sense, the order created by the Meiji Constitution contained aspects of a constitutional monarchy. One of the criticisms put forward by some members of the government toward the constitution was that the phrase "according to the provisions of the present Constitution" in the aforementioned Article 4 should be removed because it placed limits on imperial power. There was also the opinion concerning inclusion of the term "the rights of subjects," that subjects should not be acknowledged as having rights, and that this should be changed to refer to "social status" (*bunzai*) instead. Itō and the others rejected these proposed amendments, however, arguing that, without any limits on the exercise of power and recognition of some civil rights, the document couldn't be truly regarded as a constitution.

Regarding the powers of the House of Representatives, it at least had a veto over the budget and laws. The ability of the government to proceed by continuing to carry out the previous year's budget was useless for the purpose of promoting "rich country, strong army." In reality, the House of Representative's supervision of the budget frequently made it possible for the body to exert influence over the military as well.

Two views of the emperor

The Meiji Constitution thus incorporated aspects of both absolutism and constitutional monarchism. Viewed from the former perspective, the emperor had to be an entity personally making decisions on every issue that the government faced. This interpretation was known as *Tennō-shinseiron* (theory of direct imperial rule) and was supported by scholars like Hozumi Yatsuka (1860–1912) and Uesugi Shinkichi (1878–1929). Viewed from the other perspective, known as *Tennō-chōseiron* (theory of the emperor above politics), the emperor entrusted each state organ with government and did not get personally involved in actual governance. Ichiki Kitokurō (1867–1944) and Minobe Tatsukichi (1873–1948) were representative scholars of this school of thought.

The problem with Tennō-shinseiron was that, if a decision made by the Emperor was a failure, political responsibility would extend to the throne. Accordingly, the theory had little support among the actual political elite. Because it was powerful as a pretense, however, it was frequently used to threaten them. Meanwhile, Tennō-chōseiron had a major problem of its own, namely the absence of a mechanism to resolve matters when the desires of multiple state organs came into conflict. It was the *genrō*, the founders of the Meiji state, who resolved these issues by participating in the planning of important policies even when not serving in positions of responsibility within the government. Eventually, the founding fathers would age and retire, however, making it difficult for Tennō-chōseiron to be maintained.

Now, as has already been discussed, the theoretical framework of the emperor's absolute sovereignty was necessary for the creation of the constitution. To boost the emperor's image as an absolute ruler, it was necessary to implant that perception among the people. The Imperial Rescript on Education (*Kyōiku Chokugo*) in 1890 played a central role in this effort. The rescript was a listing of virtues in the words of the emperor. It ran from filial piety toward one's parents, friendship to siblings, harmony between spouses, trust between friends, and humility and respect for the law, justice, and courage. Its most distinctive characteristic is that neither God nor the emperor was credited with establishing these virtues but rather the imperial ancestors. In other words, there was a concern that attributing the virtues to a transcendental entity like God or heaven would render the emperor and the people equal in their relationship to it. This possibility was prevented by the use of the imperial ancestors. Another characteristic of the rescript was that, by enumerating Confucian values for daily use, it eliminated free interpretation. The image of the emperor supported by Tennō-shinseiron was disseminated by structuring the rescript in this way.

Taking on treaty revision

The treaty revision issue

Incidentally, the Meiji government was grappling with revising its treaties with the West at the same time that it was introducing a constitution. Treaties are of no less importance than a constitution to a country in the sense that they are all basic laws of the state. Even with the creation of a constitution, the national framework of Japan could not be regarded as complete with the unequal treaties of the Baku-matsu still in place.

One problem caused by the unequal treaties was the issue of extraterritoriality, the acknowledgment of consular jurisdiction over foreign nationals. Crimes committed by foreigners could be tried by their nation's consular courts, and appealing to higher courts was extremely inconvenient for the Japanese. To take the case of Britain as an example, appeals first went to the British Supreme Court for China in Shanghai and then went to the Privy Council in London. It goes without saying that disputes over trade often ended with results disadvantageous to the Japanese. There were also cases such as that of John Hartley in 1877–1878, a British merchant who was convicted of smuggling opium yet received only an extremely light punishment, as well as examples of foreigners rejecting the application of Japanese administrative codes, such as in the case of the *Hesperia*, a German ship that, in 1879, refused to be quarantined after coming to Japan from a cholera-stricken area.

Another problem caused by the treaties was the one-sided tariff system. While the West had sovereignty over tariffs imposed on Japanese goods, Japan did not have sovereignty over foreign goods; Japan's income from tariffs was accordingly extremely low. According to the research of Ono Azusa (1852–1886), tariffs accounted for over 50 percent of the national incomes of America and Germany; even Britain, who claimed to practice free trade, made more than 20 percent of its income from tariffs. In comparison, tariffs represented a mere 3 percent of Japan's income. Because tariffs were kept so low, the Japanese government had no choice but to implement a high land tax (see Chapter 4). This vicious cycle contributed to governmental instability. It goes without saying that Japan's lack of sovereignty over tariffs was also a hindrance to its promotion of domestic industries. Revision of the unequal treaties was thus absolutely necessary to Japan for reasons of national honor, income security, domestic stability, and the promotion of domestic industry.

Setting aside the failed attempt at treaty revision negotiations undertaken during the Iwakura Mission, it was under Foreign Minister Terashima Munenori (1834–1893, in office 1873–1879) that Japan began to truly take on the revision issue. Prioritizing the restoration of taxation authority, he decided to first negotiate with America, the country with the most cordial relations with Japan. As mentioned earlier, the government had lowered the land tax from 3 to 2.5 percent in 1877 shortly before the Satsuma Rebellion out of concern that a revolt by farmers could join forces with a samurai rebellion (see Chapter 3). How much the government desired to be able to raise tariffs can be readily understood.

Treaty revision moved from being a question of economic interest to one of national honor, however, when public opinion erupted as the Hartley and *Hesperia* incidents occurred from 1877 to 1879. Antigovernment factions used this to once again criticize the government. Later, in what became known as the Normanton Incident, the *Normanton*, a British ship, sank after encountering a typhoon in the

Kumano Sea in October 1886. Although the entire white crew safely escaped the ship, all twenty-five Japanese passengers died. A song expressing outrage at the incident became popular throughout the country.

Inoue Kaoru, who became foreign minister in 1879 and who would be in charge of Japan's foreign affairs for eight years, took the distinctive approach of attempting to secure foreign agreement to treaty revision by publicizing Japan's state as a civilized country, showing off its rapid modernization. This resulted in the famous Rokumeikan period, named after a large Western-style building constructed for social events. Regarding specific changes to the treaties, Inoue sought an increase of the tariff rate rather than a restoration of Japan's right to set its own tariffs. He also believed Japan should rapidly develop its legal system, gain foreign consent to it, and add Western judges to Japanese courts dealing with foreigners to handle the issue of extraterritoriality. His treaty policy was put together in April 1887 and received a positive reactive from the foreign powers. The policy was increasingly criticized within Japan as humiliating, however, and Inoue was forced to resign.

Ōkuma Shigenobu was faced with dealing with the treaty issue after succeeding Inoue as foreign minister in February 1888. Although his plans for revision were similar to those of Inoue, they had evolved in some ways: the number of cases that would involve Western judges was reduced, and, although foreign countries would be informed of the further development of Japan's laws, their consent would no longer be sought. Japan signed a treaty with Mexico in November, its first equal treaty with a non-Asian nation. Following the promulgation of the new constitution in February 1889, members of the government began to argue that appointing foreign judges would be unconstitutional, however. Ōkuma's plans were also leaked to the *Times* in London, leading to increased domestic opposition. Ōkuma himself was then seriously injured in a terrorist attack in October 1889. The Kuroda government resigned, and Ōkuma lost his position. His efforts thus ended in failure.

The government had promoted increasingly conservative policies since the 1881 Political Crisis, and the efforts of Inoue and Ōkuma were incompatible with the political atmosphere that this had created. Opposition to their plans had come from those who emphasized the importance of national sovereignty, both inside and outside the government. There was also a conservative faction within the government led by the imperial court that did not look kindly upon the Westernization policies of Itō and other leaders.

The Daidō Danketsu movement

Incidentally, the treaty revision issue brought about the revival of the people's rights movement, which had been briefly dormant. Strong opposition had arisen among the government's conservative faction after Inoue's plans for treaty revision had been prepared and shown to the Western powers; this in turn revived the old people's rights movement. Kataoka Kenkichi (1843–1903) of Tosa submitted a petition to the Genrōin in October 1887 in which he advocated for freedom of speech, lowering the land tax, and the restoration of equal diplomacy. This petition ultimately developed into the Petition for Three Important Matters (*San Daijiken Kenpaku*) movement, with Hoshi Tōru at its center. Hoshi supported Gotō Shōjirō as its leader and toured the country making speeches; this became the *Daidō Danketsu* (Grand Coalition) movement, which called for all factions of the people's rights movement to join together. This antigovernment movement reached its pinnacle during the Hokkaidō Colonization Office's assets scandal in 1881 (see Chapter 4).

The government made concessions to its conservative faction in response: Inoue was made to resign in September 1887, and Prime Minister Itō was replaced as imperial household minister by the conservative Hijikata Hisamoto (1833–1918). Meanwhile, harsh steps were taken against the people's rights movement: the Peace Preservation Law (*Hoan Jōrei*) was enacted, and those involved in the movement were driven from Tokyo. The government invited Ōkuma to join the cabinet in 1888 to split the former Progressive Party members who made up part of the movement and then invited Gotō Shōjirō, its head, to join in 1889.

The Daidō Danketsu movement can be seen as an eruption of energies that had been suppressed since the Matsukata Deflation (see Chapter 4). A desire to participate in the forthcoming legislature provided another source of energy; a number of the movement's participants planned to run for seats. They were fated to run against one another in the election, however, which is why the movement went into decline following the loss of Gotō, who had been symbolic for the movement. The figures that had made up the movement now began working toward the forthcoming election and the opening of the Imperial Diet.

Note

1 *Genrō* is often translated in Western literature as "elder statesmen," but they are also the founding fathers of the Meiji state. Later on, Katsura Tarō and Saionji Kinmochi were made *genrō*, but they did not have enough prestige because their contribution to the making of the Meiji state was limited compared to Itō, Matsukata, and others. After them, no one was made or treated as a *genrō*; they could not be reproduced.

6 The establishment of parliament

Hanbatsu–party relations in the early Diet sessions

The launch of parliament

Entrenching parliament is a far more difficult task than merely creating a constitution. Even today, a number of countries, having written impressive constitutions, abandoned them after only a brief period. Institutionalizing political opposition through parliament is especially difficult. It is more common for those in power, when faced with an increasingly powerful opposition, to maintain their control rather than surrender the reins of government, even if that means warping political institutions. And it is easy for the opposition to move to more radical measures and reject the entire political system when opposition from within the legislature proves ineffective. It is only natural that the early period of parliamentary government in Japan was marked by intense factional confrontation. The question that needs to be asked is how and why parliament became entrenched in the country. This chapter examines the period from the launch of the Diet, or parliament, to the founding of the Seiyūkai (Friends of Constitutional Government) in 1900 from the viewpoint of this question.

Transcendentalism

Relations between the Meiji oligarchs, or *hanbatsu* (literally, domain cliques), and the political parties during the early parliamentary period – that is, the time from the first Diet in 1890 to the First Sino-Japanese War in 1894 – developed along two confrontational axes: transcendentalism (*chōzenshugi*) vs. responsible cabinets and *fukoku kyōhei* (rich country, strong military) vs. *minryoku kyūyō* (relief for the people). The former axis will be discussed first.

On February 12, 1889, the day after the constitution's promulgation, Prime Minister Kuroda Kiyotaka told the Prefectural Governors Conference (Chihōkan Kaigi) that "the government must always hold to its established policy of standing apart from the political parties as a transcendental [body] on the path of righteousness." This is famously known as the transcendentalism speech (*chōzenshugi enzetsu*) and made clear the stance that government policy was more important

Figure 6.1 Kokkai Gijō no Zu (Picture of the Diet Chamber) by Tōshū Shōgetsu. (From the collection of the University of Tokyo Graduate Schools for Laws and Politics' Center for Modern Japanese Legal and Political Documents.)

than political opinion and that the government would not be under the control of the Diet or the political parties. The political parties responded by asserting that public opinion as reflected in the Diet should be given importance and that the cabinet should have the support from some major party. It was called the argument of responsible cabinet. The next goal for the political parties was, of course, a party cabinet, that is, to have a party leader as the prime minister.

The governments of the domain cliques adopted this policy of transcendentalism for a number of reasons. First, the leaders of the government shared an understanding that the modernization of a developing state like Japan was extremely difficult and had been made possible only by strong leadership. They were confident that it was only the Satsuma and Chōshū domains that had supported the Meiji state up to that point that were capable of providing such leadership, not any political party representing a particular faction. When the naval expansion budget was rejected during the second Diet, the furious Navy Minister Kabayama Sukenori (1837–1922) told the Diet that while they might criticize the government as being dominated by the domain cliques, it was only due to the accomplishments of the Satsuma and Chōshū domains that the Meiji state had been able to come so far (this is known as the *banyū enzetsu*, or brutal speech). Although Kabayama's words were widely derided, they accurately expressed the true feelings of the Meiji oligarchs.

Furthermore, the Meiji state used the emperor's authority to preserve its great administrative powers and gave the privileged status to its officials. Because the bureaucracy drew upon a standardized national educational system, officials were confident in their ability to assemble the most capable men in the country. There also remained a large gap in the amount of information the government and opposition had about foreign countries.

These advantages were not necessarily enough to be decisive, however. The government may have had a great amount of administrative authority, but the power of the Diet still couldn't be ignored. The possibility that the powerful bureaucracy would become independent and move beyond the grasp of the domain cliques always remained as well. And the information gap would soon close as modernization continued to progress. Absolute transcendentalism had been an impossibility from the start.

In fact, even Kuroda, who had made the transcendentalism speech, included Gotō of the Grand Coalition movement (see Chapter 5) and Ōkuma of the Progressive Party in his cabinet. And Inoue Kaoru, Kuroda's agricultural minister, was also planning to gather local elites into a new political party, the Self-Government Party (*Jichitō*). In other words, the Kuroda government was in no way transcendental; it was instead almost a national unity government incorporating figures from many political groups.

Aspects of the early Diet sessions

The first general election for the House of Representatives was held on July 1, 1890. Professing to hold to transcendentalism, the government did not interfere with the election, leaving it relatively freely to the electorate. Four hundred fifty thousand Japanese were eligible to vote, a mere 1 percent of the population. The electorate, members of the privileged classes, wore full dress as they went to vote in the long-awaited election and voted by writing down their names and addresses and stamping their ballots. As the electorate consisted of the propertied class, the government expected that the majority would be supportive to the government.

Contrary to these expectations, the antigovernment *mintō* (literally, people's parties) had overwhelming power in the new Diet when it opened. Although party affiliation was not clear at the time, roughly 130 of the 300 members formed and joined the *Rikken Jiyūtō* (Constitutional Liberal Party) before the opening of the Diet; another forty-six belonged to the *Rikken Kaishintō* (Constitutional Progressive Party); some other small parties and independent members were also on the opposition side. It should be noted that while they opposed the government, they were in fact privileged and wealthy and thus did not represent "the people" as *mintō* might otherwise imply. Indeed, few people in Japan had the right to vote at this time. The progovernment parties were given the derisive name of *ritō* (bureaucrat parties), showing their unpopularity. Against a majority held by the opposition, the primary issue facing the government was how to get their policies, especially the budget, through the Diet.

The first strategy they employed was to try to split the people's parties, including through bribery. The Yamagata government agonized over the opposition's demands for spending cuts during the first Diet (1890–1891) and only barely managed to pass a budget by splitting off the Liberal Party's Tosa faction. But this was not an especially good approach as it infuriated the party that suffered the defection, making them even more opposed to the government. And the cost of splitting off factions would only increase.

A second strategy was dissolving the Diet and calling another election. Matsukata Masayoshi's government dissolved the second Diet (November–December 1891) and then, led by Home Minister Shinagawa Yajirō (1843–1900), engaged in massive electoral interference/fraud in an attempt to break the power of the opposition. The second general election, held on February 15, 1892, was completely different from the first; the violence is believed to have resulted in twenty-five dead and 388 injured. As elections are essentially a system meant to substitute voting for violence, elections without any violence are a difficult thing to accomplish in any country. It was only during the early Shōwa period that violence stopped being a common part of Japanese elections, and even today bloody elections are not rare in the world. In that sense, the severity of the government's intervention in the second general election is less surprising than the fact that the government still couldn't win. Since the electorate was made up of the privileged classes, it was less receptive to bribes and threats.

Finally, the government could make use of imperial edicts. Believing that even the opposition would respond to sincere persuasion, Itō criticized Matsukata's confrontational approach and forced the fall of the government. He then gathered influential members of the domain cliques and formed his second government in August 1892. But the involvement of important Meiji oligarchs made the opposition all the more defiant, and the budget process again ground to a halt during the fourth Diet (1892–1893). Itō decided to resolve the situation through an imperial edict issued on February 10. In this the emperor, stating his desire for "harmonious cooperation" between the Diet and the government, imposed a 10 percent salary reduction on government officials and promised to provide 300,000 yen a year for six years from the budgeted allowance for the private expenses of the imperial family. These funds would be used to supplement the naval construction budget. This approach, in which a dispute was resolved by having all three parties (the two opposing parties and the mediator) share the burden equally, is extremely interesting as a quintessentially Japanese example of conflict resolution.

This, however, was a dangerous approach that threatened the emperor's sacred inviolability; had the Diet refused to accept the proposed solution, the authority of the emperor would have been damaged.

To summarize, there was no effective means of maintaining transcendentalism. Accordingly, only two options remained: the government could either suspend the constitution or compromise with the political parties.

One reason that the constitution remained in place was concern about Japan's reputation as a civilized country. Had it been suspended, Japan would have been seen as an uncivilized country incapable of constitutional government, and revision of the unequal treaties would then clearly have become impossible for quite some time. Another reason was that the domain cliques were not a monolithic group. Because they frequently opposed one another, any action seen as too extreme would immediately cause others within the group to act against it.

The transformation of "relief for the people"

As transcendentalism was reaching a stalemate, the opposition was also facing a dilemma over "relief for the people." *Minryoku kyūyō* was not a rejection of the doctrine of "rich country, strong military." Its fundamental goal was to reduce government spending. It called for reducing government expenditures, cutting the salaries of officials, and lowering the land tax. Since the antigovernment parties controlled a majority in the House of Representatives, they were able to cut the budget, but lowering the land tax would require revising existing laws. That needed the approval of both houses of the Diet, and there was very little chance of gaining the agreement of the domain cliques–controlled House of Peers for any reduction of the tax. Thus, even if the opposition successfully cut government spending, they wouldn't be able to make this part of relief for the people.

Even if reducing the land tax rate was impossible, "relief for the people" could still be achieved by adjusting land value estimates. And due to the accumulation of revenue surpluses, that at least seemed possible. But reactions to this proposal were mixed among the opposition because the benefits would vary; some regions would benefit while others would not.

The proposal of *minryoku ikusei* (development of the people) within the parties as an alternative to relief for the people was another issue for the opposition. This took the position that if reduction of the land tax was impossible, then the surplus revenue should be used for railroad construction, civil works, land improvement, and other activities that would benefit the people. This position was also referred to as positivism (*sekkyokushugi*).

Yet another issue was the increasingly fluid relations between the *hanbatsu* and the parties over the treaty revision issue. Despite having originally been the party most opposed to the government, the Liberal Party under the leadership of Hoshi Tōru (1850–1901) began to shift from relief for the people to development of the people and draw closer to the Itō Cabinet. At the same time the Progressive Party, which had been relatively cordial with the government prior to the creation of the Diet, became increasingly oppositional. And as the appeal of relief for the people faded, the focus of antigovernment criticism shifted toward pushing the government to adopt a more hard-line foreign policy.

The Kokumin Kyōkai (National Association) is another political group active at this time that is worth giving some attention to. Created during the Matsukata Cabinet, the National Association was a so-called bureaucrat party that fought against the people's parties during the second general election in 1892. But because Itō had been critical of Matsukata's foreign policy, the relationship between his government and the party was delicate. While the increasingly close relationship between the Liberal Party and the government because of the former's adoption of positivism brought it closer to the National Association's original position, the nature of politics meant that this was not something to be overjoyed about. This is because, as a bureaucrat party, a close relationship between the government and a people's party threatened its reason for existing. The National Association thus changed its emphasis to pushing for a hard-line foreign policy (one of its original positions) and adopted an oppositional stance.

As the fifth Diet opened in November 1893, the hard-liners on foreign policy (including the Progressive Party and National Assembly) held a majority. At this time, they advocated a policy of strict enforcement of the treaties (*jōyaku reikō*). Although foreigners had been granted privileges such as extraterritoriality under the Ansei treaties (see Chapter 2), this was in exchange for restrictions that made it difficult for foreigners to travel beyond the treaty ports. The parties thus sought to cause difficulties by having these restrictions strictly enforced. This was a dangerous policy for the Japanese government, which was in the midst of attempting to revise the treaties. The Itō Cabinet thus dissolved the Diet on December 30, 1893. The next Diet then met the same fate on June 2, 1894.

The conflict in the Diet between the government and the parties thus became fierce. While the Itō Cabinet and the Liberal Party grew closer, the Progressive Party and the National Assembly attacked it over its weak foreign policy. Accordingly, when the government succeeded in revising the unequal treaties in July 1894 and entered the First Sino-Japanese War (see Chapter 7), the parties immediately adopted a "war-time political truce" and supported the position of a national unity government. Although other elements, such as the Japanese character, were also partly responsible for national unity, the fluidity of domain clique–party relations prior to the war (the Liberal Party's increasingly progovernmental stance and the change to a hard-line position on foreign policy by the Progressive Party and the National Association) had already laid the groundwork for this.

Hanbatsu–party relations following the First Sino-Japanese War

Postwar expansion

As the specifics of the First Sino-Japanese War will be covered in the next chapter, the discussion here will move on to domain clique–party relations following the war. Although the war came to an end when a peace treaty was signed in April 1895, a wartime political truce continued to hold. The greatest issue pending for the government in the wake of the war was postwar expansion (*sengo keiei*), the plan to use reparations from China to fund a massive expansion of the country's military and industries. The first postwar expansion budget passed by the ninth Diet (1895–1896) included 250 million yen over ten years for expansion of the military and 50 million over seven years for industrial promotion. To give an idea of how significant a spending increase this was, annual spending before the war had been only 80 million yen. As a result of this additional spending, the 1896 budget swelled to 150 million yen and the 1897 budget to 240 million.

The increasing encroachment of the Western powers on China since the exposure of its weakness had made Japan uneasy about its security; this was why a massive plan of this kind had become necessary. The Triple Intervention (see Chapter 7) was an extreme example of this Western encroachment.

Even though the Chinese reparations served as the chief source of funds for this plan, they were not enough on their own to make it a reality. It was therefore essential for Japan to raise its taxes. This expansion of the budget also increasingly rendered useless the government's ability to continue the previous year's budget when no new budget was passed by the Diet (see Chapter 5).

Yamagata Aritomo (1838–1922) and the House of Peers and Privy Council

Under the Constitution of the Empire of Japan, the House of Peers possessed powers that were essentially the same as those of the House of Representatives. Its membership consisted of *kōzoku giin* (members of the imperial family), *kazoku giin* (peerage members), *chokusen giin* (members nominated by the emperor), and *tagaku nōzeisha giin* (members representing the highest taxpayers); these gradually increased in number from 250 members to roughly 400. All members of the imperial family became members of the body upon reaching a certain age but did not normally attend sessions. All princes and marquises were members, but counts, viscounts, and barons needed to be elected by those holding the same rank (and served for seven-year terms). In 1890, fourteen counts, seventy viscounts, and twenty barons were serving as members. *Chokusen giin* were chosen for life as a reward for service to the state. The *tagaku nōzeisha giin* were selected, one per prefecture, in an election held among the highest taxpayers. Memberships were added beginning in the Taishō period for the Imperial Academy (*Teikoku Gakushiin*), Korea, and Taiwan.

Former bureaucrats with great administrative experience made up the core of the House of Peers. They made up the majority of the *chokusen giin*, and since bureaucrats of great accomplishment were frequently appointed to the peerage during the Meiji period, they were also influential in the peerage member elections. The bureaucrats who opposed Itō Hirobumi's close relationships with the political parties following the First Sino-Japanese War gathered around Yamagata Aritomo and successfully gained control of the body during the first peer election in 1897.

The Privy Council was created in 1888 to review the proposed constitution; afterward, it investigated important state affairs when requested by the emperor (Article 56), as well as the constitution and laws related to the constitution, laws pertaining to the imperial household, and emergency imperial edicts. The matters that fell under its purview would occasionally be changed, and it could at times cause difficulties for the government by effectively acting as a third house of the Diet. The failure of the government of Wakatsuki Reijirō (1866–1949) to gain the body's support for its proposed emergency imperial edict to save the Bank of Taiwan in April 1927 resulted in its resignation.

Itō Hirobumi served as the first president of the Privy Council, and the body initially consisted of twelve councilors (this was later expanded to more than twenty) who were given treatment close to that accorded to cabinet ministers. Yamagata Aritomo, who became increasingly important from the late Meiji period on, served as president of the body for twenty-one months from 1893 to 1894 before going on to hold the position for the seventeen years between 1905 and his death in 1922 (excluding a gap of four months). After Yamagata, an attempt was made to depoliticize the Privy Council during the era of party governments by appointing scholars as councilors, but the actions of the powerful Itō Miyoji (1857–1934) continued to cause difficulties for the cabinets and occasionally force their resignations.

As previously shown, Yamagata was a powerful force in both the House of Peers and the Privy Council. Furthermore, by the time of his death, he also exerted influence over the army as an active duty field marshal, held power among the serving bureaucrats, had a small political party in the House of Representatives, and had become powerful enough to stand against Itō Hirobumi.

It was thus necessary for the domain cliques–led government to further amend its policy of transcendentalism if it wanted to pursue postwar expansion. The Itō Cabinet publicly declared an alliance with the Liberal Party in November 1895 and welcomed Itagaki Taisuke into the government as its new home minister in April 1896. Ōkuma was then named foreign minister in the following 2nd Matsukata government formed in September 1896. The quasi cabinet-level positions of chief cabinet secretary (*naikaku shokikanchō*) and head of the Legislation Bureau (*Hōseikyoku*), seven posts at the vice-minister, bureau chief, and deputy bureau chief levels in various ministries, and eight governorships were also given to members of the *Shimpotō* (Progressive Party, the successor to *Kaishintō* formed in March 1896).

The Itō and Matsukata cabinets also listened to the arguments of the parties and left the land tax alone, choosing instead to levy tax increases on commerce and industry, such as through the business tax or indirect taxes like the one on alcohol.

This course of postwar expansion caused two new opposition factions to form, however. The first of these was the bourgeois, who now began to participate in politics. This had previously been unnecessary as they had been under the protection of the Meiji politicians, but as they were being used as a source of funds, they now began independent political activities.

The second was the Yamagata faction. The adjustments made to transcendentalism by Itō and Matsukata had come as a major shock to the next generation of officials who feared that their position as the legitimate successors to the Meiji government would be stolen from them by the political parties. These officials gathered around Yamagata Aritomo, who was seen as the strongest believer in transcendentalism. Kiyoura Keigo (1850–1942, later prime minister), Hirata Tōsuke (1849–1925, later Lord Keeper of the Privy Seal), and Ōura Kanetake (1850–1918, later home minister) were members of this group.

The appointment of Itagaki as home minister in April 1896 served as the impetus for the formation of the Yamagata faction. The position of home minister was central to bureaucratic power and held powers that today are divided between the Ministry of Internal Affairs and Communications, the Ministry of Land, Infrastructure, Transport, and Tourism, the Ministry of Health, Labor and Welfare, the National Public Safety Commission, and the prefectural governors. The shock the officials within the home ministry felt at losing control of such a powerful position is easy to understand.

The Yamagata officials, led by Kiyoura and the others, were victorious during the July 1897 appointment of peers to the House of Peers (from the counts, viscounts, and barons) (see "Yamagata Aritomo and the House of Peers and Privy Council"), putting the body largely under their control.

The Ōkuma-Itagaki Cabinet

In addition to these complication, a new problem would surface and cause major changes to domain clique–party relations. This was the issue of increasing the land tax.

Postwar expansion had been initiated on the basis of estimates that were only just barely feasible. When a postwar recession caused revenues to fall below projections, there were immediately fiscal problems. Because it was believed that the burden caused by business and indirect taxes had reached its limit, the 2nd Matsukata Cabinet decided to raise the land tax instead. This ended its alliance with the Progressive Party; the eleventh Diet was dissolved in late 1897, and the cabinet resigned.

Increasing the land tax wasn't enough by itself to definitively sever cooperation between the domain cliques and the parties, however, and the newly formed 3rd Itō Cabinet and Liberal Party entered negotiations for a potential alliance. But the conditions for such an alliance, namely the provision of official posts to party members, presented another problem as the rise of the Yamagata faction had made it more difficult for the government to make such concessions. The 3rd Itō Cabinet was thus formed without any party allies. As a result, its plan to raise the land tax was overwhelmingly rejected during the twelfth Diet. The Diet was dissolved once again in June 1898, but it was clear that the government would be unsuccessful during the coming elections. To make matters worse, the Liberal Party and Progressive Party merged on June 22 to form the *Kenseitō* (Constitutional Party), a massive party that controlled 80 percent of the seats in the House of Representatives.

The Meiji oligarchs had no brilliant plan on how to overcome this situation. Itō considered forming his own political party to regain control. That would represent a complete break with the concept of transcendental government, however, and was questionable in terms of its likely effectiveness. There were those within the Yamagata faction who considered using an emergency imperial edict to increase the tax, but the increase would have to be approved by the next Diet, and it was feared that the emperor's authority would be damaged should it refuse to do so. It was thus ultimately decided to allow the Constitutional Party to form a government. The Meiji oligarchs believed that the party's base was still weak and that it would undoubtedly fracture before long from internal conflict; in any case, the war and naval minister positions could be used to restrain the government should it attempt to implement any dangerous policies. But most importantly, the oligarchs had no better alternative available to them. Japan's first party cabinet was thus formed with Ōkuma Shigenobu as prime and foreign minister and Itagaki Taisuke as home minister.

As the oligarchs had predicted, however, the Constitutional Party cabinet suffered from internal conflicts and proved to be short-lived. The first issue it had faced was a flood of office seekers. The long awaited party government had arrived, and many members eagerly expected it to abolish the Civil Service Appointment Law (*Bunkan Ninyō Rei*) and provide access to all government positions. Implementing such an extreme spoils system would have turned the existing bureaucracy completely against the cabinet, however, so this was not done. The cabinet thus faced criticism from both the bureaucracy for going too far and from the party for not offering enough positions; a fierce competition broke out between former members of the Liberal Party and Progressive Party over the limited number of posts made available. When Minister of Education Ozaki Yukio (1858–1954) was forced to resign after making a reference to republicanism while criticizing the rise of materialism in Japan, a struggle erupted over who would be his successor. The former Liberal Party members were also unhappy that Prime Minister Ōkuma was serving as foreign minister and demanded that the position be given to one of them.

The government also found it difficult to discard the previous governments' postwar expansion policy. Both the Liberal Party and the Progressive Party had committed to the plan and the government had promised its war and naval ministers that there would be no changes to the expansion of the military, the centerpiece of the policy. It was obvious that the government would immediate fall if it attempted to make any major revisions.

That meant that the cabinet was faced with the following three possible courses of action. First, it could continue with postwar expansion and attempt to use business and indirect taxes as sources of revenue. That would be consistent with the Constitutional Party's nature as a party of landowners and would be useful for keeping the government in power. Second, it could increase revenue by raising the land tax. That would be useful for allowing the party to continue to participate in the government and for promoting the development of cities, but it could potentially reduce their electoral base in farming areas. Finally, they could implement cuts to postwar expansion. While that would likely result in the collapse of the cabinet, it would allow them to maintain their traditional policy positions.

The cabinet pursued the first of these options, but ultimately fell due to internal conflicts. The ministers from the former Liberal Party announced their resignations on October 29, 1898. The Liberal Party branch of the Constitutional Party then drove the former Progressive Party members from the party by holding a general party meeting in which only the Liberal Party branch was in attendance. At this meeting, they voted to dissolve the party and then immediately formed a new Constitutional Party with themselves as the sole members. This heavy-handed approach took advantage of the fact that Itagaki Taisuke of the Liberal Party branch was serving as home minister. Prime Minister Ōkuma submitted his resignation on October 31, and the former Progressive Party members reluctantly carried on, taking the name Kensei Hontō (literally, True or Main Constitutional Party) on November 3.

The Yamagata Cabinet

The 2nd Yamagata Cabinet was formed on November 8 following the fall of the Ōkuma-Itagaki Cabinet. It chose the second of the Constitutional Party's options, passing a land tax increase during the thirteenth Diet that opened shortly afterward (on December 30). This was made possible by the close relationship between the cabinet and the Constitutional Party promoted by Hoshi Tōru. Hoshi viewed the role of a political party as participating in government administration and accomplishing its policy goals rather than engaging in criticism of the government and forcefully dragging the rest of the Constitutional Party along.

The government had also made a number of concessions; it had originally planned to increase the land tax (then at 2.5%) to 4 percent but instead compromised on a rate of 3.3 percent for a period of just five years and also began adjusting land values in a number of regions. The result of these concessions was that the land tax was effectively raised to only 2.9 percent. But even given these factors, the ability of a government to actually successfully increase the land tax within a mere eight years of the Diet's creation represented a revolutionary change given how intense the opposition had been. (See Tables 6.1 and 6.2.)

For the Constitutional Party, cooperation with the Yamagata Cabinet was intended to merely serve as a first step toward the party's participation in the government. But Yamagata was not inclined to make many concessions to the parties. In March 1899, immediately after passing the land tax increase, the government used an imperial edict to amend the Civil Service Appointment Law to prevent members of political parties from becoming important officials; a number of positions, including vice-minister, the heads of important bureaus, and prefectural governors, were changed to be available only to those with certain qualifications. The government then went a step further in 1900 by making the amendment of laws such as the Civil Service Appointment Law subject to consultation with the Privy Council, a stronghold of the Yamagata faction and outside the touch of the parties. It also adopted the active duty military ministers (*gunbu daijin geneki*

Table 6.1 Presidents of the Privy Council.

Itō Hirobumi	4/30/1888–10/30/1889	Prime minister
Oki Takatō	12/24/1889–6/1/1891	President, Genrōin
Itō Hirobumi	6/1/1891–8/8/1892	Councilor, imperial household
Oki Takatō	8/8/1892–11/22/1892	Minister of education
Yamagata Aritomo	3/11/1893–12/18/1894	Minister of justice
Kuroda Kiyotaka	3/17/1895–8/25/1900	Minister of communications
Saionji Kinmochi	10/27/1900–7/13/1903	Councilor, Privy Council
Itō Hirobumi	7/13/1903–12/21/1905	President, Seiyūkai
Yamagata Aritomo	12/21/1905–6/14/1909	Councilor, Privy Council
Itō Hirobumi	6/14/1909–10/26/1909	Resident-general of Korea
Yamagata Aritomo	11/17/1909–2/1/1922	Councilor, Privy Council
Kiyoura Keigo	2/8/1922–1/7/1924	Vice president, Privy Council
Hamao Arata	1/13/1924–9/25/1925	Vice president, Privy Council
Hozumi Nobushige	10/1/1925–4/8/1926	Vice president, Privy Council
Kuratomi Yuzaburō	4/12/1926–5/3/1934	Vice president, Privy Council
Ichiki Kitokurō	5/3/1934–3/13/1936	Imperial household minister
Hiranuma Kiichirō	3/13/1936–1/5/1939	Vice president, Privy Council
Konoe Fumimaro	1/5/1939–6/24/1940	Prime minister
Hara Yoshimichi	6/24/1940–8/7/1944	Vice president, Privy Council
Suzuki Kantarō	8/10/1944–4/7/1945	Vice president, Privy Council
Hiranuma Kiichirō	4/9/1945–12/3/1945	Home minister
Suzuki Kantarō	12/15/1945–6/13/1946	Prime minister
Shimizu Tōru	6/13/1946–5/3/1947	Vice president, Privy Council

Source: Adapted from Nihon Kingendaishi Jiten Henshū Iinkaihen, *Nihon Kingendaishi Jiten* (Dictionary of Modern Japanese History) (Tokyo: Tōyō Keizai Shimpōsha, 1978), p. 803).

Table 6.2 Vice presidents of the Privy Council.

Terashima Munenori	5/10/1888–9/10/1891	Councilor, Privy Council
Soejima Taneomi	9/10/1891–3/11/1892	Councilor, Privy Council
Higashikuze Michitomi	3/17/1892–1/4/1912	Councilor, Privy Council
Yoshikawa Akimasa	1/9/1912–3/20/1917	Councilor, Privy Council
Kiyoura Keigo	3/20/1917–2/8/1922	Councilor, Privy Council
Hamao Arata	2/15/1922–1/13/1924	Councilor, Privy Council
Ichiki Kitokurō	1/14/1924–3/30/1925	Councilor, Privy Council
Hozumi Nobushige	3/30/1925–10/1/1925	Councilor, Privy Council
Okano Keijirō	10/1/1925–12/23/1925	Minister of Education
Kuratomi Yuzaburō	12/28/1925–4/12/1926	Councilor, Privy Council
Hiranuma Kiichirō	4/12/1926–3/13/1936	Councilor, Privy Council
Arai Kentarō	3/13/1936–1/29/1938	Councilor, Privy Council
Hara Yoshimichi	2/3/1938–6/24/1940	Councilor, Privy Council
Suzuki Kantarō	6/24/1940–8/10/1944	Councilor, Privy Council
Shimizu Tōru	8/10/1944–6/13/1946	Councilor, Privy Council
Ushio Shigenosuke	6/13/1946–5/3/1947	Councilor, Privy Council

Source: Adapted from Nihon Kingendaishi Jiten Henshū Iinkaihen, *Nihon Kingendaishi Jiten* (Dictionary of Modern Japanese History) (Tokyo: Tōyō Keizai Shimpōsha, 1978), p. 803.

bukan) system, which restricted the positions of war and navy ministers to active duty general and flag officers holding the rank of at least lieutenant general or vice admiral. The cabinet thus severed its alliance with the Constitutional Party by strengthening the bulwarks against the parties.

The establishment of the Seiyūkai

Hoshi and the Constitutional Party discovered a new partner in Itō Hirobumi, however. Itō hadn't abandoned his previous ideal of a transcendentalism that incorporated the political parties, and that concept was compatible with Hoshi's plans to a degree. After trying and failing to convince Itō to become president of the Constitutional Party, Hoshi decided to dissolve it and join the political party that Itō was attempting to create. At first glance, this development may make it seem like the domain cliques had defeated the political parties. Upon the founding of Itō's party, the Seiyūkai (Friends of Constitutional Government), on September 15, 1900, the socialist journalist Kōtoku Shūsui (1871–1911) wrote "*A* Requiem for the Liberal Party (*Jiyūtō o Matsuru Bun*)" in which he lamented that the Liberal Party, the inheritors of the glorious traditions of the people's rights movement, had died. But the formation of the Friends of Constitutional Government should really be considered a victory for the parties, at least in the sense of securing party participation in the government.

A political party that had been in the opposition had taken one of the most powerful of the oligarchs responsible for the creation of the Meiji state as its president. Until this point, the antioligarchs had essentially served as framework for opposition to the government. But because of a fracturing of the domain cliques and a softening of the parties' position, the Japanese political world became dominated by two great forces: the Friends of Constitutional Government, a political party that had joined with the oligarchs, and the Yamagata faction, a group within the domain cliques who persevered with transcendentalism. Depending on your perspective, this state of affairs would continue for the following eleven to twenty years.

7   The First Sino-Japanese and Russo-Japanese Wars

The First Sino-Japanese War

The line of sovereignty and the line of interest

In his first speech to the Diet in December 1890, Prime Minister Yamagata Aritomo stated that Japan needed to secure influence over not just the "line of sovereignty" (*shukensen*, Japan's territory) but over the "line of interest" (*riekisen*) as well—the line of regions that were closely connected to the security of the line of sovereignty. In more specific terms, it referred to the Korean Peninsula. Yamagata was saying that the Korean Peninsula falling under the influence of a great power hostile to Japan would endanger Japan's security.

This type of thinking was not particularly uncommon at the time. Britain had long considered the Low Countries (today's Benelux countries) on the European mainland to serve as its line of interest. It disliked when the area was invaded by a third party and frequently attempted to intervene to restore their independence when this occurred. Britain believed that things were going well so long as the balance of power on the European mainland was maintained but that its security was threatened when a country (Spain, France, Germany) upset that balance and attempted to unify the continent. The independence of the Low Countries served as a barometer for the balance of power. The Americas for the United States and Eastern Europe for the Soviet Union during the Cold War are other areas where this philosophy applied.

The Sino-Japanese confrontation over Korea

China and Russia were the countries capable of threatening the Korean Peninsula in this sense.

The situation in Korea prior to the 1875 Ganghwa Island Incident and the signing of the Japan-Korea Treaty of Amity in 1876 has already been covered (see Chapter 4). Korea had opened up further under the rule of Empress Myeongseong (Queen Min, 1851–1895), and a Treaty of Peace, Amity, Commerce and Navigation was signed in May 1882 between Korea and the United States. Korea had initiated military reforms in 1881 and had begun to create a modern military

Figure 7.1 U.S. President Theodore Roosevelt (center), Komura Jutarō (to his right), and Sergei Witte (far left) in Portsmouth. (August 1905. Photo provided by Photo12.)

based on the Japanese model. This invited a backlash from Korean conservatives, however, and domestic discontent increased due to the late payment of wages to the old military. Heungseon Daewongun (1820–1898, father of King Gojong,) used this discontent to launch a coup d'etat in July 1882. The Japanese legation was attacked, and Minister Hanabusa Yoshimoto (1842–1917) barely managed to escape by sea in what is known as the Imo Incident. The Qing intervened decisively, however, and the Daewongun was arrested and confined in Tientsin in China. Korea then signed the Treaty of Chemulpo in which they apologized to

Japan and paid compensation. The failure of the coup cemented Korea's policy of opening its doors, but the events also made Japan's powerlessness in Korea and China's superiority there clear. The Qing Dynasty was attempting to increase its influence over the country and effectively reestablish its former suzerain relationship.

Following the Imo Incident, a rivalry developed between the Sadaedang faction, who sought to maintain and strengthen the country's traditional relationship with China, and the Gaehwadang faction, who wanted independence from China and the creation of a modern state using Japan as a model. Taking advantage of China's involvement in a war with France over Indochina (the Sino-French War), members of the Gaehwadang including Park Yeonghyo (1861–1939) and Gim Okgyun (1851–1894) launched a coup in December 1884 with the aid of Japan. China again intervened rapidly and decisively, however, and the attempt ended in failure (this event is known as the Gapsin Coup). The Sadaedang would thus continue to lead the government until the First Sino-Japanese War.

The Treaty of Hansung was signed between Japan and Korea in January 1885 in the coup's aftermath, and the Tientsin Convention dealing with Sino-Japanese relations over Korea was signed in April. The Tientsin Convention included a clause stating that Japan and China needed to notify each other before sending troops to Korea.

Chinese naval power had been responsible for Japan's two setbacks. At the time, China possessed the *Dingyuan* and *Zhenyuan*, two world-class, 7,000-ton battleships, and towered over Japan, whose largest ships didn't even reach 4,000 tons. The Chinese Beiyan Fleet visited Japan from 1886 to 1887 and performed demonstrations of its capabilities.

Having received a shock from the Gapsin Coup's failure, Japan immediately set out on a course of naval expansion. This was the reason that the cost of ship construction became a frequent point of contention during the early Diets. The army also began to emphasize operational capabilities on the Asian mainland after the Gapsin Coup.

Russia was another reason that Japan continued to take a strong interest in the Korean Peninsula.

Japan had been aware of the Russian threat since Russia had occupied Tsushima in the 1861 Tsushima Incident during the Bakumatsu. The belief that Japanese influence on the Korean Peninsula had to be secured quickly to counter the eastern expansion of Russia had also been a factor behind the 1873 debate over the invasion of Korea (see Chapter 4). Russia announced its plans for the Trans-Siberian Railway in 1885; when work on the railroad began in 1891, it seemed to the Japanese that the Russian threat was increasingly becoming a reality. The Ōtsu Incident, in which the Russian crown prince (the future Tsar Nikolai II, 1868–1918, reigned 1894–1917) was attacked by police officer Tsuda Sanzō (1854–1891) during his 1891 visit to Japan, and the pressure the government placed on the Supreme Court to order the officer's execution is well-known. Although the body did not comply, the government and much of the public panicked; messages of apology came to the Russian crown prince in Kyoto from all over the country; one woman even committed suicide. The incident and its aftermath show the degree to which Russia was feared by Japan. There were many who felt that something must be done about the Korean problem before Russian power extended that far.

Achieving revision of the unequal treaties

As Japan moved to strengthen its military, envisioning a Russian advance into Asia and a clash with China, this spurred on the revision of the unequal treaties.

Aoki Shūzō (1844–1914) took on the task following Ōkuma's failure (see Chapter 5). Aoki was Japan's first foreign minister to come from a diplomatic background and had extensive experience with Europe. The most distinctive feature of Aoki's approach was that he began his negotiations with Britain, the most challenging country with respect to the issue. Aoki's negotiations ended in failure due to the Ōtsu Incident and a few other factors, but his basic policy was continued by Mutsu Munemitsu (1844–1897), the foreign minister in the 2nd Itō government.

Mutsu considered the failure of past attempts at negotiations to have largely been caused by domestic opposition and therefore emphasized achieving domestic agreement on the issue. At the same time, Aoki, who had become minister to Britain (as well as minister to Germany), made the best use of his copious experience in his negotiations with Britain. The Anglo-Japanese Treaty of Commerce and Navigation, which agreed to the revocation of extraterritoriality after five years, was signed in July 1894 as the result of these efforts. The issue of the restoration of Japanese sovereignty over tariffs went more poorly than Aoki had planned, however; although the treaty included an increase in the tax rate, no agreement on sovereignty was reached. Japan would have to wait until 1911 for a complete revision of the unequal treaties that included tariff sovereignty.

Changes in the international environment were the greatest factor making treaty revision possible. Russia's advance east with the construction of the Trans-Siberian Railway had a massive effect on international relations. Until that point, European advances into Asia had been by sea; control had been made possible by Britain's colonies and sea power. In that sense, the construction of the Trans-Siberian Railway shook the entire Anglo-centered international order. Russia was also constructing the Trans-Caspian Railway, thereby threatening Britain's control of India from the flank. And Russia's position was being strengthened by the negotiations over a Franco-Russian alliance that began in 1891 (the alliance would be formed in 1894). In fact, it had been French capital that had made the beginning of construction on the Trans-Siberian Railway possible.

Britain had originally planned to use the Ottoman Empire to resist Russia in western Asia and China in the east, but it now began to focus on Japan instead.

Economic interest was another factor in the change in Britain's attitude toward Japan. When Ōkuma's treaty negotiations fell through in 1889, *The Times* had criticized the British government's attitude, asserting that it had already become clear that increasing commerce with Japan would be beneficial to Britain and that privileged trade limited by extraterritoriality was becoming a hindrance to the expansion of trade.

The First Sino-Japanese War

The spark for the First Sino-Japanese War was provided by the Donghak Rebellion in Korea that took place in March 1894. Donghak (Eastern learning) was a syncretic Korean folk religion opposed to Westernization that incorporated elements of Confucianism, Buddhism, and Taoism. Although the Donghak Rebellion had already been largely suppressed, Foreign Minister Mutsu decided to use the opportunity to fight China. He proposed to China that both countries jointly issue a series of demands on the reform of Korean domestic politics on June 16; when China rejected this proposal, Japan issued the demands independently on July 10, 1894, and, when Korea did not comply, Japan occupied the Korean royal palace on July 23.

The fighting between Japan and China, which began with the Battle of Pungdo on July 25, 1894, ended in an overwhelming victory for both the Japanese army and navy. This was partially due to a large gap in the military technology of the two forces, including in terms of their organization and training. Even more important was the difference in the countries' degree of political modernization. There were many among the Western powers who had predicted that the war would end in China's favor. While the Japanese army had 120,000 men in all, the Chinese had 50,000 just under the command of Li Hongzhang (1823–1901) and were believed to have almost limitless reserves to draw upon. In truth, however, they had no more troops to mobilize. Several years after the war, traveling even slightly onto the Chinese mainland, one would find that many Chinese were unaware of Japan's existence, let alone of the First Sino-Japanese War. Japan had many more citizens in the modern sense – those who equated the fate of their country with that of themselves – than China did.

Mutsu Munemitsu (1844–1897)

Mutsu Munemitsu was born the son of Kii samurai Date Munehiro. His father was a prominent historian and thinker but had been defeated in internal domain politics, and Munemitsu had an impoverished childhood. He became friends with Sakamoto Ryōma, Kido Takayoshi, Itō Shunsuke (Hirobumi), and Katsu Kaishū while studying in Edo. He became a member of the Kaientai and often worked alongside Sakamoto.

Following the Restoration, Mutsu served as governor of Hyogo and Kanagawa Prefectures and as head of the Bureau for Land Tax Reform (*Chisō Kaisei Jimukyoku*) before resigning in anger at the despotism of the Satsuma and Chōshū factions. When the Tosa Risshisha plotted against the government in connection with the Satsuma Rebellion in 1877, Mutsu joined. He was then arrested and imprisoned in Yamagata and Miyagi. While in prison, he read and translated the works of Jeremy Bentham (1748–1832) and was pardoned and released in 1883 due to the efforts of Itō Hirobumi. He traveled to Britain that same year and then studied under Stein in Austria before returning to Japan in 1886.

Once home, he joined the foreign ministry and became minister to the United States in 1888. Simultaneously serving as minister to Mexico, he successfully signed the first equal treaty while serving there. He returned home in 1890, was appointed minister of agriculture and commerce, and became active in setting the government's Diet policy. He knew Nakajima Nobuyuki of Tosa from his time in the Kaientai, and Hoshi Tōru of the Jiyūtō had long served under Mutsu. Mutsu's dislike of bureaucratic, autocratic government remained unchanged, and he became a member of the Diet.

Mutsu became foreign minister in the 2nd Itō cabinet, and his activities toward treaty revision and during the First Sino-Japanese War are covered in the main text. *Kenkenroku*, his memoirs of being at the helm of Japanese diplomacy during the First Sino-Japanese War, are unparalleled as an example of Japanese diplomatic accounts and shows the zenith of realist thought. He died shortly after the war from tuberculosis. Hara Takashi was among those deeply influenced by Mutsu, and his lengthy diary keenly lays bare his feelings on Mutsu's death.

The Treaty of Shimonoseki was signed in April 1895, ending the war. In addition to paying an indemnity, China ceded Taiwan and the Liaodong Peninsula to Japan. However, Russia, France, and Germany immediately intervened, saying that the ceding of the Liaodong Peninsula would threaten the capital of Quin, the independence of Korea, and the peace in the Far East and forced Japan to return the peninsula to China. This Triple Intervention was a great shock for a Japanese public drunk on victory and "enduring hard times for the sake of future success" (*gashin shōtan*) became a national slogan. These events provided the context for the political parties' cooperation with the government on postwar management (see Chapter 6).

The partition of China

Until the First Sino-Japanese War, China had been regarded as "a sleeping lion" due to its latent strength. Now the great powers mercilessly sought to expand into the country.

Using the opportunity provided by Li Hongzhang's attendance at Nikolai II's coronation in May 1896, the two countries signed a secret treaty of defensive alliance (the Li-Lobanov Treaty) in which they agreed to handle the threat of Japan together. Using that as a pretext, Russia received the right to construct and manage a railroad that branched off from the Trans-Siberian Railway and cut across Chinese territory until it reached Primorsky Kral.[1] This was the Chinese Eastern Railway and meant that Russia secured a route to Vladivostok without having to follow the Russian-Chinese border. In 1898, Russia then leased the Liaodong Peninsula that Japan had been forced to return to China just three years earlier and received the right to construct and manage a southern branch of the Chinese Eastern Railway to run from Harbin to Lushun/Dalian on the tip of the peninsula. Russia thus achieved its long held ambition for a warm water port. (See Figure 7.2.)

Germany leased the Shandong Peninsula that same year using the murder of two German missionaries as justification, and France leased Guangzhouwan. Britain then leased Weihaiwei to counter Lushun/Dalian and Qingdao, as well as Kowloon to counter Guangzhouwan. By way of comparison, Japan only managed to secure a proclamation that Fujian, located across from Taiwan, would not be ceded to any foreign country.

The Open Door Note

These developments made the United States uneasy. The country had been victorious in the 1898 Spanish-American War fought over Cuba and had unexpectedly gained the Philippines during the conflict. With its interest in Asia thus heightened, America had grave misgivings about the ongoing colonization of China. Its history made it antagonistic toward European colonial control, and it was also concerned that the great powers would divide up China, cutting out American capital. It thus opposed further colonization of China and sought guarantees of

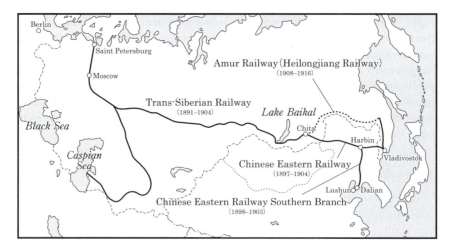

Figure 7.2 Trans-Siberian and Chinese Eastern Railways.

equality of opportunity for commerce in the country, including within already established spheres of influence. This was the 1899 Open Door Note issued by Secretary of State John M. Hay (1838–1905). The majority of the countries concerned agreed to this as a principle without much concrete commitment. Although the note did not have any particular weight in terms of international law, America took this as a diplomatic victory and used this policy to further its advance into East Asia.

The Russo-Japanese war

The Hundred Days Reform and the Boxer Rebellion

Incidentally, no one reacted more fiercely to the division of China than China itself. In June 1898, Kang Youwei (1858–1927), Liang Qichao (1873–1929), and others began the Hundred Days Reform, a reform movement modeled on Japan's Meiji Restoration (see Chapter 3). It differed from China's earlier Self-Strengthening Movement, which had sought to import Western technology but leave the Chinese system as it was. That difference meant that it suffered an even stronger conservative backlash, however. Empress Dowager Cixi (1835–1908) launched a coup d'etat, and the Guangxu Emperor (1871–1908, reigned 1874–1908) was placed under house arrest; the reforms thus came to a halt after a mere three months.

If the Hundred Days Reform represented the rational response to China's colonization, then the Boxer Rebellion was the irrational one. The Boxers were an antiforeign movement that began gaining strength in May 1900 and that had adopted "Support the Qing, annihilate the West" (*Fuqing Mieyang*) as their slogan. The conservative-led Chinese government of the time gave the movement its sanction, and the group surrounded the foreign powers' Beijing legations in June.

Russia and Japan were the only powers in a position to immediately dispatch troops in response. The Japanese were requested to dispatch troops because Russian ambitions were an issue and the country played a major role in the suppression of the incident. Although Japan received little directly out of the event (only 7.7% of the indemnity paid by the Chinese), it was significant that Japan had been able to participate as a member of the great powers. The argument over whether Japan should act as an Asian nation or seek to become a Western, civilized one had been a recurring one throughout the nineteenth century, and the issues of Pan-Asianism and *Datsua-ron* (Call to Leave Asia) ran throughout modern Japanese political thought. The Boxer Rebellion, in which Japan had fought with the West against China, was an important step toward making the philosophy of Leaving Asia and Entering Europe (*datsua nyūō*) a reality.

The Anglo-Japanese Alliance

An important consequence of the end of the Boxer Rebellion was the Russian occupation of Manchuria (what is now Northeast China). Russia had sent over

160,000 men into Manchuria under the pretext of maintaining order and was not disposed to simply remove them now that the rebellion had ended. The situation was extremely serious; although China had suffered partial colonization, until this point this had only concerned relatively small coastal areas. Now a massive amount of territory close to Beijing and contiguous with Russia was involved. The situation was responsible for America's 1900 restatement of its Open Door Policy in which it especially emphasized maintaining the territorial integrity of China.

Britain, who had been wary ever since Russia had leased the Liaodong Peninsula in 1898, also took the situation extremely seriously. British Colonial Secretary Joseph Chamberlain (1836–1914) stated in a speech in Parliament shortly after Russia's occupation that British interests in Asia, especially those in China, might come into conflict with the country's traditional policies in the future. In other words, Britain had begun to reexamine its "splendid isolation." But despite this concern, Britain had few options available to it. France was an ally of Russia, and America was an isolationist sea power when a land power was needed to check Russian expansionism. The only remaining options were Germany and Japan. Britain's initial plan was to create an Anglo-Japanese-German alliance, an idea that met a degree of favor within Germany. It was to Germany's benefit to have Russian interests focused on the East, however, and an Anglo-German alliance would lead to an undesirable tense confrontation with the Russo-French alliance.

Japan was the only option left. Domestically, there was a debate within Japan between those who supported an Anglo-Japanese alliance and those who wanted to reach a Russo-Japanese Entente. Britain was concerned that if the latter camp won out, Russian pressure on Britain would increase. Japan had proven its capabilities during the First Sino-Japanese War and the Boxer Rebellion, and it possessed a powerful navy in addition to its army. Germany was attempting to close its naval gap with Britain at the time; if Britain joined with Japan, it would likely have spare sea power in Asia and be able to redeploy some of its forces there to Europe. Britain's foreign policy of splendid isolationism had been linked to its so-called two-power standard policy for its navy: if British naval strength was better than that of the next two strongest navies combined, there was little need for it to have any alliances. Germany's rapid increase in naval power (such as in the 1898 Naval Law) made this policy difficult to maintain, however.

Katsura Tarō (1847–1913) was Japan's prime minister at the time, and he, Foreign Minister Komura Jutarō (1855–1911), and Minister to Britain Katō Takaaki (1860–1926) were proponents of an Anglo-Japanese alliance. Meanwhile, *genrō* such as Itō and Inoue favored reaching an understanding with Russia. The two policies were not irreconcilable; even the proponents of an alliance desired improvements in Russo-Japanese relations, and the *genrō* were not opposed to a closer relationship with Britain. There was a significant gap between the two groups' judgment of whether an alliance with Britain was possible and whether, in a worst-case scenario, a confrontation with Russia could result. The driving force behind the Anglo-Japanese Alliance was the younger generation of Japanese who had gained confidence from the country's power; it's symbolic that it was the Katsura government, the first not led by a Meiji *genrō* (founding father), who signed the alliance in January 1902.

The Russo-Japanese War

Although the Anglo-Japanese Alliance was effective to a certain extent and Russia's policies became flexible for a time, the balance of power within the government soon changed, and a hard-line anti-Japanese faction came to power. Seeing Russian preparations for war steadily progress, Japan decided to launch hostilities and began the war in February 1904 with a surprise attack. The circumstances of the Russo-Japanese War were as poor for Japan as the Pacific War would be later. As in that war, there was utterly no chance of a total Japanese military victory, and Japan decided to begin hostilities while circumstances were still somewhat favorable. But the international environment and how the Japanese leaders approached that environment were quite different.

First, Britain, Japan's ally, responded favorably to the Japanese attack. It refused the use of the Suez Canal to the Russian Baltic Fleet as it headed to the Far East and severely restricted the fleet's ability to refuel at British colonies. Not only did this significantly delay its arrival in Asia, it also meant that the ships were in poor condition and losing speed and that their crews were exhausted when they finally did arrive. Britain also used diplomatic influence to prevent the Black Sea Fleet from entering the Mediterranean Sea. Without this cooperation from the British, the overwhelming Japanese naval victory at the Battle of Tsushima in May 1905 would have been impossible.

The United States was also favorable toward Japan. It felt that it had a stake in the situation as it wished to maintain and expand its trade in Manchuria and was critical of Russia's actions due to their violation of the principle of the Open Door.

Aid in the procurement of foreign loans represented the greatest facet of Anglo-American support for Japan. The Russo-Japanese War cost Japan over 1.74 billion yen, a massive sum equivalent to 8.5 times the cost of the First Sino-Japanese War and 3.5 times Japan's annual revenues. Only a small portion of this sum could be raised through taxes, and Japan thus had no choice but to raise 85 percent of it by issuing bonds. Of these, half were foreign loans obtained on the American and British markets. Fortunately for Japan, America's Jewish financiers disliked Russia's oppression of Jews and were thus inclined to be favorable toward Japan.

The government also viewed the securing of foreign loans as essential and thus engaged in a strategy of emphasizing its war achievements during their sale to prevent them from losing popularity. It also paid the utmost attention to maintaining friendly international relations. In other words, military affairs were made subordinate to politics during the Russo-Japanese War, a decisive difference from the situation during the Pacific War.

In comparison, Russia's international support was quite weak. Its ally France didn't want Russia becoming overly invested in Asian issues because that would distract it from Germany. And Germany wasn't entirely supportive of Russia due to Jewish opposition to providing financing.

Yet even with this favorable international environment, Japan was able to secure only a tentative victory. Japan won the Battle of Mukden in March 1905 but was unable to strike a decisive blow. The military balance was shifting; the further north the front moved, the more favorable conditions became for Russia.

In accordance with traditional Russian strategy, it planned to force a decisive battle at Harbin and then roll back Japanese gains once its Baltic Fleet arrived.

The Japanese leaders were fully aware of this danger, however, as were the Americans. Seizing the Japanese victory in the Battle of Tsushima as an opportunity, American President Theodore Roosevelt (1858–1919, in office 1901–1909) offered to mediate a peace in May. He believed that if things remained as they were, Russia would ultimately be victorious.

At the same time, the domestic revolutionary conditions within Russia played a large role in convincing it to agree to peace, as there was the possibility that these would worsen if the war continued. Its ally France was also concerned about this and was pushing Russia to make peace.

The peace conference between the two nations began in August 1905 in Portsmouth, New Hampshire, in the United States. The conference was a difficult one, but peace was agreed to in the following month. In September, under the terms of the peace, Russia acknowledged Japan's controlling position in Korea, ceded to Japan its lease of the Liaodong Peninsula and most of the southern branch of the Chinese Eastern Railway (from Changchun south), as well as the southern half of Sakhalin. As is well-known, the Japanese public, who had borne massive sacrifices during the war and had the war described to them as nothing but a series of Japanese victories, were outraged at the "humiliating" treaty. This led to rioting in Tokyo (the Hibiya Incendiary Incident). The government leadership was well aware that the war needed to be ended, however, regardless of the popular dissatisfaction.

The Russo-Japanese War was a major event in world history in that it brought Western expansion in Asia to a halt. Many of the leaders of the newly independent countries that appeared after the Second World War knew of and were inspired by Japan's victory in the war during their youth.

The war was a major event for Japan as well, one that demarcated their modern history. Japan's goal had long been ensuring that its independence was entirely secure. But the Russo-Japanese War marked the end of that phase of Japanese history. Japan's goal had been self-evident until the war; determining what path Japan should follow now became more difficult.

Note

1 China had the right to purchase this railroad thirty-six years after it began operations, and it would revert to China at no cost after eighty years.

8   Imperial expansion

The annexation of Korea

As a result of the Russo-Japanese War, Japan succeeded in obtaining recognition from the great powers of its controlling position in the Korean Peninsula. America, Britain, and Russia all recognized Japan's position: America in the July 1905 Taft-Katsura Agreement, Britain in their renewal of the Anglo-Japanese Alliance in August, and Russia in the Treaty of Portsmouth in September.

This support from the powers in hand, Japan pressured Korea into signing the Japan-Korea Treaty of 1905 in November. The Japan-Korea Protocol of August 1904, under which Korea agreed to employ advisers put forward by Japan and promised to consult with Japan in advance over important diplomatic matters, had already been signed during the Russo-Japanese War. This new treaty went further, however; Japan was now granted control over Korea's financial and diplomatic rights. It established the Office of the Resident-General of Korea (*Kankoku Tōkanfu*) to exercise this control, and Meiji founding father Itō Hirobumi was appointed as the first resident-general.

Emperor Gojong of Korea (1852–1919, reigned 1863–1907) secretly sent emissaries to the Second Hague Conference held in the Netherlands in June 1907 to appeal to the powers against this Japanese oppression (this is known as the Hague Secret Emissary Affair). Japan condemned this attempt to escape its control and turned Korea into even more of a protectorate, seizing control of Korean internal affairs, forcing the emperor to abdicate, signing the Japan-Korea Treaty of 1907, and dissolving the Korean military.

Former Resident-General Itō was assassinated by Korean independence activist An Chung-gun (1879–1910) in Harbin while traveling to Russia in October 1909. Japan used this as an opportunity to increase pressure on Korea and to force through its annexation in August 1910. In place of the Office of the Resident-General of Korea, the Japanese government strengthened its administration by establishing the position of governor-general (*Chōsen Sōkanfu*), appointing War Minister Terauchi Masatake (1852–1919) as the first governor-general of Korea. Korean resistance thus backfired and actually accelerated Japan's colonization of Korea. Although so-called righteous armies (*uibyeong*) resisted Japanese rule during this period, they were steadily suppressed, and Korea was shown little sympathy by the great powers.

Figure 8.1 Gotō Shimpei. (Photo provided by Jiji Press Photo.)

The primary goal of Japanese diplomacy from the early Meiji period on had been securing the independence of Korea to ensure that the Korean Peninsula did not fall under the control of a hostile third party. This had also been a primary objective of the First Sino-Japanese and Russo-Japanese Wars. Yet Japan ultimately placed Korea under its own control. While that would seem to be incredibly contradictory, during the age of imperialism, preventing an area from falling under the control of another country frequently meant placing it under your own.

With the Korean Peninsula, previously part of Japan's line of interest (see Chapter 7), now within its line of sovereignty, Manchuria now became Japan's new line of interest. Manchuria was a frontier of international politics that drew the interest of more powers than Korea had. While securing Japan's independence had been the basic task of Japanese foreign policy until this point, it now gradually turned to maintaining and strengthening Japan's interests in Manchuria.

Japan's Manchuria policy

The Manchurian issue and international relations

The key concessions in Manchuria that Japan had secured from Russia were the rights to lease Lushun and Dalian and to manage most of the southern branch of the Chinese Eastern Railway (from Changchun to Lushun/Dalian). Japan assigned the name the Kwantung Leased Territory (*Kantōshū*) to Lushun/Dalian in August 1906 and established the Office of the Kwantung Governor-General (*Kantō Tōtokufu*; the position of governor-general was held by a lieutenant or full general) to administer the territory. The South Manchuria Railway Company (Mantetsu) was formed in November and was allowed to engage in a number of economic activities related to railroads. Gotō Shimpei (1857–1929), who had excelled at managing Taiwan, was appointed as its first director.

Gotō Shimpei (1857–1929)

Gotō Shimpei was born in the domain of Mizusawa. Defeated in the Boshin War, he diligently studied medicine and became the director of a hospital and head of the medical school in Nagoya as a young man. He came to believe that preventing disease was more important than healing patients, however, and entered the Home Ministry hoping to help administrate public health. He became head of the ministry's public health bureau after studying in Germany but lost his position after becoming involved in the Sōma Incident (a scandal concerning the treatment of mental illness). He reentered the workforce and was successful in administering quarantine operations for demobilized soldiers following the First Sino-Japanese War. When Kodama Gentarō, who had become acquainted with Gotō at this time, was appointed governor-general of Taiwan, Gotō was hired to serve as the head of civilian affairs for the office.

Gotō was well-known for conducting thorough studies during his time in the public health bureau, and he did the same in Taiwan. He also helped plan the transplantation of modern civilization. He believed that civilization should not be introduced mechanically, that it needed to be implanted in a way that respected old customs. Gotō stated that this was a principle of biology (as opposed to physics). Using this method, he stamped out opium in Taiwan, built infrastructure such as city planning, railroads, and schools, and fostered the sugar cane industry.

Gotō was appointed director of Mantetsu because there was confidence in his abilities. As director, he immediately got Mantetsu's operations on track, pursuing bold and effective methods of railroad management. He also emphasized the importance of supporting the local inhabitants and engaged in large-scale urban planning and the construction of schools and hospitals. Gotō was appointed minister of communications and director of the Railway Bureau (*Tetsudōin*) during the 2nd Katsura government. As the *de facto* first director of Japanese Government Railways, he implemented many new ideas.

Gotō again served in the 3rd Katsura cabinet and joined his new party, although he soon left over disagreements with Katō Takaaki. He joined Terauchi Masatake's government in 1916 as home minister and then foreign minister. He oversaw many failures at this time, however, such as the Siberian Intervention.

Afterward, he engaged in city planning as the mayor of Tokyo (a position that would be governor of Tokyo Prefecture today) but was unsuccessful due to opposition from the Friends of Constitutional Government Party (Seiyūkai) and others. He served as home minister in the 2nd Yamamoto Gonnohyōe administration following the Great Kanto Earthquake and took on the task of reconstructing the capital but was unable to achieve significant success. Later in life, he grappled with restoring relations between Japan and the Soviet Union.

Gotō can be considered an outstanding political entrepreneur, a product of modern Japan. He did not have sufficient political power on his own, however, and it was only when supported by powerful politicians like Kodama that he was first able to show his excellence. In an interview late in his life, the Shōwa Emperor fondly remembered the grand scale of Gotō's work.

Incidentally, Japan's interests in Manchuria were not based on a particularly firm foundation; the right to lease Lushun/Dalian, for example, extended only to 1923. Japan was not strong economically, and it faced Chinese resistance and competition from other powers. Furthermore, that resistance was frequently backed by diplomatic and financial support from the great powers, and Japan needed to introduce foreign investment. Japan thus needed to give especially careful consideration to its relations with the other powers.

The relationship Japan was most concerned about following the Russo-Japanese War was that with Russia. The Russian Far Eastern Army was still strong, and

Japan was deeply concerned about a potential war of vengeance. Russia's ally France was also concerned about this possibility, however, as it didn't want Russia to become too deeply involved in Asia. It thus mediated the reconciliation of the two countries, offering a loan to Japan with the *de facto* requirement that it accept this mediation. The result was the Franco-Japanese Treaty of 1907 in June and the First Russo-Japanese Agreement (*Nichiro Kyōyaku*) in July.

Meanwhile, Sino-Japanese and American-Japanese relations had worsened since the Russo-Japanese War. The war had hastened the awakening of oppressed peoples around the world, and the Chinese were no exception. Although the Qing Dynasty had previously given Manchuria special treatment as the land of their ancestors and severely restricted the migration of ethnic Han there, it introduced systems equivalent to those in the rest of the Chinese mainland in 1907. Xu Shichang (1855–1939) was appointed viceroy of the Three Northeast Provinces (an alternative name for Manchuria and equivalent to the modern provinces of Liaoning, Jilin, and Heilongjiang) and Tang Shaoyi (1860–1938) was made governor of Fengtian (Mukden). Both were influential figures close to Yuan Shikai (1859–1916), the most powerful man in the Qing Dynasty at the time. Their appointment shows the strong desire of the Qing to recover Manchuria.

America had taken a favorable position toward Japan until this point because of the Open Door, but Japan's policies in Manchuria following the war hadn't been as open as America had expected. Military administration of the area continued for a year after the end of the war, during which time the activities of foreigners were severely restricted. And even after that ended, the special feelings Japan had toward the land that it had made so many sacrifices for caused it to frequently take a unwelcoming attitude toward foreigners. Although whether or not the closed nature of Japanese policy deviated from the acceptable boundaries of the international relations of the time is debatable, criticism grew within the U.S. State Department that Japan's actions in Manchuria violated the Open Door.

No one welcomed America's criticism of Japan more than China. Tang Shaoyi, who had studied at Columbia University and was pro-American, in particular sought to prevent Japan from incorporating Manchuria into its sphere of influence by introducing American capital. He became close to Willard D. Straight (1880–1918), the U.S. consul in Fengtian, and drew the interest of railroad king Edward H. Harriman (1848–1909), who was considering establishing operations in Manchuria.

Incidentally, the anti-Japanese immigration movement appeared on the American mainland in 1906, making Japanese-American relations more acrimonious. Although President Theodore Roosevelt showed understanding toward Japan's feelings and opinions on the issue, he felt that it was necessary to permit an outlet for Japanese expansionism away from the United States so as to preserve America as a white nation. He therefore suppressed the opinion of the State Department and took an approach of tacit acknowledgment toward Japan's policies in Manchuria. The Root-Takahira Agreement, signed in November 1908 toward the end of his administration, spelled out this stance.

The development of dollar diplomacy and
Russo-Japanese rapprochement

When William Howard Taft (1857–1930, in office 1909–1913) became president in March 1909, however, he accepted the State Department's proposals for the Far East as they were.

The key to the State Department's plan was the idea of using American capital to construct a north-south railroad in Manchuria parallel to the Mantetsu line. Mantetsu had immediately assumed monopolistic control over cargo shipping in Manchuria following the beginning of its operations in 1907 and was earning profits exceeding expectations. State believed that breaking the Mantetsu monopoly with a parallel railroad would be the most effective means of achieving an Open Door in Manchuria. The proposal put forward in 1909 for a Jinai Railway running between Jinzhou and Aihun is an example of such a railway. The Mantetsu neutralization plan formulated later that year, which involved providing American capital to China so that it could purchase Mantetsu and the Chinese Eastern Railway, was similar. This approach was referred to as dollar diplomacy because it involved challenges making use of dollars as weapons.

Japan had received a promise from China in 1905 that no parallel-running railroads would be built near the Mantetsu line and had already used this agreement to defeat a proposed Xinfa Railway that would have run from Xinmintun to Fakumien. It was difficult to describe the proposed Jinai Railway as being close to the Mantetsu line, however, and Japan, largely reliant on foreign capital, wanted to avoid coming into conflict with American capital if at all possible. The Japanese thus decided that, although construction of a Jinai Railway was undesirable, it was impossible to oppose.

America's plan also invited strong Russian opposition by threatening its North Manchurian Railway, however. Japan and Russia thus jointly resisted America's dollar diplomacy and signed the Second Russo-Japanese Agreement in July 1910, which mutually guaranteed the two countries' interests in northern and southern Manchuria. Although America would continue to repeatedly attempt to use dollar diplomacy in Manchuria, it was prevented by Russo-Japanese cooperation, backed by the silent support of Britain and France. As a result, an understanding spread among the powers that investment projects in Manchuria and Inner Mongolia that ignored Japan and Russia were difficult to pursue. Russia and Japan reached a third agreement in 1912 in which they recognized each other's spheres of influence not only in Manchuria but also in Inner Mongolia, with the eastern half belonging to Japan and the west to Russia. (See Figure 8.2.)

During the period from the end of the Russo-Japanese War to 1908, the Japanese government had only perceived its sphere of influence in southern Manchuria as including the area east of the Liao River, extending to its western bank at the most. But due to America's rather sudden and clumsy diplomacy and the unyielding attitude of Russia, they soon came to see all of southern Manchuria and even eastern Inner Mongolia as part of their sphere of influence. The phrases

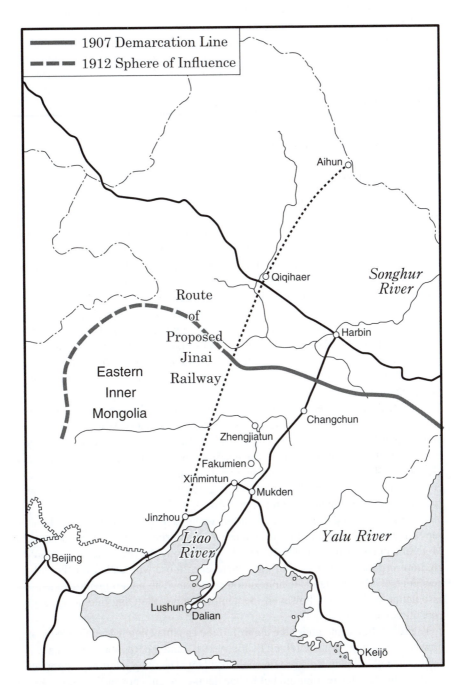

Figure 8.2 Russo-Japanese spheres of influence in Manchuria.

"interests in Manchuria" (*manshū keneki*) and "interests in Manchuria and Mongolia" (*manmō keneki*) now came into frequent use.

As can be seen from all this, Russia had become Japan's most important diplomatic partner. The support of Britain, who placed importance on its relationship with America, had become rather lukewarm in comparison. Japan did not rely on the Russians alone, however, as Russia was, in the end, a latent massive military threat, and British capital was indispensable.

The First World War and Japan

The Xinhai Revolution

Japan's China policy reached a turning point in the fall of 1911. It had achieved almost all of the interests set out in the Treaty of Portsmouth (see Chapter 7) and the Treaty of Beijing that recognized Japan's succession of Russian rights and interests in South Manchuria. With the failure of America's dollar diplomacy, its aims had now turned to incorporating Manchuria and Inner Mongolia into its sphere of influence. The minimum necessary rail network for this had been established, including a direct rail line between Korea and Manchuria, and the next goal for Japan thus became rather uncertain. It could now take a number of potential courses. Should it attempt to further strengthen its interests in Manchuria and Inner Mongolia, should it attempt to push south rather than concentrating on the northeast alone, or should it attempt to increase its influence over the Chinese government? It was just as this decision was being made that the Xinhai Revolution broke out.

There had been movements in China seeking to bring down the Qing Dynasty and establish a republic ever since the First Sino-Japanese War, and Chinese nationalism had been further strengthened by the Russo-Japanese War. Armed revolts began to break out across the country, and one of these in Wuchang in October 1911 finally succeeded and spread. Provinces began declaring independence from the Qing. Sun Yat-sen (1866–1925) was soon selected as provisional president and confronted the Qing in the north.

As this was going on, there were those within Japan who felt that it should support the Qing and use this to acquire further privileges in Manchuria and Mongolia in compensation. Others felt that supporting the revolutionaries would be more in Japan's interest, and there were even those who called for the independence of Manchuria or its annexation by Japan. The government decided in association with Britain, however, to attempt to guide the Qing into accepting a constitutional monarchy.

The revolution came under the control of the capable Qing leader Yuan Shikai, however; the Qing Dynasty fell on February 1912, and the Republic of China was established with Yuan as its provisional president. The Qing court had appointed Yuan to suppress the revolution, but he had decided to gain power by compromising with the revolutionaries. Britain was partially behind this as it wanted a united and stable China.

The divisions between Yuan and the revolutionaries soon became intense, however, and the so-called Second Revolution began in July 1913. Many policies were once again debated within Japan, but it was unable to take advantage of the situation as Yuan immediately suppressed his opposition.

The unrest in China was thus unconnected to Japanese expansion. Britain was the country most concerned about the unity and stability of China; as long as it supported Yuan Shikai, Japan's ability to expand into China was limited. This was because, as already mentioned, British diplomatic support and financial cooperation were indispensable to Japan.

The Twenty-One Demands and the anti-Yuan policy

The summer of 1914 brought decisive changes. A war between Austria and Serbia broke out in July and soon sucked in Britain, France, Germany, and Russia, developing into an unprecedented world war. The European powers thus no longer had any energy to spare for interfering in Asian issues and instead had to seek favors from Japan. The ability of Yuan's government, which was largely dependent on diplomatic and financial support from Europe, to resist Japan was hampered, and Japan's economy boomed during the war. The three basic factors that had restrained Japanese policy toward China had been greatly altered, and its continental expansion became more active.

First, the Ōkuma government proactively joined the war under the leadership of Foreign Minister Katō Takaaki. Britain was wary of Japan's ambitions and attempted to place conditions on its entry into the war, but Japan pushed past these and declared war on Germany in August. Once Germany's base of operations in the Jiaozhou Bay concession fell in November, Japan then issued multiple demands to China in January 1915 and entered into negotiations with the intention of resolving all of its long-standing issues with China in one fell swoop. These were the infamous Twenty-One Demands.

The demands were divided into five groups: the first involved the transfer of most German rights and privileges in the Shandong Province to Japan; the second increased Japanese rights in Manchuria and Inner Mongolia by, for example, extending the lease of Mantetsu and the Kwantung Leased Territory, clarifying Japan's preferential rights relating to railroads and loans in the two areas and recognizing the Japanese right to own land; the third related to the Hanyeping Company in the Yangtze Valley; the fourth declared that the Chinese coast would not be further divided; and the fifth covered other miscellaneous items, such as the hiring of Japanese advisors, police reforms, and the purchase of Japanese weapons.

Although the Twenty-One Demands are now often spoken of as an aggressive act representative of Japanese imperialism, they were not especially so by the standards of the world at the time. Indeed, the government was fiercely criticized at the time for not going far enough.

If we set aside the items relating to the Shandong Peninsula, the emphasis of the Twenty-One Demands was on the Manchuria–Inner Mongolia issues put forward in the second group. Japan already *de facto* enjoyed many of these rights; as such, the Japanese view was that they were merely seeking confirmation of an already existing situation. That the Chinese still resisted is only natural, however, as they foresaw that explicitly confirming these rights in writing would only give rise to further "customary" privileges later. This difference in views caused negotiations to go poorly. China expected a power to intervene, especially America. That expectation, combined with Japan's unskilled diplomacy, caused Japanese-American relations to become extremely complicated. The negotiations ended with Chinese acceptance of Japan's final note in May. Although the demands had ended with Japan receiving a number of new rights, they also left behind many unresolved major problems such as the deep distrust by America and China that had been fostered.

Shortly after the Twenty-One Demands were concluded, a scandal broke out involving Home Minister Ōura Kanetake that led to Foreign Minister Katō leaving the cabinet over differing opinions with Prime Minister Ōkuma. With his departure, the army general staff now had the most influence in setting policy on China. This would become especially strong after the powerful Tanaka Giichi (1864–1929) and Uehara Yūsaku (1856–1933) became vice-chief and then chief of the general staff in late 1915.

At this time in China, Yuan Shikai was planning to restore the imperial government with himself as the new emperor. It was foreseen that this would be accompanied by a certain amount of disorder. Some in Japan wanted to support him and put him in Japan's debt so that it would be at an advantage in the future. Others argued that it was in Japan's best interests to let Yuan fall as his skillful use of foreign threats to promote national unity made him dangerous to deal with. After vacillating between the two positions, the Ōkuma Cabinet settled on the latter and, in a March 1916 cabinet meeting, made the historically unusual reckless decision of seeking Yuan's fall.

The army general staff then took the lead in a grand strategy formulated to simultaneously provide support to a number of groups in China: the southern anti-Yuan military cliques; the Kuomintang; the Zongshedang in Manchuria, who sought a Qing restoration; the Mongolian royal family, who sought to split away from China; and Zhang Zuolin (1875–1928), who sought to become an independent power. Yuan was placed in a difficult position as a result and suddenly died in June 1916. Coming after the Twenty-One Demands, this threw Sino-Japanese relations into disarray.

The Terauchi Cabinet and its China policy

The new Terauchi Cabinet, formed in October 1916, attempted to change Ōkuma's China policy. Its goal was to improve Sino-Japanese relations as well as those with the great powers, America in particular. The government stopped interfering in Chinese domestic politics and avoided coercive policies. It also attempted to strengthen ties between the two countries by offering loans to the pro-Japanese Duan Qirui (1865–1936) after he formed a government. To improve relations with the other powers, it increased its level of participation in the world war in exchange for a promise to support Japan's demands for the Shandong Peninsula and Germany's South Seas islands north of the equator at the postwar peace conference.

For America, Japan's most difficult relationship among the powers, the government dispatched former foreign minister Ishii Kikujirō (1866–1945) to the United States as an envoy once it entered the war in April 1917 against Germany. The two countries signed the Lansing-Ishii Agreement, which included the passage "The government of the United States and Japan recognize that territorial propinquity creates special relationships between countries, and, consequently, the government of the United States recognizes that Japan has special interests in China, particularly in the part to which her possessions are contiguous." This was the moment when America, who had criticized Japan for many years over its special interests in Manchuria and Mongolia because of the Open Door, came closest to the Japanese position.

A policy of simultaneously seeking both Sino-Japanese cooperation and partnerships with the great powers was one filled with contradictions, as Sino-Japanese cooperation meant having China develop a close relationship with Japan than with other powers. But this is what the Terauchi government sought to accomplish using the favorable conditions produced by the world war.

The Siberian Intervention and the Nishihara Loans

The Russian Revolution of October 1917 (November by the Gregorian calendar) greatly changed these circumstances. The new Bolshevik government ended its fighting against Germany, rejected the war as imperialistic, and signed the Treaty of Brest-Litovsk in March 1918. It was considered a victory by the pro-German faction in Russia, and within Japan, it was even feared that the Germans and Russians would join forces and advance east.

A fear of Western countries, especially nearby Russia, had formed the basis of the Terauchi Cabinet's foreign policy. If these countries advanced on East Asia in full force, Japan's only option would be to join with China. This was why the government had emphasized increasing Sino-Japanese cooperation. Of course, Terauchi also believed that Japan should build up friendly relationships with the powers, especially Russia, to avoid such a situation from coming about. But Russia, who was intended to form the cornerstone of Japanese cooperation with the great powers, had fallen in the Russian Revolution, and it now appeared that a Russo-German force could be coming east. Strengthening Japan's cooperation with China was necessary to respond to this. This was why the Terauchi Cabinet began offering China massive loans (known as the Nishihara Loans), an act that greatly diverged from the understanding reached by the powers.

The Siberian Intervention was also related to this understanding of the situation. When Russian withdrawal from the war became definite with the October Revolution, Britain and France launched a military intervention, judging that Germany would be able to move all its forces to the western front if they didn't topple Russia's revolutionary government and reestablish the front in the east. The argument that the revolutionary government should be overthrown was present in Japan as well, as was the argument that Japan should take advantage of the chaos to expand its territory or sphere of influence. There were, of course, those who advocated caution as well, but when America proposed a joint expedition to save the Czechoslovak Legion, the Terauchi Cabinet decided to send troops.[1] It began doing so in August 1918.

The idea of a Russo-German alliance and an advance east were mere illusions, however, and the Nishihara Loans and the Siberian Intervention were both failures for this reason. The massive sum invested in China through the loans was irrecoverable, and the Siberian Intervention lasted years and wasted hundreds of millions of yen and thousands of lives. The Terauchi had achieved a number of accomplishments during its first year but lost direction following the Russian Revolution.

Since its victory in the Russo-Japanese War, Japan had focused its energies on foreign expansion, especially that of its rights in Manchuria. And, thanks in part to clumsy American diplomacy and an unexpected Russian repulsion, Japan exceeded its initial expectations and managed to successfully build a sphere of influence for itself in southern Manchuria and eastern Inner Mongolia. But this was imperialism with a weak foundation, built using conflicts among the other powers and covering up a lack of capital with power. And even imperialism itself now came under criticism as the imperial powers were either destroyed or weakened following the First World War. What was particularly a problem for Japan was that the strength of the United States, its greatest critic, was now unrivaled. Japan now faced a completely new task.

Note

1 The Czechoslovak Legion had defected from the Austro-Hungarian army and joined with Russia, seeking independence from the Austro-Hungarian Empire. With the Russian Revolution, they now had nowhere to go.

9   The development of party government

Hanbatsu–party relations following the Russo-Japanese War

From Itō to Saionji

Chapter 6 described the development of party politics prior to the founding of the Friends of Constitutional Government Party (Seiyūkai) in September 1900. Once the party was founded, Prime Minister Yamagata Aritomo immediately resigned and recommended that Itō Hirobumi serve as his successor. This was intended to throw the newly founded party into confusion by forcing it to take power before it was ready. Itō thus reluctantly formed his fourth government in October but was plagued by opposition from the Yamagata-influenced House of Peers. Hoshi Tōru, an influential member of the former Progressive Party (*Kenseitō*), then became embroiled in a bribery scandal involving the Tokyo municipal assembly and was forced to resign as communications minister. Unable to control the party, the government resigned in May 1901, a mere seven months after taking power.

Inoue Kaoru, a founding father of the Meiji state, then tried and failed to form a government; the task ultimately fell to Katsura Tarō of the Yamagata faction, who became prime minister in June. As Inoue was an ally of Itō, this failure was an indication of the decline of Itō and the rise of Yamagata within the Meiji oligarchy. The Katsura Cabinet was given the nicknames of the "little Yamagata government" and the "vice-minister cabinet," reflecting the perception that it consisted of men of little importance backed by Yamagata. But it also marked the arrival of a new generation; the significance this change had on foreign policy has already been discussed.

The Friends of Constitutional Government Party had difficulty working against the Katsura Cabinet. As Itō was a member of the Meiji founding fathers as well as the president of the Friends of Constitutional Government Party, he had to use care when criticizing the cabinet. This was especially true as tax increases to support military expansion became an issue in the run-up to the Russo-Japanese War (see Chapter 7). Itō ultimately resigned as party president as war approached in July 1903 and became president of the Privy Council. He was succeeded by Saionji Kinmochi (1849–1940). The Friends of Constitutional Government Party

Figure 9.1 Hara Takashi. (Photo provided by Jiji Press Photo.)

suffered a number of defections during this period as Itō forced it to side with the cabinet; by 1903, its share of seats had dropped to 34 percent.

With the outbreak of war with Russia in February 1904, however, the political parties cooperated with the government in the name of national unity. The Friends of Constitutional Government Party notably supported the government at the end of the war when it suffered fierce criticism from the public over the peace treaty. This then became an opportunity for an agreement between the government and the Friends of Constitutional Government Party to transfer power; the 1st Saionji Cabinet was formed in January 1906. Although the 4th Itō Cabinet had theoretically been a party government, it had actually been one led by a Meiji founding father. The creation of the Saionji Cabinet, however, signified the acceptance of the political party as a legitimate part of the political system, as can be seen from their key role in responding to the peace issue.

The Keien era and the hanbatsu

The period from Katsura's agreement to transfer power to Saionji in the fall of 1905 to late 1912 is known as the Keien (Katsura-Saionji) era because it saw the 1st Saionji, 2nd Katsura, and 2nd Saionji cabinets. This was the most politically stable era under the Meiji constitution. Both general elections during this period were held due to the members of the Lower House reaching the end of the term, and there were largely smooth transfers of power because of an understanding between the sides.

One of the reasons for this stability was a general agreement over foreign policy. The most important task facing Japan at the time was entrenching its rights in Manchuria, and while the Katsura Cabinet was more proactive in taking this on, the Saionji Cabinets also promoted the same policy. Another factor was that the bureaucracy and political parties, the two major spheres of the political world, were under the control of the stable Yamagata faction and Friends of Constitutional Government Party majorities, respectively. While the two groups did compete with each other, on the whole they cooperated and supported the government. Let's now examine the situation of each group, beginning with the domain cliques.

The ascendancy of Yamagata was the chief distinguishing characteristic of the Meiji oligarchs in the period following the Russo-Japanese War. With the Satsuma faction's decline and the Chōshū faction's Itō group suffering setbacks, the Yamagata faction became the leaders of the oligarchs. Katsura Tarō was a key member of the faction, as was Terauchi Masatake, who served as war minister in three cabinets from 1902 to 1911. With the departure of Yamagata from active participation in politics, the power to hold together a massive group like the Yamagata faction passed to these two men.

Incidentally, Yamagata, Katsura, and Terauchi were all army generals, and it was the army who served as the greatest stronghold of the Yamagata faction. Terauchi controlled the army throughout the Keien period. Appointed war minister before the Russo-Japanese War, he would hold that position for nine years and build up overwhelming authority within the army, aided in part by the death of his rival Kodama Gentarō (1852–1906). Notably, Terauchi placed many trusted confidantes from Chōshū in the war ministry, reducing the authority of the army general staff and strengthening the ministry as he did so.

Although the army thus successfully placed leaders in top positions in the government, there are rather few cases of the army's policies being proactively pursued. Katsura, who also served as finance minister during his second cabinet, sought a policy of austerity and was therefore not inclined toward further expansion of the army; Terauchi also conformed to Katsura's policy as a national leader.

The arrival of dreadnought battleships brought great innovations in naval technology, and expansion of the navy was prioritized in order to keep up. This new style of battleship, first commissioned by Britain in 1906, boasted a speed of 21 knots, surpassing the previous standard of 18, and had more than twice the number of cannon. This became the new world standard and was soon followed by the arrival of so-called super dreadnoughts in 1912. All existing battleships had suddenly been rendered obsolete. (See Figure 9.2.)

Similarly, while the army had high hopes for continental expansion, the policies of Katsura and Terauchi, although more proactive than those of Saionji and his allies, followed the most moderate view within the army. In summary, Katsura and Terauchi prioritized their status as members of the *hanbatsu* and as national leaders over their positions as leaders of the army and actually worked to restrain proactive policies for expansion of the army in China.

This situation soon gave rise to opposition from within the army. Led by the formerly powerful Satsuma faction, this group supported the influential Satsuma general Uehara Yūsaku and pushed for the implementation of policies such as personnel changes, strengthening the general staff, and a proactive continental policy. Despite being seen as the likely next Chōshū leader, Tanaka Giichi was sympathetic to these positions and became close to the movement. Tanaka became director of the Bureau of Military Affairs in 1911, and Uehara was made war minister in 1912. The rise of an oppositional force within the army, the stronghold of the Yamagata faction, had the potential to greatly upset the stability of the Keien era and would in fact ultimately break the link between Katsura and Saionji through the debate over expanding the army by two divisions.

Satsuma (primary armament of two twin turrets)

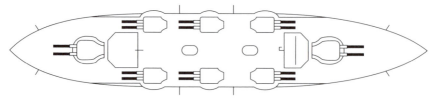

HMS Dreadnought (primary armament of five twin turrets)

Figure 9.2 Battleships *Satsuma* and HMS *Dreadnought*.

The Keien era and the parties

Turning to the parties, there was a conspicuous decline in those groups that drew from the people's rights movement. The Original or Main Constitutional Party (*Kensei Hontō*), which was closer to the original people's party than was the Friends of Constitutional Government Party, had been unable to participate in a government since its formation and had steadily waned in power; in the tenth general election, its share of seats fell to almost a third of the Friends of Constitutional Government Party. And the power of the former Liberal Party (*Jiyūtō*) faction within the Friends of Constitutional Government Party was collapsing as well. It was Matsuda Masahisa (1845–1914) of the Kyūshū faction and Hara Takashi (1856–1921), the leader of the Tōhoku and Kantō factions, who came to hold power in the party during the presidency of Saionji. Hara in particular was the successor to Hoshi Tōru's Kantō base and vision following Hoshi's assassination in 1901.

To Hara, a political party had to be more than a merely oppositional force; it had to be something that actively took up national governance. It was thus necessary for strong leadership to be established within the party because effectively compromising and dealing with other political forces would be impossible without it. To achieve this, Hara concentrated an abundant amount of political funds within the party (Saionji had deep ties to the Sumitomo *zaibatsu* and Hara to the Furukawa *zaibatsu*) and was prepared to spread posts and privileges widely. Hara's plan was successful, and it became standard for members of the party to obediently follow the party president and other party executives. The remarkable expansion of the electorate during this period was another factor behind this. By this time, the electorate had swelled to 3.5 times that of the first Diet due to the 1900 electoral reform law and tax increases put in place during the Russo-Japanese War. This increase meant that elections had become significantly more expensive and members were thus increasingly reliant on the party leadership. (See Table 9.1.)

Hara actively encouraged those with backgrounds in the bureaucracy and the business community to join the party. The parties had alienated the bureaucracy in the past by attempting to work their way into their organizations, but Hara was now trying to get the bureaucrats involved. This was connected to improving the party's ability to take up the burdens of national governance. And including the business community in the party would be beneficial for obtaining political funds. Hara twice served as home minister during the Saionji governments and conducted sweeping personnel changes in the name of "weeding out the old and promoting the up-and-coming" (*rōkyū tōta shinshin batteki*). Many of those chosen for promotion became *de facto* members of the Seiyūkai as a result, and a number would later join the party.

He also actively pursued industrial promotion policies at the local level and used them to strengthen the base of the Friends of Constitutional Government Party. A typical example of this was his railroad policy. By 1906, the country's major railroads had been established for the most part, and most had been nationalized.

Table 9.1 Major increases in the electorate.

Election	Electorate (thousands)	Comment
1st (1890)	451	15 yen or more paid in direct tax needed
6th (1898)	502	
7th (1902)	983	10 yen or more paid in direct tax needed
9th (1904)	762	
10th (1908)	1,599	Largely due to Russo-Japanese War tax increases
13th (1917)	1,422	
14th (1920)	3,069	3 yen or more paid in direct tax needed
15th (1924)	3,288	
16th (1928)	12,409	First election with general male suffrage

Note: Elections with large increases from the preceding election are listed for comparison. Numbers are rounded to the nearest thousand.

The next tasks were the targeted improvement of the shipping capabilities of the main rail lines and further expansion of the rail network. Gotō Shimpei, who became the President of the Railway Bureau during the 2nd Katsura Cabinet after serving as the first director of Mantetsu, viewed the first of these tasks as more important. He believed that the major lines like the Tōkaidō Main Line (running between Tokyo and Kobe) should be converted to standard gauge track (which was superior for shipping) and linked to the continental rail network. Hara, however, prioritized the expansion of the rail network into local areas, a policy that strengthened support for the Friends of the Constitutional Government Party. This would later be referred to as "drawing rails to one's own fields," a play on words based on the expression "drawing water to one's own fields" (meaning to be self-serving). Hara similarly supported the creation of local industrial bases through the construction of roads, bridges, and ports in a way that strengthened the party. Although these types of policy had existed in the past, Hara was the first to develop them in such a large-scale and systematic fashion.

Hara Takashi (1856–1921)

Hara Takashi was born into the household of an elder advisor in Nambu domain. He suffered discrimination and poverty as one of those defeated in the Boshin War but studied hard and entered the foreign ministry in 1882 after working for a number of newspapers. After being stationed in areas such as Tientsin and Paris, he transferred to the Ministry of Agriculture and Commerce, where he came to know Mutsu Munemitsu. When Mutsu became foreign minister, Hara was appointed as head of the foreign ministry's International Commerce Bureau and as vice-minister of foreign affairs. He retired after serving as minister to Korea and became president of the newspaper *Osaka Mainichi Shimbun*.

He participated in the founding of Itō Hirobumi's Friends of Constitutional Government Party in 1900 and served as communications minister in the 4th Itō Cabinet until he resigned and was replaced by Hoshi Tōru. He was later home minister in the 1st and 2nd Saionji Cabinets and the 1st Yamamoto Cabinet, during which time he built up a large following by selecting bureaucrats who had college educations.

Along with Matsuda Masahisa of the Kyōshō faction, Hara was part of the so-called triumvirate of the Friends of Constitutional Government during Saionji's presidency, and he was the one who actually put forward important policies and engaged in negotiations with figures such as Katsura Tarō. The laying of rail lines became especially important to building the Seiyūkai's base (as already mentioned).

Hara became president of the Friends of Constitutional Government Party in 1914 after Saionji's resignation the previous year and became the first prime minister serving in the Lower House after the Terauchi Cabinet fell in 1918. All cabinet posts in his government except for the positions of war, navy, and foreign ministers were held by party members, making it to first true party government.

The Hara government promoted industry and higher education by constructing middle schools, high schools, and universities. Hara had had high regard for the influence of America since the late Meiji period. He was the first pro-American Japanese diplomatic leader, and his policies on China were often undertaken from the position of collaboration with America.

Hara's original pen name was Ichizan (One Mountain), which he took to signify his frustration at hearing the expression "a mountain north of the Shirakawa gate is only worth a hundred mon" (*Shirakawa ihoku hitoyama hyakumon*), a saying that was derogatory toward the Tōhoku region from which he came from, but he later changed it to Itsuzan (a great mountain, although its pronunciation was quite similar) as the first name was too blunt. From at least the late Meiji period on, Hara declined to become a peer so as to remain in the House of Representatives. The real reason was, however, that he did not like the hierarchical system like the peerage. Many of his policies were aimed at eradicating the authoritarian nature of the Meiji state that Satsuma and Chōshū had built. He wrote in his will that his grave was to read only "the grave of Hara Takashi"; it bears no mention of his rank or positions.

Hara well understood the weaknesses of politicians and was a steel-willed prime minister who did not flinch using money and posts to tame office seekers. Criticism led to his assassination in 1921, making him the first serving prime minister to so die.

He himself was an uncorrupted man and left behind many debts after his death. The detailed diary that Hara left behind is a masterpiece of modern Japanese political history. It would be impossible to analyze the politics of the era in which he was active without it. In that sense, Hara continues to spellbind researchers even today.

The Friends of Constitutional Government Party was thus able to secure a stable majority under Hara's leadership, a situation that continued steadily. This growth backed the Original Constitutional Party against a wall and sparked debate within the party as to whether it should continue with its traditional antioligarch (domain cliques) positions or adopt a new stance of prioritizing opposition to the Friends of Constitutional Government Party. The former was known as the horizontal position because it emphasized cooperation with the Friends of Constitutional Government Party and the latter as the vertical position since it meant drawing closer to the domain cliques. This internal conflict over policy would continue undiminished after the Original Constitutional Party became the *Rikken Kokumintō* (Constitutional Nationalist Party) in 1910; while the reform faction gained in strength, it never became strong enough to overcome its opponents. This was the context for the later formation of Katsura's new party, *Rikken Dōshikai* (Association of Allies of the Constitution).

Hanbatsu–party relations during the Taishō period

The Taishō Political Crisis

The alliance between Katsura and Saionji was severed in late 1912, sparking a major Political Crisis. This was triggered by a proposal to add an additional two divisions to the army.

The army had a few reasons for demanding additional divisions. The first was that it wanted to create two new divisions in Korea to prepare for the disorder that it predicted would follow the outbreak of the Xinhai Revolution and the fall of the Qing Dynasty (see Chapter 8). The army had also taken notice of Russia's conversion of the Trans-Siberian Railway to double track and the construction of the Amur Railway. It believed that preparations should be taken in response as these significantly increased Russian freight transport capabilities between European Russia and Primorsky Krai in Siberia (see Chapter 7).

But a more fundamental reason for the expansion plan was that Japan was approaching a turning point in its foreign policy. As mentioned previously, Japan had largely accomplished its principle foreign policy objective, securing its interests in Manchuria, by the fall of 1911 (see Chapter 8). It now needed a new objective. But the government had prioritized naval expansion for the previous several years, and, from the eyes of middle-grade army officers (*chūken shōkō*) at least, Japanese expansion on the continent was lacking vigor. Uehara and Tanaka's middle-grade officers proposed this increase in the number of the army's divisions in the fall of 1912 (in preparation for the 1913 budget) to overcome this state of affairs.

The Saionji cabinet, wanting to concentrate on administrative reform, did not accept the army's arguments, however. Uehara accordingly resigned as war minister, and the army then refused to put forward a successor, causing the government to fall in December. Forming a new government was a difficult task, but ultimately Katsura created his third cabinet. Katsura had been appointed Lord Keeper of the Privy Seal and Grand Chamberlain in August following the Meiji Emperor's death, on the grounds that there was a need for influential figures near the new emperor. This had been done in accordance with the wishes of Yamagata, who disliked that Katsura had taken some of his real power. The politically ambitious Katsura had no desire to be locked away in the imperial palace, however, and seized this opportunity to escape.

Katsura was sharply criticized by the public for this, however, as he was seen as having orchestrated the change in government. He had received an imperial edict to leave the palace and made use of another to force the naval minister to remain in the government; this further enraged the public, whose anger developed into a fierce popular movement, the first *goken undō* (movement to defend constitutional government).

Katsura prepared a number of progressive policies to compromise with the public. These included suspending the army and naval expansion plans and abolishing the requirement that military ministers be active duty officers (see Chapter 6), as well as the requirement that colonial governor-generals be officers. He also formed his own political party, the Association of Allies of the Constitution, in late 1913 and attempted to use his long friendship with Saionji to suppress criticism from the Friends of Constitutional Government Party. But all this backfired in the face of an angered public, and he had no choice but to resign after a mere two months in office. This is known as the Taishō Political Crisis (*Taishō Seihen*).

The crisis was the result of a number of overlapping rivalries such as those between the parties and the bureaucracy, between the army and the navy, between the Friends of Constitutional Government Party and the new party, between the Association of Allies of the Constitution and Satsuma and Chōshū. But the most important was probably the argument over what China policy should be adopted now that Japanese rights and interests in Manchuria had been secured. The conflict between the proactive and gradualist factions on the issue, especially the actions of the army's middle-grade officers, was the key.

Navy Admiral Yamamoto Gonnohyōe (1852–1933) of Satsuma succeeded Katsura, forming a government with the backing of the Friends of Constitutional Government Party. Although Yamamoto was a member of the domain clique, he embarked on policies that reduced the privileges of the military and bureaucracy, such as the abolition of the active duty officer requirement for military ministers (allowing reserve and auxiliary officers to serve) and revision of the Civil Servant Appointment Law. The Siemens Scandal, which involved corruption within the navy over procurements, came to light in early 1914, however, and this was used to force his resignation.

Ōkuma Shigenobu then formed a cabinet, fifteen years since his last. The Association of Allies of the Constitution, the new party formed by Katsura (who had died in October 1913), now became the party in power. The Association included the Constitutional Nationalist Party's reform faction and the former Katsura bureaucrats, as well as the Yamagata-aligned bureaucrat Ōura Kanetake. The government was close to the Chōshū faction and the army and supported a proactive continental policy.

The two years following the 1912 proposal that the army be expanded by two divisions were thus a turbulent period caused by disagreement over the direction of continental policy.

Hanbatsu *and parties during the First World War*

The Ōkuma Cabinet had initially been a minority government. But with the outbreak of the First World War in July 1914, a situation favorable to those supporting a proactive continental policy was born. Buoyed by this situation, the government dissolved the Diet in late 1914, seeking to defeat the Friends of Constitutional Government and add two divisions to the army. The government vigorously took on the general election with Prime Minister Ōkuma at its head. He was seventy-six but seemed in the best of health, campaigning around the country and giving speeches to the crowds that gathered to meet his train. His associates dispatched telegrams and recordings of his speeches to his supporters across the country. The election was unprecedented in that members of the cabinet actively campaigned, and it resulted in a landslide victory for the government. Although it was extremely common for Japanese elections to result in government victories, there had never been a result quite as dramatic as this one. Factors in this include the so-called Ōkuma boom, a surge of sympathy for Ōkuma, who had been in an unfortunate state for many years, and the introduction and skillful use of modern election tactics.

After Ōkuma resigned in October 1916 due to his advanced age and an impasse over China policy, a new government was formed by Terauchi Masatake of the Yamagata faction. At about the same time, the three factions led by the Association of Allies of the Constitution that had supported the Ōkuma Cabinet merged to form the *Kenseikai* (Constitutional Association) and brought pressure to bear on Terauchi. Terauchi drew close to the Friends of Constitutional Government Party and Constitutional Nationalist Party and dissolved the Diet in early 1917, breaking the Constitutional Association's majority in the April elections.

Saionji had resigned as president of the Friends of Constitutional Government Party in 1913 and had been replaced by Hara Takashi in June of the following year. Although the party had suffered a great blow from the election of the Ōkuma

Cabinet, it worked to overcome the situation by becoming close to Yamagata. With the formation of the Terauchi Cabinet and the 1917 election, it was finally able to recover its position as the most important political party and exert influence over the government. When the Terauchi Cabinet was unable to make progress in 1918 due to the prime minister's illness and the rice riots, the party was able to use its position to form a new government to replace it.

The failure of the triangular parties theory

Meiji founding father Yamagata held the following, which he called the theory of triangular parties (*santō teiritsu-ron*), to be ideal situation: while there would usually be two large parties in the Diet, the domain cliques should ensure the existence of a third party under their influence that would work to ensure that neither of the two larger parties was able to secure a majority. A cabinet could be formed through a coalition between one of the larger of parties and the third party, but this could be severed if the party opposed the government. The third party would then join with the other large party. This situation would mean that the government could escape the "tyranny" of party control and would be able to implement its policies.

And, in fact, a situation close to this ideal did develop during the Ōkuma and Terauchi Cabinets. The Friends of Constitutional Government and the Association of Allies of the Constitution both sought Yamagata's favor, and thus, from his perspective, he was able to use each party to defeat the other. But his theory broke down at the end of the Terauchi cabinet, leaving Yamagata no choice but to accept the party governments that he had hated for so long.

One of the reasons that the triangular party theory had failed was that power in the Association of Allies of the Constitution and Constitutional Association was held by party president Katō Takaaki and his supporters like Wakatsuki Reijirō (1866–1949) and Hamaguchi Osachi (1870–1931), relatively young politicians with backgrounds in the bureaucracy. These men, most notably the anglophile Katō, were bureaucratic progressives who held British-style party government to be the ideal and disliked becoming close to the Meiji oligarchs. This meant that when the cabinet and Friends of Constitutional Government fell out at the end of the Terauchi Cabinet, it was impossible to have the Constitutional Association take its place. (See Table 9.2.)

Another factor that caused the theory to fail was that the army, who had made up the core of the domain cliques, broke away. It has already been mentioned that the middle-grade army leadership, based around Tanaka and Uehara, had been dissatisfied with the army's situation during the Keien era, when Katsura and Saionji dominated and the army's self-assertiveness had been responsible for proactive continental policies such as the anti-Yuan policy discussed in the previous chapter. This hostility between the middle-grade officers and the top leadership that Terauchi represented became clear during his government. When the army drew up a plan for actively strengthening the army due to the tremendous military developments of the First World War, Terauchi rejected it out of a desire to reduce

Table 9.2 Changes in the number of seats in the House of Representatives by party (%).

	Seiyūkai	Kensei Hontō	Teikokutō	Other/No Party	Total
September 1900: Formation of the Seiyūkai	155 (52)	67 (22)	12 (4)	66 (22)	300
August 1902: 7th General Election	190 (51)	95 (25)	17 (5)	73 (19)	376
March 1903: 8th General Election	175 (47)	85 (23)	17 (5)	99 (26)	376
March 1904: 9th General Election	133 (35)	90 (24)	19 (5)	137 (36)	379
	Seiyūkai	Kensei Hontō	Daidō Club	Other/No Party	Total
December 1905: Formation of the Daidō Club	149 (39)	98 (26)	76 (20)	56 (15)	379
May 1908: 10th General Election	187 (49)	70 (18)	29 (8)	93 (25)	379
	Seiyūkai	Kokumintō	Chūō Club	Other/No Party	Total
March 1910: Formation of Kokumintō and Chūō Club	204 (54)	92 (24)	50 (13)	33 (9)	379
May 1912: 11th General Election	211 (55)	95 (25)	31 (8)	46 (12)	381
	Seiyūkai	Kokumintō	Rikken Dōshikai	Other/No Party	Total
February 1913: Formation of Rikken Dōshikai	188 (49)	43 (11)	93 (24)	57 (15)	381
March 1915: 12th General Election	108 (28)	27 (7)	153 (40)	93 (24)	381
	Seiyūkai	Kokumintō	Kenseikai	Other/No Party	Total
October 1916: Formation of Kenseikai	111 (29)	28 (7)	197 (52)	45 (including vacancies) (12)	381
April 1917: 13th General Election	165 (43)	35 (9)	121 (32)	60 (16)	381

the burden on the public and to maintain balance with the navy. The Friends of Constitutional Government Party, who advocated for the country's industrial base to be actively built up, was actually closer to the army's position. The army had also come to realize that such an industrial base would be necessary for the modernization of the country's arms and thus drew close to the party in 1918. When the Hara government was formed, Tanaka became war minister.

The majority factions of the domain cliques and the parties had allied during the Keien era and the Friends of Constitutional Government had expanded its power as a result. This was because, despite the Meiji oligarchs' attempts to manipulate them, neither the Original Constitutional Party nor the Constitutional Nationalist Party actively sought to become close to them. But with the formation of Katsura's new party, the Association of Allies of the Constitution, both major parties attempted to enter into an alliance with the domain cliques, leading to fierce competition between them and their manipulation by the oligarchs from 1913 to 1917. When the Constitutional Association took an anti–domain clique stance, however, manipulation of the parties became difficult. Additionally, the army, the core of the domain cliques, began to move away from them. The oligarchs and Friends of Constitutional Government Party cooperation of the earlier Katsura-Saionji alliance was thus restored, albeit in a relationship that was clearly more favorable to the party than the previous one had been.

Public opinion and the activities of intellectuals were in the background of this. Yoshino Sakuzō published his "On the Meaning of Constitutional Government and the Methods by Which It Can Be Perfected" in the January 1916 issue of *Chūō Kōron*; he advocated for party cabinets and diplomacy based on international cooperation and would come to be an opinion leader during the 1920s.

10 International cooperation and party cabinets

The Hara Cabinet

Formation of the Hara Cabinet

Hara Takashi formed a Friends of Constitutional Government Party (Seiyūkai) cabinet in September 1918. Although a number of previous governments had been based on political parties, the prime minister had always been a member of the peerage: Count Ōkuma Shigenobu (his title while in office; this is true for the others as well); Marquis Itō Hirobumi; Prince Saionji Kinmochi. Hara Takashi was the first prime minister without a title and the first to hold a seat in the House of Representatives. Supremacy of the lower house is an indispensable requirement for party government, and in that sense, it is only natural that Hara reaped praise from the public for being the "commoner prime minister" (*heimin saishō*).

The First World War came to an end shortly after Hara assumed office. Germany joined Russia in collapse, and Britain and France were exhausted; America was now the dominant power of the world in terms of both power and ideology. In light of these changes to the international environment, the arrival of a new age of party government in Japan was felt all the stronger.

Hara's policies have traditionally been considered proactive. His promotion of regional industrialization since the Keien era through policies such as aggressive expansion of the Japanese rail network has already been described (see Chapter 9), but his promotion of middle and higher education was another of his proactive policies worthy of attention. Prior to Hara's government, there were only five imperial universities in Japan (Tokyo, Kyoto, Tōhoku, Kyushu, and Hokkaidō), and while private universities existed, they were not acknowledged as granting equivalent qualifications. There were also only eight high schools (which were numbered from one to eight). The Hara government established national and public universities and granted private universities like Keio and Waseda essentially the same rights as the imperial universities. A large number of high schools were also built, and many technical and middle schools were constructed and expanded. This policy was undertaken both in response to Japan's tremendous industrial development during the First World War and as an attempt to increase access to higher education due to a rise in the educational level of the public.

Figure 10.1 Shidehara Kijūrō. (January 1931. Photo provided by the *Mainichi Shimbun*.)

Another distinguishing characteristic of the Hara government's policies was the increasing importance of political parties to the political structure. Under the political system of the Meiji state, party members and other private citizens were excluded from being eligible for appointment in a number of areas for reasons such as maintaining national standards and protecting state secrets. The governor-generals of Korea and Taiwan were required to be general or flag officers on active duty, for example. Hara reformed this system, appointing retired Admiral Saitō Makoto (1858–1936) as governor-general of Korea (traditionally a stronghold of the army) and Den Kenjirō (1855–1930), a Yamagata faction bureaucrat, as governor-general of Taiwan (see Chapter 16). He also named politicians, businessmen, and scholars to the Privy Council and as *chokusen giin* in the House of Peers. These positions had previously generally gone to those with backgrounds in the bureaucracy. He also worked hard to reform the disproportionate awarding of peerage titles and decorations to bureaucrats.

Hara thus weakened the Meiji state's extremely centralized and bureaucratic character and attempted to make it less authoritarian. The Seiyūkai was the tool he used to do so, however, and promoting regional benefits was ultimately tied to strengthening the party's base. Laying railways and constructing new high schools were both means to the same end in this sense. And reducing restrictions on access to political bodies also ultimately meant inserting Seiyūkai members or party sympathizers. When the leadership of Mantetsu became dominated by the Seiyūkai, for example, it became a source of funds for the party.

By the time Hara was assassinated in November 1921, public opinion toward him had turned cool. While the assassination was condemned, many also felt that Hara also bore some responsibility for it. While he had increased his party's power, he had simultaneously inspired distrust in it. That Japan's first so-called commoner prime minister was also the first to be assassinated in office symbolizes the unfortunate fate that awaited the country's party governments.

After Hara's death

The negative legacy that Hara left behind didn't end there. As an extremely powerful politician, he had been able to significantly weaken his rivals. He had amended the Election Law in 1919 to expand the franchise and to introduce the single-member electoral district system. He dissolved the Diet as the movement seeking universal male suffrage grew in strength in the following year and won a great victory in the fourteenth general election that May. The result was an extremely lopsided Diet; of the 464 seats, the Friends of Constitutional Government Party held 278 and the Constitutional Association, the second largest party, 110. Hara also hounded and weakened the Yamagata faction, the government's latent opposition outside the Diet.

As a result, there was no one skilled enough to take over the government when Hara was gone. Hara's finance minister Takahashi Korekiyo (1854–1936) succeeded him as prime minister after the assassination, but he was a relative newcomer to the Friends of Constitutional Government Party and was incapable of leading the massive party. An anti-Takahashi faction rose within the party, and his cabinet fell after only six months due to the party infighting.

The next cabinet was formed by Admiral Katō Tomosaburō (1861–1923), who had been the chief Japanese commissioner at the Washington Conference and was close to the Friends of Constitutional Government Party. The party was dissatisfied that the prime minister wasn't a member of their party but reluctantly supported the cabinet as they feared that the Constitutional Association would be given the chance to form a cabinet if Katō declined.

When Katō died in August 1923, Yamamoto Gonnohyōe formed his second cabinet. The 2nd Yamamoto Cabinet included many politicians of prime ministerial caliber such as Gotō Shimpei, Tanaka Giichi, Inukai Tsuyoshi (1855–1932), and Den Kojirō. It sought to implement universal male suffrage and put forth grand plans for reconstruction following the September 1923 Great Kanto Earthquake. Opposition from the Friends of Constitutional Government Party greatly hindered its reconstruction plans, however, and the government resigned after taking responsibility for an assassination attempt on Prince Regent Hirohito known as the Toranomon Incident. The post-Hara Friends of Constitutional Government Party was thus unable to produce responsible leadership commensurate to the power of its absolute majority.

It truly came as a shock to the party, however, when Kiyoura Keigo turned to the House of Peers when ordered to form a cabinet in January 1924. The faction of Takahashi, who was serving as president of the Friends of Constitutional Government Party, asserted that having three consecutive nonparty cabinets was unacceptable and that the party should join with the other parties under the banner of opposition to the government and support for universal male suffrage. The anti-Takahashi faction disagreed and said that the party should wait one more time. Taking the name *Seiyū Hontō* (True Friends of Constitutional Government), the faction left the party and supported the government. The Friends of Constitutional Government Party, Constitutional Association, and the Reformist (*Kakushin*) Club formed the *Goken Sanpa* (Three Parties to Protect the Constitution) and led a second protect-the-constitution movement in the name of universal male suffrage and reform of the House of Peers. Despite lacking the naturally arising energy of the first such movement of the early Taishō period (see Chapter 9), it was victorious in the May elections. The Kiyoura Cabinet resigned and the three parties entered into a coalition, marking the beginning of the era of true party governments. Before examining this new era, however, let's first move to the foreign policy of the early 1920s.

The Washington system

Creation of the Washington system

The First World War brought major changes to the nature of the world order. Not only did it alter the balance among the great powers, but it brought about the embrace of and advocacy for new ideas that would have been unthinkable before the war such as self-determination of the people, pacifism, and open diplomacy. The Versailles Peace Treaty of June 1919 gave shape to this new world order, but that was very much primarily concerned with Europe. It was the Washington Conference (November 1921–February 1922) that established the postwar world order for East Asia and the Pacific. A number of treaties and exchanges of notes were made at the conference such as the Nine-Power Treaty concerning China and the Washington Naval Treaty (also known as the Four-Power Treaty, the Five-Power Treaty, and the Nine-Power Treaty). The world order created via these treaties is referred to as the Washington system, just as its counterpart in Europe is called the Versailles system.

When America first proposed the conference in July 1921, many Japanese harbored great unease at its invitation. America had traditionally been the power most critical of Japanese foreign policy, and they feared that Japanese policy – from the Twenty-One Demands to the Siberian Intervention (see Chapter 8) – would be subjected to attacks. And a number of items appearing disadvantageous to Japan were indeed decided upon at the conference. The Open Door was adopted as a principle of the East Asian world order more strictly, and Japan gave up a number of its special rights and interests. The Anglo-Japanese Alliance, which America had criticized as having supported Japanese expansion, was discontinued and replaced with the not particularly meaningful Four-Power Treaty concerning the Pacific. But if the Washington system was so disadvantageous for Japan, why did Japan accept it?

The first reason that can be raised was the absence of a convincing alternative for Japan to cooperation with America. Japan had been able to fend off American criticism since the Russo-Japanese War by joining with Russia, France, and Britain. But now, with Russia having fallen and a weakened Britain drawing closer to America, there were no longer any powers with which Japan could ally to resist America. China was also closer to America than ever. America had become prominent not just in terms of its power but in its intellectual and moral influence as well, with many in the world looking to it as a model for the world to learn from. It seemed imprudent for Japan to attempt to resist such a country.

Second, Japan and America had reached compromises over a number of important points of contention. The issue of Manchuria and Inner Mongolia (South Manchuria and Eastern Inner Mongolia) was one of these. There appeared to be a great distance between the position of Japan, who saw Manchuria and Inner Mongolia as part of its sphere of influence and sought to secure this status, and America, who sought to make the principle of the Open Door even clearer and rejected spheres of influence. This same issue had arisen earlier, during the formation of the new Four-Power Consortium in 1920. Because loans had frequently been used in China as a form of imperialism, this consortium was intended to make all loans to China a joint enterprise among the great powers. Many in Japan had argued that loans related to Manchuria and Inner Mongolia should be exempt, but Prime Minister Hara managed to resolve the issue by striking a compromise: in exchange for not excluding Manchuria and Inner Mongolia, Japan's already enacted rights, such as those for Mantetsu, would be exempt from the consortium's activities. Those rights not yet acted upon would be submitted to the consortium.

This was essentially the approach adopted during the Washington Conference as well. While the Nine-Power Treaty concerning China laid out the principles of the Open Door and equality of opportunity in China even more rigorously than ever, there was also an understood compromise that the powers wouldn't infringe upon one another's already established interests.

Naval disarmament was another point of contention. America proposed a U.S.-Britain-Japan capital ship tonnage ratio of 5:5:3, and many in the Japanese navy argued that, from a technological viewpoint, Japan needed to possess ships equivalent to 70 percent of the U.S. Navy to resist it. But since a prohibition on strengthening military bases in the Pacific was agreed to as well, Japan's position in the western Pacific became relatively advantageous. Additionally, America was the country with the largest ship construction plans at the time; Japan had no chance of competing with its economic power, and the 5:3 ratio was clearly more beneficial to Japan than a naval arms race would be. Navy Minister Katō Tomosaburō, one of the leaders of the navy and a commissioner at the conference, took the broader perspective and accepted the 5:5:3 ratio, overcoming the narrow technical argument and unifying the navy.

Shidehara diplomacy and Tanaka diplomacy

Shidehara Kijūrō (1872–1951) was born in Osaka. He graduated from Tokyo Imperial University in 1895 and entered the foreign ministry the following year. His wife was a member of the Iwasaki family, and Katō Takaaki was his brother-in-law. He followed the elite course, serving as vice-minister of foreign affairs and ambassador to America and was active as a commissioner at the Washington Conference. He served as foreign minister in five cabinets: 1st and 2nd Katō Takaaki, 1st Wakatsuki Reijirō, Hamaguchi Osachi, 2nd Wakatsuki. The policies he pursued during these governments are known as Shidehara diplomacy and centered on cooperation with Britain and America, nonintervention in internal Chinese politics, and economic expansion. He emphasized the treaty rights that formed the basis for economic activity and took a relatively hard approach toward the increase of Chinese tariffs and strikes in factories financed by Japanese capital.

In comparison, Tanaka Giichi (1864–1929) was from Chōshū and served as war minister in the Hara and 2nd Yamamoto administrations. While in office, Tanaka organized the *Zaigō Gunjinkai* (Veterans' Association) and worked to strengthen the relationship between the military and the public. When he became president of the Friends of Constitutional Government Party in 1925, he criticized the Constitutional Association cabinet's China policy as weak and called for a more proactive diplomacy. When he became prime minister in 1927, he served as foreign minister as well. He held the Eastern Conference (*Tōhō Kaigi*) to develop a general policy on China and dispatched troops to the Shandong Peninsula. But in practice Tanaka took a hard-line policy that was still within the framework of the Washington system and worked to expand Japanese power by compromising with Chiang Kai-shek on the Chinese mainland and supporting Zhang Zuolin in Manchuria.

The idea that Japan should seize control of Manchuria through force gained a following in the army, however. One such believer was Kōmoto Daisaku, who arranged the assassination of Zhang Zuolin in June 1928. Tanaka briefly considered punishing Kōmoto but changed his mind due to strong opposition from the army. He was rebuked for this by the emperor and resigned in July 1929.

Later, in 1945, the Potsdam Declaration stated that Japan's democratic tendencies should be restored and strengthened. As the Japanese believed that being unlikely to be tried for war crimes was a requirement for candidates to become prime minister, two possibilities that came to everyone's mind were Shidehara Kijūrō and Yoshida Shigeru, who had been vice-minister under Tanaka Giichi when he was foreign minister. The two had opposed each other prior to the Manchurian Incident but actually had a number of positions in common during the period of fierce foreign policy that followed the incident.

A third important reason for Japan to cooperate was the U.S.-Japan economic relationship. Japan had managed to become a creditor nation due to the First World War, but it had procured massive foreign loans from Britain and America during the Russo-Japanese War and was still in debt to both countries. Japan's trade revenues also fell back into deficit following the war, making its situation difficult. Exports of raw silk to America were Japan's salvation. Experiencing a postwar boom, the American middle class sought to buy luxury goods that had previously been the purview of the wealthy and the nobility. Although the chronic postwar recession of Japan's farming villages continued, these exports were one of the reasons that this did not become fatal.

The export of cotton goods to China provided another source of hope for foreign economic relations, and the raw cotton for these was imported from America. In other words, relations with America were a major factor in preventing Japan's foreign trade relations from becoming critical. It was believed that Japan's economic future lay in continued friendly relations with the United States.

The weakening of China and the Soviet Union was a final reason for cooperation. If China had been strong or if the Soviet Union had been powerful, the Japanese miliarty wouldn't have accepted the Washington system without explicit assurances of Japan's rights in Manchuria and Inner Mongolia. The fact that Chinese and Soviet power resistance was negligible was an important prerequisite for the creation of the Washington system.

The collapse of the Washington system

These conditions for cooperation steadily disappeared during the late 1920s, however. And as they did so, the Washington system headed toward collapse.

First, Chinese nationalism grew. The Kuomintang government in Guangzhou, which had been essentially powerless in terms of capabilities (even if not necessarily so ideologically) until the early 1920s, rapidly began to increase its power due to support from the Soviet Union following the formation of the First United Front in 1924 between the Kuomintang and the Communist Party. It launched the Northern Expedition under Chiang Kai-shek (1887–1975) in 1926 and defied world expectations by repeatedly defeating the warlords and successfully unifying China in 1928. Anti-imperialism became the greatest rallying cry of the period, and Chinese demands grew to include the return of the Kwantung Leased Territory and Mantetsu. Although Japan had managed to secure guarantees of her interests in Manchuria and Inner Mongolia from the other powers, they were now threatened by China.

Second, the Soviet Union also began to recover as a military power in the late 1920s. The Soviets concentrated on building up heavy industry after Josef Stalin (1879–1953) cemented his dictatorship in 1928, and this effort steadily produced results. When a war broke out with China over the Chinese Eastern Railway in 1929, the Soviets did not hesitate to use this strength to win a crushing victory. Thus, just as Japanese interests in Manchuria and Inner Mongolia were coming under threat from the south, another threat appeared to their north.

The London Naval Conference then opened in 1930 to place restrictions on auxiliary ships. America's goal was to again achieve a 5:5:3 ratio as it had in the Washington Naval Treaty. Improvements in shipping technology had made it relatively more powerful in the western Pacific than it had been at that time, however, and Japan had comparatively more advanced auxiliary ship construction technology. This meant that accepting a cap of 60 percent of American naval strength was more painful than the restriction on capital ship tonnage had been. The navy also lacked a powerful leader like Katō Tomosaburō. Although the treaty itself was ratified in April through the efforts of the Hamaguchi Osachi Cabinet, Japan had been unable to achieve the 70 percent ratio that the navy had wanted. The navy was thus strongly opposed to the treaty and joined with outside groups in a movement against it. This would leave behind significant acrimony afterward.

The Great Depression began in the United States in October 1929, and this also had deep influences on Japan as it directly attacked the silk industry by causing exports of raw silk to America to decline dramatically. Additionally, the Great

Depression unfortunately overlapped with the enactment of the Hamaguchi Cabinet's policy to return to the gold standard in January 1930, which magnified its impact on the Japanese economy. America then passed the Smoot-Hawley Tariff Act in June 1930, adopting a policy of extremely high tariffs, which dealt another heavy blow to Japanese exports to America.

These weren't the only effects of the Great Depression. America had previously been seen as a model for the world in a number of ways, but that image was now greatly tarnished. Notably, since Marxism was influential in Japan, a number of intellectuals came to believe that the collapse of capitalism had finally begun. At the same time, the Italy of Benito Mussolini (1883–1945), Stalin's Soviet Union, and the German Nazis (who had not yet assumed power) all appeared to be on the rise. Many believed that democracy and capitalism had come to an end and that a new age of totalitarianism was beginning.

And by this point, there were no longer any figures capable of exercising strong leadership like Hara Takashi had been. That was the final reason for the Washington system's collapse. How did this leadership vacuum come to be? Let's examine the era of party cabinets from the viewpoint of this question.

The era of party cabinets

Table 10.1 briefly summarizes the seven party cabinets in office from the 1st Katō Takaaki Cabinet of 1924 to the resignation of the Inukai Cabinet in 1931, giving the political party and the reason for the cabinets' fall.

The first noticeable trend is the extremely short lives of the cabinets. Their greatest characteristic is that they were short-lived and unstable.

Table 10.1 Party cabinets and their collapse.

Cabinet	Reason for Fall	Date Formed
1st Katō Takaaki (Kenseikai, Seiyūkai, Kakushin Club also known as the Reformist Club)	Dissolution of the Sanpa coalition	1924/6/11
2nd Katō Takaaki (Kenseikai)	Katō's death	1925/8/2
1st Wakatsuki Reijirō (Kenseikai)	Rejection of request for emergency imperial edict by Privy Council	1926/1/30
Tanaka Giichi (Seiyūkai)	Imperial distrust due to mishandling of the assassination of Zhang Zuolin	1927/4/20
Hamaguchi Osachi (Minseitō)	Hamaguchi seriously injured in assassination attempt	1929/7/2
2nd Wakatsuki Reijirō (Minseitō)	Cabinet disunity over the political situation that followed the Manchurian Incident	1931/4/14
Inukai Tsuyoshi (Seiyūkai)	Inukai assassinated in the May 15th Incident	1931/12/13

Additionally, their short lives were not due either to motions of no confidence in the House of Representatives or to general election defeats. In fact, if the 1st Katō Cabinet is set aside because it was based on a three-party coalition, all of these were formed as minority governments yet managed to secure a majority if an election was held: the Friends of Constitutional Government Party went from 190 to 207 seats in the sixteenth general election held during the Tanaka Cabinet; the Constitutional Democratic Party (*Rikken Minseitō*), founded in June 1927 through the merger of the Constitutional Association and the original Friends of Constitutional Government Party (*Seiyū Hontō*), went from 173 to 273 in the seventeenth general election under the Hamaguchi Cabinet; and the Friends of Constitutional Government Party went from 171 to 301 in the eighteenth general election under the Inukai Cabinet. In each case, the cabinet party emerged victorious. Universal male suffrage went into effect with the sixteenth general election, but there were no changes in election style despite the participation of the proletariat parties. Instead, since the increase in the size of the electorate made it difficult to win elections relying solely on the traditional bases of the parties, there was a marked increase in parties using their positions in the government to procure funds and the use of state organs to interfere with elections.

For this reason, when in the opposition parties prioritized becoming the government party above all else. They did not abstain from becoming close to the elder statesman Saionji Kinmochi (who had the final say on recommendations to the emperor on who to name as prime minister), from exposing scandals involving their opposition, or from dragging an ill prime minister to the Diet. They were also willing to ally with groups hostile to party government, such as the military and the Privy Council, and to appeal to principles that ran counter to the idea of party government.

As soon as the three-party effort to protect the constitution (the 1st Katō Takaaki government) passed the universal male suffrage law that it had campaigned on in March 1925, the Friends of Constitutional Government attempted to cause the government to fall. Takahashi Korekiyo was forced to retire as party president and was replaced with Tanaka Giichi in April, and the party merged with the Kakushin Club (The Reformist Club) in May to increase its number of seats. When the government fell over disagreements regarding tax reform, however, the emperor ordered Katō Takaaki to form another cabinet, causing the plans of the Friends of Constitutional Government Party to go awry.

The 2nd Katō Cabinet came to an end after half a year due to Katō's death from pneumonia, however, and Wakatsuki Reijirō of the Constitutional Association formed the next cabinet in January 1926. The Friends of Constitutional Government Party attacked the Wakatsuki Cabinet incessantly, accusing it of scandals and decrying the Constitutional Association's China policy as worthless. In the end, it borrowed the power of the Privy Council to bring the cabinet down in April 1927.

This led to the formation of the Tanaka Cabinet, but it struggled with low popularity and Home Minister Suzuki Kisaburō (1867–1940) argued during the sixteenth general election that changing the cabinet on the basis of the election's results would violate the emperor's authority. This was a rejection of the idea of party cabinets. The government attempted to change the country's China policy but was unsuccessful. It dispatched troops to Shandong where they clashed with the National Revolutionary Army in May 1928 in what is known as the Jinan Incident. The government ultimately lost the emperor's confidence when it mishandled the aftermath of the June 1928 assassination of Zhang Zuolin and resigned in July 1929.

Hamaguchi Osachi, the president of the Constitutional Democratic Party, formed the next government. When it concluded the London Naval Treaty, the Friends of Constitutional Government Party charged the cabinet with having inappropriately ignored the opinions of the navy general staff and infringing upon the emperor's prerogative of supreme command (see Chapter 5). Prime Minister Hamaguchi was seriously injured in an assassination attempt in November 1930 and had to resign in April the following year. (He died in August.) The 2nd Wakatsuki Cabinet that succeeded him was then unable to handle the Manchurian Incident and resigned over disunity within the government.

The Friends of Constitutional Government Party cabinet of Inukai Tsuyoshi that succeeded Wakatsuki won a great victory in the eighteenth general election in February 1932 due to the unpopularity of the Constitutional Democratic Party but was toppled by the May 15th Incident launched by naval officers.

This excessive political fighting between the parties invited public distrust, strengthened political organizations hostile to them, and attempted to make use of political principles that contradicted party cabinets. It was thus the parties themselves who destroyed the foundations of party cabinets. The parties were utterly unable to respond when, beginning in the 1930s, the Japanese economy stalled and the military rose, asserting that national defense was in a state of crisis and that Japanese rights in Manchuria and Inner Mongolia were threatened.

The phrase "*kensei no jōdō*" ("the normal course of constitutional government") was often used throughout the era of party cabinets. This held that, when a cabinet reached an impasse in policy, it should resign and turn power over to the opposition. However, this *kensei no jōdō* concept was never institutionalized and was most often invoked by the opposition party in an attempt to gain power. Once the said party achieved this goal, they would usually immediately forget their past arguments and firmly attempt to hold onto power.

In any case, however, it was actually the relative fairness on the part of the founding fathers who made recommendations to the emperor regarding whom to name as prime minister that caused the transfer of power between the parties to continue. After the death of Yamagata Aritomo in 1922, the only remaining members of the *genrō* were Matsutaka Masayoshi and Saionji Kinmochi. Saionji then became the last *genrō* when Matsutaka died in 1924. Saionji, who unlike Yamagata did not have a large amount of personal power, was primarily concerned with maintaining stable cabinets, and transferring power between parties was one way to achieve this. International cooperation, especially with Britain and America, was also important to Saionji, however. Saionji can be considered to have been a believer in the "normal course of constitutional government" so long as it involved cooperation with Britain and America.

11 The rise of the military

The Manchurian incident

Disarmament and the modernization of the military

It was the military, and the army in particular, who gave the *coup de grace* to the Washington system (see Chapter 10) and party government. The road to the Manchurian Incident and the Pacific War cannot be discussed without the army.

The source of the army's political rise can be found in two legacies of the First World War. The first of these was the tremendous improvement in military technology and the development of a system for total war. The fierce fighting in Europe had given rise to tanks, airplanes, poison gas, and submarines, and firepower had increased remarkably. And attempts had been successfully made to realize systems of total war, mobilizing the entirety of society for the purpose of war. Japan had been left behind, however, and was largely disconnected from both this improvement in technology and the preparation for total war.

The other legacy of the war was pacifism. Heralded as the "end of nationalism" and the arrival of a new age of democracy, the postwar era was one in which military men must have felt small. The 1920s were the only period between the Bakumatsu and the Second World War in which disarmament was advocated for and made progress.

When a naval disarmament treaty was agreed upon at the Washington Conference in 1922 (see Chapter 10), the public immediately began to support a reduction in the size of the army as well. The army began making efforts toward disarmament in August under War Minister Yamanashi Hanzō (1864–1944) in response. The result was a two-part reduction in the size of the army totaling 60,000 men (about a quarter of the entire army) and 13,000 horses. This so-called Yamanashi reduction wasn't enough to satisfy public opinion, however. War Minister Ugaki Kazushige (1868–1956) thus decided in 1925 to pursue a second round of reductions and embarked on a plan to eliminate four of the army's twenty-one divisions (these cuts dealt a greater blow to the military bureaucrats than those under Yamanashi had as the elimination of four divisions and sixteen regiments meant that many officers lost their posts). The army attempted to retain as much of the money saved by these cuts as possible, however, using it instead for modernization such

Figure 11.1 Ugaki Kazushige. (August 1929. Photo provided by the *Mainichi Shimbun*.)

as increasing firepower. The Ugaki reduction (*Ugaki gunshuku*) was one of the approaches adopted by the army to address the difficult problem of how to modernize in the face of the pacifist trend.

Yamanashi had served as vice-minister under War Minister Tanaka during the Hara Takashi Cabinet and had been chosen to be his successor. Ugaki had also served as vice-minister under Tanaka (during the 2nd Yamamoto Gonnohyōe Cabinet) and accordingly became war minister at his recommendation in the following Kiyoura Keigo Cabinet. Ugaki would serve in the subsequent three cabinets, as well as during the Hamaguchi Osachi Cabinet, and built up entrenched influence within the army leadership. It would not be unreasonable to say that the first half of the 1920s was the "age of Tanaka" for the army and the second half was the "age of Ugaki." Both men cooperated closely with the parties and sought to modernize the army while accepting a certain degree of disarmament.

The rise of the Shōwa military factions

The results achieved through this modernization policy were insufficient, however. The postwar Japanese economy continued to perform poorly, and the Great Kanto Earthquake gave it another heavy blow in 1923. Regardless, Tanaka Giichi became president of the Friends of Constitutional Government Party in 1925 and then prime minister in 1927. There were rumors that Ugaki was a candidate for the presidency of the Constitutional Democratic Party and could potentially become prime minister as well. Criticism rose within the army that military leaders like these were using the army as a stepping-stone for their own advancement.

Another criticism was aimed at the very concept of military modernization. These critics argued that large numbers of trained soldiers would be more important than modernization, given Japan's expected battlefields and hypothesized opponents. Many close to Uehara Yūsaku held to this view. Uehara had opposed War Minister Tanaka while serving as chief of the general staff during the Hara government and had led the largest opposition groups against Tanaka and Ugaki ever since. There were also those who supported modernization but believed that it would be impossible to do so sufficiently through Tanaka and Ugaki's strategy of working with the parties.

Finally, there were also those who criticized Tanaka and Ugaki over their policies on China. Broadly speaking, both men viewed these within the framework of the Washington system and in the context of cooperation with Britain and America. A faction opposing their policies formed, with many members overlapping with the aforementioned critical groups.

Ugaki Kazushige (1868–1956)

Ugaki Kazushige was born into a farming family in Okayama Prefecture but managed to enter the Imperial Army Academy (graduating in its first class in 1890) and the Army War College (graduating in 1900) despite his family's poverty. He studied in Germany and was repeatedly promoted. As a colonel, he was demoted for distributing a document opposing the abolition of the requirement that military ministers be active duty officers (see Chapter 9). He became war minister in the Kiyoura Keigo

Cabinet in 1924 and remained in place during the 1st and 2nd Katō Takaaki Cabinets and the 1st Wakatsuki Cabinet. During this time, he oversaw the Ugaki [arms] reduction. He was reappointed as war minister in the Hamaguchi Osachi Cabinet in 1929. During the March Incident of 1931, the coup members intended for him to become prime minister afterward, and his involvement in the incident was suspected. He retired from active duty and became governor-general of Korea in June.

After the Hirota Kōki Cabinet resigned in January 1937, he was ordered by the emperor to form a government but failed to do so because of strong opposition from the army (see Chapter 12). The army believed that Ugaki would oppose the massive military expansion plans then being formulated and therefore blocked his attempts to assemble a cabinet. The palace was also uncooperative with Ugaki at this time.

He became foreign minister in May 1938 when the Second Sino-Japanese War stalled during the Konoe Fumimaro Cabinet. He attempted to break through the stalemate through negotiations with the Kuomintang and Britain. He also worked to resolve the border conflicts with the Soviet Union in a practical manner.

Ugaki was frequently considered a dark horse in political circles and was eyed as a powerful candidate for prime minister. Although he was heavily involved in political machinations including securing funds, he ultimately never served as prime minister.

Many reasons have been given for this, including the many enemies he created within the army due to his arms reduction, which had eliminated posts for many high-ranking officers. He acted arrogantly and never concealed his ambitious nature, which caused many to be wary of him (including the imperial palace). The middle-grade officers of the army were also concerned about his likely ability to achieve cuts in military spending.

For a military officer of his time, Ugaki possessed an outstanding breadth of vision and an energy that encompassed both military affairs and diplomacy. This could be seen in his attempts to modernize the military and to improve relations with China and Britain. That he was never given the chance to exercise those skills as prime minister was a great tragedy not only for Ugaki but for Japan as well.

A force among the middle-grade officers of the army thus arose in opposition to Tanaka and Ugaki that was convinced that both the political parties and the Washington system had to be destroyed. Nagata Tetsuzan (1884–1935), Obata Toshishirō (1885–1947), and Itagaki Seishirō (1885–1948) were leaders of this group. All three were members of the Imperial Japanese Army Academy's six-teenth graduating class (1904). (See Table 11.1.) This group of colonels and lieu-tenant colonels, which also included the younger Ishihara Kanji (1889–1949) of the twenty-first graduating class, held regular meetings during the early Shōwa period. They agreed in 1929 to support Araki Sadao (1877–1966), Mazaki Jinzaburō (1876–1956), and Hayashi Senjūrō (1876–1943), all members of Ueha-ra's factions, in pushing through reform of the army and a resolution of the issue of Manchuria and Inner Mongolia.

When the Hamaguchi Cabinet was formed in July 1929, Ugaki once again served as war minister. He embarked on reforms and attempted to further push for military modernization. Given the austerity finances of the Hamaguchi Cabi-net, however, it was doubtful how much could be achieved. Moreover, Ugaki

Table 11.1 Army leaders by their year of graduation from the Imperial Army Academy.

Class	Name	Birth	Origin	Major Positions
1 (1890)	Ugaki Kazushige	1868	Okayama	War minister under Kiyoura, Katō, Watatsuki, Hamaguchi, governor-general of Korea
	Shirakawa Yoshinori	1868	Ehime	War minister under Tanaka
	Suzuki Sōroku	1865	Niigata	Chief of staff (1926–1930)
5 (1894)	Kanaya Hanzō	1873	Ōita	Chief of staff (1930–1931)
6 (1895)	Minami Jirō	1874	Ōita	War minister under Wakatsuki, governor-general of Korea
8 (1896)	Hayashi Senjūrō	1876	Ishikawa	Inspector-general of military education, war minister under Saitō, Okada, prime minister
9 (1897)	Araki Sadao	1877	Tokyo	War minister under Inukai, Saitō
	Abe Nobuyuki	1875	Ishikawa	Acting war minister under Hamaguchi, prime minister
10 (1898)	Kawashima Yoshiyuki	1878	Ehime	War minister under Okada
11 (1899)	Terauchi Hisaichi	1879	Yamaguchi	War minister under Hirota
12 (1900)	Ninomiya Harushige	1879	Okayama	
	Sugiyama Hajime	1880	Fukuoka	War minister under Hayashi, Konoe, Koiso
	Hata Shunroku	1879	Fukushima	War minister under Abe, Yonai
	Koiso Kuniaki	1880	Tochigi	Colonial minister under Hiranuma, Yonai, prime minister
13 (1901)	Nakamura Kōtarō	1881	Ishikawa	War minister under Hayashi
15 (1903)	Umezu Yoshijirō	1882	Ōita	Chief of staff (1944–1945)
16 (1904)	Nagata Tetsuzan	1884	Nagano	Head, Bureau of Military Affairs
	Okamura Yasuji	1884	Tokyo	Commander, China Expeditionary Army
	Obata Toshishirō	1885	Kochi	Head, General Staff 3rd Section
	Itagaki Seishirō	1885	Iwate	War minister under Konoe
17 (1904)	Tōjō Hideki	1884	Tokyo	War minister under Konoe, prime minister
21 (1907)	Ishihara Kanji	1889	Yamagata	Head, General Staff 1st Section

had ambitions toward a government of his own, and his actions lacked clarity. Although all bureau and department heads in the war ministry and the general staff were members of Ugaki's faction, distrust spread among the section heads. There was a coup attempt in March 1931 (known as the March Incident) in which Lieutenant Colonel Hashimoto Kingorō of the *Sakurakai* (a nationalist secret society) attempted to make Ugaki prime minister. Although Ugaki's degree of involvement in the incident is unclear even today, many of those involved in the coup believed he had been involved but had cold feet as the coup was ongoing. The incident caused Ugaki to lose supporters and further strengthened his critic's distrust of him. When Hamaguchi resigned as prime minister in April and was succeeded by the Wakatsuki Cabinet, Ugaki stepped down as war minister and recommended that Minami Jirō (1874–1955) be his successor. Expectations for Ugaki within the army rapidly faded away.

The Manchurian Incident and Japanese withdrawal from the League of Nations

Around the time of Ugaki's resignation, Ishihara Kanji of the Kwantung Army Staff was putting together a scheme in Manchuria intended to provide an opportunity for Japan to occupy the entire region. Kōmoto Daisaku (1882–1955) had already made a similar attempt in 1928 (the assassination of Zhang Zuolin), but Ishihara's plan was more carefully prepared and included analysis of domestic and international conditions and efforts to shape public opinion. It also had wide support among middle-grade officers. The Kwantung Army of the time was only a small force about the size of a division and was quite unlike the large force it would later become (it had 740,000 men in 1941). Despite its small size, it included capable and ambitious middle-grade officers.

In what is known as the Liutiaohu (or Mukden) Incident, the Kwantung Army blew up a section of the Mantetsu rail line in September 1931 and claimed that this had been the work of men under Zhang Xueliang (1901–2001). The army immediately occupied strategic points along the rail line and moved on Jinzhou, the stronghold of Zhang's army, in October. It advanced into northern Manchuria, part of the Soviet sphere of influence, in November, and by early 1932 the three eastern provinces were completely under its control (the Manchurian Incident).

In Tokyo, Prime Minister Wakatsuki and Foreign Minister Shidehara Kijūrō (1872–1951) worked to regain control of the situation and to limit its spread but were unable to control the actions of the Kwantung Army. The cabinet soon tried to ally with the Friends of Constitutional Government Party to handle the difficult situation, but it ultimately fell in December due to disunity in the cabinet.

Although the army leadership under War Minister Minami and Army Chief of Staff Kanaya Hanzō (1873–1933) was not necessarily working in concert with Wakatsuki and Shidehara's plans, it did work to try to somehow contain the situation as the Kwantung Army's advance toward Jinzhou and Harbin (the center of Soviet power in Manchuria) drew strong opposition from the other great powers. The prestige of both men was significantly damaged as the situation continued to surpass their expectations. When the Wakatsuki Cabinet resigned and was replaced by the new Inukai Tsuyoshi Cabinet, Araki Sadao of the anti-Ugaki faction became war minister. Thus the Manchurian Incident not only was a direct attack upon the Washington system and party government but also struck a strong blow against the Ugaki faction that had cooperated with them.

Foreign response to the incident was relatively calm at this point. The Chinese Kuomintang was fighting the communists and therefore didn't embark on a policy of total resistance against the Japanese. The Soviet Union, the foreign country with the greatest interests in Manchuria, proposed a nonaggression pact. And Britain and America also initially abstained from harsh criticism due to the trust they had in Wakatsuki and Shidehara.

The attack on Jinzhou put the foreign powers on edge, however. In January 1932, U.S. Secretary of State Henry L. Stimson (1867–1950) criticized Japan's actions as being in violation of the Nine-Power Treaty (see Chapter 10) and the Kellog-Briand Pact and issued the Stimson Doctrine, which stated that America would not recognize any illegal changes made to the status quo in China through the use of force. This was followed by a military clash later that month over the anti-Japanese movement there (the Shanghai Incident) which significantly hardened popular opinion in Britain and America against Japan. Neither nation took further steps, however. In March 1932, the Kwantung Army embarked on the creation of the puppet state of Manchukuo with the final emperor of the Qing Dynasty, Puyi (1906–1967, reigned 1908–1912), serving as its chief executive. The Inukai Cabinet abstained from recognizing the new state, but the following Saitō Cabinet was inclined to do so. Its foreign minister, Uchida Yasuya (1865–1936), gave a speech in the Diet in August in which he stated that he "would not surrender a single inch, even if it reduces the country to scorched earth" (an approach known as scorched earth diplomacy). As Uchida was a veteran diplomat who had served as foreign minister twenty years earlier and been involved in the creation of the Versailles-Washington system during the Hara Cabinet, this drastic change of character shocked those involved.

The Saitō Cabinet took the plunge and recognized Manchukuo in September. A framework was created under which the commander of the Kwantung Army would also serve as the Japanese ambassador to Manchukuo and as head of the Kwantung Territory Government (*Kantōchō*). The League of Nations' Lytton Commission under Victor Alexander Lytton (1876–1947) was visiting Japan as this step was taken. Recognizing Manchukuo during their visit was an obviously provocative act.

Incidentally, this commission released its report in October. Although it rejected Japan's assertion that it had acted in self-defense, it acknowledged that Manchuria was a special area. And while it requested that the Japanese army withdraw, it also proposed self-rule for Manchuria. The report's contents were in no way disadvantageous to Japan alone and could have possibly served as a basis on which to resolve the situation. The army, public opinion, and Foreign Minister Uchida were no longer flexible enough to seek a compromise, however. At the League of Nations' general meeting in Geneva in March 1933, Japan announced its withdrawal from the League. This decision was caused by the extreme character of Ambassador Matsuoka Yōsuke (1880–1946), a number of acts of chance, and the defiance of the Kwantung Army.

The February 26 incident

International relations after the departure from the League of Nations

At the time, the Kwantung Army was eliminating the remaining resistance in Rehe Province and pushing south of the Great Wall. The Tanggu Truce was signed in the end of May 1933, however, bringing the Manchurian Incident to an end. Japan then went to work rebuilding its foreign relations.

This task fell to Hirota Kōki (1878–1948), who was appointed foreign minister in September. Hirota would remain in office during both the Saitō and Okada Cabinets and then become prime minister after Okada. Although out of government for the four months of the Hayashi Senjūrō Cabinet, he then served as foreign minister once again in the 1st Konoe Cabinet and remained until the May 1938 cabinet reorganization. This lengthy time in office was extraordinary, given the tumultuous times.

Hirota first attempted to improve relations with America. He tapped Saitō Hiroshi (1886–1939), the foreign ministry's foremost expert on America, to serve as ambassador to the United States in late 1933 and sent a message to U.S. Secretary of State Cordell Hull (1871–1955) expressing his desire for goodwill between the two countries. He also worked to eliminate potential sources of conflict with the Soviet Union by trying to purchase the North Manchurian Railway (Chinese Eastern Railway), the remaining Soviet interest in Manchuria. He succeeded in this in January 1935. He also made efforts to improve relations with China beginning in late 1934 and adopted a friendly posture toward them by, for example, raising the status of the Chinese presence in Japan from legation to embassy in 1935.

There were major problems with Hirota's diplomacy, however, one of which was inherent to it. When a diplomatic course was adopted at the Five Ministers Conference in October 1933 attended by the prime minister and the foreign, finance, war, and naval ministers, this included a statement that "cooperation and mutual assistance between the three nations of Japan, Manchukuo, and China will be realized under the guidance of the Japanese Empire, thus ensuring lasting peace in the East and contributing to the promotion of world peace." And Hirota himself stated in a January 1934 speech in the Diet that Japan bore total responsibility for maintaining peace in East Asia. In other words, the concept of an "Asian Monroe Doctrine," an East Asian international order in which Japan was the leading power, was inherent to Hirota's foreign policy.

Hirota accordingly took a dim view toward other powers becoming closer with China. In April 1934, Amō Eiji (1887–1968), the head of the foreign ministry's Information Bureau, made waves by stating that Japan was, in principle, opposed to any joint actions by the Western powers toward China (this is known as the

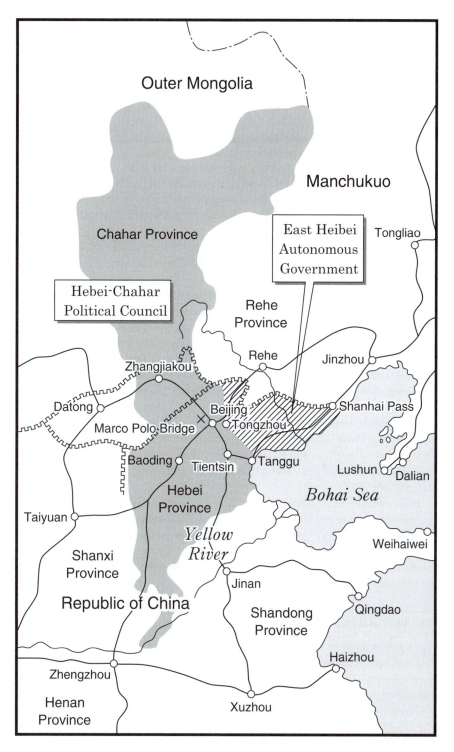

Figure 11.2 Manchukuo and autonomy operations in North China.

Amō Statement). And when Britain planned reforms of China's monetary system from 1934 to 1935 and invited Japanese participation, Hirota was cool to this proposal. It was unlikely that Sino-Japanese goodwill of this sort, which required the exclusion of any third countries, would be accepted by others. It certainly wouldn't be accepted by America, who continued to emphasize the principle of the Open Door.

The attitude of the military presented another problem for Hirota's diplomacy. By late 1933, the military had begun to repeatedly assert that a "Crisis of 1935–1936" existed, arguing that military expansion needed to be accelerated in order to be prepared for the crisis that would accompany the 1935–1936 expiration of the naval limitation treaties. Japan ultimately announced its renunciation of the treaties at the end of 1934, an action that was not desirable in terms of reducing tensions with the United States.

The army's attitude also restricted Hirota's China policies to a remarkable extent. The Kwantung Army, which had a strong interest in the security of Manchukuo's rear, and the China Garrison Army (*Shina Chūtongun*, a force stationed near Tientsin as a result of the Boxer Rebellion and also known as the Tientsin Army) began in 1935 to demand the demilitarization and independence from the central Chinese government of the area south of the Great Wall and a halt to anti-Japanese activities. The Chinese government reluctantly acceded to most of these in the Umezu-He Yingqin and Doihara-Qin Dechun Agreements in June. The Kwantung and Tientsin Armies used these agreements to move forward with their operations aimed at achieving the autonomy of northern China, however, and established the East Heibei Autonomous Council in November (this would be renamed the East Heibei Autonomous Government in December) and the Hebei-Chahar Political Council in December. They then claimed that the extent of these administrations and their degree of autonomy from the Kuomintang government were still insufficient and continued to push for further concessions.

Hirota's diplomacy emphasized improving relations with Japan's neighbors, as can be seen from its nickname of *wakyō gaikō* (diplomacy of peace and cooperation). It was overly optimistic regarding improving relations with America, however, given that it took an Asian Monroe Doctrine as its premise and was hindered by the policies of the army and the navy. It was unable to achieve any significant results.

The Saitō and Okada Cabinets

Let's now turn to the character of the Saitō and Okada Cabinets in office during this period. After the Inukai Cabinet fell due to the May 15 Incident, the *genrō* Saionji chose Saitō Makoto to become prime minister. He had wanted to maintain party government if possible but decided to create a national unity government under the moderate Saitō (a senior figure in the navy) because of the strength of the military's opposition to the parties and his wariness toward the ultranationalist tendencies of the new Friends of Constitutional Government president Suzuki Kisaburō.

The Saitō Cabinet included three members of the Friends of Constitutional Government (Takahashi Korekiyo and two others) and two members of the Constitutional Democratic Party (Yamamoto Tatsuo, 1856–1947, and one other). It had been eight years since the last nonparty government (the 1924 Kiyoura government), and that Takahashi and Yamamoto held the important posts of finance and foreign ministers showed that the power of the parties still could not be ignored.

Of the two, Finance Minister Takahashi, who remained from the Inukai Cabinet, played an especially important role. He had put the prohibition on gold exports back into effect during the Inukai Cabinet and now caused the economy to rapidly recover by weakening the foreign exchange rate (increasing the competitiveness of Japanese exports), creating domestic demand by relaxing the money supply, and expanding government spending. This was known as the Takahashi fiscal policy. If each country's total exports in 1929 are assigned a value of 100, Japan had recovered to its pre-1929 level by 1934 while Britain was still at 54 and America at 41. Japan's annual economic growth from 1933 to 1935 surpassed 8 percent.

When the Saitō Cabinet resigned in July 1934 due to the Teijin Incident (a financial scandal in which government officials were accused of stock manipulation), Okada Keisuke (1868–1952), another member of the moderate naval faction, formed the new government. Although this government included two members of the Constitutional Democratic Party including Machida Chūji (1863–1946) and three members of the Friends of Constitutional Government Party, the latter party refused to cooperate and expelled the three ministers from the party.

With the decline of the parties, the bureaucrats rose in prominence. The Okada Cabinet created the Cabinet Deliberation Council (*Naikaku Shingikai*) to advise on policy and the Cabinet Research Bureau (*Naikaku Chōsakyoku*) to serve as its secretariat. The Cabinet Deliberation Council achieved little and was soon abolished, but the Cabinet Research Bureau became a stronghold of the young bureaucrats. It later became the Planning Agency (*Kikakuchō*) and then the Planning Board (*Kikakuin*; see Chapter 12) and played a large role in the government's control over the economy.

The Saitō and Okada Cabinets were both of basically the same nature: cabinets with a moderate senior member of the navy serving as prime minister and including a few members from each established political party. They were governments intended to prevent the army from making radical changes to the status quo rather than ones meant to produce accomplishments.

Saionji and the imperial palace were behind these governments. As shown in Table 11.2, the important posts within the palace were firmly within the grasp of the naval, foreign, and home ministries. As a whole, they were moderates who held favorable views of Britain and America. The large number of individuals from distinguished families, such as Makino (son of Ōkubo Toshimichi), Kido, and Matsudaira (relative to Tokugawa), is also particularly noticeable. And the Home Ministry was responsible for maintaining public order and was always on guard against alarming moves within the military. The structure of the Saitō and Okada Cabinets was an attempt to mobilize moderates within the navy, the established political parties, the bureaucracy, and the distinguished peer families to join with the cabinet in containing radical moves by the army.

Table 11.2 Important imperial palace positions from the 1930s to the end of the war.

Lord Keeper of the Privy Seal		
1925–1935	Makino Nobuaki	Foreign Ministry, 2nd son of Ōkubo Toshimichi, Education minister, foreign minister
1935–1936	Saitō Makoto	Navy, Satsuma faction, governor-general of Korea, prime minister
1936–1940	Yuasa Kurahei	Home Ministry, Chōshū faction
1940–1945	Kido Kōichi	Ministry of Agriculture and Commerce, adopted grandson of Kido Takayoshi
Imperial Household Minister		
1925–1933	Ichiki Kitokurō	Home Ministry, education minister, home minister
1933–1936	Yuasa Kurahei	(as above)
1936–1945	Matsudaira Tsuneo	Foreign Ministry, 4th son of Matsudaira Katamori
Grand Chamberlain		
1929–1936	Suzuki Kantarō	Navy
1936–1944	Hyakutake Saburō	Navy
1944–1946	Fujita Hisanori	Navy

This containing function clearly weakened over time, however, and received a heavy blow in the 1935 incident concerning the so-called organ theory of the emperor (*tennō kikan setsu*). This was an attack by the right on the academic theory, put forward by Minobe Tatsukichi, that the emperor was an organ of the state. As already mentioned in the section discussing transcendentalism (see Chapter 5), the organ theory was considered to be self-evidently true by the elite. As such, this attack was also aimed at those close to the emperor.

Factional conflict within the army

So what was the state of the army at this time? The appointment of Araki Sadao as war minister for the Inukai Cabinet was initially widely welcomed by the middle-grade officers of the army, but his later actions soon caused divisions among them. First, Araki handled personnel appointments in an extremely partisan fashion. Many of the important positions within the army general staff and the war ministry were filled by members of the Araki/Mazaki faction (known as the Imperial Way faction, or *Kōdō-ha*). Most notably, Araki's sworn friend Mazaki Jinzaburō was appointed as deputy chief of staff in January 1932. Second, under Araki the army's policy of strengthening its defenses against the Soviets came to a halt. Araki emphasized fighting spirit (*seishinshugi*) and was ideologically opposed to communism. But while this made him hate communism, it also produced a tendency to underestimate Soviet military capabilities. He instead took the view that developments like the devastation of farming villages endangered the foundations of the army. This is why he diverted the army budget toward operations to save rural villages (*jikoku kyōkyū hi*) and wasn't inclined toward putting full effort into preparations against the Soviets. The influence of Araki and the Imperial Way faction is also partially responsible for the failure of the Soviet-Japanese nonaggression pact, proposed by the Soviets in 1932–1933, to come to fruition. His attitude also caused the delay of Japan's purchase of the North Manchurian Railway to 1935.

A group of staff officers of the army uneasy about the state of anti-Soviet preparedness began to gather around Nagata Tetsuzan (these are known as the *Tōsei-ha*, the Control faction). Nagata drew close to Minami Jirō and the Ugaki faction, with whom he shared the goal of military modernization, and sought to purge the army of the Imperial Way faction. First, Mazaki was promoted to full general in June 1933 and made a member of the Supreme Military Council (*Gunji Sangikan*). He was then appointed Inspector General of Military Education in January 1934, pushing him away from the army leadership. Araki then resigned as war minister due to illness that same month and was replaced by Hayashi Senjūrō. Nagata became head of the Bureau of Military Affairs (*Gunmukyoku*) under Hayashi and went to work eliminating Imperial Way faction members. As part of this effort, he dismissed Mazaki as Inspector General of Military Education in July 1935.

This rise of the Control faction was related to the army's operations aimed at autonomy in northern China in 1935. Minami, who was close to the faction, became commander of the Kwantung Army at this time. He had strong misgivings about the state of anti-Soviet military affairs and was very concerned with Manchukuo's rear security. Hirota's diplomatic efforts, which emerged at the same time as the Imperial Way faction, were thus in a sense impeded by the rise of the Control faction.

The embattled Imperial Way faction struck back in a number of ways. Although it had become a minority group within the central staff officers, it was strong ideologically and had extensive support among regimental officers. The Imperial Way faction counterattack first took the form of an ideological battle. The attack on the organ theory of the emperor was part of this. It also took the form of force. In the Aizawa Incident (named after Lieutenant Colonel Aizawa Saburō, 1889–1936), Nagata was assassinated in his office in August 1935. This incident was then followed by the February 26 Incident.

Before dawn on February 26, 1936, 1,500 men of the 3rd Infantry Regiment and other army units attacked Prime Minister Okada, Finance Minister Takahashi Korekiyo, Lord Keeper of the Privy Seal Saitō Makoto, Grand Chamberlain Suzuki Kantarō (1867–1948), former Lord Keeper of the Privy Seal Makino Nobuaki (1861–1949), and Inspector General of Military Education Watanabe Jōtarō (1874–1936) under the leadership of young officers of the Imperial Way faction. Though Okada and Makino barely escaped, Saito, Takahashi, Watanabe were killed and Suzuki was seriously injured. They also attacked police headquarters and other buildings, and Saionji had initially been targeted by their plans as well. In other words, the February 26 Incident was a direct assault on the aforementioned encirclement of the army. Although they had no plans for after the *coup d'état* ended, their plan of destruction was skilled. The emperor was enraged by the murder of his close advisors, however, and because he personally displayed the desire to suppress the coup, the military leadership also decided to do so. The revolt failed. Thus, the coup, undertaken for the subjective goal of eliminating "enemies to the throne," was halted by the will of the emperor. Even though it failed, the incident was the largest armed revolt in Japan since the Satsuma Rebellion (see Chapter 4) and shook the leadership. While the coup itself ended in failure, it had a decisive influence on the later nature of Japanese politics.

12 The collapse of the empire

The Second Sino-Japanese War

Formation of the Hirota Cabinet

When the Okada Keisuke Cabinet resigned following the February 26 Incident (see Chapter 11), Hirota Kōki formed a new cabinet. The army interfered in the creation of the cabinet, opposing five potential members, such as Yoshida Shigeru (1878–1967), the candidate for foreign minister, claiming they were too inclined toward Britain and America. Three of these men ultimately withdrew. This interference by the army in the appointment of posts other than war minister was unprecedented.

At the time, the army leadership was concerned about the occurrence of another February 26 Incident. Its interference with the formation of the cabinet was a sign of the leadership's lack of confidence in its ability to maintain internal discipline. This concern is also why the army attempted during its post-Incident purge to eliminate all politicized officers likely to cause internal instability. Those forced into the reserves thus included not just the members of the Imperial Way faction but also those in the Ugaki Kazushige faction that had opposed them. The restoration of the requirement that military ministers be active duty officers (see Chapter 9) was also intended to prevent the return of elements like the Imperial Way faction.

Both Ugaki and Araki Sadao had been officers possessing the ability to unify the army to a degree and to negotiate with the other groups in the government. Such men were eliminated in this purge, however, and external control of the army thus became considerably more difficult. With the ouster of the politicized officers and the increased bureaucratization of the army, checks on its demands became increasingly ineffective.

The greatest of these demands was for an increased budget to fund expansion. Finance Minister Takahashi Korekiyo had issued bonds during the Saitō Cabinet and put together an expansionary budget but had begun clamping down on the issuing of these bonds in 1934 due to concerns about inflation. Finance Minister Baba Eiichi (1879–1937) of the new Hirota Cabinet reversed Takahashi's policies, however. He began to release bonds to fund military spending, embarking

Figure 12.1 Konoe Fumimaro. (Photograph provided by Jiji Press Photo.)

on an enormous expansion of the military. The budget for 1937 was 31.6 percent larger than that for 1936, with direct military spending accounting for 46 percent of the budget. Japan's international balance of payments thus rapidly worsened, and financial policy began to become impossible. It was at this point that attempts to control the very movement of goods appeared.

The Hirota Cabinet represented a turning point for Japan's diplomacy as well, in that it signed the Anti-Comintern Pact in November 1936. The Nazis had assumed power in Germany in January 1933 and followed Japan in withdrawing from the League of Nations that same year. They embarked on large-scale rearmament in violation of the Versailles Treaty and had begun making diplomatic approaches to Japan that summer.

The Hirota Cabinet fell in January 1937. Responding to a question in the Diet from Hamada Kunimatsu (1868–1939) of the Friends of Constitutional Government Party, War Minister Terauchi Hisaichi (1879–1946) stated that the question had included an insult to the army. Enraged at this accusation, Hamada stated that the transcript should be reviewed; if there was any insult then he would commit *seppuku*, but if none was found, then it was Terauchi who should do so (this exchange is known as the *harakiri mondō*). Terauchi was angered, and ultimately the government fell. By this point, exchanges like this were the only form through which the established parties could vent their frustration.

From Ugaki to Konoe

After Hirota resigned, Saionji Kinmochi recommended to the emperor that Ugaki become the next prime minister. Saionji viewed Ugaki as a trump card for restoring government control over the situation. As described in Chapter 11, the Saitō and Okada governments had been structured to make use of various moderate factions in containing the radicalism of the army. All that had been missing was a moderate faction within the army itself. That was what Saionji hoped that Ugaki could provide.

The middle-grade officers of the army fiercely resisted the formation of an Ugaki Cabinet, however, and as a result he was unable to obtain a war minister and had to abandon his attempt to create a government. This shows how quickly the restoration of the requirement that military ministers be active duty officers made an impact. Ugaki still persisted, however, devising three potential solutions: take over the duties of war minister while serving as prime minister; restore a suitable general serving in the reserves to active duty; or use an imperial edict to order a suitable active duty general to serve in the cabinet. But when he attempted to obtain the cooperation of Lord Keeper of the Privy Seal Yuasa Kurahei (1874–1940), Yuasa demurred out of a fear that the emperor would become embroiled in the issue.

One of the reasons for the army's opposition to an Ugaki government was lasting enmity from the forced retirement of a number of influential officers during the reductions he had implemented as war minister. There were also dissatisfaction and criticism of his involvement in the March Incident (see Chapter 11). Finally, Ugaki was a forceful leader, and it was feared that his appointment as prime minister would threaten various plans that were then under way. At the time, the army general staff, under the lead of Ishihara Kanji, head of its operations section, was finalizing an ambitious plan to almost double the country's military strength within five years through a tremendous expansion of its military industries in order to be ready for a war with the Soviet Union by 1941. This was known as the Ishihara Plan (*Ishihara Kōsō*). The army wanted a robotic figure as prime minister who would accept this plan without any resistance.

With Ugaki's failure to form a government, Saionji recommended Hiranuma Kiichirō (1867–1952) and Hayashi Senjūrō as his first two choices for prime minister. When Hiranuma declined, Hayashi assumed office. Ishihara expected Hayashi to support his plan, but the two argued over the formation of the new cabinet and Ishihara was expelled from Hayashi's presence. The Hayashi Cabinet soon came into conflict with the parties, however, and fell a mere four months, having accomplished nothing.

Saionji recommended Konoe Fumimaro (1891–1945) as Hayashi's successor. The Konoe family was the most famous one in the nation with the exception of the imperial house, and the young, intelligent Fumimaro had long been considered a future star of the peerage. He had written an article entitled "Rejecting Anglo-American Centered Pacifism" (*Eibei Honi no Heiwashugi o Haisu*) in 1918, however, in which he had asserted that the postwar trend toward pacifism was intended to benefit Britain and America. The pro–Anglo-American Saionji was concerned that Konoe might show a similar attitude toward cooperation with the two countries, but Konoe was his final trump card now that Ugaki had failed to form a government. People welcomed the appointment of this tall and young (45-year-old) noble with his distinguished background.

The Second Sino-Japanese War and general mobilization

The Marco Polo Bridge Incident occurred near Beijing on July 7, 1937, just a month after the formation of Konoe's cabinet, however. Unlike the previous Liutiaohu Incident (see Chapter 11), the Marco Polo Bridge Incident was an accident, and both the government and local military initially attempted to contain it. The argument soon arose that China should be attacked to resolve the status of Northern China in one blow, however, and Ishihara Kanji, now head of the army general staff office's first bureau and an opponent of expansionism, became isolated. Dragged along by this situation, Prime Minister Konoe and Foreign Minister Hirota both accepted this argument for expansionism and decided to dispatch reinforcements on the 11th. When a clash erupted in Shanghai, they decided to dispatch an army (on August 13).

The fighting in Shanghai was longer and fiercer than had been expected. Negotiations for peace were opened while the battle was going on, mediated by German Ambassador to China Oskar P. Trautmann (1877–1950). Germany was close to both countries and wanted them to cooperate and restrain the Soviet Union. The government and military were initially favorably inclined toward the Trautmann negotiations, but as the war situation turned in Japan's favor in early November, they began to hope that, if the Chinese capital of Nanjing could be taken, Chiang Kai-shek could be forced to surrender. Their requirements for peace thus became increasingly demanding. Within the army, the general staff office hoped that Trautmann's efforts would succeed as they feared the war becoming a quagmire. But Prime Minister Konoe and Foreign Minister Hirota were more in step with the antipeace faction, and the peace efforts were cut off in January 1938 with the release of the 1st Konoe Statement (January 16, 1938), in which Konoe stated that Japan "would no longer negotiate with the Kuomintang government." Thus it was not just the judgment of the army but that of Konoe and Hirota as well that bore a large responsibility for the expansion of the Second Sino-Japanese War.

The Konoe Cabinet also represents a major turning point in domestic Japanese politics as well. Konoe accepted Ishihara's plans for increasing the country's industrial capacity. But it would be impossible to undertake these while also attempting to improve Japan's balance of trade unless the provision of goods was directly controlled by the state. And this type of control became all the more necessary with the outbreak of the Second Sino-Japanese War. The Planning Agency (created in May 1937 from the Cabinet Research Bureau; see Chapter 11) and the Cabinet Resources Bureau (*Naikaku Shigenkyoku*) merged in October 1937 to form the Planning Board. This body consisted of powerful economic bureaucrats and was charged with conducting research for important policies and formulating material mobilization plans. Military demand was thus naturally prioritized, and civilian demand was significantly suppressed. When black market transactions that violated the government's control began to spread, the Economic Police (*Keizai Keisatsu*) were activated to counter this. Social conditions in Japan became extremely dark.

The government further expanded its economic controls in 1938, passing the National Mobilization Law (*Kokka Sōdōin Hō*) and the Electricity Management Law (*Denryoku Kanri Hō*). The established political parties were greatly opposed to these laws; their greatest supporters were the proletariat parties, which, while formerly critical of imperialist wars, had increasingly moved toward the right since the Manchurian Incident (see Chapter 11). This was especially noteworthy in the case of the Social Masses Party (*Shakai Taishūtō*) formed in 1932. This party, which elected eighteen Diet members in the 1936 general elections and thirty-seven in the following year, was the most progovernment party while Konoe was in office.

The state of the parties at the time is reflected by the expulsion of Nishio Suehiro (1891–1981) from the Diet in 1938. A member of the Social Masses Party, Nishio gave a speech in the Diet in support of the National Mobilization Law in which he called on Konoe to be "a leader of firm convictions like Hitler, Mussolini, and Stalin." This speech drew criticism for its apparent praise of Stalin and resulted in his expulsion. This was an expression of the parties' anger at their inability to successfully oppose the National Mobilization Law and their jealousy of the Social Masses Party. Even the army had found it difficult to make the Diet act, but Konoe's popularity made it possible. There were moves around Konoe toward the formation of a new party, and his extreme popularity with the public made the established parties very wary of showing any hostility toward him.

A new order in East Asia

Konoe reshuffled his cabinet in May 1938, naming Ugaki as his foreign minister and adding Ikeda Shigeaki (1867–1950), the head of the Mitsui financial combine, as finance minister and minister of commerce and industry. Realizing that his January statement that he would "no longer negotiate" with the Kuomintang government had been a failure, he began formulating a change. Ugaki entered negotiations with Britain, who had many interests in China, and began peace talks with Premier Kong Xiangxi (1880–1967) of the Kuomintang. But these moves gave rise to opposition not just from the army but from the foreign ministry as well. The ministry had previously been inclined toward Britain and America but had now entered a period when an Asian faction had become influential and a majority of its young and midlevel members of the bureaucracy belonged to a "reform" faction that sought to have Japan join with the Axis powers of Germany and Italy. Konoe also gave Ugaki insufficient support; he resigned in September.

The war was entering an important phase as this was going on. Japan had taken Hankou and Guangdong in October, but the Kuomintang government had moved farther inland to Chongqing. A military solution to the war was no longer possible, and even the army now changed to a long, drawn out war footing.

This was the situation in which Konoe unveiled his vision for a new order in East Asia on November 3. Stating that the purpose of the war was "the construction of a new order ensuring the eternal stability of East Asia," Konoe stated that even the Kuomintang government would not be refused if it sought to join in this effort (this is known as the 2nd Konoe Statement). The government's plans for Wang Jingwei (1883–1944) were an indispensable component of this plan for a new order in East Asia. Efforts proceeded to have Wang, the most influential member of the Kuomintang after Chiang Kai-shek, escape from Chongqing and form a new government, which Japan could then sign a peace agreement with.

But this announcement of a new order sparked fierce criticism from the United States. It censured Japan with unprecedented severity in December, stating that no country had the right to plan the construction of a new order for areas over which it was not sovereign and that America would not recognize any new order formed in violation of the principles of the Open Door. It also began providing China with *de facto* loans around this time. While America had supported China emotionally, it had maintained its neutrality since the outbreak of the Second Sino-Japanese War; it now clearly turned toward a policy of aiding China. It would not be an overstatement to say that the ideological origins of the Pacific War lay in the statement declaring a new order in East Asia.

Incidentally, Pan-Asianism wasn't the only area where the Konoe government rushed ahead; there was also the issue of strengthening its ties with Germany. Italy had joined the previously mentioned Anti-Comintern Pact in November 1937. Germany successfully annexed Austria in March 1938 and then recognized Manchukuo in May, withdrew its military advisors from China and stopped providing it with arms. Germany appeared to be developing magnificently and to be the only ally still available to the isolated Japan. Strengthening ties with Germany was also attractive because Japan had been militarily defeated by the Soviet Union during a July 1938 dispute over the Soviet-Manchurian border (the Battle of Lake Khasan). The navy strongly opposed this, however, because it was gravely concerned that it would worsen relations with Britain and America. The Konoe government was unable to resolve this argument and resigned in January 1939.

The Pacific War

The outbreak of the Second World War

Hiranuma Kiichirō became prime minister following Konoe's resignation. Relations with America were becoming notably more difficult at this time. As mentioned earlier, America had decided to support China in reaction to the 1938 announcement of a "new order in East Asia," and Britain followed suit. Furthermore, America announced its abrogation of the Treaty of Commerce and Navigation between Japan and the United States in July 1939. Japan suffered crushing defeats by the Soviets in military clashes along the border between the Mongolian People's Republic, a Soviet satellite, and Manchukuo in May and then again in July and August. These are known as the Nomonhan Incident (although recent scholarship has made it clear that the Soviet Union suffered significant losses in these battles as well, they were still unquestionably utter defeats for Japan).

Proceeding with the Wang Jingwei scheme was one way of responding to these strained foreign relations, but doing so was filled with difficulties. Strengthening the Anti-Comintern Pact was another, but opposition from the navy prevented agreement on this. This changed with the signing of the German-Soviet Nonagression Pact in August. Hiranuma famously stated that "the world of Europe has produced a complicated and puzzling phenomenon" and resigned following the treaty.

In any case, Germany invaded Poland in September immediately after signing the pact. Britain and France declared war on the 3rd and thus began the Second World War. The outbreak of war provided Japan's foreign policy with a golden opportunity to change direction.

And in fact the cabinet of Abe Nobuyuki (1875–1953) that followed Hironuma was a break with the strongly reformist governments from Hirota to Hirunuma. It adopted a posture in favor of restoring cooperation with Britain and America, which can be seen in the selection of Nomura Kichisaburō of the navy's pro-American faction to serve as foreign minister. The government reached an impasse over the creation of the Wang Jingwei government, however, and failed in its attempt to restore diplomatic relations with the United States; the abrogation of the Treaty of Commerce and Navigation went into effect in January 1940. Soaring commodity prices and other sources of social unrest caused problems as well, and the government resigned in January 1940 over a trivial matter.

Yonai Mitsumasa (1880–1948) of the navy was the next to form a government. The Yonai Cabinet was concerned with preserving the status quo as the previous Saitō and Okada Cabinets had been and included, for examples, two members each from the Friends of the Constitutional Government Party and Constitutional Democratic Party. The long awaited Wang Jingwei government was also finally established in March in China.

Germany launched its blitzkrieg attack on the stalemated Western front in April, and the Netherlands, Belgium, and Luxembourg surrendered in May, followed by France in June. This sudden change in the state of the war caused Japanese public opinion to change utterly. The fall of the Netherlands and France created a clear power vacuum in Southeast Asia, one that would grow even larger if Britain surrendered as well. The Treaty of Commerce and Navigation with the United States no longer existed, and Japan desperately wanted the resources available to its south.

Voices calling for a closer relationship with Germany and a southern advance thus became louder, as did criticism of the Yonai Cabinet, who took a dim view of these arguments. At the time, Konoe was forming a new party, and there were great public expectations about this. When the army caused the Yonai Cabinet to fall by having the war minister resign, Konoe once again became prime minister. This was July 1940.

The road to the Pacific War

With the formation of Konoe's cabinet, his new party movement became markedly active; the established parties, fearing being left behind, dissolved one after another and joined up. He suddenly became fainthearted, however, when he began to receive criticism from the right wing that he was attempting to create an "entity like the shogunate" that would take over the power of the Emperor to control national politics. When the Imperial Rule Assistance Association (*Taisei Yokusankai*) was founded in October, it was a massive organization but was in fact weak. A majority that did not hold any ideology could not be used to wield power.

Matsuoka Yōsuke, the "hero" behind Japan's withdrawal from the League of Nations, was chosen as foreign minister for the 2nd Konoe Cabinet. The midlevel reform bureaucrats of the ministry were responsible for his selection. He immediately went to work strengthening relations with Germany, which resulted in the signing of the Tripartite Pact with Germany and Italy in September. Matsuoka next began negotiations with the Soviet Union, which ended with the signing of the Japan-Soviet Neutrality Pact in April 1941. Matsuoka's plan was to open negotiations with America backed by the strength of this Japanese-German-Soviet cooperation.

Japan occupied northern French Indochina immediately prior to signing the Tripartite Pact. This allowed Japan to interdict supply routes to Chiang Kai-shek passing through Indochina and to use the power vacuum that had resulted from Germany's victories to gain favorable developments in territory and resources. This triggered an American response of prohibiting the export of scrap iron to Japan, however, and relations between the two nations grew markedly worse.

As Matsuoka had been successfully arranging a treaty with the Soviets, secret negotiations with America to improve relations had been proceeding under Konoe. When Matsuoka showed little interest in these negotiations upon his return to Japan, Konoe briefly resigned in July 1941. He then received a new imperial mandate and formed a new cabinet. He thus removed Matsuoka for the sake of negotiations with America.

Konoe was still imperceptive when it came to relations with America, however, and Japan occupied southern Indochina in July shortly after he formed his third government. This time America responded by freezing all Japanese assets within the United States and prohibiting the export of oil to Japan. This was an unexpectedly strong response.

Amidst the increasing suppression of free speech, the commentator Kiyosawa Kiyoshi (1890–1945) continued to harshly criticize the course of U.S.-Japan relations and argued that Japan should avoid taking a confrontational stance toward America. Despite his criticism, Kiyosawa believed that war with America could be avoided so long as Japan did not move beyond China. This was because, while American support for China was strong, he believed that it was primarily interested in Europe. But in signing the Tripartite Pact and occupying French Indochina, Japan had already moved two steps beyond that constraint.

And America's attitude toward Japan did indeed become increasingly severe beginning in July due to the German invasion of the Soviet Union. The outbreak of the German-Soviet War in June made it unnecessary for America to make undesired concessions to Japan. Japan still had hope for negotiations, however, and Konoe sought to hold a summit with U.S. President Franklin D. Roosevelt (1882–1945, in office 1933–1945). America did not accept this proposal.

The Japanese government decided in a September 6, 1941, meeting held in the presence of the emperor to begin preparations for a war against the United States, Britain, and the Netherlands. These plans were to be completed by late October. When negotiations with America deadlocked, the 3rd Konoe Cabinet resigned and Tōjō Hideki (1884–1948) became prime minister on October 18. The selection of a leader of the army, the greatest impediment to peace, to serve as prime minister was made in an attempt to force it to act responsibly. A final proposal for the negotiations with America was adopted on November 5 in another imperial council. If it failed, Japan was resolved to use force in early December.

This proposal was rejected by U.S. Secretary of State Hull on November 26, who also introduced the Hull Note, which effectively reset all previous negotiations between the countries and demanded Japan's withdrawal from all of Indochina and China. The Americans had also composed a different compromise plan, but this was not adopted, at least partly due to the efforts of Britain, China, and the Soviet Union, who all hoped for an American entry into the war. The Hull Note was not necessarily America's final position, however, and it did not include a deadline. Yoshida Shigeru and others believed that further negotiations had thus not been rendered impossible. The great majority of those involved felt that the note made war inevitable, however.

Kiyosawa Kiyoshi (1890–1945)

Kiyosawa Kiyoshi was born into a farming family in Nagano Prefecture. He was unable to attend middle school due to his family's circumstances and instead studied at a local Christian private school. He emigrated to

America at age sixteen and became known for his skill with words as he worked as a reporter for a Japanese-language newspaper on the West Coast. He returned to Japan in 1918. He retired in 1929 after working for the *Chūgai Shōgyō Shimpō* (the predecessor to the modern *Nihon Keizai Shimbun*) and the *Asahi Shimbun* and then became an independent commentator.

Based on his experiences in America, Kiyosawa was an advocate for so-called abacus-based diplomacy, that is, diplomacy that abandoned theory and concentrated on economics. He believed that Japan's interests in Korea and Manchuria were weak and dependent on government protection. Adhering to these interests and thereby damaging trade with China and relations with America was thus against the national interest. This was similar to the argument put forward by his later ally, Ishibashi Tanzan, for abandoning Japan's colonies.

Chūō Kōron served as the primary vehicle for Kiyosawa's pieces. He fiercely criticized Foreign Minister Uchida Kōsai's scorched earth diplomacy following the Manchurian Incident and that of Matsuoka Yōsuke, who was viewed as a hero after he announced Japan's withdrawal from the League of Nations. Kiyosawa compared the cheers that would greet Matsuoka following his return from Geneva to the storm of criticism that had met Komura Jutarō after Portsmouth, asking which men's efforts had actually contributed to the national interest.

As it became difficult to publish criticism of foreign policy because of controls on free speech, Kiyosawa turned to the field of diplomatic history shortly afterward. One of the fruits of these labors was *Gaiseika to shite no Ōkubo Toshimichi* (Ōkubo Toshimichi as a Diplomatist), published in 1942. In this work, he praised Ōkubo for taking on every adversity the nation faced, beginning with the calls to invade Korea in the 1870s and for engaging in responsible diplomacy. This was a criticism of Konoe and the other diplomatic and military figures who had abandoned the Second Sino-Japanese War while it was still going on.

Yoshida Shigeru immediately sent a reply to Kiyosawa after receiving a copy of the work in which he stated that the greatness of Ōkubo (who was Yoshida's grandfather-in-law) was that he would "take it upon himself to deal with difficulties with an awareness of how important it was to volunteer oneself for the nation." Yoshida also stated that he hoped that "a diplomat would appear who took the desires of the public to heart." In light of Yoshida's postwar actions, these comments are very interesting.

Kiyosawa died suddenly of illness in 1945, three months before Japan's defeat. A diary he kept during the war on the conditions of Japan's political society was published and widely read after the war under the title of *Ankoku Nikki* (Diary of Darkness).

There is a frequently voiced theory that Roosevelt knew that Japan was going to attack and allowed it to happen. But while there's no question that he had become indifferent to a potential Japanese attack by June 1941, that doesn't mean that he predicted the attack on Pearl Harbor. He had no intention of compromising with Japan over the issues of the renunciation of the Tripartite Pact and withdrawal from Indochina and the Chinese mainland. But if, as Kiyosawa had stated, Japan had been willing to make bold concessions on these issues and produced a schedule for them, then there was still a possibility that war could be avoided.

The collapse of the empire

The decision to enter into a total war with Britain and America despite military tensions with the Soviet Union having only barely been papered over by the neutrality pact and a four-year stalemate in China was irrational in every sense of the word. If "militarism" is a political system in which military logic is emphasized over everything else, then the Japan of 1941 can't even be considered a militarist country. It would not be an exaggeration to say that the Japanese Empire, as a body capable of conducting unified, rational decision making, had been destroyed long before 1945. How did this happen?

The Meiji Restoration and the Meiji Constitution had, in principle, adopted a theory of direct rule by the emperor. The Restoration's ideological underpinnings had been the removal of those who obstructed the will of the emperor, "the true sovereign." And the extremely decentralized nature of the system established by the Meiji Constitution (see Chapter 5) was also related to this theory. There could not be anyone who took the place of the emperor and unified the will of the state.

The Meiji state, however, had also required someone to unify the will of the various state organs and produce a national will. This role was first fulfilled by the Meiji oligarchs from the domain cliques, and after their fall it was assumed by the political parties. But when the founding fathers and political parties began to decline, no one remained to take over for them. The politically influential military officers had been driven from the military. While there were multiple attempts at creating a body to unify national policy, they all ultimately failed. Using a bureaucratic structure to generate political will was a fundamentally impossible task in the first place. And the criticism of Konoe's new system as being a "Bakufu" was truly symbolic.

Toward the end of the war, Ishibashi Tanzan (1884–1973) cried out, saying "Please come forth, Prince Itō, Prince Yamagata!" Ishibashi had been a harsh critic of Yamagata Aritomo during the Taishō period, but he realized that, regardless of their ideology, a strong figure reminiscent of the oligarch leaders was necessary to end the war. While the wartime period is not covered here in detail, responsible leadership was not easily produced despite the tremendous sacrifices being made on a daily basis. The decision to surrender in 1945 was only barely achieved, and even it required the extraordinary means of an imperial decision.

13 Defeat, occupation, and peace treaty

Early occupation policies

Defeat

The Second World War was a gigantic conflagration even in comparison with its predecessor. No fewer than four-fifths of the world's nations participated in the war, and the destructive power of the weapons they employed increased tremendously over its course. The conflict involved fierce warfare not just on the battlefield but on the home front as well, as the combatants sought to utterly eliminate their enemies' ability to continue to fight. And unlike the wars that had preceded it, the majority of the Second World War's victims were noncombatants.

It also marked the first time that the Japanese homeland had been exposed to the horrors of war. Nearly a hundred cities all over the country were bombed from late October 1944 on. Seventy percent of them did not contain any military facilities. Tokyo in particular was subjected to four major air raids between March and May 1945. In the March 10 bombings, 325 B-29 bombers dropped 380,000 incendiary bombs, resultingin more than 100,000 dead or missing and reducing the center of the city to ruins. In total, Tokyo was bombed 106 times during the course of the war. And as a further extension of these bombings came the use of the atomic bombs on Hiroshima and Nagasaki. In attempting to understand Japan's defeat and the occupation that followed, it is important to keep in mind just how horrific the war had been.

Franklin D. Roosevelt, Winston Churchill (1874–1965), and Stalin met at Yalta in February 1945 and reached some understandings about the postwar world. The agreements regarding Japan included an understanding that Japan's territorial gains following the Russo-Japanese War (Lushun, Dalian, the South Manchuria Railway, and southern Sakhalin) would be returned to the Soviet Union, that the Soviets would also receive the Kuril Islands (although what exactly these included was left ambiguous), and that they would join the war against Japan within ninety days of the end of hostilities in Europe.

Germany surrendered in Europe on the 7th of May (Reims) and again on the following day (Berlin); these are considered as marking the date of Allied victory in the Second World War, including within the United States. Meanwhile,

Figure 13.1 Yoshida Shigeru. (February 1949. Photo provided by the *Mainichi Shimbun*.)

August 15, Victory over Japan Day, is largely forgotten today. Japan continued to fight after the German surrender, however, and it was believed, given the seemingly strong Kwantung Army and other Japanese forces, that mobilizing a massive number of additional troops would be necessary to compel a Japanese surrender. Given the prevailing sentiment in America that the war was already over and the importance of public opinion in the country, such a mobilization represented an extremely difficult task. The American government's leaders thus agonized over finding some way to end the war quickly and without the needless (from their perspective) sacrifice of lives.

Essentially, three options were available to them: the Soviet entry into the war, the atomic bomb (which had only just been completed and tested in July), and, finally, using the emperor (that is, guaranteeing the *kokutai*, or Japan's national polity centered on the emperor). If a fourth option were to be conjectured, it would be blockading Japan and then merely awaiting the complete destruction of the nation's economy and increasing starvation.

The American, British, and Soviet leadership met in Potsdam on the outskirts of Berlin on July 17. On the 26th, they released the Potsdam Declaration, which demanded the immediate surrender of Japan's military (see Table 13.1).[1] After Prime Minister Suzuki Kantarō stated that he would ignore (*mokusatsu*) the declaration, the Allies interpreted this as a rejection. The atomic bombs were dropped on

Table 13.1 Text of the Potsdam Declaration (abbreviated).

5. Following are our terms. We will not deviate from them. There are no alternatives. We shall brook no delay.
6. There must be eliminated for all time the authority and influence of those who have deceived and misled the people of Japan into embarking on world conquest, for we insist that a new order of peace, security and justice will be impossible until irresponsible militarism is driven from the world.
7. Until such a new order is established and until there is convincing proof that Japan's war-making power is destroyed, points in Japanese territory to be designated by the Allies shall be occupied to secure the achievement of the basic objectives we are here setting forth.
8. The terms of the Cairo Declaration shall be carried out and Japanese sovereignty shall be limited to the islands of Honshu, Hokkaido, Kyushu, Shikoku and such minor islands as we determine.
9. The Japanese military forces, after being completely disarmed, shall be permitted to return to their homes with the opportunity to lead peaceful and productive lives.
10. We do not intend that the Japanese shall be enslaved as a race or destroyed as a nation, but stern justice shall be meted out to all war criminals, including those who have visited cruelties upon our prisoners. The Japanese Government shall remove all obstacles to the revival and strengthening of democratic tendencies among the Japanese people. Freedom of speech, of religion, and of thought, as well as respect for the fundamental human rights shall be established.
11. Japan shall be permitted to maintain such industries as will sustain her economy and permit the exaction of just reparations in kind, but not those which would enable her to re-arm for war. To this end, access to, as distinguished from control of, raw materials shall be permitted. Eventual Japanese participation in world trade relations shall be permitted.
12. The occupying forces of the Allies shall be withdrawn from Japan as soon as these objectives have been accomplished and there has been established in accordance with the freely expressed will of the Japanese people a peacefully inclined and responsible government.
13. We call upon the government of Japan to proclaim now the unconditional surrender of all Japanese armed forces, and to provide proper and adequate assurances of their good faith in such action. The alternative for Japan is prompt and utter destruction.

Source: National Diet Library (www.ndl.go.jp/constitution/e/etc/c06.html).

Hiroshima on August 6 and then Nagasaki on the 9th; the Soviet Union also invaded Manchukuo before dawn that morning, breaking its neutrality pact with Japan.

The Japanese government was shocked by the terms, but nevertheless decided at a council held on the 9th (with the emperor in attendance) to accept the Postdam Declaration on the sole condition that "the *kokutai* be preserved." This was conveyed to the Allies on the 10th, and America replied on the following day that the ultimate form of the Japanese government would "be established by the freely expressed will of the Japanese people" and that "from the moment of surrender the authority of the Emperor and the Japanese government to rule the state shall be subject to the Supreme Commander of the Allied Powers." This response provoked fierce arguments within the Suzuki Cabinet and military over whether this meant that the national polity would be preserved or not, but ultimately an imperial decision was made to accept it at a council held on August 14.

There were arguments within the American government as well over whether or not the Japanese should be given an explicit guarantee that the national polity would be preserved. Guaranteeing the position of the emperor, who was considered one of the leaders of the war, was not easily done, however, and as such no explicit message could be sent. Even so, with the two atomic bombings and the Soviet entry into the war, Japan finally decided to surrender on the basis of the abstract guarantee of the national polity.

Occupation

The first distinguishing feature of the occupation of Japan was that it was effectively an operation of the United States alone.

Although Japan's sovereignty now lay in the hands of SCAP (the Supreme Commander for the Allied Powers), its General Headquarters (GHQ) was, with a few exceptions, entirely composed of Americans. The British Commonwealth had only a minor presence, and when Stalin proposed that the Soviet Army occupy Hokkaidō, this was flatly rejected. In theory, the Soviet Union and other Allied nations were guaranteed the right to express their opinions on the occupation. But although the Far Eastern Commission in Washington was supposed to make the highest-level policy decisions on Japan and an Allied Council for Japan was established in Tokyo to serve as an advisory body for GHQ, in practice these groups' roles existed only on paper. America had been the primary power in the war against Japan and had absolutely no intention of yielding its dominant position to anyone else. The occupation operated as a near dictatorship by GHQ's Supreme Commander Douglas MacArthur (1880–1964).

Two of GHQ's subdivisions, General Staff–2 (G2), in charge of intelligence, and Government Section (GS), in charge of civil administration, played particularly large roles within the organization. G2 emphasized military affairs and public security and was concerned about the activities of the Japanese Communist Party and labor groups. Meanwhile, GS contained a large number of New Dealers who were enthusiastic about the democratization of Japan. They believed in the ideals of President Roosevelt's New Deal and had been disappointed by the conservatism of Harry S. Truman (1884–1972). They sought in Japan a place where they could enact their policies. The two groups frequently clashed over the direction of the occupation's reforms.

The second distinguishing feature of the occupation was the indirect nature of its governance. In the case of Germany, the eastern half of the country had already fallen under the *de facto* control of the Soviet Union by the time the fighting had come to a halt, and the national government had effectively ceased to function. But the situation in Japan was completely different. The occupation authorities were already faced with the serious problem of finding a way to feed 75 million Japanese with an economy in ruins. While there was criticism of their decision to maintain and use Japan's existing systems to govern, the choice was an unavoidable one in terms of efficiency and stability.

This decision meant that important parts of Japan's domestic administration were carried out through negotiations and coordination with GHQ. Of the five prime ministers who served between the defeat and the restoration of Japanese independence following the signing of the peace treaty, three (Shidehara Kijūrō, Yoshida Shigeru, and Ashida Hitoshi [1887–1959]) were former diplomats. That no prime minister since has possessed a diplomatic background highlights just how unusual this was. Japan's internal governance during this period was essentially diplomacy: diplomacy undertaken with the United States.

Demilitarization and democratization

The most significant objectives of the American occupation of Japan were demilitarization and democratization. It was only natural, given the fierce fighting that had preceded the occupation, that America planned to render Japan harmless through thorough demilitarization. Elements of this demilitarization policy included (1) the disarmament of the army and navy; (2) the elimination of all bodies and laws related to the military; (3) the prohibition of military research and production; (4) trials for war crimes; (5) a purge of professional military personnel and the wartime leadership; and (6) the dissolution of militarist and nationalist organizations. These quite thorough measures included items that were ambiguous and arbitrary in scope. For example, Tokyo University's aviation department was dissolved under the third criterion, and judō and kendō were banned under the sixth.

Democratization was also an inevitable consequence of the war, given the way that the conflict had been framed as a struggle between fascism and democracy. And that democracy would, of course, be an American liberal democracy so that Japan would stand against the Soviet Union. Another factor behind the policy of democratization was that following the war, America was bursting with confidence and convinced that democracy meant peace. Democratization was thus another element of the occupation's aforementioned policy of demilitarization.

Democratization involved a number of areas. First, existing restrictions on freedom of speech were lifted (anti-GHQ and anti-American speech was excluded from this, however, and was strictly controlled). Second, the education and legal

systems were democratized. Examples of the former include the purge of milita-
ristic education, the democratization of textbooks, the enactment of the Fundamental Law of Education, and the decentralization of education. Reform of the
Code of Criminal Procedure and the laws on families and inheritance are examples of the latter. Third, the political system was democratized. The enactment of
revolutionary changes through a drastic revision of the constitution was central
to this. Under the new constitution, Japan became a *de facto* republic. Not only
was the national polity not preserved, but it hardly needs to be stated that the
current emperor system is of a completely different nature from that of the prewar period. Meanwhile, attempts were also made to strengthen local governments
outside the capital as the Americans believed that local government served as a
"school of democracy." The dissolution of the Home Ministry, the introduction of
popular elections for the heads of local government, and the transfer of control
over education and police matters to local governments were major elements of
this effort. Given that Japanese governance had been quite centralized ever since
the Edo period, however, this policy experienced only mixed success. By the time
of the peace treaty, America had largely given up on promoting local government
in Japan.

It was democratization of the economy – farmland reform, the breaking up of
the financial conglomerates (*zaibatsu*), and the promotion of labor unions – that
greatly changed Japan beyond American intentions.

Farmland reform was introduced because it was believed that the feudal inter-
personal relationships present in farming villages had served as a spawning ground
for fascism and that the poverty of the villages had been one cause for Japan's
external expansion. It was felt as well that the food crisis facing the country would
be insurmountable unless something was done to stimulate the village's desire to
produce. There were also concerns, in light of the rise of the Chinese Communist
Party, that the villages would become dens of communism unless the occupation
authorities took the initiative in engaging with the Japanese farmer movements.
The Japanese government had previously also made plans for "farmland eman-
cipation" (*nōchi kaihō*) in order to increase productivity and counter the increase
in absentee landlordship. The thorough land reforms twice-performed by GHQ
thus met a latent need in Japan and were extremely successful. The emancipa-
tion of farmland changed farming villages from have-nots to haves. As a result of
the reforms, productivity increased, domestic demand expanded, the basis for the
later stable conservative control of the government was created, and the foundation for high-speed economic growth was formed.

The *zaibatsu* were economic organizations consolidated around holding companies and controlled by specific families. In the case of Mitsui Gōmei, for example,
the holding company for the Mitsui *zaibatsu*, only those from the eleven house-
holds of the Mitsui family were able to become members. America, believing that
the *zaibatsu* had served as a base for Japanese militarism, broke up the holding
companies and released their shares to the public. The *zaibatsu* were thus eliminated, at least in the form they had traditionally existed in. Although the Americans had been mistaken in linking the *zaibatsu* with militarism, the dissolution of

the *zaibatsu* rapidly fostered a "managerial revolution" (the separation of capital and management and the ascendancy of managers) in Japan similar to those that had already occurred in the United States and elsewhere. Managers had traditionally been relatively powerful in Japan since the Edo period, and that tendency had been further strengthened by the economic controls enacted during the war. Now the managerial revolution had been made complete and would serve as a driving force behind Japan's later economic growth. America had a tradition of antitrust laws, however, and there were those, especially among the New Dealers in GHQ, who argued that the dissolution of the *zaibatsu* still needed to be taken further. But there was also strong opposition to the breaking up of large companies, and America would, for various reasons, cease being as assertive in its efforts in this area. Despite this, the realization of a managerial revolution and the introduction of a certain amount of market competition would have a greater than expected impact on the Japanese economy.

The policy of fostering labor unions came from the same thought process that had pushed for farmland reform. It was believed that the Japanese domestic market had been limited because workers had been unprotected and had had no choice but to accept low wages. The limited domestic market was also seen as having been one of the triggers for foreign expansion. It was thought that fostering labor unions would serve as a check on any return of fascism. Three major labor laws were thus passed between 1945 and 1947, and a policy of promoting labor union membership was adopted. However, the Greater Japan Patriotic Industrial Association (*Dai Nippon Sangyō Hōkoku Kai*) was the basis for the development of labor unions. Formed in 1940, this was a union organized on a company-by-company basis that did not differentiate between blue- and white-collar workers. It was in that environment that a cycle arose in which wages were increased, causing workers to increase their efforts for the company, which in turn caused the company to grow.

These reforms, particularly farmland reform, the breaking up of the *zaibatsu*, and the fostering of labor unions, resolved problems that had burdened Japan; they set the nation's dormant strength free. All, however, were initially undertaken with the intention of rendering Japan harmless.

Still, of all the reforms undertaken, it was constitutional revision that has had the greatest and most long-standing influence. MacArthur had initially waited for the Japanese to revise their constitution themselves, but their efforts moved slowly and amounted to little more than proposing minor amendments to the Meiji Constitution. After learning this, he provided GHQ with the basic principles for a constitution (in the form of the MacArthur Note; see Table 13.2) in February 1946 and had it create a draft. GHQ completed this task over a period of nine days and then sought Japanese acceptance of the document. Although the Shidehara government found the status of the emperor (now a symbol of the unity of the Japanese people) and the renunciation of war (or, more correctly, the renunciation of both war and maintaining a military) especially problematic, it accepted the draft after it was suggested that failure to do so might lead to the emperor being summoned to the International Military Tribunal for the Far East (Tokyo War Crimes

Table 13.2 The MacArthur Note.

I. Emperor is at the head of the state. . . .
II. War as a sovereign right of the nation is abolished. Japan renounces it as an instrumentality for settling its disputes and even for preserving its own security. It relies upon the higher ideals which are now stirring the world for its defense and its protection.
No Japanese Army, Navy, or Air Force will ever be authorized and no rights of belligerency will ever be conferred upon any Japanese force.
III. The feudal system of Japan will cease. . . .

Source: National Diet Library (www.ndl.go.jp/constitution/e/shiryo/03/072/072tx.html).

Trials). The government was more fixated on the question of the emperor's status than on the renunciation of war, however. And the public, having just experienced such a horrific war, welcomed the renunciation.

MacArthur felt that he needed the emperor's cooperation to make the occupation function smoothly. However, seeking that cooperation was something that both the other Allied countries and the American people would find difficult to accept. It was therefore necessary for MacArthur to show that the status of the emperor had been greatly altered and that Japan no longer posed a military threat. That purpose provided the political rationale for the two contentious parts of the new constitution.

Politics under the occupation

All of Japan's industries had suffered major damage during the war, and with the defeat, they had also lost their overseas resources; at the same time, the country also had to absorb the large number of people who were being repatriated from overseas. Inflation and unemployment were thus particularly severe problems facing Japan. And it was under these conditions that the government had to implement the reforms just described, reforms that surpassed the expectations of almost every Japanese in terms of their scope and radicalness.

An additional factor was that, at the same time that democratization had increased the importance of elections and the Diet, the large number of new members in the body meant that it would take time for responsible leadership to emerge there. Another result of democratization was the spread of mass movements; these groups became fierce critics of the government over the economic problems. The government was thus forced to undertake the immense tasks it was faced with under tense circumstances, facing off against inexperienced Diet members and vitriolic mass movements while also lacking the backing authority that had existed under the previous imperial system. Let's briefly look at this chaotic situation.

Prince Higashikuni Naruhiko (1887–1990) formed a cabinet following Japan's defeat in an attempt to soften the shock by having a member of the imperial family lead the cabinet. The Higashikuni Cabinet resigned after two months, having made tentative steps toward coping with the defeat. It was replaced by a new government under Shidehara. The return of the largely forgotten Shidehara, who had been absent from the political stage since the Manchurian Incident (see Chapter 11), showed that Japan had a past legacy of democracy and cooperative diplomacy that should now be revived.

The tasks facing Shidehara included implementing GHQ's reforms, most notably constitutional revision, and overcoming the economic crisis. A food crisis caused by the worst weather in forty years was an especially serious problem. When the first general election of the postwar period was held in April 1946 amid these conditions, no party succeeded in achieving a majority, and Shidehara resigned when he was unable to assemble one.

Yoshida Shigeru (1878–1967)

Yoshida Shigeru was born the fifth son of Takenouchi Tsuna, a Tosa people's rights activist. He was adopted by Yoshida Kenzō, a Yokohama trader, and succeeded to an immense inheritance at age 11 following his adoptive father's death. After attending a number of other schools, he studied at Gakushūin (The Peers' School) before graduating from Tokyo Imperial University in 1906 and entering the foreign ministry. Although he married the daughter of Makino Nobuaki, most of his work assignments were in China, and he was not necessarily on the path to success. He opposed Shidehara during the heyday of Shidehara diplomacy, calling for a more hard-line diplomatic approach, and became vice-minister when Tanaka Giichi became foreign minister. As previously mentioned, however, while he advocated a more hard-line course, it was still one within the framework of the Washington treaties. He was critical of the Manchurian Incident and became close with Shidehara afterward.

Yoshida consistently pursued collaboration with Britain before the war and was strongly opposed to Japan joining the Axis. Although he retired from the foreign ministry after serving as ambassador to Britain, he still had connections through Gakushūin and actively engaged in political activities and attempts to end the war. He was taken into custody by the military police in 1945.

Following the end of the war, Yoshida replaced Higashikuni's first foreign minister, Shigemitsu Mamoru, who resigned after clashing with GHQ. He continued to hold the position when Shidehara became prime minister. At the time, the only individuals who had had a chance to become prime minister were those who had good relations with the Americans, were unlikely to be tried for war crimes, and were experienced in diplomacy;

not many met those criteria. Additionally, unlike Shidehara, who had essentially retired following the Manchurian Incident, Yoshida was close to both Konoe Fumimaro and Hatoyama Ichirō (1883–1959).

When Hatoyama was purged in May 1946 before he could form a cabinet, Yoshida was the one chosen to serve as his replacement. Despite having no experience with party politics, he was able to build a trusting relationship with MacArthur and skillfully lead the Liberal Party. And while he lost his position after being defeated in the April 1947 general election, the period of moderate cabinets that followed lasted for only eighteen months. Yoshida returned to power in October 1948, having witnessed the decline of the moderates, and watched intently as the Cold War developed. He won a landslide victory in the twenty-fourth general election in January 1949, reaching the height of his power. He established the base for his faction during the election by recruiting a large number of figures with bureaucratic backgrounds, such as Ikeda Hayato (1899–1965) and Satō Eisaku (1901–1975), to serve as candidates.

Yoshida signed the San Francisco Peace Treaty and the Security Treaty between the United States of America and Japan in September 1951, creating the foundation for postwar Japan. Although Yoshida was seen as a haughty and arrogant reactionary conservative and frequently fell under criticism from intellectuals, his figure – wearing a traditional Japanese *haori*, *hakama*, and white *tabi* and smoking a cigar – inspired public confidence. Although the method Yoshida advocated for protecting and expanding trade differed depending on the period, he had consistently placed the highest emphasis on trade since his time as a prewar diplomat. His postwar policy of pursuing minimal rearmament and prioritizing the economy was one form this emphasis took; it was nothing so rigid as to be considered a "doctrine." Even so, however, the basic points of Yoshida's approach were maintained by his disciples, Ikeda Hayato and Satō Eisaku, and had a long-standing and deep influence.

After Shidehara's resignation, the largest party in the Diet, the Liberal Party (*Jiyūtō*), attempted to form a cabinet under Hatoyama. This fell through when Hatoyama was purged from holding public office by GHQ, however. As a result, Yoshida Shigeru took Hatoyama's place as leader of the Liberal Party and formed his first cabinet in May. The food crisis had also endangered the formation of the Yoshida Cabinet, but this was narrowly averted after GHQ warned of the radicalization of the mass movements and released food supplies to the public. The labor movement became increasingly radicalized as inflation continued to rise, but the general strike called for on February 1, 1947 would prove to be its zenith. GHQ ordered the strike canceled, thus allowing the government to weather its greatest crisis. The Socialist Party (*Shakaitō*) made gains in the second postwar general election held in April, however, and became the largest party in the Diet. With the Liberal Party reduced to second place, Yoshida resigned.

Yoshida was followed by two governments backed by a coalition between the Socialist Party, Democratic Party (*Minshutō*), and the National Cooperative Party (*Kokumin Kyōdōtō*). The first of these was formed in May by Katayama Tetsu (1887–1978) of the Socialist Party. When internal party conflicts caused this government to fall in February 1948, Ashida Hitoshi of the Democratic Party formed a new government in March with the backing of the same parties. This government also proved to be short-lived, however, and ended in October after former Deputy Premier Nishio Suehiro was arrested in connection with the Shōwa Denkō bribery scandal.

It is frequently remarked that America's occupation policy shifted or backed away from democratization. This overrates the initial American enthusiasm for reform, however, and is a viewpoint born out of a sense of disappointment at having been betrayed. In truth, the primary goal of the initial phase of the American occupation was ending the Japanese threat, not democratization.

Although the economic crises of the early occupation were particularly severe, GHQ initially showed little interest in rebuilding the Japanese economy. Instead, its basic policy was that Japan should not be allowed to have a standard of living higher than that of the countries that it had invaded. But it couldn't permit Japan to fall into chaos, either, as that would interfere with the goals of the occupation. The reason that America opposed the radicalization of the labor movement and ultimately intervened was that the movement had grown strong enough to threaten America's policies for the occupation, not because those policies had become reactionary.

GHQ placed its hopes on the moderates in Japan, including the Socialist Party. Compared to the post-1955 party, the Socialists at the time were moderate and flexible and had many right-wing members. Groups like the Liberal Party, in comparison, were seen as a reactionary force, the remnants of militarism; after its fierce war with Japan, America was not about to support such groups. The moderates thus appeared to be the safest choice, existing between the extremes of both the right and the left. As already mentioned, however, America's hopes for the moderates were never all that strong, either.

The Cold War and peace treaty

A shift in occupation policy

Just as a moderate government collapsed in October 1948, however, America's policies toward Japan made a clear shift toward fostering Japan as a partner (and accordingly, emphasizing economic reconstruction) rather than punishing it. The background to this change was, naturally, the Cold War.

Churchill's Iron Curtain speech, famous for its proclamation of a coming Cold War, was given in March 1946. And it was in March 1947 that President Truman put forth the Truman Doctrine, arguing for armed resistance to the Soviet Union. No policy opposing the Soviets had yet been adopted for Asia, however. George F. Kennan (1904–2005) of the Policy Planning Staff, famous for calling for a policy of containment toward the Soviet Union, played a major role in the Japan policy change.

With the new policy toward Japan adopted in October 1948, America embarked on a major revival of the Japanese economy. The Dodge Line (so named because it was put forward by Detroit banker Joseph M. Dodge [1890–1964]) was introduced to that end as an attempt to first conquer inflation through a balanced budget with surplus. The economy worsened dramatically as a result, and economic rationalization and workforce reductions proceeded apace. And when this caused the labor movement to intensify, the suppression of the Japan Communist Party (*Nihon Kyōsantō*) began.

The next shock for America was the establishment of the People's Republic of China in October 1949. The Open Door and Sino-American collaboration had served as the core of American policy on Asia ever since the Russo-Japanese War (see Chapter 7); to have China itself reject the United States was a great shock. America's frontier in Asia now moved from China to Japan, and its policies toward Japan became more assertive.

The Korean War then began in June 1950 (see Chapter 16). Although they were briefly pushed all the way to Pusan by the North Korean surprise attack, America (and the United Nations forces) soon counterattacked and drove north until it arrived near the Chinese border. This caused the Chinese People's Volunteer Army to enter the war in late October under the direction of Peng Dehuai (1898–1974), however, and America was thus forced to fight China.

The Korean War caused America to embark on the construction of an anticommunist military alliance. This marked a shift from a policy of containment to one of rollback. This applied to China as well; America now set out to preserve Taiwan, something that it had previously given up on, by dispatching the Seventh Fleet.

And in Japan, it commenced the near-total suppression of the Japan Communist Party. GHQ had interpreted certain actions of the Communist Party as having been made in concert with the North Korean drive south and thus began cracking down on the party. The Communist Party had won thirty-five seats in the January 1949 general election and pursued a moderate course, but it moved away from the path of peaceful revolution after it came under criticism from the Cominform in January 1950. This was during the same period that Stalin was supporting Kim Il-Sung's (1912–1994) push south and immediately predated the signing of the Sino-Soviet Treaty of Friendship, Alliance and Mutual Assistance in February.

Toward peace treaty

America also began pushing for Japan to rearm and moving toward the conclusion of a peace treaty. Although many in Japan called for a peace treaty with all countries (including the Soviet Union), given America's overwhelming position at the time, it seems fair to conclude that Japan never really had any other option but to go along.

As this was being done, Yoshida led the Japanese government. He had formed his second cabinet in October 1948, following the fall of Ashida, and had won the first postwar outright majority in the Diet (for the Democratic Liberal Party, or *Minshu Jiyūtō*) in the January 1949 general election.

Former high-level bureaucrats like Ikeda and Satō ran for seats during the election and won, strengthening Yoshida's position within the party. Supported by the American change in policy and the boost provided by the Korean War special procurements, Yoshida oversaw the signing of a Peace Treaty in September 1951 (see Chapter 14) and would continue in office until December 1954. The special procurements were an especially fortunate piece of luck for a Japanese economy suffering under the recession caused by the Dodge Line. Japan surpassed its prewar economic level in 1951. The Korean War served as one of the springboards for Japan's high-speed economic growth.

Yoshida was not merely subservient to America, however. He resisted its demands for Japanese rearmament, claiming that the state of the economy and public opinion made it impossible, and stuck to a course of minimal rearmament. There were, of course, limits to what he could do, however. Pressure from Secretary of State John Foster Dulles (1888–1959) forced him to acknowledge the Republic of China on Taiwan as the legitimate government of China, for example. But despite this, Yoshida's path of prioritizing the economy and adopting only minimal rearmament would serve as the basis for Japan's postwar development.

Note

1 The Soviet Union did not sign the declaration due to its neutrality pact with Japan. It was considered a joint statement by America, Britain, and China (which was not represented at the conference).

14 The Development of the Liberal Democratic Party (LDP)

High economic growth

The creation of the 1955 system

The signing of the 1951 Peace Treaty with Japan and its subsequent going into effect in 1952 greatly changed Japanese politics. With some exaggeration, Japanese politics until that time was essentially diplomacy toward the United States (see Chapter 13). However, with the return of sovereignty, not only did Japan's political and diplomatic options expand, but the political situation also became unstable with the departure of the occupation forces.

The Yoshida Shigeru Cabinet began first to prepare the basic governing foundations for post-Occupation Japan. These included legislation for domestic security including the Anti-Subversive Activities Act, the centralization of the police, and the establishment of nomination systems for textbook review committees and local boards of education. These moves were done because Yoshida felt he could not secure the proper governing structure without them. In response to these measures, the reformists strongly criticized Yoshida's actions as a "reverse course."

What made the political situation even more unstable was the return of prewar politicians who had been purged during the Occupation by the General Headquarters of the Supreme Commander for the Allied Powers. The men who succeeded Yoshida – Hatoyama Ichirō, Ishibashi Tanzan, and Kishi Nobusuke (1896–1987) – had all been released from prison just before or slightly after the San Francisco Peace Conference. They had each already been in influential positions in the prewar and were critical of Yoshida's postwar reforms. In particular, Hatoyama, who was purged shortly before he was to become prime minister in 1946, sought early on to seek the premiership from Yoshida, to whom he had turned over the running of the Liberal Party.

The battle between the pro-Yoshida forces and those around Hatoyama continued for some time. Eventually, in November 1954, the anti-Yoshida forces, including Hatoyama, Kishi, and Ishibashi, formed the Japan Democratic Party. Gaining the cooperation of the Japan Socialist Party, they were successful in bringing an end to the Yoshida administration and establishing the Hatoyama Cabinet.

In doing all of this, the Hatoyama forces, the Democratic Party, and the Hatoyama Cabinet itself openly pushed for the correction of Yoshida's politics and called for constitutional revision, rearmament, and an end to dependence on the United States.

Figure 14.1 (a) The signing of the Security Treaty on January 19, 1960, with Prime Minister Kishi Nobusuke (center left) and President Dwight D. Eisenhower (center right) at the White House in Washington, D.C. (b) Demonstrations outside the Diet Building on May 19, 1960 in Tokyo. (Photo provided by Jiji Press Photo/*Mainichi Shimbun*.)

As a way to end Japan's dependence on the United States, the first order of business the Hatoyama administration sought was to restore relations with the Soviet Union. Japan and the Soviet Union were still legally in a state of war, as the latter had not signed the Allied peace treaty with Japan, and only a few of the nearly 600,000 Japanese who had been taken prisoner in Siberia had been returned. Moreover, due to the Soviet's veto power as a Permanent Member of the Security Council, Japan had been unable to join the United Nations. Moreover, there had been an endless series of disputes in the Sea of Okhotsk over fishing rights. In order to end this, the Hatoyama Cabinet undertook negotiations with the Soviet Union, the result of which was the Japan-Soviet joint statement of October 1956 restoring relations. However, the territorial dispute over the so-called Northern Islands between the two countries was left unresolved. Former Prime Minister Yoshida remained critical of the negotiations, stating it would benefit only the Soviet Union and hurt Japan's relations with the United States.

The Socialist Party was concerned with the Hatoyama cabinet for reasons other than simply the restoration of relations with the Soviet Union. The *de facto* rearmament that had begun as a result of the Korean War breaking out caused people in Japan to be concerned, having not forgotten their recent war experiences, and gave rise to a peace movement. The public was worried that the postwar reforms would come to naught under the efforts of the depurged prewar politicians who had begun openly calling for constitutional revision and rearmament as a way to correct Occupation policies. This fear led to a dramatic rise in support for the Socialist Party, in particular its Left Wing. The Socialist Party had been damaged by the Katayama Tetsu and Ashida Hitoshi coalition Cabinets but recovered shortly thereafter and began to grow again. In particular, the combined wings of the Socialist Party reached a total of one-third the number of seats in the Diet in the 1955 general election, being able to block any efforts to revise the constitution. With these numbers in hand, the left and right wings of the Socialist Party reunited in October 1955.

There were movements among the conservatives as well to unite. These efforts increased with Yoshida's resignation, and the reunification of the Socialist Party provided an additional stimulus. In November that same year, the conservatives merged to form the Liberal Democratic Party.

It appeared that a two-party system would emerge with the respective mergers of smaller groups to become the Japan Socialist Party (JSP) and (Liberal Democratic Party) LDP, respectively. However, the Socialist Party never became strong enough to take over, and thus throughout the decades after this, Japan simply had the appearance of a two-party system, or a so-called 1.5 Large Party System, without there ever being a routine change in administrations. This political structure that dominated the postwar years afterward is called the 1955 System. (See Table 14.1.)

The Kishi Cabinet and the revision of the Japan-U.S. Security Treaty

Hatoyama Ichirō became the first LDP president and used the restoration of relations with the Soviet Union as his way to leave the stage while everyone was still

Table 14.1 Changes in Lower House representation of the Japan Socialist Party, 1946–1960.

General Election	Left Wing	Right Wing	Combined	Overall Total (Diet)
No. 22 (April 1946)	n/a	n/a	93	466
No. 23 (April 1947)	n/a	n/a	143	466
No. 24 (January 1949)	n/a	n/a	48	466
No. 25 (October 1952)	54	57	111	466
No. 26 (April 1953)	72	66	138	466
No. 27 (February 1955)	89	67	156	467
No. 28 (May 1958)	n/a	n/a	166	467
No. 29 (November 1960)	(DSP 17)		145	467

clapping. After a heated party election to succeed him, Ishibashi Tanzan was chosen party president and became prime minister. However, he became ill shortly after that and had to resign, with Kishi becoming the party president and premier in February 1957.

Kishi had long called for constitutional revision and other changes to Occupation policies. After becoming prime minister, he further took a hawkish stance on domestic security and labor disputes and used the postwar reparations issue as a way to make advances into Southeast Asia. In bilateral relations, he called for a "New Era in Japan-U.S. Relations" and wanted to make the relationship with the United States, which had worsened under Hatoyama, more equal and friendlier.

In order to do this, Kishi sought the revision of the Japan-U.S. Security Treaty. The Security Treaty had been signed at the same time as the peace treaty and gave the strong appearance of being no more than an agreement permitting the stationing of U.S. forces in Japan following the peace treaty and end of the Occupation. Kishi wanted to make it a more mutual, more holistic friendship treaty.

However, a large opposition movement emerged against revision of the Security Treaty. One view was based on nationalism – while the Occupation was unavoidable, it was long over, and some Japanese did not want the United States to have any role in post-treaty Japan. A second group consisted of those who felt that democracy was threatened under the hawkish Kishi cabinet and that the attempts to force ratification were dangerous to democracy. A third element was comprised of those who had a personal antipathy toward Kishi himself, due to his having been a member of the Tōjō Cabinet (see Chapter 12) and once named as a Class A War Criminal (but released before being indicted at the Tokyo War Crimes Tribunal). His policies as prime minister invited suspicion from the opposition parties, as well as from many people in the general public. Kishi was able to see the revised security treaty barely ratified in June 1960 but had to resign shortly after that to take responsibility for the political disturbances, the result of which he had to suspend the visit of U.S. President Dwight D. Eisenhower that was scheduled in June.

Kishi Nobusuke (1896–1987)

Kishi Nobusuke was born the son of Satō Shūsuke, a government official for Yamaguchi Prefecture. He was adopted by the Kishi family and became Kishi Nobusuke. His older brother, Satō Ichirō, was in the Imperial Japanese Navy, later becoming a vice admiral, and his younger brother, Satō Eisaku, a prime minister. Nobusuke studied at Tokyo Imperial University and graduated near the top of his class in 1920. He entered the Ministry of Agriculture and Commerce, and when the ministry was divided into two separate organizations in 1925, he joined the Ministry of Commerce and Industry. In 1935, Kishi became the director of the Bureau of Public Works, and in 1936, he entered the Manchukuo Government's Industrial Bureau as the deputy director. He played a large role in the development of the economy of Manchukuo. He became the vice-minister of Commerce and Industry in the Tōjō Hideki Cabinet in 1941 and subsequently became minister. Kishi was not an ordinary bureaucrat at all. He ran for a Lower House seat in the 1942 general election and was elected while minister. It was not impossible technically, but it was very rare. In July 1944, he played an important role opposing Tōjō and bringing down the cabinet.

In the postwar, he was arrested as a Class A War Criminal, incarcerated in Sugamo Prison, but released in 1948. He was still purged from holding public office, but in 1952, the purge was lifted, and he returned to the political world. He helped Hatoyama Ichirō form the Japan Democratic Party and became its secretary general in 1954, and, after working toward the merger of the conservatives into the Liberal Democratic Party (*Jiyū Minshutō*), he became its secretary general as well. Following Hatoyama's stepping down in 1956, Kishi ran in the party presidential contest, losing to Ishibashi Tanzan by a slight margin. He became the foreign minister in the Ishibashi Cabinet and succeeded Ishibashi when the latter resigned for health reasons.

The main issue Kishi chose to deal with was the revision of the Japan-U.S. Security Treaty. While Japan provided bases to the United States as per the original treaty, the United States was not obligated to defend Japan or even consult with the Japanese government on the operation of its bases. Kishi successfully sought its revision and was able to sign a new mutual Security Treaty in January 1960 but had to resign in June when the treaty went into effect due to daily demonstrations by protesters who had risen up against it.

Kishi increased Japan's defense strength and deepened its relations with the United States, while on the other hand resolving most of the wartime reparation issues with the countries in Southeast Asia. He also saw the United Nations as important. The Kishi Cabinet also greatly contributed to Japan's high economic growth. He looked toward constitutional revision as well. But some feared his prewar record, as well as his power and ambition, and there was opposition even from within the party, so he focused only on revising the Security Treaty.

The revised Security Treaty has for a long time been the basis for Japan's security policies. In this sense, Kishi's legacy is huge. However, at the same time, the Kishi cabinet was viewed as too pushy, and leaders of the LDP afterward tended to avoid addressing constitutional revision or security matters. The LDP, which had been formed in part to pursue constitutional revision, had to in effect give up on it and sought to gain the public's support through pursuing economic growth instead. This was another of Kishi's legacies, albeit one he probably did not wish to leave.

The Ikeda and Satō Cabinets

Ikeda Hayato became LDP president and prime minister following Kishi. It appeared that with the peak of the anti–security treaty movement and the advances of the Socialist Party since its reunification in 1955, the LDP was facing a crisis that summer. However, Ikeda, calling for "Tolerance and Forbearance," adopted a low political posture overall and a conciliatory stance toward the opposition parties. Furthermore, he saw that the economy, which had entered a period of high growth starting around 1955, was going to continue and to grow and thus announced to the Japanese public an "income-doubling plan." With this, Ikeda's LDP did well in the general elections that November and overcame the crisis that had befallen the party that summer with the security treaty revision and ratification crisis.

This change in political fortunes was not a temporary phenomenon. Although constitutional revision remained on the LDP's party platform, Ikeda avoided contested such issues and focused instead on an economy centric, "interest-based politics" in order to get the public's support. The Satō Cabinet, described later in this chapter, adopted a similar style, with the LDP enjoying stable support from the voters. Thus, 1960 was more important a year in postwar Japanese politics than 1955 when the conservative parties merged to create the LDP and the two wings of the Socialist Party merged again. While scholars call the political system since 1955 the 1955 System, the author calls the political system after 1960 the 1960 System and regards the latter as more important than the former.

Ikeda resigned for health reasons in 1964, and Satō, who had traditionally been critical of Ikeda's approach, became party president. However, although he dealt swiftly with some high-politics issues after becoming prime minister, such as the signing of the Treaty on Basic Relations between Japan and the Republic of Korea in 1965, Satō agreed not to pursue constitutional revision and instead focused on governing through interest-based politics being supported by the period of high growth, much as Ikeda had done.

At the end of the 1960s, pollution and welfare issues garnered much attention, and the government was criticized for the distortions caused to society by the pursuit of high economic growth. Ironically, this was one of the points that Satō criticized Ikeda about. However, these problems were resolved by expanding the budgets thanks to the ever increasing economy. Within the party, Satō's rivals had all passed away, and he was reelected as president four times. He was able to then focus on his long held desire to see the reversion of Okinawa to Japan. He continued in office until July 1972. This is the longest continuous administration in modern Japanese political history and is only slightly less than the total number of years Katsura Tarō (see Chapter 9) served as prime minister.

The Socialists were unable to respond to the LDP's successes following the security treaty crisis. The JSP had trouble being a credible opposition party, criticizing the security treaty while benefiting from the very system it was opposing. There were those who saw the JSP eventually taking power if urbanization, which started in the latter half of the 1950s, continued, as the Socialists were strong in the cities. However, the JSP was unable to do well in the 1960 election or even after the LDP faced a number of scandals on the eve of the 1967 general elections. Its criticism of the Vietnam War, of which the Satō administration was supportive, and the environmental problems resulting from the high economic growth, resonated with many voters but were not enough to take over the reins of government from the LDP.

What developed instead, however, was the increase in the number of opposition parties. In 1960, the right wing of the Socialist Party criticized the antiestablishment nature of the party and left it, forming with Nishio Suehiro the Democratic Socialist Party, with a total of forty Lower House members. The DSP sought to take power within five years and fielded 105 candidates (with the JSP fielding 186), but it lost, seeing only seventeen elected. Afterward, it recovered somewhat, eventually regaining in the 1980s the strength it had when it originally formed the party two decades before but did no better. Next, the Clean Government Party (*Kōmeitō*) ran in the 1967 general elections and by 1969 became the second largest opposition party. However, its broader advancement was limited by its connection to the new religion, *Sōka Gakkai* (Value-Creating Society). Next, the Communist Party lost all of its seats in the 1952 election due to its revolutionary doctrine adopted in 1950 but, after revising its approach, was able to regain seats in the 1955 general election and continued gradually to make gains among people disenchanted with the LDP's long grip on power. In 1969, it tripled the number of seats to fourteen and in 1972 almost tripled that number again to thirty-eight. In any case, under the Ikeda-Satō line, the LDP's majority was never seriously in danger. (See Table 14.2.)

Table 14.2 Changes in Lower House representation, 1958–1969.

General Election	LDP	JSP	DSP	CGP	JCP	Total
No. 28 (May 1958)	287	166	n/a	n/a	0	467
No. 29 (November 1960)	296	145	17	n/a	3	467
No. 30 (November 1963)	283	144	23	n/a	5	467
No. 31 (January 1967)	277	140	30	25	5	486
No. 32 (December 1969)	288	90	31	47	14	486

LDP politics

The development of factions

With the stabilization of the majority by the LDP, the battle for control shifted from one that would normally be between the ruling and opposition parties to one between the factions within the ruling LDP.

Factions have existed since time immemorial, certainly since the formation of the Liberal Party (*Jiyūtō*) in 1881 and the Constitutional Reform Party (*Kaishintō*) in 1882 during the Meiji Period. The Tosa faction of the Liberal Party and the Kantō faction of the Friends of Constitutional Government Party (Seiyūkai), founded in 1900, were referred to in Chapters 4 and 9. The Constitutional Association (*Kenseikai*), founded in 1916, saw the existence of a faction around President Katō Takaaki and another faction around his opponents within the party. Furthermore, during the early years of the Shōwa period, the rivalry between the Hatoyama faction and that of Kuhara Fusanosuke was another one. It was quite natural in a large party for people to form an association with people from the same hometown or of the same political views, or with someone might act as a political sponsor.

However, the factions that developed with the creation of the LDP were very much different. In the prewar, many politicians did not belong to factions whatsoever, and even for those who did, their allegiance was somewhat vague. However, by the time of the Ikeda-Satō years, almost every member of the LDP belonged to one faction or another. The factions even had a physical office, staff, and an organized process for the succession of leaders of the group.

The biggest reason for the promotion of the factional system was the existence of the electoral districts. Since 1925, the Lower House constituencies were comprised of three to five candidates each, in which the Friends of Constitutional Government and Constitutional Democratic Party (*Minseitō*) battled it out. However, the meaning of these electoral districts changed in the postwar, especially following the formation of the all-powerful Liberal Democratic Party in 1955. Rather than the LDP battling it out with the opposition parties, the real contests tended to take place between the candidates of the LDP itself. Rather than trying to appeal to voters of different ideological or policy persuasions, the conservative candidates tended to eat into each other's base.

One more important aspect is the dissolution of the traditional order in local areas after the war. First, due to the farmland reform (see Chapter 13) during the Occupation, it was no longer possible to rely on the local leaders when campaigning due to the impact that the reforms had on the traditional structure of the countryside by which one landlord or family controlled things. The decline of traditional local leaders quickened during the period of high economic growth when more and more people left the countryside, and the economy further industrialized. Thus, candidates had to develop their own political organizations in their districts. The result was groups of supporters known as *kōenkai*. Initially, these supporters' groups began not in the rural districts or in the large metropolises but in the small and midsized cities. In the rural communities, the traditional structure was still in place, and in the large cities, it was difficult to bring voters into such an organization due to the fluidity of people's lives in urban areas. But over time, it became easier to organize around the country.

One of the original reasons that factions came to exist was a regional identity. However, due to the situation of the electoral districts, the factions tended to become not based on regional connections. Candidates in the same district would fight viciously against one another. Each candidate in turn belonged to a different faction, and the candidate, while adding to the numbers and strength of the faction, was supported by the faction leader in his or her elections, party leadership and committee assignments, and cabinet appointments. As long as the midsized electoral districts continued, at least three to four factions would exist.

Another reason contributing to the development of factions was the advancements of the parliamentary cabinet system and the national bureaucratic structure, which led to the ruling party possessing overwhelming power and influence. First was the status of the LDP's president. Until the LDP lost power temporarily in August 1993, the LDP president always immediately became the prime minister of the country. Party heads in the prewar were no more than a candidate for the premiership – they did not automatically become the prime minister. Even if they did manage to become premier, they still had to contend with the army and navy and other elements in the government and were woefully restricted in their powers. In contrast, the prime minister in postwar Japan, especially that of a ruling party with a clear majority, was basically almighty. It was the election for the party president that decided the leader of Japan, and often the person with the largest influence within the party who was elected, and thus it was natural for him to build the largest base or faction from which to receive this support. When the LDP was formed, there were approximately eleven moderately aligned groupings, but by the presidential elections in December 1956, the number had decreased into a handful of strongly cohesive factions.

For those who were not candidates for party president, there were still reasons to form or belong to factions. As the position of the ruling party grew in importance, the number of posts given to members of the parliament grew dramatically. In the prewar, the number of cabinet ministers varied between fifteen and sixteen, and the posts of Army and Navy ministers, as well as foreign minister, went to officers or officials not in the party. Thus, the number of party cabinet positions for party members was usually between seven and nine. In the postwar, however, the number of cabinet positions grew to about twenty-one, and almost all of them were usually assigned to LDP Diet members. Moreover, the LDP's top three (secretary general, chairman of the General Council, and chair of the Policy Affairs Research Council) or top four posts just below the party president (the preceding three, as well as sometimes the position of vice president of the party) were also available and usually more sought after than a cabinet position. In addition, there were the positions of director of the general affairs, finance, national chapters, and other important bureaus. There were the positions of secretary general and the like in the prewar, but they do not compare in importance to their postwar counterparts. Furthermore, within the Diet, whose importance grew in the postwar, there are the speakers of the House of Representatives and of the House of Councilors, as well as the chairs of the various standing and special committees in both houses. As long as honor and fame, as well as actual power and benefits, accrue to these positions, it is natural that party members will seek the protection and assistance of influential members of the party in order to acquire those posts.

As seen from this discussion, the postwar LDP factions were not the traditional leader-follower relationships of the past but instead developed into a rational structure due to a variety of reasons, including the realities of the (then) mid-sized electoral districts, policy and ideological distances between the ruling and opposition parties, and parliamentary cabinet system. The attention of journalists similarly shifted from the contests between the ruling LDP and opposition parties to factional conflicts within the LDP itself.

The LDP and bureaucracy in policy decisions

Another significant special characteristic that developed due to LDP politics was the close relationship that developed between the ruling party, the bureaucracy, and the business community, otherwise known as the Iron Triangle. This was not necessarily self-evident or expected in the context of Japanese political history. Indeed, the relationship between the parties and the bureaucracy was one of the conflict, one that continued from the Meiji period; similarly, that between the bureaucracy and the business community lacked cooperation, particularly due to the former's efforts to control the economy.

However, with the formation of one single conservative party, the economic world, LDP, and bureaucracy all belonged to one camp. The business community provided political funds. The bureaucracy prepared the policies. The LDP provided the capitalist order for the economic world to function and for the bureaucracy the necessary political guarantees to implement their policies. Furthermore, when bureaucrats retired, they were given positions in the LDP or in the business community (the so-called descent from heaven). This was the relationship for much of the postwar, and the degree of cooperation grew even more in the latter half of the period of high growth.

Until the beginning of the 1960s, the LDP, which had comprised party politicians in its early years, depended overwhelming on the policy-making capabilities of the bureaucracy. Even the Policy Research Council of the LDP in the beginning simply listened to explanations provided by the bureaucracy. As former bureaucrats entered the LDP's ranks, the party's ability to develop policy increased. Even those parliamentarians who were not from the bureaucracy developed an expert-like grasp of policy making since they served in the Diet for a long time due to the party's repeated success in the polls. Moreover, the divisions of the Policy Affairs Research Council were matched with the respective government agencies, and thus parliamentarians who served in these divisions for a long time were able to develop policy savvy that surpassed that of the bureaucrats, who often ended up rotating every couple of years.

It was at this juncture that the special teamwork between the LDP and the bureaucrats emerged. When the bureaucracy wished to make an important policy decision, especially when it wished to see legislation passed, the responsible officials would meet with the leadership of the PARC divisions in order to gain their support. The senior politicians, in turn, would either represent the business community's interests to the bureaucrats or represent the bureaucracy's stance to the business community, serving as a facilitator between the two (coming to become known as policy tribe members). Moreover, the bureaucracy and business world would look to these politicians to secure more funding for their projects, coming to depend on them. The business community would help the politicians by providing political funds and votes through their companies and industries and help the bureaucrats by providing positions following retirement.

Amid the tradition of statism, in other words, the revering of the bureaucrats and the denigrating of the ordinary citizen, the role of the politicians in making the relationship between the bureaucracy and the economic world go smoothly was quite significant.

In this way, the coexistence-like or interdependent relationship between the LDP parliamentarians and the bureaucracy developed amid the period of high economic growth and led to the bureaucratization of the Japanese state. This, in turn, led to the Diet becoming a mere façade.

15 Changes in the international order and the end of the Cold War

Japanese politics in the years of turbulence

Changes in international relations

What guaranteed the political stability of the long period of high economic growth, especially during the Ikeda Hayato and Satō Eisaku Cabinets, was America's overwhelming superiority in international politics and the world economy. As this changed in the early 1970s, Japanese politics were also greatly affected.

A sign of these changes to come was seen in the bilateral textile problem. At the November 1969 summit meeting between Prime Minister Satō and U.S. President Richard M. Nixon (1913–1994; in office 1969–1974), the Japanese leader seems to have promised some sort of self-restraint on textile exports to the United States in exchange for the return of administrative rights over Okinawa (see Chapter 14). It is unclear what exactly Satō promised at this time, but the problem began at this juncture as the United States understood it to be a promise from the prime minister. Because the implementation of this agreement did not go well at all, criticism toward Japan grew in the United States. The relationship was rocky until Japan actually began to implement these restraints in January 1972.

While this textile problem in and of itself should not have been a big problem, there were three things of note here. First, it was the first example of postwar Japan saying "no." Japan's mass media at the time praised the government's hard-line stance toward the United States. Second, U.S.-Japan relations until this point had been predicated on America's preeminence, but changes began to be seen in the relationship, including more competition and conflict. Third, the focus of international politics began to shift from high-policy issues of security matters to low-policy matters such as economic problems.

An even bigger challenge came at the time of the so-called Nixon Shocks of July and August 1971. President Nixon on July 15 announced that the United States and the People's Republic of China were seeking rapprochement and that he would be visiting Beijing the following year (he did so in February 1972). This announcement was made without any forewarning to Japan and came as a big surprise to its officials. It was said the friction of the textile issue was behind the lack of prior warning.

Figure 15.1 Prime Minister Nakasone Yasuhiro (right) and U.S. President Ronald W. Reagan walking at Camp David in April 1986. (Photo provided by Nakasone Yasuhiro Office.)

Japan had until then recognized the Republic of China (ROC), or Taiwan, as the legitimate representative of China (see Chapter 13). This was a choice Prime Minister Yoshida Shigeru reluctantly made at the strong request of John Foster Dulles, who was President Harry S Truman's special representative. This was an unnatural situation, but Japan could not change its policy unless the United States itself changed its anti-China stance. However, it was the United States that suddenly changed its policy, without informing Japan. This initiative was even a bigger shock to the Japanese public because it was reminiscent of previous U.S.-China cooperation against Japan in the prewar period.

Next, in August, President Nixon announced a new economic policy that would take the United States off the gold standard and place a 10 percent surcharge on imported goods to protect the dollar. Throughout the postwar, under the Bretton Woods System, the dollar had a fixed value of $35 against one ounce of gold. Worldwide, there were fixed exchange rates as well, with $1 equaling 360 yen in Japan's case. For the Japanese public, 360 yen to the dollar was second nature. It was only as a result of Nixon's New Economic Policy that Japan came to realize once again the international economic order was something that humans maintained. In December that year, the Smithsonian Agreement was signed, which adjusted fixed exchange rates under the Bretton Woods Conference, with the dollar being set at 308 yen.

The Tanaka Cabinet and foreign relations

This change in American policy had a great effect on Japanese politics. It particularly affected Fukuda Takeo (1905–1995), who was the foreign minister at this time and who was viewed as Prime Minister Satō's likely successor. In particular, in the matter of the China problem, public opinion called for a change in policy, and the People's Republic of China (PRC) as well called on Satō to change his stance, placing Fukuda in a very difficult position. The race to succeed Satō heated up in 1972, and four candidates – Tanaka Kakuei (1918–1993), Ōhira Masayoshi (1910–1980), Miki Takeo (1907–1988), and Nakasone Yasuhiro (1918–) – formed an anti-Fukuda alliance, the commonality being a change in China policy. It was the first time since the issue of the restoration of relations with the Soviet Union and the revision of the U.S.-Japan security treaty for this sort of foreign policy matter to affect Japanese politics so deeply. In the postwar, foreign policy did not intervene in politics that much, but in the prewar, it was a regular occurrence. In this sense, it can be understood how the 1960s were a unique period in Japanese history.

Tanaka, who succeeded in becoming prime minister in July 1972, was a product of the domestic politics–first type of politician of the 1960s. One of his campaign pledges when he ran in the Liberal Democratic Party presidential election was to "a bottle of free milk every day to small children and expectant mothers." It is almost astonishing that he brazenly made such small, yet concrete promises, publicly, that could be seen as bribes. Moreover, his main policy – the Remodeling Plan for the Japanese Archipelago – was similarly a reflection of the high economic growth of the time. However, this sort of domestically focused policy based on the assumption of high growth was unsustainable as the international environment changed suddenly and drastically, eventually becoming his downfall.

One issue was the currency problem. In September 1972, the U.S. trade deficit with Japan had reached $4 billion, a new record. The Japanese Ministry of Finance determined the yen would have to be appreciated against the dollar. However, the Tanaka cabinet postponed a decision on yen appreciation due to general elections scheduled for December that year and the situation in the Diet afterward. However, in February 1973, a frenzied selling of the dollar began, necessitating Japan's move to a floating exchange rate. Initially, it began at 280 yen to the dollar, moving to somewhere between 263 and 265. At this time, Japan's response was the slowest among the advanced countries – and the least appropriate. As a result of a continued effort to force the international balance of payments through financial relaxation policies, excessive liquidity emerged, causing high inflation from 1973 to 1974.

With the outbreak of the fourth Middle East War (or Yom Kippur War, also known as the Arab-Israeli War of 1973) in October 1973, the Organization of Arab Petroleum Exporting Countries (OAPEC) adopted an oil embargo policy. While the United Kingdom and France were seen as friendly countries, Japan, West Germany, and Italy were branded as unfriendly ones. Petroleum exports to the United States and the Netherlands were forbidden outright. It became difficult for these countries, resource-dependent Japan especially, to secure a stable supply of oil. The Japanese government quickly adopted a pro-Arab, anti-Israel policy, thus earning the ranking of a "friendly" nation. However, this caused relations with the United States to worsen. For Japan, cooperative relations with the United States and the securing of cheap natural resources were two prerequisites to high economic growth, but, in this case, the two premises came into conflict.

What's more is that, by the time of the spring of 1974, the price of petroleum had jumped nearly five times what it was in 1972, from $2.50 a barrel to $11.70. This, in turn with the excessive liquidity facing Japan from the previous year, caused inflation. The increase in the consumer price index went from 4.5 percent, which was below the Organization of Economic Cooperation and Development (OECD) average, to 11.7 percent in 1973 and an actual 24.5 percent in 1974. Both of these percentages were the worst among the twenty-five countries then making up the OECD at the time.

Dealing with both the currency problem and the Oil Crisis would probably have been difficult for anyone, but the Japanese government at the time was unprepared for the problems of the Middle East, particularly the Oil Crisis. Moreover, the cabinet was focused on Tanaka's plan to reform the Japanese archipelago, which necessitated a great deal of spending. Inflation was further worsened by the failure to change the budget for this project. The Tanaka Cabinet was forced to resign en masse due to the money in politics scandal in November 1974, but it had already been greatly damaged. This situation was largely caused by the structural priority given to domestic politics that had been established in the 1960s.

Parity in the number of conservatives and reformists

Shortly after the Tanaka Cabinet ended, which was earlier than anticipated, Miki Takeo (in office December 1974–December 1976), Fukuda Takeo (in office December 1976–December 1978), and Ōhira Masayoshi (in office December 1978–July 1980), each became president of the LDP and prime minister. Each of them was a losing candidate in the 1972 party presidential election following Satō's resignation and had long aggressively sought to become prime minister in their own right. Moreover, each of their respective factions had led the fight to criticize one another's administrations as the cabinets weakened amid the worsening international situation.

In July 1974 Upper House elections, the LDP lost seats as a result of the Tanaka Cabinet's having invited inflation. Both Miki and Fukuda criticized Tanaka and left the cabinet. After Tanaka's resignation due to the money scandal, Miki was named party president after consultations between the factions. He was nominally chosen, at least, because he was seen as the most appropriate one in light of public criticism of the LDP because of his calls over the years to clean up politics.

Miki's policies would come under attack from within the LDP due to his efforts to seek limits on political funds and outlaw monopolies. In February 1976, the Lockheed Scandal came to light, and former Premier Tanaka was arrested. The factions of Ōhira, Fukuda, and Tanaka banded together and formed the

Coordination Council to Strengthen the Party Structure in an effort to bring the crusading Miki down. With the help of Nakasone and others, Miki resisted, but the party lost badly in the December 1976 general elections and the cabinet was forced to resign.

After this, Fukuda formed a cabinet with the support of Ōhira. It is said that there had been a secret agreement between the two that Fukuda would step down in favor of Ōhira after a term of two years. However, Fukuda chose to run for a second term but was defeated in the primary of the party presidential race in November 1978 and had to resign as premier. The Tanaka-Ōhira alliance had been the stabilizing force within the LDP since 1972, but, due to public criticism of Tanaka's money scandal, Ōhira was not entirely able to be out in front until then.

However, Ōhira as well invited problems when he tried to introduce a general consumption tax at the time of the general elections of 1979, leading to the party's poor showing. The Fukuda, Miki, and Nakasone factions all called for his resignation, and at an extraordinary session of the Diet, Fukuda actually ran against Ōhira in the hopes to be named prime minister again. With the help of the New Liberal Club, a breakaway group of the LDP, Ōhira was barely able to overcome this crisis, known as the 40-Day Struggle. Nevertheless, in May 1980, the opposition parties submitted a motion of no confidence against the Ōhira cabinet in the Upper House, which passed due to the absence of members of the Fukuda and Miki factions and others who opposed Ōhira. The result was a general election again, but Ōhira died during the campaign due in part to his worsening health.

These factional battles were the result of these groups organizing as essentially combat brigades in an effort to make their leaders prime minister. However, these internal conflicts ended up weakening overall confidence in the LDP. Moreover, the years from 1974 to 1978 saw the largest recession in the postwar (until that time). As the economy became a slow growth one, the politics based on high economic growth no longer applied, and support for the LDP similarly and understandably dropped. (See Table 15.1.)

The era when the conservatives and reformists were roughly equal numerically paralleled this time. In June 1976, a group of party members split from the LDP and formed the New Liberal Club (NLC). The reformists, on the other hand, lacked appeal, and with the improvement in the economy beginning in 1978, a return to the conservatives was seen with a rise in support for the LDP. Although the LDP lost seats in the 1979 election due to the problem of the attempted introduction of the consumption tax and in 1983 with Tanaka's guilty verdict in the Lockheed Scandal in the courts and lost support due to the 40-Day Struggle, overall support for the LDP remained relatively high and stable.

The consolidation of identity as a member of the West

The developed industrialized countries were all challenged with the problem of stagflation after the Oil Crisis. The G6 Economic Summit was begun in 1975 to overcome this problem. Because the gathering focused on economic matters rather than on security and political issues, Japan's role naturally grew. Furthermore,

Table 15.1 Changes in Lower House representation, 1972–1986.

General Election	LDP	JSP	CGP	DSP	NLC	JCP	Total
No. 33 (December 1972)	271	118	29	19	n/a	38	491
No. 34 (December 1976)	249	123	55	29	17	17	511
No. 35 (October 1979)	248	107	57	35	4	39	511
No. 36 (June 1980)	284	107	33	32	12	29	511
No. 37 (December 1983)	250	112	58	38	(8)	26	511
No. 38 (July 1986)	300	85	56	26	(6)	26	512

Source: NLC became a caucus within the LDP by the early 1980s and formally dissolved in August 1986.

Liberal Democratic Party (LDP); Japan Socialist Party (JSP); Clean Government Party (CGP); Democratic Socialist Party (DSP); New Liberarl Club (NLC); Japan Communist Party (JCP)

Miki, Fukuda, and Ōhira all actively participated in the summit meetings. The summits also gave them an advantage when firming up their base within the party.

For example, in 1978 at the time of the Bonn Summit, Prime Minister Fukuda made an appeal about the importance of international cooperation in overcoming the recession. He explained the role that high economic growth rates for Japan, the United States, and Germany had for the global economy, much like a locomotive engine pulls the rest of the train (locomotive engine theory), and promised Japan would seek an annual growth rate of 7 percent. Using this international pledge and the global expectations toward Japan, Fukuda decided to run again for the party presidency. Using foreign policy issues for domestic political gain was common in prewar Japan, and, internationally, it had been rare in the previous decade-plus of the Ikeda-Satō years.

In any case, Japan's international role grew dramatically through these summits. The locomotive engine theory of growth was based on Japan's understanding of Europe's situation and was the first time since the Tripartite Pact (see Chapter 12) or since the time it sent a destroyer to the Mediterranean Sea during First World War that Japan was so directly involved in European matters.

It was during the Ōhira Cabinet that this identity of Japan as a member of the West grew from simple economic matters to the strategic realm. The genesis for this was the Iranian Islamic Revolution, the Second Oil Shock, and the Soviet invasion of Afghanistan, all in 1979.

In February that year, a revolution in Iran began, and in November, radical students demanding the handover of the former monarch, Muhammad Redā Shāh Pahlevī (1919–1980; on throne 1941–1979), overran the U.S. Embassy in Tehran and took American diplomats hostage. In response, U.S. President James E. Carter, Jr. (1924–; in office 1977–1981) placed strong sanctions on Iran, including the banning of its imports to the United States. However, Japanese trading firms saw the rise in petroleum prices as inevitable and purchased two-thirds of Iranian oil at a high price. It was this time when Secretary of State Cyrus R. Vance (1917–2002) criticized Japan's actions as "insensitive" to Foreign Minister Ōkita Saburō (1914–1993). This was an unusually strong criticism of an alliance partner. The Ōhira Cabinet quickly announced its support of the U.S. position, and the friction dissipated.

Shortly after this, the Soviet Union invaded Afghanistan. In response, the Ōhira Cabinet actively cooperated in the sanctions proposed by the United States against the Soviets, even joining in the boycott of the July 1980 Moscow Olympics. The public's interest in the Olympics was the highest it had been since the 1964 Tokyo Olympics, and the cabinet's decision for Japanese athletes not to participate was a crisis-filled one affecting the popularity of the administration, but Ōhira viewed participating in the sanctions as more important.

Ōhira was foreign minister at the time of the first Oil Crisis and struggled with the conflict between cooperation with the United States and securing natural resources for the country. In the challenging times of 1979–1980, Ōhira chose cooperation with the United States as the paramount objective. In the area of the global economy, cooperation with the West had shown impressive gains through the summits. However, in the area of strategic problems, cooperation among the Western states was more difficult for Japan's leaders as the subject had been taboo so long amid the pacifism of public opinion in the postwar period. Ōhira set out to address this problem.

However, Ōhira died suddenly during the election, and his successor, Suzuki Zenkō (1911–2004; in office July 1980–November 1982), from the same faction, was more focused on domestic issues. As a result, Japan's proactive international stance shown by Ōhira was put on a back burner under Suzuki. This became clear at the May 1981 bilateral summit meeting with U.S. President Ronald W. Reagan (1911–2004; in office 1981–1989) in Washington, D.C. After Suzuki returned to Tokyo, he stated that the U.S.-Japan security treaty did not imply a military alliance, causing consternation in bilateral relations. Foreign Minister Itō Masayoshi (1913–1994) even took responsibility for the imbroglio and resigned.

It was Suzuki's successor as prime minister, Nakasone (in office November 1982–November 1987), who continued with Ōhira's policies, positioning Japan firmly as a member of the West. Shortly after taking office, Nakasone traveled to South Korea to restart economic assistance, negotiations of which had taken a long time due to a variety of conditions and concerns on the Japanese side. After this, Nakasone went to the United States to meet with Reagan, developing a close relationship with him. In May, for example, at the G-7 Summit held in Williamsburg, Virginia, Nakasone took the initiative to rally the participants on the issue of the Soviet's Intermediate Nuclear Force by explaining that it concerned not only the nations of Europe but also of Asia. This proactive stance of Nakasone's was memorable for the other participants, who had been conditioned to expect Japan's leaders to be reactive on military and strategic matters.

A new international responsibility

The basic conditions for Japanese diplomacy were changing, however, around the time of the formation of the Nakasone cabinet. Japan was the first country to overcome the Second Oil Crisis, strengthening its economic structure in the process.

Moreover, because its trade surplus continued to grow, it was criticized by the United States and other nations. As a result, over the two years following the Plaza Accords of September 1985, the yen appreciated very quickly, going from 250 yen to the dollar to 125 yen. This high rate for the yen caused changes in Japan's manufacturing industry. Japan's GNP rose to 14 percent of the global economy, and its GNP on a per capita basis surpassed that of Americans to become the highest in the world. Even if this statistic of being the wealthiest group of people in the world did not necessarily match the feelings of the average Japanese citizen, it is an undeniable fact that Japan was a huge presence on the international scene. This was clearly a major development in tracing the modern history of Japan since the Meiji period.

Even with the rapid rise in the yen, Japan's trade surplus did not go down, and U.S. demands for Japan to open its markets continued to grow. Around this time in 1985, Mikhail Sergeyevich Gorbachev (1931–) became general secretary of the Communist Party of the Soviet Union and began reforms in reaction to which voices in the United States started describing Japan, not Soviet military power, as the biggest threat to the country. Furthermore, a revisionist debate started, with people calling Japan fundamentally and inherently different. Japan expanded its internal demand and opened its markets, but these efforts were not enough. Nakasone was successful, however, with privatizing Japan Railways and enjoyed high popular support. Furthermore, he had potential successors (Takeshita Noboru, 1924–2000; Abe Shintarō, 1924–1991; and Miyazawa Kiichi, 1919–2007) compete among themselves and thus was able to stay in power for five years, becoming, at the time, the third longest serving prime minister in the postwar after Satō and Yoshida.

The Takeshita cabinet, formed in November 1987, which succeeded Nakasone's, was a strong one party-wise, and Takeshita succeeded in introducing the consumption tax, which had been pending since the time of the Ōhira administration. It was passed in December 1988 and went into effect in April 1989. Moreover, in the area of foreign policy, Takeshita raised the issue of international contributions to peacekeeping, sending civilians in the summer of 1988 to United Nations' missions to broker a peace between Afghanistan and Pakistan, as well as to monitor the ceasefire between Iran and Iraq. While it was only two people, it was a new start for Japan.

However, in July 1988, Takeshita found himself in a tough situation when it became known he took stocks from the Recruit Company before they were publicly offered. The scandal was a result of the bubble economy and impacted almost all the major players in the LDP. It was a crisis not only for Takeshita and his cabinet but for the LDP as a whole.

Nineteen eighty-nine was a year of many challenges. On January 7, Emperor Hirohito (1901–1989; reigned 1926–1989), posthumously known as the Showa Tennō, passed away. In April, the consumption tax went into effect. That same month, amid the controversy of the Recruit Scandal, Takeshita resigned as prime minister while calling for political reform. The LDP, under his successor Prime Minister Uno Sōsuke (1921–1998), lost badly in the July Upper House election, and he resigned. It was the largest defeat in LDP history, and it was the first time for the LDP to lose its majority in the Upper House. Kaifu Toshiki (1931–), who succeeded him, became prime minister with the support of the Takeshita faction. It was very unusual for someone who was not even the head of a small faction to suddenly become premier, but this was because just about none of the better known faces of the LDP were acceptable to the voters at the time.

Later that fall, there were big changes internationally in East-West relations. Open demonstrations against Soviet domination in Eastern Europe grew, and in November, the Berlin Wall was torn down. Subsequently Gorbachev and U.S. President George H. W. Bush (1924–; in office 1989–1993) declared the Cold War over at a December summit on Malta.

While it appears there was no simple connection between these events, there was in fact a deeply close relationship between the end of LDP politics and that of the Cold War. During the Cold War, the LDP led Japan and helped it to develop and prosper as a junior partner of the United States amid the bilateral security relationship. However, that period had to end with the end of the Cold War. Yet this end did not necessarily or immediately mean the start of a new era. Japan entered a long period of economic stagnation and struggled with finding a role in international conflicts such as the Gulf Crisis and Gulf War. It is still seeking to clarify the path it wishes to take. The changes of 1989, in that sense, simply represented the start of a long inertia.

16　Japan's colonies and their fates

Before 1945

Modern Japan ruled over the following colonies. First, in 1895 it gained Taiwan through its victory in the First Sino-Japanese War. Then, following its 1905 victory in the Russo-Japanese War, it gained the southern half of Sakhalin from Russia as well as the right to lease the tip of the Liaodong Peninsula (consisting of Lushun, Dalian, and their surroundings, for a total of 3,462 square kilometers). Strictly speaking, the latter was not a colony but a leased territory. However, because these were the areas controlled by Japan within China, we should discuss it as a colony together with the South Manchuria Railway Company (Mantetsu) and the land attached to it. Next, it placed the Korean Peninsula under its control in 1910. After the First World War, Japan also obtained a League of Nations mandate over Germany's former South Sea islands holdings in the northern hemisphere. These became *de facto* Japanese colonies. Finally, Japan created Manchukuo in 1932. While Manchukuo had nominally declared independence from the Republic of China of its own volition in accordance with the desires of its inhabitants, this was merely a fiction; in truth, it was actually under Japanese administration.

Japanese rule over these colonies was very short-lived relative to that of the West over its colonies. The longest held, Taiwan, was possessed for fifty years and the shortest, Manchukuo, was controlled for just thirteen. And while Western colonies were located in areas remote from their home countries and were considerably different from them in terms of culture, all of Japan's colonies were located along its periphery and had relatively small cultural differences with Japan except for the South Sea Islands.

Looking at the population of each colony, Taiwan's population was 2,627,656 in 1896 (10,584 of whom were Japanese). This increased considerably over the course of its colonization, reaching 6,249,468 (including 368,221 Japanese) in 1941.

Japan created an administrative district called the Kwantung Leased Territory (*Kantōshū*) at the tip of the Liaodong Peninsula. Its population was 384,755 (including 16,613 Japanese) in 1906 and 1,273,526 (194,933 Japanese) in 1939. These figures also include those living in areas affiliated with the South Manchuria Railway Company, which had limited administrative authority.

Figure 16.1 Headquarters of the Government General of Korea. (Circa 1931. Photo provided by the *Mainichi Shimbun*.)

The population of Sakhalin was 12,361 in 1906 and 406,557 in 1941 (almost all of whom [405,826] were Japanese).

The population of Korea was 13,313,017 (171,543 Japanese) in 1910 and had effectively doubled by 1942, reaching 26,361,401 (752,823 Japanese).[1]

Taiwan

Japanese interest in Taiwan can be traced back to at least 1871, the year in which Ryūkyūan islanders were massacred after washing ashore on the island (as described in Chapter 4). The Qing Dynasty's position at this time was that, while Taiwan was Chinese territory, it lay outside the Chinese cultural sphere and China bore no responsibility for what occurred there. This position was, from the perspective of modern international law, arguably an abdication of responsibility, meaning that Taiwan was not actually Chinese territory. This consequently led to arguments that Japan could potentially take possession of Taiwan.

Afterward, when Japan was victorious in the First Sino-Japanese War, it gained Taiwan as a foothold toward later southern expansion. This is not to say that a concrete vision of such expansion was necessarily already in place at the time, however.

Taiwan was, from the Chinese perspective, a "barbarian" land. It had come under the control of first the Dutch and then Zheng Cheng-gong (1624–1662), a former Ming vassal, in the seventeenth century, and Qing control of the island only began in 1683. The dispatch of Japanese troops to Taiwan in 1874 awakened China to the necessity of having real control over the island, however, and Taiwan Province was created in 1885 (the island had previously been part of Fujian Province). Even after this point, however, Chinese rule did not extend to either the native population or the eastern part of the island.

The Japanese also found Taiwan to be a difficult territory to govern. It established the Government General of Taiwan (*Taiwan Sōtokufu*) and limited the position of governor-general to active duty flag officers. The first three men to hold the position were unsuccessful, however (Katsura Tarō, the second of these, did not actually assume the post and was replaced after four months); Japanese rule over the island only became stable after Kodama Gentarō became the fourth governor-general in 1898 and appointed Gotō Shimpei as his head of civilian affairs.

Gotō was a former physician who had helped administer public health in Japan while serving as the head of the Home Ministry's public health bureau. He had adopted the "principles of biology" (*seibutsugaku no gensoku*) as his motto; that is, he believed it was necessary to respond flexibly, in accordance with actual local conditions, when governing. This he contrasted with the "principles of physics," that is, applying universal principles uniformly. He felt it was abhorrent to have a situation where "the surgery was successful but the patient died," that is, where process was emphasized over results. He also put the police rather than the military at the forefront of the pacification of Taiwan, adopting an approach rooted in gentle persuasion rather than the use of force.

One of Gotō's greatest successes was the eradication of opium addiction in Taiwan. He advocated a gradual prohibition of opium; through a policy of providing high-quality opium to serious addicts, providing treatment for less severe cases, and strictly prohibiting the drug for nonusers, opium use fell gradually and was ultimately eliminated.

He also undertook a thorough land survey of Taiwan. Land ownership rights in Taiwan had been complicated; by thoroughly investigating them and making ownership definite, he made it possible to levy taxes and create new businesses.

Finally, he poured his energies into improving Taiwan's infrastructure, undertaking large-scale urban planning in Taipei, expanding the water supply and sewage networks and laying down roads and railways throughout the island. This was accompanied by a remarkable expansion of schools and hospitals. He also worked to improve the sugar refining industry.

Japan's colonial system was reformed in 1919 (as will be touched on when discussing the situation in Korea), and civilians served as governor-general from then on until 1936. The position was later returned to the hands of military officers under the rationale that Japan was facing emergencies.

That the post was left to civilians shows that the Japanese government did not feel it was necessary to be coercive in Taiwan; it felt no sense of danger regarding the island. Despite this, oppression and rebellions are an unavoidable part of colonial administration, and the Wushe Incident (a revolt by some of the island's native population) broke out in October 1930. Approximately 700 natives lost their lives in this incident (as did about 200 Japanese). The governor-general and other officials resigned afterward. This was then followed by another conflict (known as the Second Wushe Incident), which was fought between those natives who had revolted against the Japanese and those who had cooperated. The roots of these incidents can be found in the insulting behavior of the Japanese toward the native population and their discriminatory views toward them.

Korea

The Japanese colonization of Korea was, above all else, motivated by security concerns. It was not pushed by a desire for colonists, natural resources, or markets. Throughout the Meiji period, there was a pervasive understanding among the contemporary Japanese elite that Japan would be endangered should the Korean Peninsula fall into the hands of a hostile power.

China was seen as the hostile power most likely to gain control of Korea, with Russia as the next most likely. In an attempt to turn its traditional suzerain relationship with Korea into something more suitable to the modern international order, China was trying to strengthen its hold over the peninsula. The Imo Incident (1882) and Gapsin Coup (1884) occurred as it was doing so, and in both cases Chinese power overwhelmed the Japanese (see Chapter 7).

Japan successfully drove Chinese influence from Korea with its victory in the First Sino-Japanese War in 1895. Seeing Japan submit to the Triple Intervention, however, the Korean royal court now attempted to turn to Russia. Russian influence in the country increased, and the Korean king and crown prince resided in the Russian legation for a year from February 1896.

Later, as Russia worked to entrench itself in Manchuria, it appeared that a *modus vivendi* under which Manchuria would be Russian and Korea would be Japanese might be possible. This compromise ultimately failed to come to fruition, however, and Japan went to war with Russia. Korean independence was the primary goal of the Russo-Japanese War.

Japan signed the Japan-Korea Protocol of 1904 during the war to ensure Korean cooperation. And, once the war had ended, Japan secured British, American, and Russian acknowledgment of its preeminent position in Korea through diplomatic moves such as the renewal of the Taft-Katsura Agreement, the Anglo-Japanese Alliance, and the Portsmouth Peace Treaty.

With the war over and a peace treaty concluded, Japan signed the Japan-Korea Treaty with Korea in November 1905 and thereby gained control of Korea's diplomatic and military affairs. It then established the Office of the Resident-General of Korea (*Kankoku Tōkanfu*). Meiji founding father Itō Hirobumi was appointed as the first resident-general and expressly given command over Japan's military units in Korea. When Itō, who had already left office, was assassinated by the Korean independence activist An Chung-gun in 1909, it led to the Japan's annexation of Korea the following year (see Chapter 8). International criticism of the annexation was, by modern standards, surprisingly scarce. Such actions were not regarded as particularly unusual by the imperialist world of the day.

While there was a certain amount of Korean resistance against the Japanese annexation in the form of so-called righteous armies (*uibyeong*), led by former members of the disbanded Korean military, this had been suppressed by about 1914. There was also another Korean movement, known as the *Isshinkai* (Iljin-hoe), which sought the establishment of an equal confederation between Japan and Korea rather than an annexation and collected a considerable number of signatures in support of this. As Itō had actually been opposed to annexation, his assassination in 1909 effectively strengthened the position of those seeking annexation.

Following the annexation, the Office of the Resident-General was replaced by the Government General of Korea (*Chōsen Sōtokufu*). For defense purposes, the position of governor-general was limited to active duty flag officers. The first man to serve in the position was General (later Marshal) Terauchi Masatake, who also held the position of war minister.

Including Terauchi, eight men were appointed as governor-general (one of whom served in the position twice). Of these, Terauchi, Saitō Makoto, and Koiso Kuniaki (1880–1950) would go on to serve as prime minister. Another, Abe Nobuyuki, was appointed governor-general after having served as prime minister. And, while this was ultimately blocked by the army, Ugaki Kazushige had been ordered by the emperor to form a government. The post of governor-general was extremely important politically.

From the army's perspective, the role of the Korean Peninsula was to guard against Russia and support the Japanese advance into China. This view was not necessarily supported by the entire country, however. A proposed plan to expand the army by adding two divisions to the Korean Peninsula was a major point of contention from 1912 to 1915, disrupting Japanese politics and leading to the fall of three governments (see Chapter 9). The administration of Korea served a focal point for the struggles between the army and its opponents.

In 1918, at the tail end of the First World War, American President Woodrow Wilson (1856–1924, in office 1913–1921) announced his Fourteen Points in which he extolled the spirit of self-determination. This had a major impact on Korea and helped spark the large-scale independence movement known as the March 1st Movement in 1919. The Government General of Korea cracked down on the movement, causing considerable casualties.

While it is difficult to grasp the entire scope of the event, one researcher estimated that there were 7,509 deaths and 46,948 arrests.[2] In fact, however, according to police and Government General records, on the other hand, 12,668 were arrested and sent to the prosecutor; more than half of these (6,417) were actually prosecuted. Of those tried, 3,967 were found guilty, none of whom were sentenced to death, life imprisonment, or a term of fifteen years or more. Only eighty were sentenced to terms of three years or more.

The March 1st Movement had major repercussions. It was seen in Japan as a failure of oppressive, army-centered administration, and Prime Minister Hara Takashi, seeing a good opportunity to reduce the army's power, eliminated the requirement that governor-generals be active duty flag officers in 1919, thereby allowing the appointment of civilians. Admiral Saitō Makoto was brought back on to active duty from the reserves and appointed as the new governor-general.

At the time of Saitō's appointment, considerable changes were being planned for Korea. In what came to be referred to as his cultural rule (*bunka seiji*), there was a move toward more normal governance and away from reliance on the use of the military police. Meiji founding father Saionji Kinmochi toasted Saitō at a banquet celebrating his appointment with the words, "I have high hopes for your civilized rule, Your Excellency." It was during Saitō's administration that *hangul*-language newspapers such as the *Chosun Ilbo* began publication.

There were calls among Japanese intellectuals and journalists to abolish cultural assimilation policies in Korea and to grant it self-government or even independence.

Although much of the administration of Korea was undertaken with an emphasis on security, the stabilization of government, development of natural resources, and a certain degree of civilized rule also brought about an increase in the public welfare.

The average lifespan increased from twenty-four to forty-eight. The literacy rate had been about 30 percent prior to annexation, and Chinese was used for formal writing; *hangul* became accepted for official letters under Japanese rule, and the literacy rate increased. There was also considerable industrial development, although the Korean economy was folded into that of Japan.

One of the tragedies of the period was the massacre of Koreans in Japan in the wake of the 1923 Great Kanto Earthquake. Stirred up by wild rumors that Koreans were attacking and panicked by the earthquake, a number of Japanese formed vigilante groups and killed Koreans. While the number of victims was estimated shortly afterward as numbering in the thousands, the exact figure is unknown as there were many cases of duplicate reports, people who were mistakenly assumed dead but were actually alive, and people who had actually fallen victim to the earthquake rather than mobs. Still, given that the police sent out condolence payments to hundreds of people, the number of victims is believed to have been higher than that.

Despite this event, the flow of Koreans to Japan continued, as did the development of the Korean economy and the increase in standard of living. Japan's rule over Korea became harsher in the 1930s, however, especially as the Second Sino-Japanese War worsened in 1938. The Japanization of Korea became more emphasized, with policies introduced promoting the adoption of Japanese names and abolishing Korean language education. It was also during this period that the procurement of the so-called comfort women began, a practice that left a massive scar in Korean-Japanese relations that has lasted to this day.

Manchuria

Precisely speaking, Manchukuo was not a Japanese colony; it was a puppet state.

Manchukuo's origins lay in the rights that Japan had taken from Russia in 1905 after the Russo-Japanese War. As mentioned earlier, these were primarily related to Lushun, Dalian, and Mantetsu.

Russia had only had the right to lease the tip of the Liaodong Peninsula for a twenty-five-year period from 1898, however, meaning that Japan's lease would thus expire in 1923.

In January 1915, the Ōkuma Shigenobu Cabinet issued the so-called Twenty-One Demands to China. While these included a variety of items, they were fundamentally about strengthening Japanese rights in Manchuria. Extending Japan's right to the Kwantung Leased Territory, which had fewer than ten years remaining, was a particularly important demand (as was inheriting German rights in Shandong Province).

This goal was achieved via the Treaty Concerning Southern Manchuria and Eastern Inner Mongolia (1915) and backed at the Washington Conference (1921–1922).

China steadily increased its nationalist claims, however, and by about 1928 it had begun calling for the return of Lushun, Dalian, and Mantetsu. It also began pursuing policies intended to counter Mantetsu.

In response, a group calling for the seizure of Manchuria through force came to prominence within the Japanese army; in an attempt to secure Japanese control of southern Manchuria, Kōmoto Daisaku of the Kwantung Army set off an explosive along the Mantetsu line in 1928, killing Zhang Zuolin. While this scheme ended in failure, the Kwantung Army caused the Liutiaohu Incident three years later; falsely claiming that Chinese had bombed the Mantetsu line, they used this to justify invading Manchuria in the name of maintaining order. This invasion is known as the Manchurian Incident (see Chapter 11).

Manchukuo was consequently established in March 1932. This state extolled the virtues of the five races in harmony (*gozoku kyōwa*; this referred to the Han Chinese, Manchu, Mongol, Koreans, and Japanese), although actual power was, of course, held by the Japanese. Japan's recognition of Manchukuo caused it to come into conflict with the international community, and it ultimately left the League of Nations in 1933 as a result. The Manchurian Incident was the first major blow to the post–First World War international order.

Development proceeded in Manchukuo under the guidance of the army. The heavy and chemical industries were expanded. At the center of this effort stood the new generation of bureaucrats that had risen with the decline of party politics. One of the most influential of these was Kishi Nobusuke; wielding great power with the support of the army, he became vice-minister of the Ministry of Commerce and Industry in 1939 and later served as commerce minister in Tōjō Hideki's government. In this respect, politics in Manchukuo were headed in the opposite direction of Japan.

Numerous emigrants were also sent to the Manchukuo border to serve as a front line against the Soviets. They would meet a cruel fate following Japan's defeat; many were killed, robbed of their possessions, or interned in Siberia.

After 1945

After the defeat

Manchuria experienced the greatest change. While the Soviet-Japanese Neutrality Pact was still in force, the Soviet Union declared war on Japan and invaded Manchukuo. Many Japanese were killed, and 650,000 soldiers and civilians were forcibly transported to Siberia; of these, some 10 percent would die of starvation or the cold.

The Sino-Soviet Treaty of Friendship and Alliance was signed on August 14, 1945, the day before Japan accepted the Potsdam Declaration. While this treaty returned Manchuria to China, it also granted the Soviet Union privileges in Lushun and Dalian and rights over the management of Mantetsu and the Chinese Eastern Railway. The rationale given for this was the need to prepare against a potential Japanese attack. This can be considered a restoration of the state of affairs that had existed from 1898 to the Russo-Japanese War. Whenever possible, the Soviets also removed the heavy industrial facilities that the Japanese had established in Manchuria and had them transported back to the Soviet Union.

The People's Republic of China (PRC) was founded in 1949, and the Sino-Soviet Treaty of Friendship, Alliance, and Mutual Assistance was signed in 1950. This treaty eliminated the Soviet special privileges in Lushun, Dalian, and those concerning the railways. The independence of Mongolia, which the Republic of China had not recognized, was upheld in line with Soviet demands. This treaty would later essentially exist in name only as the Sino-Soviet split became more serious. It expired in 1980.

Meanwhile, the northeast was developed into China's industrial region. Recently, it has also become the region in most need of reform, however, as changes are made to state-owned enterprises. The region has a deep interest in Japan; nearly half of all Chinese researchers on Japan originate from the northeast.

Postwar Taiwan

American, Britain, and China decided at the 1943 Cairo Conference that Taiwan would be returned to the Republic of China, and the Potsdam Declaration stated that "the terms of the Cairo Declaration shall be carried out."

With the Japanese defeat in 1945, the Chinese military moved into and recovered Taiwan. In 1949, however, Chiang Kai-shek, having been defeated in the Chinese Civil War, fled to Taiwan and took it over with Taipei as its capital.

The standard of living in the Republic of China at the time was far lower than what Taiwan had reached under Japanese rule. To make matters worse, the Chiang government operated as a dictatorship, declaring martial law so as to be able to prepare to recover the Chinese mainland. A system was put in place under which those who had fled from the mainland (*waishengren*) enjoyed special privileges. Given these circumstances, it is not difficult to understand that the Taiwanese were nostalgic about the time of Japanese rule.

The issue of which government would represent China, the Republic of China in Taiwan or the PRC on the mainland, was a major problem. Prime Minister Yoshida Shigeru wanted to leave Japan room for improving relations with the mainland but was pressured by the fiercely anticommunist United States into choosing Taiwan. Japan acceded to this, which the Republic of China repaid with a *de facto* renunciation of compensation.

Although it soon became clear that regaining control of the mainland would be a difficult task for the Republic of China, America's anticommunist policies meant that it enjoyed the recognition of the international community, including China's seat on the UN Security Council. It also strengthened its economic ties with Japan and achieved a considerable amount of economic growth.

When America moved to improve its relationship with the PRC in 1971, however, Japan did likewise. It restored diplomatic relations with China in 1972, ahead of the United States. And when America recognized the PRC in 1979, Taiwan became increasingly isolated.

In the meantime, Chiang Kai-shek died and was succeeded by his son, Chiang Ching-kuo (1910–1988). The new president chose Lee Teng-hui (1923–), a native-born Taiwanese who had studied in Japan, to serve as his vice president and embarked on ambitious reforms. The special privileges of the *waishengren* were reduced in 1988, and when the first national election in Taiwanese history was held in 1996, Lee Teng-hui was elected. The Democratic Progressive Party (DPP) won the presidency in the 2000 and 2004 elections, and the Kuomintang (KMT) won in 2008 and 2012; the DPP won again in 2016. Taiwan has thus become a country where government change is achieved through elections.

At the same time, in the face of China's massive economic development, Taiwan has been severely limited in the ways it can function as a state. And, amidst all this, a Taiwanese identity is in the process of maturing.

Postwar Korea

The Allies didn't make any definite plans for the Korean Peninsula after the war. It had been agreed in the Cairo Declaration that Korea would become independent, but no agreements were made regarding how, specifically, that was to happen or what form of government would be put in place.

It was decided that, for the time being, the Soviets would be stationed in the north and the Americans in the south and that a joint election would be held at some later point. Concerned about the north's strength, America rejected the joint election, however, and the Republic of Korea (South Korea) was founded in August 1948. Rhee Syngman (1875–1965), who had worked in America for Korean independence, became the country's president. The Democratic People's Republic of Korea (North Korea) was then founded in September with Kim Il-sung, who had worked for Korean independence in Manchuria, as its leader.

Kim launched an attack on the south in June 1950 with the intention of unifying the peninsula through force (the Korean War). The Soviet Union and China were not favorably inclined toward this but ultimately tacitly accepted it. The North

Korean army advanced rapidly and drew near to Pusan. In response, America successfully convinced the UN Security Council to adopt a resolution recognizing North Korea as an aggressor and forming a United Nations military force to oppose it. This was made possible by the long-term absence of the Soviet Union from the Security Council over the issue of Chinese representation; it is the only time that the UN has been able to organize a UN military force.

With MacArthur as its commander, the UN forces (which were primarily an American force, although many nations contributed) landed west of Seoul at Incheon in September and pushed north until it had cornered the North Korean forces against the Yalu River. Viewing this with apprehension, Mao Zedong (1893–1976) decided to have China enter the war. Pushing south using human wave tactics, communist forces again crossed the 38th parallel and gained control of Seoul.

The Americans counterattacked, and the war entered a stalemate. An armistice was signed in 1953. The war had greatly devastated Korea's land.

For a time, North Korea was considered the more advanced of the two Koreas. One reason for this is that much of Japan's colonial investment had gone into the north, with the south generally regarded as agricultural.

South Korea's development began after Park Chung-hee (1917–1979) became president, signed the Treaty on Basic Relations between Japan and the Republic of Korea in 1965, and began pursuing a so-called developmental dictatorship.

Concluding the treaty took fourteen years; even so, the two governments still needed to push through the remaining domestic opposition to finalize it. Particularly contentious issues included the question of whether the 1910 Japan-Korea Annexation Treaty had ever been valid, the ownership of Takeshima, and compensation. An agreement was reached over compensation under which Japan provided a $300 million grant, $200 million in loans, and more than $300 million in private loans. These were provided in the form of economic cooperation (quasi reparations) rather than compensation. The contemporary South Korean national budget was $350 million; no other former colony has ever received economic assistance on such a scale.

The Park administration continued until 1979, achieving the economic growth referred to as the Miracle on the Han River. While military administrations such as that of Chun Doo-hwan (1931–) would continue to hold office after Park, in late 1987, Roh Tae-woo (1932–) ran for and won the presidency. Roh had a military background but ran for office as a civilian. A democratic system has been in place in Korea ever since. This occurred at roughly the same time that democracy was also taking hold in Taiwan.

South Korea had a per capita annual income of about $105 in 1965, making it poorer than Sub-Saharan African nations. The Korean War was a major reason why. Its per capita income is now about $28,000. While there are many former colonies in the world, only the United States, Australia, and Canada have experienced the same degree of postindependence development as South Korea.

On the other hand, North Korea continued with its system of extreme military dictatorship; the contrast between it and the south is striking.

There are many similarities and differences between South Korea and Taiwan. Similarities include their pursuit of development via developmental dictatorships, the framework provided by the various systems put in place during their time as Japanese colonies, their close relationships with Japan, and their contemporaneous democratization.

One difference is that, while Taiwan is pro-Japanese, Japan's relationship with South Korea has been a difficult one. The numbers of victims from the colonial period are not that different between the two countries, numbering in the tens of thousands in both cases if those who participated and died during the war as imperial subjects are excluded. Compared to the roughly 200,000 who died in the American subjugation of the Philippines between 1899 to 1902, this is a relatively small number.

There are a number of reasons for this difference, but the basic difference between the two is that there was little in the way of indigenous culture and tradition in Taiwan, and Japan's rule of the island was undertaken in a flexible, enlightened manner (as represented by Gotō Shimpei). In Korea, on the other hand, Japanese rule was oppressive due to military demands, and the country had long-held traditions and a long history. There are other reasons as well, but they won't be covered here.

Briefly turning to Japan's other former colonies, southern Sakhalin became part of the Soviet Union and later Russia. And as for Japan's Pacific islands, the Federated States of Micronesia, the Marshall Islands, and Palau became independent states; the Northern Marianas have remained American territory but maintain friendly relations with Japan.

Postwar Japan and its former colonies

In the 1920s, Ishibashi Tanzan, a journalist who later became prime minister, was thoroughly critical of Japan's colonial rule. While he had been critical of the Twenty-One Demands in 1915 as well, it was only after the First World War that he made his arguments more explicit. His criticism was based less on idealism than on fundamental realism.

Ishibashi calculated the amount of investment that Japan had put into ruling Korea and the management of Manchuria and Japan's other colonies (in a broad sense) and thought that the returns it had received were extremely low. He felt that administering colonies was meaningless from an economic standpoint. And in terms of strategic importance, he rejected claims that the Korean Peninsula served as Japan's first line of defense, asserting that the Sea of Japan was sufficient. In response to the claim that Japan was overpopulated and needed colonies, he argued that developing export-oriented industries would support more population than colonization would, needless to say that colonization would cause friction with other nations. In short, he called for a "small Japanism" (*shōnihonshugi*).

The foreign policy commentator Kiyosawa Kiyoshi put forth a similar argument. Kiyosawa, who had experience as an immigrant living in America, opposed emigration, arguing that emigration to places with low standards of living was unfeasible in the absence of a considerable amount of state backing. He also pointed out that much of the economic efforts undertaken by Japanese in Korea and Manchuria had been achieved with government support rather than on their own basis. Such efforts were not, in other words, firmly rooted. He felt that this was in sharp contrast to Japanese emigration to America, which had been undertaken without any government backing and had taken hold through the efforts of the emigrants themselves.

While they did not express themselves as clearly as Ishibashi and Kiyosawa, a certain number of other intellectuals and politicians with similar views existed in the 1920s. Japan as a whole had attempted to develop through economic means, but this had been made impossible by the domestic rise of the army and the destruction of the international economic order that began with the Great Depression.

Ishibashi immediately welcomed Japan's surrender (Kiyosawa had died during the war). He believed that a Japan free of the military and unburdened by colonies could rebuild and develop. Yoshida Shigeru made similar arguments as well. And, with America's now unwavering commitment to South Korea due to the Korean War, Japan's exposure to a threat from the north via the Korean Peninsula was eliminated. Ishibashi's words thus became reality.

Notes

1 Sōmuchō Kanshū, Nihon Tōkei, and Kyōkai Henshū, *Nihon Chōki Tōkei Sōran* (General Survey of Long Term Statistics), Vol. 1 (*Kokudo, Gyōsei Chiiki, Jinkō, Rōdō* [Territory, Jurisdictional Area, Population, and Labor]) (Tokyo: Nihon Tōkei Kyōkai, 1987), pp. 58–65.

2 Park Eun-sik, trans. by Gang Deok-sang, *Chōsen Dokuritsu Undō no Kesshi* (The Bloody History of the Korean Independence Movement), Vol. 1 (Tokyo: Heibonsha Tōyō Bunko, 1972), p. 183. This book is often quoted as a reference, but its sources are questionable. Park himself has admitted that the number of victims and other data are all based only on what he heard, and thus it is unclear if the numbers here are exaggerated and, if so, to what degree. I only cite this book to show the higher end of the "estimates." For other estimates, see Kondō Kenichi, ed., *Banzai Sōjō Jiken (San-Ichi Undō)* (Long Live the March First Movement), Vol. 1 (Tokyo: Yūhō Kyōkai Chōsen Shiryō Hensankai, 1964), pp. 103, 121, 174; and Yamabe Kentarō, "Nihon Teikokushugi to Shokuminchi (Japanese Imperialism and Its Colonies)," in Ienaga Saburō, et al,. eds., *Iwanami Kōza Nihon Rekishi 19 Gendai 2* (Iwanami's Japan History Course, Vol. 19, Modern Day 2) (Tokyo: Iwanami Shoten, 1963), p. 240.

Bibliography

This book covers more than 150 years of Japanese history in approximately 200 pages. But it really only scratches the surface. For details on what happened beneath the surface, I prepared the following bibliography of relevant books in Japanese and English. Following a list of a general reference books and those that cover the theme of modern Japanese history, foreign policy, and politics, I then introduce approximately twenty books per chapter for further reading. For books that are related to two or more chapters, I introduce the book in the list for the chapter that it is most relevant or comes earliest period-wise. Please be aware that, in this case, I do not reintroduce the book in a later list, although it may still be relevant. I have introduced books and writings that are highly specialized but have also tried to list as many that are more general in nature but are backed by solid evidence. Where the books have been translated into English, I have attempted to provide the English title and publisher in place of the Japanese. I also included books and writings from the respective periods written by journalists and other observers or by the participants at the time in the form of, for example, treatises and memoirs. These period works ably articulate what was happening at the time. In order to make the acquisition of the books in this bibliography easier to acquire, I have sought to list, in addition to the original version, where the older works have been reissued or revised, when that occurred, and which publisher has brought out the newer version.

Reference books

Gaimushō, Gaikōshiryōkan, Gaikōshi Jiten, and Hensan Iinkaihen. *Shinpan Nihon Gaikōshi Jiten* (New Japanese Diplomatic History Dictionary) (Tokyo: Yamakawa Shuppansha, 1992).

Hunter, Janet E. *Concise Dictionary of Modern Japanese History* (Berkeley: University of California Press, 1984).

Itō, Takashi, and Momose, Takashi, eds. *Jiten Shōwasen Zenki no Nihon: Seido to Jittai* (Dictionary on Prewar Showa Japan: Institutions and the Actual Situation) (Tokyo: Yoshikawa Kōbunkan, 1990).

Iwanami, Shoten Henshūbuhen. *Kindai Nihon Sōgō Nenpyō* (Comprehensive Chronology of Modern Japan), 4th ed. (Tokyo: Iwanami Shoten, 2001).

Momose, Takashi, ed. *Jiten Shōwasen Zenki no Nihon: Senryō to Kaikaku* (Dictionary on Prewar Showa Japan: Institutions and the Actual Situation) (Tokyo: Yoshikawa Kōbunkan, 1995).

Overall works

Gordon, Andrew. *A Modern History of Japan: From Tokugawa Times to the Present*, 3rd ed. (London: Oxford University Press, 2013).

Ikeda, Kiyoshi. *Nihon no Kaigun* (Japan's Navy), Vols. 1 & 2 (Tokyo: Gakūshū Kenkyūsha, 2002, originally published by Shiseidō, 1966).

Iriye, Akira. *Nihon no Gaikō: Meiji Ishin kara Gendai Made* (Japanese Diplomacy: From the Meiji Restoration to Today) (Tokyo: Chūkō Shinsho, 1966).

Jansen, Marius B. *The Making of Modern Japan* (Cambridge, MA: Harvard University Press, 2000).

Masumi, Junnosuke. *Japanese Politics, 1945–1955* (Berkeley: University of California, 1985).

Neumann, William L. *America Encounters Japan: From Perry to MacArthur* (Baltimore: Johns Hopkins University Press, 1963).

Pyle, Kenneth B. *The Making of Modern Japan* (Lexington, MA: D. C. Heath and Co., 1978).

Suetake, Yoshiya, and Takeda, Tomomi, ed. *Nihon Seitōshi* (A History of Japanese Political Parties) (Tokyo: Yoshikawa Kōbunkan, 2011).

Tobe, Ryōichi. *Nihon no Kindai 9 Gyakusetu no Guntai* (Modern Japan 9: The Paradoxical Military) (Tokyo: Chūō Kōronsha, 1998).

Tsuji, Kiyoaki, and Hayashi, Shigeru, ed. *Nihon Naikakushiroku* (The Historical Record of Japanese Cabinets), Vol. 6 (Tokyo: Daiichi Hōki Shuppan, 1981).

Uchida, Kenzō, Kinbara Samon, and Furuya Tetsuo, eds. *Nihon Gikaishiroku* (A Historical Record of Japanese Parliament) (Tokyo: Daiichi Hōki Shuppan, 1990).

Wang, Yun-sheng (Suehiro Shigeo, ed., trans. by Nagano Isao and Hatano Kanichi). *Nicchū Gaikō Rokujūnenshi* (Tokyo: Ryūkei Shosha, 1987, originally published by Kensetusha as *Nisshi Gaikō Rokujūnenshi*, 1936).

Preface

Carr, Edward H. *What Is History?* (London: Vintage, 1967).

Elton, Geoffrey R. *The Practice of History*, 2nd ed. (Indianapolis: Wiley-Blackwell, 1991).

Huntington, Samuel P. *The Soldier and the State: The Theory and Politics of Civil-Military Relations* (Cambridge, MA: Harvard University Press, 1957).

Kennedy, Paul. *The Rise and Fall of the Great Powers* (London: Vintage, 1989).

Vagts, Alfred. *A History of Militarism: Civilian and Military* (Santa Barbara, CA: Greenwood Press, 1981).

Chapter 1

Bellah, Robert. *Tokugawa Religion* (New York: Free Press, 1985).

Boulding, Kenneth. *A Premier on Social Dynamics: History as Dialectics and Development* (New York: Free Press, 1970).

Cipolla, Carlo M. *Guns, Sails, and Empires: Technological Innovation and the Early Phases of European Expansion, 1400–1700* (New York: Sunflower University Press, 1985).

Dore, Ronald P. *Education in Tokugawa Japan* (Berkeley: University of California Press, 1972).

Dore, Ronald P. *The Diploma Disease: Education, Qualification and Development* (Berkeley: University of California Press, 1976).

Fujita, Satoru. *Bakumatsu no Tennō* (The Emperor at the End of the Tokugawa Period) (Tokyo: Kōdansha Gakujutsu Bunko, 1994).

Hayami, Akira. *Rekishi Jinkōgaku de Mita Nihon* (Japan as Seen from Historical Population Studies) (Tokyo: Bungei Shunjū, 2001).

Hayami, Akira, and Miyamoto, Matao, eds. *Keizai Shakai no Seiritsu, 17–18 Seiki Nihon Keizaishi 1* (The Development of Economic Society in the 17–18th Centuries, Vol. 1, Japan Economic History Series) (Tokyo: Iwanami Shoten, 1988).

Hirano, Satoshi. *Daishin Teikoku to Chūka no Konmei Kōbō no Sekaishi 17* (The Great Qing Dynasty and China's Chaos World History on the Rise and Fall [of Empires] 17) (Tokyo: Kōdansha Gakujutsu Bunko, 2007).

Jansen, Marius B., ed. *Changing Japanese Attitudes Toward Modernization* (Princeton, NJ: Princeton University Press, 1965).

Karube, Tadashi. *Ishin Kakumei e no Michi* (The Road to the Restoration Revolution) (Tokyo: Shinchōsha, 2017).

Kito, Hiroshi. *Jinkō kara Yomu Nihon no Rekishi* (Japanese History as Seen from Its Population) (Tokyo: Kōdansha Gakujutsu Bunko, 2000, originally published by PHP Kenkyūsho as *Nihon Nisennen no Jinkōshi* [Japan's Population History in 2000], 1983).

Parker, Geoffrey. *The Military Revolution: Military Innovation and the Rise of the West, 1500–1800*, 2nd ed. (London: Cambridge University Press, 1996).

Passin, Herbert. *Society and Education in Japan* (Tokyo: Kodansha International, 1983).

Shinbo, Hiroshi, and Saitō, Osamu, eds. *Kindai Seichō no Shidō* (The Beginning of Modern Growth), *Nihon Keizaishi*, Vol. 2 (Tokyo: Iwanami Shoten, 1989).

Toby, Ronald P. *State and Diplomacy in Early Modern Japan: Asia in the Development of the Tokugawa Bakufu* (Princeton, NJ: Princeton University Press, 1984).

Watanabe, Hiroshi. *Higashi Ajia no Ōken to Shisō* (Royal Prerogative and Political Thought in East Asia) (Tokyo: University of Tokyo Press, 1997).

Watanabe, Hiroshi. *Nihon Seijishisōshi, 17–19 Seiki* (The History of Japanese Political Thought from the 17–19th Centuries) (Tokyo: University of Tokyo Press, 2010).

Weber, Max, trans. by Guenther Roth and Claus Wittich. *Economy and Society* (Berkeley: University of California Press, 1996, originally published in 1922).

Chapter 2

Alcock, Rutherford. *The Capital of the Tycoon: A Narrative of a Three Years' Residence in Japan* (New York: Harper & Brothers, 1863).

Craig, Albert M. *Choshu in the Meiji Restoration* (Cambridge, MA: Harvard University Press, 1961).

Doi, Ryōzō. *Kanrinmaru Umi o Wataru* (The Kanrin Maru Sails the Oceans) (Tokyo: Chūkō Bunko, 1998, originally published by Miraisha, 1992).

Haga, Tōru. *Taikun no Shisetsu: Bakumatsu Nihonjin no Seiō Taiken* (The Tycoon's Delegation: The Western Experience of Japanese at the End of the Tokugawa Period) (Tokyo: Chūkō Shinsho, 1968).

Iechika, Yoshiki. *Bakumatsu no Chōtei: Wakaki Kōmei Tei to Takatsukasa Kampaku* (The Imperial Court at the End of the Tokugawa Era: The Young Emperor Kōmei and the Regent Takatasukasa) (Tokyo: Chūkō Gyōsho, 2007).

Iechika, Yoshiki. *Saigō Takamori: Hito o Aite ni Sezu, Ten o Aite ni Seyo* (Saigō Takamori: Not Worrying About What Other People Think but Only About What Heaven Commands) (Kyoto: Minerva Shobō, 2017).

Inoue, Isao. *Ōsei Fukko Keio Sannen Jūnigatsu Nichi no Seihen* (Restoring the Monarchy: The December 9, 1867 Political Change in Government) (Tokyo: Chūkō Shinsho, 1991).

Inoue, Isao, ed. *Kaikoku to Bakumatsu no Dōran Nihon no Jidaishi 20* (The Opening of Japan and the Upheaval at the End of the Tokugawa Period Japanese Period History 20) (Tokyo: Yoshikawa Kōbunkan, 2004).

Ishii, Takashi. *Meiji Ishin no Butaiura Dai Niban* (Behind the Scenes of the Meiji Restoration) (Tokyo: Iwanami Shinsho, 1975, originally published in 1960).

Jansen, Marius B. *Sakamoto Ryoma and the Meiji Restoration* (New York: Columbia University Press, 1995).

Katō, Yūzō. *Bakumatsu Gaikō to Kaikoku* (Diplomacy at the End of the Tokugawa Years and the Opening of the Country) (Tokyo: Chikuma Shinsho, 2004).

Matsuzawa, Hiroaki. *Kindai Nihon no Keizai to Seiyō Keiken* (The Formation of Modern Japan and the Western Experience) (Tokyo: Iwanami Shoten, 1993).

Mitani, Hiroshi, trans. by David Noble. *Escape from Impasse: The Decision to Open Japan* (Tokyo: International House of Japan, 2006).

Mitani, Hiroshi. *Meiji Ishin to Nashonarizumu: Bakumatsu no Gaikō to Seiji Hendō* (The Meiji Restoration and Nationalism: Diplomacy at the End of the Tokugawa Period and Political Changes) (Tokyo: Yamakawa Shuppansha, 2009, originally published in 1997).

Mizutani, Mitsuhiro. *Shōgun no Tei: Hama Rikyū to Bakumatsu Seiji no Fūkei* (The Shogun's Garden: Hama Rikyū and the Political Landscape at the End of the Tokugawa Period) (Tokyo: Chūkō Sosho, 2002).

Noguchi, Takehiko. *Bakufu Hoheitai: Bakumatsu o Kakenuketa Hohei Shūdan* (The Tokugawa Infantry: An Infantry Group That Made It Through the End of the Tokugawa Period) (Tokyo: Chūkō Shinsho, 2002).

Onodera, Ryūta. *Iwase Tadanari: Goshū Nanzo Tōshi to Iwan* (Iwase Tadanari: Five Continents Are in My Reach) (Kyoto: Minerva Shobō, 2018).

Onodera, Ryūta. *Kurimoto Joun: Ōsuji o Kenji Shita Bokoku no Ishin* (Kurimoto Joun: A Former Official of the Old Nation Who Stuck with His Principles) (Kyoto: Minerva, 2010).

Osaragi, Jirō. *Tennō no Seiki* (The Emperor's Century), Vols. 1–12 (Tokyo: Bunshun Bunko, 2010).

Sasaki, Suguru. *Boshin Sensō: Haisha no Meiji Ishin* (The Boshin War: The Losers' Meiji Restoration) (Tokyo: Chūkō Shinsho, 1977).

Satō, Seizaburō. *"Shi no Chōyaku" o Koete: Seiyō no Shōgeki to Nihon* (Beyond the Great Leap: Japan and the Shock from the West) (Tokyo: Chikura Shobō, 2009, originally published by Toshi Shuppan, 1992).

Satow, Ernest M. *Diplomat in Japan* (New York: Oxford University Press, 1968).

Sims, Richard. *French Policy Towards the Bakufu and Meiji Japan 1854–1895* (New York: Psychology Press, 1998).

Somura, Yasunobu. *Perii ha, Naze Nihon ni Kita ka* (Why Did Perry Come to Japan?) (Tokyo: Shinchō Sensho, 1987).

Takamura, Naosuke. *Nagai Naoyuki: Kōkoku no Tame Tokugawake no Tame* (Nagai Naoyuki: For the Empire, for the Tokugawa House) (Kyoto: Minerva Shobō, 2015).

Chapter 3

Banno, Junji. *Mikan no Meiji Ishin* (The Incomplete Meiji Restoration) (Tokyo: Chikuma Shinsho, 2007).

Craig, Albert M. *Civilization and Enlightenment: The Early Thought of Fukuzawa Yukichi* (Cambridge, MA: Harvard University Press, 2009).

Fukuzawa, Yukichi, trans. by David A. Dilworth. *An Encouragement of Learning* (Tokyo: Keio University Press, 2012).

Fukuzawa,Yukichi, trans. by David A. Dilworth. *An Outline of a Theory of Civilization* (Tokyo: Keio University Press, 2008).

Katsuta, Masaharu. *Haihan Chiken: "Meiji Kokka" ga Umareta Hi* (Dissolving the Domains and Establishing the Prefectures: The Day the "Meiji State" Came into Being) (Tokyo: Kōdansha Gakujutsu Bunko, 2000).

Kitaoka, Shinichi, trans. by James M. Vardaman. *Self-Respect and Independence of Mind: The Challenge of Fukuzawa Yukichi* (Tokyo: JPIC, 2017).

Kume, Kunitake, edited by Chushichi Tsuzuki and R. Jules Young. *Japan Rising: The Iwakura Embassy to the USA and Europe* (London: Cambridge University Press, 2009).

Miyamoto, Matao. *Kigyōka no Chōsen Nihon no Kindai 11* (The Entrepreneurs' Challenge Modern Japan 11) (Tokyo: Chūō Kōron Shinsha, 1999).

Nakae Chomin, trans. by Tsukui Nobuko. *A Discourse by Three Drunkards on Government* (Fairfield, CT: Weatherhill, 1992).

Ōkubo, Toshiaki. *Meirokusha* (Meirokusha) (Tokyo: Kōdansha Gakujutsu Bunko, 2007, originally published by Rittaisha as *Meirokushakō* [Considering Meirokusha], 1976).

Oka, Yoshitake. *Kindai Nihon Seijishi 1 Oka Yoshitake Chosakushū Dai 1 Kan Meiji Seijishi 1* (Modern Japanese Political History 1, Collection of Oka Yoshitake's Works, Vol. 2, Meiji Political History 1) (Tokyo: Iwanami Shoten, 1992).

Ochiai, Hiroki. *Chitsuroku Shobun: Meiji Ishin to Bushi no Risutora* (Ending the Privileges: The Meiji Restoration and the Laying Off of the Samurai) (Tokyo: Chūō Kōronshinsha, 1999).

Sakamoto, Takao. *Shijō, Dōtoku, Chitsujo* (Markets, Morality, and Order) (Tokyo: Chikuma Gakugei Bunko, 2007, originally published by Sōbunsha, 1991).

Sakamoto, Takao. *Meiji Kokka no Kensetsu, 1871–1890 Nihon no Kindai 2* (The Building of the Meiji State Modern Japan 2) (Tokyo: Chūō Kōronsha, 1999).

Sasaki, Kanji. *Chiso Kaisei: Kindai Nihon e no Tochi Kaikaku* (The 1873 Land Tax Reform: Land Reforms for a Modern Japan) (Tokyo: Chūkō Shinsho, 1989).

Sasaki, Suguru. *Ōkubo Toshimichi to Meiji Ishin* (Ōkubo Toshimichi and the Meiji Restoration) (Tokyo: Yoshikawa Kōbunkan, 1998).

Shinohara, Hiroshi. *Kaigun Sōsetsushi: Igirisu Gunji Komondan no Kage* (The History of the Establishment of the Imperial Japanese Navy: The Influence of the British Military Advisors) (Tokyo: Libro Port, 1986).

Shinohara, Hiroshi. *Rikugun Sōsetsushi: Furansu Gunji Komondan no Kage* (The History of the Establishment of the Imperial Japanese Army: The Influence of the French Military Advisors) (Tokyo: Libro Port, 1983).

Suzuki, Jun. *Shingijitsu no Shakaishi Nihon no Kindai 15* (Social Journal of New Technology Modern Japan 15) (Tokyo: Chūō Kōron Shinsha, 1999).

Suzuki, Jun. *Ishin no Kōsō to Tenkai Nihon no Rekishi Nihon no Rekishi 20* (The Concept and Development of the Restoration Japanese History 20) (Tokyo: Kōdansha Gakujutsu Bunko, 2010, originally published by Kōdansha Gakujutsu Bunko, 2002).

Tanaka, Akira. *Iwakura Shisetsudan: Beiō Kairan Jikki* (Iwakura Mission: Actual Records of the Travels to America and Europe) (Tokyo: Iwanami Gendai Bunko, 2002, originally published by Kōdansha Gakujutsu Bunko, 1977).

Tanaka, Akira. *Meiji Ishin* (The Meiji Restoration) (Tokyo: Kōdansha Gakujutsu Bunko, 2003, originally published by Shōgakukan as volume 24 in the Japan History series, 1976).

Umetani, Noboru. *Oyatoi Gaikokujin: Meiji Nihon no Wakiyakutachi* (Foreign Advisors: Supporting Characters in Meiji Japan) (Tokyo: Kōdansha Gakujutsu Bunko, 2007, originally published by Nihon Keizai Shimbunsha, 1965).

Umemura, Mataji, and Yamamoto, Yūzō, ed. *Kaikō to Ishin* (Opening the Ports and the Restoration Japan Economic History 3) (Tokyo: Iwanami Shoten, 1989).

Chapter 4

Arai, Katsuhiro, ed. *Jiyū Minken to Kindai Shakai Nihon no Jidaishi 22* (The People's Rights Movement and Modern Society Japanese Period History 22) (Tokyo: Yoshikawa Kōbunkan, 2004).

Ariizumi, Sadao. *Hoshi Tōru* (Hoshi Tōru) (Tokyo: Asahi Shimbunsha, 1983).

Banno, Junji. *Kindai Nihon no Gaikō to Seiji* (Modern Japanese Diplomacy and Politics) (Tokyo: Kenbun Shuppan, 1985).

Banno, Masataka. *Kindai Chūgoku Gaikōshi Kenkyū* (Research on Modern Chinese Diplomatic History) (Tokyo: University of Tokyo Press, 1973).

Banno, Masataka. *Kindai Chūgoku Seijigaikōshi: Vasuko da Gama kara Goshi Undō Made* (Research on Modern Chinese Political and Diplomatic History: From Vasco de Gama to the May Fourth Movement) (Tokyo: University of Tokyo Press, 1973).

Gabe, Masao. *Meiji Kokka to Okinawa* (The Meiji State and Okinawa) (Tokyo: Sanichi Shobō, 1979).

Hagihara, Nobutoshi. *Baba Tatsui* (Baba Tatsui) (Tokyo: Asahi Shinbunsha, 2007, originally published by Chūō Kōronsha, 1967).

Hasegawa, Noboru. *Bakuto to Jiyū Minken Nagoya Jiken Shimatsuki* (Criminals and the People's Rights Movement: A Record of the Entire Nagoya Incident) (Tokyo: Heibonsha Raiburarii, 1995, originally published by Chūkō Shinsho, 1977).

Harada, Tamaki. *Chōsen no Kaikoku to Kindaika* (The Opening and Modernization of Korea) (Hiroshima: Keisuisha, 1997).

Inada, Masahiro. *Jiyū Minken no Bunkashi: Atarashii Seiji Bunka no Tanjō* (The Cultural History of the People's Rights Movement) (Tokyo: Chikuma Shobō, 2000).

Inoue, Kōji. *Chichibu Jiken: Jiyū Minkenki no Nōmin Hōki* (The Chichibu Incident: Peasant Revolt During the Period of the People's Rights Movement) (Tokyo: Chūkō Shinsho, 1968).

Irokawa, Daikichi, trans. edited by Marius B. Jansen, *The Culture of the Meiji Period* (New Jersey, NJ: Princeton University Press, 1988).

Nagai, Hideo. *Jiyū Minken Nihon no Rekishi 25* (The People's Rights Movement Japanese History 25) (Tokyo: Shōgakukan, 1976).

Okamoto, Takashi. *Zokukoku to Jishu no Aida: Kindai Shinkan Kankei to Higashi Ajia no Meiun* (Between a Tributary State and Autonomous One: Modern Sino-Korea Relations and the Fate of East Asia) (Nagoya: University of Nagoya Press, 2004).

Okamoto, Takashi. *Sekai no Naka no Nisshinkan Kankeishi: Kōrin to Zokukoku, Jishu to Dokuritsu* (A History of Japan-Sino-Korean Relations in the World: Neighbors and Tributaries, Autonomous and Independent) (Tokyo: Kōdansha Sensho Meche, 2008).

Ogawara, Masamichi. *Seinan Sensō: Saigō Takamori to Nihon Saigo no Naisen* (The Satsuma Rebellion: Saigō Takamori and Japan's Last Civil War) (Tokyo: Chūkō Shinsho, 2007).

Sasaki, Yō. *Shinmatsu Chūgoku ni Okeru Nihonkan to Seiyōkan* (Views of Japan and the West at the End of the Qing Dynasty) (Tokyo: University of Tokyo Press, 2000).

Tabohashi, Kiyoshi. *Kindai Nikkan Kankei no Kenkyū Fukkokuban* (Research on Modern Japan-Korea Relations), Vols. 1 & 2. Reprinted Edition (Tokyo: Sūkō Shobō, 1972, originally published by Bunka Shiryō Chōsakai, 1963).

Yoshizawa, Seiichirō. *Shinchō to Kindai Sekai: 19 Seiki Shiriizu Chūgoku Kingendaishi 1* (China-Korea Relations and the Modern World in the 19th Century) (Tokyo: Iwanami Shoten, 2010).

Chapter 5

Akita, George. *Foundations of Constitutional Government in Modern Japan, 1868–1900* (Cambridge, MA: Harvard University Press, 1967).

Ariizumi, Sadao. *Meiji Seijishi no Kisūo Katei: Chihō Seiji Jōkyōshiron* (The Foundational Process Meiji Political History: An Historical Explanation of the Situation of Local Politics) (Tokyo: Yoshikawa Kōbunkan, 1980).

Banno, Junji. *Kindai Nihon no Kokka Kōsō: 1871–1936* (The National Concept of Modern History from 1871–1936) (Tokyo: Iwanami Gendai Bunko, 2009, originally published by Iwanami Shoten, 1996).

Inada, Masatsugu. *Meiji Kenpō Seiritsushi* (The History of the Establishment of the Meiji Constitution), Vols. 1 & 2 (Tokyo: Yūhikaku, 1960, 1962).

Iokibe, Kaoru. *Okuma Shigenobu to Seitō Seiji: Fukusū Seitōshi no Kigen Meiji 14-Taishō 3 Nen* (Okuma Shigenobu and Party Politics: The Origins of the Multiple Party System, 1881–1914) (Tokyo: University of Tokyo Press, 2003).

Iokibe, Kaoru. *Jōyaku Kaiseishi: Hoken Kaifuku e no Tenbō to Nashonarizumu* (History of Revising the Treaties: Prospects for Restoring Jurisdiction and Nationalism) (Tokyo: Yūhikaku, 2010).

Matsuda, Kōichirō. *Kuga Katsunan: Jiyū ni Kōron o Daihyō Su* (Kuga Katsunan: Representing the Freedom to Debate) (Kyoto: Minerva Shobō, 2008).

Mikuriya, Takashi. *Meiji Kokka o Tsukuru: Chihō Keiei to Shuto Keikaku* (Making the Meiji State: Regional Development and Capital Planning) (Tokyo: Fujiwara Shoten, 2007).

Ōkubo, Yasuo. *Bowasonaado: Nihon Kindaihō no Chichi* (Boissonade: The Father of Modern Japanese Law) (Tokyo: Iwanami Shinsho, 1977).

Ōsawa, Hiroaki. *Kindai Nihon no Higashi Ajia Seisaku to Gunji: Naikakusei to Gunbi Rosen no Kakuritsu* (Modern Japan's East Asia Policy and Military: The Establishment of the Cabinet System and Militarization Road) (Tokyo: Seibundō, 2001).

Sakai, Yukichi. *Inoue Kowashi to Meiji Kokka* (Inoue Kowashi and the Meiji State) (Tokyo: University of Tokyo Press, 1983).

Sakamoto, Kazuto. *Itō Hirobumi to Meiji Kokka Keisei: "Kyuchu" no Seidoka to Kenpōsei no Dōnyū* (Itō Hirobumi and the Formation of the Meiji State: The Establishment of the Imperial Court System and the Introduction of the Constitutional System) (Tokyo: Yoshikawa Kōbunkan, 1991).

Takeuchi, Yō. *Gakureki Kizoku no Eikō to Zasetsu Nihon no Kindai 12* (The Glory and Frustrations of the Schooled Nobility Modern Japan 12) (Tokyo: Kōdansha Gakujutsu Bunko, 2011, originally published by Chūō Kōronshinsha, 1999).

Takii, Kazuhiro, trans. by David Noble. *The Meiji Constitution: The Japanese Experience of the West and the Shaping of the Modern State* (Tokyo: International House of Japan, 2007).

Titus, David. *Palace and Politics in Prewar Japan* (New York: Columbia University Press, 1974).

Chapter 6

Banno, Junji. *Kindai Nihon no Shuppatsu Taikei Nihon no Rekishi 13* (The Start of Modern Japan: Outline of Japanese History 13) (Tokyo: Shinjinbutsu Ōraisha Jinbutsu Bunko, 2010, originally published by Shōgakukan, 1989).

Banno, Junji. *The Establishment of the Japanese Constitutional System* (London: Routledge, 1992).

Itō, Yukio. *Itō Hirobumi: Kindai Nihon o Tsukutta Otoko* (Itō Hirobumi: The Man Who Made Modern Japan) (Tokyo: Kōdansha Gakujutsu Bunko, 2009).

Mikuriya, Takashi. *Meiji Kokka no Kansei, 1890–1905 Nihon no Kindai 3* (The Completion of the Meiji State, 1890–1905 Modern Japan 3) (Tokyo: Chūō Kōron Shinsha, 1999).

Mizutani, Mitsuhiro. *Kanryō no Fūbō Nihon no Kindai 13* (The Bureaucrat's Appearance Modern Japan 13) (Tokyo: Chūō Kōron Shinsha, 1999).

Muroyama, Yoshimasa. *Kindai Nihon no Gunji to Zaisei: Kaigun Kakuchō o Meguru Seisaku Keisei Katei* (Modern Japanese Military and Finance: The Policy Formation Process of Expanding the Navy) (Tokyo: University of Tokyo Press, 1984).

Oka, Yoshitake, trans. by Andrew Fraser, and Patricia Murray. *Five Political Leaders of Modern Japan: Ito Hirobumi, Okuma Shigenobu, Hara Takashi, Inukai Tsuyoshi, and Saionji Kinmochi* (Tokyo: University of Tokyo Press, 1986).

Oka, Yoshitake. *Yamagata Aritomo: Meiji Nihon no Shōchō* (Yamagata Aritomo: The Symbol of Meiji Japan) (Tokyo: Iwanami Shinsho, 1958).

Oka, Yoshitake. *Kindai Nihon Seijishi 2 Oka Yoshitake Chosakushū Dai 2 Kan Meiji Seijishi 2* (Modern Japanese Political History 2, Collection of Oka Yoshitake's Works, Vol. 2, Meiji Political History 2) (Tokyo: Iwanami Shoten, 1992).

Sasaki, Takashi. *Media to Kenryoku Nihon no Kindai 14* (Media and Authority Modern Japan 14) (Tokyo: Chūō Kōron Shinsha, 1999).

Suetake, Yoshiya. *Senkyō Ihan no Rekishi Ura Kara Mita Nihon no 100 Nen* (The History of Election Violations: 100 Years of Japan Behind the Scenes) (Tokyo: Yoshikawa Kōbun, 2007).

Takii, Kazuhiro. *Itō Hirobumi: Japan's First Prime Minister and Father of the Meiji Constitution* (London: Routledge, 2014).

Ubukata, Toshirō. *Meiji Taishō Kenbunshi* (Recollections on the Meiji and Taisho Eras) (Tokyo: Chūkō Bunko, 2005, originally published by Shunjūsha, 1926).

Chapter 7

Feis, Herbert. *The Diplomacy of the Dollar: First Era, 1919–1932* (Baltimore: Johns Hopkins University Press, 1970).

Hagihara, Nobutoshi. *Mutsu Munemitsu* (Mutsu Munemitsu) (Tokyo: Asahi Shimbunsha, 2007, originally published in 1997).

Kawashima, Shin. *Kindai Kokka e no Mōsaku, 1894–1925 Shiriizu Chūgoku Kingendaishi 2* (Toward a Modern State, 1894–1925 Series on Chinese Modern and Contemporary History 2) (Tokyo: Iwanami Shinsho, 2010).

Kobayashi, Michihiko. *Nihon no Tairiku Seisaku, 1895–1914: Katsura Tarō to Gotō Shimpei* (Japan's Continental Policy, 1895–1914: Katsura Tarō to Gotō Shimpei) (Tokyo: Nansōsha, 1996).

Langer, William L. *The Diplomacy of Imperialism, 1890–1902*, 2nd ed. (New York: Alfred A. Knopf, 1951).

Mutsu, Munemitsu, ed. and trans. by Gordon M. Berger. *Kenkenroku: A Diplomatic Record of the Sino-Japanese War, 1894–1895* (Princeton, NJ: Princeton University Press, 1983).

Mitsuishi, Zenkichi. *Chūgoku, 1900: Giwadan Undō no Kōbō* (China in 1900: The Highlights and Lowpoints of the Boxer Rebellion) (Tokyo: Chūkō Shinsho, 1996).

Moriyama, Shigenori. *Kindai Nikkan Kankeishi Kenkyū: Chōsen Shokumenchika to Kokusai Kankei* (Tokyo: University of Tokyo Press, 1987).

Moriyama, Shigenori. *Nikkan Heigō Shinsōban* (Japan's Annexation of Korea, New Ed.) (Tokyo: Yoshikawa Kōbunkan, 1995, originally published in 1992).

Nish, Ian H. *The Anglo-Japanese Alliance: The Diplomacy of Two Island Empires, 1894–1907* (London: Athlone Press, 1966).

Okazaki, Hisahiko. *Komura Jutarō to Sono Jidai* (Komura Jutarō and His Era) (Tokyo: PHP Bunko, 2003, originally published by PHP Kenkyūsho, 1998).

Okazaki, Hisahiko. *Mutsu Munemitsu to Sono Jidai* (Mutsu Munemitsu and His Era) (Tokyo: PHP Bunko, 2003, originally published by PHP Kenkyūsho, 1999).

Osatake, Takeki, and Mitani, Taiichirō. *Ōtsu Jiken: Roshia Kōtaishi Ōtsu Sōnan* (The Otsu Incident: The Attempted Assassination of the Russian Tsarevich) (Tokyo: Iwanami Shoten, 1991).

Sakata, Masatoshi. *Kindai Nihon ni Okeru Taigaikō Undō no Kenkyū* (Research on the Activities of the Hardliners in Modern Japanese Diplomacy) (Tokyo: University of Tokyo Press, 1978).

Shimada, Kinji. *Roshia ni Okeru Hirose Takeo* (Hirose Takase in Russia) (Tokyo: Asahi Sensho, 1976).

Shimada, Kinji. *Amerika ni Okeru Akiyama Saneyuki* (Akiyama Saneyuki in America) (Tokyo: Asahi Bunko, 2009, originally published by Asahi Sensho, 1975).

Tani, Hisao. *Kimitsu Nichiro Senshi Shinsōban* (Secret Russo-Japanese War History, New Ed.) (Tokyo: Hara Shobō, 2004, originally published, 1971).

Yamada, Akira. *Gunbi Kakuchō no Kindaishi: Nihongun no Bōchō to Hakai* (The Modern History of Military Expansion: The Enlargement of the Japanese Military and Its Collapse) (Tokyo: Yoshikawa Kōbunkan, 1997).

Chapter 8

Asakawa, Kanichi, and Yura, Kimiyoshi. *Nihon no Kaki [Fukugenban]* (Japan's Ill Omen [reprinted edition]) (Tokyo: Kōdansha Gakujutsu Bunko, 1987, originally published by Jitsugyō no Nihonsha, 1909).

Chiba, Isao. *Kyūgaikō no Keisei: Nihon Gaikō, 1900–1919* (The Formation of Old Diplomacy, 1900–1919) (Tokyo: Keisō Shobō, 2008).

Griswold, A. Whitney. *Far Eastern Policy of United States* (New Haven, CT: Yale University Press, 1962).

Hata, Ikuhiko. *Taiheiyō Kokusai Kankeishi: Nichibei Oyobi Nichiro Kiki no Keifu, 1900–1935* (The History of International Relations of the Pacific: The Lineage of Japan-U.S. and Japanese-Russian Crises, 1900–1935) (Tokyo: Fukumura Shuppan, 1972).

Hosoya, Chihiro. *Shiberia Shuppei no Shiteki Kenkyū* (Historical Research on the Siberian Dispatch) (Tokyo: Iwanami Gendai Bunko, 2005, originally published by Yūhikaku, 1955).

Hough, Richard. *Dreadnought: A History of the Modern Battleship* (New York: MacMillan Publishing, 1975).

Hunt, Michael. *Frontier Defense and the Open Door: Manchuria in Chinese-American Relations, 1895–1911* (Ann Arbor, MI: University Microfilms, 1972).

Inose, Naoki. *Kurobune no Seiki: Gaiatsu to Nichibei Miraisenki* (The Century of the Black Ships: Outside Pressure and Notes on the Future Japan-America War) (Tokyo: Bunshun Bunko, 1998, originally published by Shōgakukan, 1993).

Kawashima, Shin. *Chūgoku Kindai Gaikō no Keisei* (The Formation of Modern Chinese Diplomacy) (Nagoya: University of Nagoya Press, 2004).

Kennan, George F. *American Diplomacy*, expanded ed. (Chicago: University of Chicago Press, 1984).

Kitaoka, Shinichi. *Nihon Rikugun to Tairiku Seisaku, 1906–1918 Nen* (The Japanese Army and Continental Policy, 1906–1918) (Tokyo: University of Tokyo Press, 1978).

Kitaoka, Shinichi. *Gotō Shimpei: Gaikō to Bijon* (Gotō Shimpei: Diplomacy and Vision) (Tokyo: Chūkō Shinsho, 1988).

Kurihara, Takeshi. *Taimanmo Seisakushi no Ichimen: Nichiro Sengo Yori Taishōki ni Itaru* (An Aspect of the History of [Japan's] Policy Toward Manchuria and Mongolia from the Russo-Japanese War to the Taishō Period) (Tokyo: Hara Shobō, 1966).

Mahan, Alfred T. *Mahan on Naval Warfare* (Mineola, NY: Dover Publications, 2011).

Masumi, Junnosuke. *Nihon Seitōshiron Daisankan* (On the History of Japan's Political Parties), Vol. 3 (Tokyo: University of Tokyo Press, 1967).

Nagata, Akifumi. *Seodoa-Ruuzuberuto to Kankoku: Kankoku Hogō Kokka to Beikoku* (Theodore Roosevelt and Korea: The Making of a Korean Protectorate and the United States) (Tokyo: Miraisha, 1992).

Nagata, Akifumi. *Nihon no Chōsen Tōchi to Kokusai Kankei: Chōsen Dokuritsu Undō to Amerika, 1910–1922* (Japan's Administration of Korea and International Relations: The Korean Independence and America, 1910–1922) (Tokyo: Heibonsha, 2005).

Nish, Ian H. *Alliance in Decline: A Study in Anglo-Japanese Relations, 1908–1923* (London: Athlone Press, 1972).

Sakurai, Ryōju. *Shingai Kakumei to Nihon Seiji no Hendō* (The Chinese Revolution of 1911 and Japan's Political Flux) (Tokyo: Iwanami Shoten, 2009).

Takeuchi, Yoshimi, and Hashikawa, Bunsō, ed. *Kindai Nihon to Chūgoku* (Modern Japan and China) (Tokyo: Asahi Sensho, 1974).

Tsunoda, Jun. *Manshū Mondai to Kokubō Hōshin: Meiji Koki ni Okeru Kokubō Kankyō no Hendō* (The Manchurian Problem and the Direction of National Defense Direction: Changes in the Defense Environment in the Late Meiji Era) (Tokyo: Hara Shobō, 1967).

Yoshimura, Michio. *Zōhoban Nihon to Roshia* (Enlarged Edition, Japan and Russia) (Tokyo: Nihon Keizai Hyōronsha, 1991).

Chapter 9

Ando, Yoshio. *Burujowajii no Gunzō Bunkoban Nihonshi no Shakai Shūdan 6* (Bourgeoisie's Gunzō Magazine) (Tokyo: Shōgakukan, 1990, originally published by Shōgakukan as volume 28 in the *Nihon no Rekishi* [Japanese History] series, 1976).

Banno, Junji. *Meiji Kokka no Shūen: 1900 Nen Taisei no Hōkai* (The End of the Meiji State: The Collapse of the 1900 System) (Tokyo: Chikuma Gakugei Bunko, 2010, originally published by Minerva Shobō as *Taishō Seihen* [Taishō Political Crisis], 1994).

Duus, Peter. *Party Rivalry and Political Change in Taisho Japan* (Cambridge, MA: Harvard University Press, 1968).

Kano, Masanao. *Taishō Demokurashii Nihon no Rekishi 27* (Taishō Democracy Japanese History 27) (Tokyo: Shōgakukan, 1976).

Kitaoka, Shinichi. Seitō Seiji Kakuritsu Katei ni Okeru Rikken Dōshi-Kenseikai: Seiken Kōsō to Seiji Shidō (The Association of Allies of the Constitution and Constitutional Association During the Process of Establishing Party Politics: Concept to Form a Government and Party Leadership), *Rikkyō Hōgaku* (Rikkyo University Law Review), No. 21 (1983) and No. 25 (1985).

Kobayashi, Michihiko. *Katsura Tarō: Yoga Seimei de Aru* (Katsura Tarō: A Political Biography) (Kyoto: Minerva Shobō, 2006).

Matsuo, Takayoshi. *Taishō Demokurashii* (Taishō Democracy) (Tokyo: Iwanami Gendai Bunko, 2001, originally published by Iwanami Shoten, 1974).

Matsuzawa, Hiroaki. *Nihon Shakai Shugi no Shisō* (Japanese Socialist Theory) (Tokyo: Chikuma Shobō, 1973).

Mitani, Taiichirō. Zōho *Nihon Seitō Seiji no Keisei: Hara Takashi no Seiji Shidō no Tenkai* (Expanded Edition the Formation of Japanese Party Politics: The Development of Hara Takashi's Political Leadership) (Tokyo: University of Tokyo Press, 1995, originally published in 1967).

Mitani, Taiichirō. *Shinpan Taishō Demokurashiiron: Yoshino Sakuzō no Jidai* (New Edition on Taisho Democracy: The Age of Yoshino Sakuzō) (Tokyo: University of Tokyo Press, 1995, originally published in 1974).

Mitani, Taiichirō. *Seiji Seido to Shite no Baishinsei: Kindai Nihon no Shihōken to Seiji* (The Jury System as a Political System: Modern Japan's Judiciary and Politics) (Tokyo: University of Tokyo Press, 2001).

Najita, Tetsuo. *Hara Kei in the Politics of Compromise, 1905–1915* (Cambridge, MA: Harvard University Press, 1967).

Nakamura, Masanori. *Rōdōsha to Nōmin Nishonshi no Shakai Shūdan 7* (Laborers and Farmers: Social Groups in Japanese History 7) (Tokyo: Shōgakukan, 1990, originally published by Shōgakukan as No. 29 in the series *Nihon no Rekishi* [Japanese History], 1976).

Naraoka, Sōchi. *Katō Takaaki to Seitō Seiji: Nidai Seitōsei e no Michi* (Katō Takaaki and Party Politics: The Path Toward a Two-Party System) (Tokyo: Yamakawa Shuppansha, 2006).

Oka, Yoshitake. *Tenkanki no Taishō Oka Yoshitake Chosakushū Daisankan Shoshū* (Taishō in the Age of Change: The Writings of Oka Yoshitake) (Tokyo: Iwanami Shoten, 1992, originally published by University of Tokyo Press, 1969).

Oka, Yoshitake, ed. *Yoshino Sakuzō Hyōronshū* (The Collection of Yoshino Sakuzō's Writings) (Tokyo: Iwanami Bunko, 1975).

Sakurai, Ryōju. *Taishō Seijishi no Shuppatsu: Rikken Dōshikai no Seiritsu to Sono Shūhen* (The Beginning of Taisho Political History: The Formation of the Association of Allies of the Constitution and Surrounding Events) (Tokyo: Yamakawa Shuppansha, 1997).

Yoshino, Sakuzō, and Matsuo, Takayoshi, ed. *Chūgoku-Chōsenron* (On China and Korea) (Tokyo: Heibonsha Tōyō Bunko, 1970).

Chapter 10

Hosoya, Chihiro, and Saitō Makoto, eds. *Washinton Taisei to Nichibei Kankei* (The Washington Treaty System and Japan-U.S. Relations) (Tokyo: University of Tokyo Press, 1978).

Inoue, Kiyoshi, ed. *Taishōki no Seiji to Shakai* (Politics and Society During the Taisho Period) (Tokyo: Iwanami Shoten, 1969).

Inoue, Kiyoshi, and Watanabe, Tōru, eds. *Kyōto Daigaku Jinbun Kagaku Kenkyūsho Kenkyū Hōkoku Taishōki no Kyūshinteki Jiyū Shugi: "Tōyō Keizai Shimpō" o Chūshin to Shite* (Research Report of the Kyoto University Institute for Research in Humanities Rapid Liberalism in the Taishō Period with a Focus on the *Toyo Keizai Weekly*) (Tokyo: Tōyō Keizai Shimpōsha, 1972).

Iriye, Akira. *After Imperialism: The Search for a New Order in the Far East, 1921–1931* (Cambridge, MA: Harvard University Press, 1965).

Itō, Takashi. *Shōwa Shoki Seijishi Kenkyū Rondon Kaigun Gunshuku Mondai o Meguru Shoseiji Shūdan no Taikō to Renkei* (Research on Political Historical of the Early Showa Period: Clash and Cooperation of the Different Political Groups Concerning the London Naval Conference) (Tokyo: University of Tokyo Press, 1969).

Koshizawa, Akira. *Tōkyō no Toshi Keikaku* (City Planning for Tokyo) (Tokyo: Iwanami Shinsho, 1991).

Koshizawa, Akira. *Tōkyō Toshi Keikaku Monogatari* (The Story of the City Planning for Tokyo) (Tokyo: Chikuma Gakugei Bunko, 2001, originally published by Nihon Keizai Hyōronsha, 1991).

Kurosawa, Fumitaka. *Taisenkanki no Nihon Rikugun* (The Japan Imperial Army in the Interwar Period) (Tokyo: Misuzu Shobō, 2000).

Masumi, Junnosuke. *Nihon Seitōshiron Dai 5 Kan* (On the History of Japanese Political Parties), Vol. 5 (Tokyo: University of Tokyo Press, 1979).

Matsuo, Takayoshi, ed. *Ishibashi Tanzan Hyōronshū* (Collection of Ishibashi Tanzan's Works) (Tokyo: Iwanami Bunko, 1984).

Minohara, Tosh. *Hainichi Undō to Nichibei Kankei: "Haniwara Shokan" no Shinsō to Sono "Jūdai Naru Kekka"* (The 1924 Immigration Act and Japan-U.S. Relations: The Truth About "The Haniwara Letter" and "Grave Consequences") (Tokyo: Iwanami Shoten, 2002).

Mitani, Taiichirō. *Uooru Sotoriito to Kyokutō: Seiji ni Okeru Kokusai Kinyū Shihon* (Wall Street and the Far East: International Financial Capital in Politics) (Tokyo: University of Tokyo Press, 2009).

Murai, Ryōta. *Seitō Naikaku no Seiritsu, 1918–1927* (The Establishment of Party Cabinets, 1918–1927) (Tokyo: Yūhikaku, 2005).

Nagai, Kazu. *Seinen Kunshu Shōwa Tennō to Genro Saionji* (Youthful Monarch Showa Emperor and Elder Statesman Saionji) (Kyoto: Kyōto University Press, 2003).

Nakamura, Takafusa. *Shōwashi* (The History of Showa), Vols. 1 (1926–1945) and 2 (1945–1989) (Tokyo: Tōyō Keizai Shinpōsha, 1993).

Nakamura, Takafusa. *Keizai Seisaku no Unmei* (The Fate of Economic Policy) (Tokyo: Nikkei Shinsho, 1967).

Nolte, Sharon A. *Liberalism in Japan: Ishibashi Tanzan and His Teachers, 1905–1960* (Berkeley: University of California Press, 1987).

Shidehara, Kijūrō. *Gaikō Gojūnen* (50 Years of Diplomacy) (Tokyo: Chūkō Bunko, 2007 reprint, originally published by Yomiuri Shimbunsha, 1951).

Smethurst, Richard J. *From Foot Soldier to Finance Minister: Takahashi Korekiyo, Japan's Keynes* (Cambridge, MA: Harvard University Press, 2007).

Usui, Katsumi. *Nihon Gaikōshi: Hokubatsu no Jidai* (Japanese Diplomatic History: The Northern Expedition Period) (Tokyo: Hanawa Shobō, 1971).

Usui, Katsumi. *Nihon to Chūgoku: Taishō Jidai Kindai Nihon Gaikōshi Gyōsho* (Japan and China: The Taishō Period Book Series on Modern Japanese Diplomatic History) (Tokyo: Hara Shobō, 1972).

Wakatsuki, Reijirō. *Meiji, Taishō, Shōwa Seikai Hishi: Kofūan Kaikoroku* (The Secret Political History of Meiji, Taishō, and Shōwa: Kofūan's Reminiscences (Tokyo: Kodansha

Gakujutsu Bunko, 1983, originally published by Yomiuri Shimbunsha as *Kofūan Kaikoroku: Meiji, Taishō, Shōwa Seikai Hishi* [Kofūan Reminiscences: The Secret Political History of Meiji, Taishō, and Shōwa], 1950).

Waldron, Arthur N. *From War to Nationalism: China's Turning Point, 1924–1925* (London: Cambridge University Press, 2003).

Chapter 11

Dower, John W. *Empire and Aftermath: Yoshida Shigeru and the Japanese Experience, 1878–1954* (Cambridge, MA: Harvard University Press, 1979.

Hata, Ikuhiko. *Rokō Kyōjiken no Kenkyū* (Research on the Marco Polo Incident) (Tokyo: University of Tokyo Press, 1996).

Kitaoka, Shinichi. *Kanryōsei to Shite no Nihon Rikugun* (The Japanese Army as Bureaucrats) (Tokyo: Chikuma Shobō, 2012).

Kitaoka, Shinichi. *Seitō kara Gunbu e, 1924–1941 Nihon Kindai 5* (From Political Parties to the Military, 1924–1941, Modern Japan 5) (Tokyo: Chūō Kōronsha, 1999).

Kitaoka, Shinichi. *Kiyosawa Kiyoshi: Gaikō Hyōron no Unmei Zōhoban* (Kiyosawa Kiyoshi: The Fate of a Diplomatic Commentator Expanded Edition) (Tokyo: Chūkō Shinsho, 2004, originally published in 1987).

Kobayashi, Michihiko. *Seitō Naikaku no Hōkai to Manshū Jihen, 1918–1932* (The Collapse of Party Cabinets and the Manchurian Incident, 1918–1932) (Kyoto: Minerva Shobō, 2010).

Mitani, Taiichirō. *Kindai Nihon no Sensō to Seiji* (Modern Japanese War and Politics) (Tokyo: Iwanami Jinbunsho Serekushon, 2010, originally published by Iwanami Shoten, 1997).

Nagai, Kazu. *Kindai Nihon no Gunbu to Seiji* (Modern Japanese Military and Politics) (Kyoto: Shibunkaku Shuppan, 1993).

Ogata, Sadako. *Defiance in Manchuria: Making of Japanese Foreign Policy, 1931–1932* (Berkeley: University of California Press, 1964).

Oka Yoshitake. *Konoe Fumimaro: A Political Biography* (Tokyo: University of Tokyo Press, 1983).

Sakai, Tetsuya. *Taishō Demokurashii Taisei no Hōkai: Naisei to Gaikō* (The Collapse of the Taishō Democracy Structure: Domestic Politics and Diplomacy) (Tokyo: University of Tokyo Press, 1992).

Shimada, Toshihiko. *Kantōgun: Zaiman Rikugun no Bōsō* (Kwantang Army: The Recklessness of the Imperial Japanese Army in Manchuria) (Tokyo: Kōdansha Gakujutsu Bunko, 2005, originally published by Chūkō Shinsho, 1965).

Takahashi, Masae. *2.26 Jiken: "Shōwa Ishin" no Shisō to Kōdō Zōho Kaiban* (The 2.26 Incident: Ideology and Actions of the "Showa Restoration" Expanding Edition) (Tokyo: Chūkō Shinsho, 1994, originally published in 1965).

Takahashi, Masae. *Shōwa no Gunbatsu* (The Military Faction of the Shōwa Period) (Tokyo: Kōdansha Gakujutsu Bunko, 2003, originally published by Chūkō Shinsho, 1969).

Thorne, Christopher G. *The Limits of Foreign Policy: The West, the League, and the Far Eastern Crisis of 1931–1933* (New York: Putnam, 1973).

Tobe, Ryōichi. *Nihon Rikugun to Chūgoku: "Shinatsu" ni Miru Yume to Satetsu* (The Imperial Japanese Army and China: The Dreams and Failures of the "Sinologists") (Tokyo: Kōdansha Gakujutsu Bunko Sensho Meche, 1999).

Tsutsui, Kiyotada, ed., trans. by Noda Makito and Paul Narum. *Fifteen Lectures on Showa Japan: Road to the Pacific War in Recent Historiography* (Tokyo: JPIC, 2016).

Usui, Katsumi. *Manshū Jihen: Sensō to Gaikō* (The Manchurian Incident: War and Diplomacy) (Tokyo: Chūkō Shinsho, 1974).

Usui, Katsumi. *Chūgoku o Meguru Kindai Nihon no Gaikō* (Modern Japanese Diplomacy and China) (Tokyo: Chikuma Shobō, 1983).

Usui, Katsumi. *Manshūkoku to Kokusai Renmei* (Manchukuo and the League of Nations) (Tokyo: Yoshikawa Kōbunkan, 1995).

Yamamoto, Yoshihiko, ed. *Kiyosawa Kiyoshi Hyōronshū* (Collection of Kiyosawa Kiyoshi's Writings) (Tokyo: Iwanami Bunko, 2002).

Yamamuro Shinichi, trans. by Joshua A. Fogel. *Manchuria Under Japanese Dominion*, (Philadelphia: University of Pennsylvania Press, 2006).

Young, Louise. *Japan's Total Empire: Manchuria and the Culture of Wartime Imperialism* (Berkeley: University of California Press, 1999).

Chapter 12

Asada, Sadao. *From Mahan to Pearl Harbor: The Imperial Japanese Navy and the United States* (Annapolis, MD: Naval Institute Press, 2006).

Berger, Gordon M. *Parties out of Power in Japan, 1931–1941* (Princeton, NJ: Princeton University Press, 1977).

Borg, Dorothy, and Okamoto, Shumpei, eds. *Pearl Harbor as History: Japanese-American Relations, 1931–1941* (New York: Columbia University Press, 1973).

Furukawa, Takahisa. *Senji Gikai* (The Parliament During Wartime) (Tokyo: Yoshikawa Kōbunkan, 2001).

Grew, Joseph C. *Ten Years in Japan: A Contemporary Record Drawn from the Diaries and Private and Official Papers of Joseph G. Grew, United States Ambassador to Japan, 1932–1942* (New York: Simon & Schuster, 1944).

Hata, Ikuhiko. *Nanjin Jiken: "Gyakusatsu" no Kōzō* (The Nanjing Incident: The Making of a "Massacre") (Tokyo: Chūkō Shinsho, 2007).

Hatano, Sumio. *Taiheiyō Sensō to Ajia Gaikō* (The Pacific War and Asian Diplomacy) (Tokyo: University of Tokyo Press, 1996).

Hattori, Ryūji. *Hirota Kōki: "Higeki no Saishō" no Jitsuzō* (Hirota Kōki: The Real Face of the "Tragic Prime Minister") (Tokyo: Chūkō Shinsho, 2008).

Heinrichs, Waldo H. *American Ambassador: Joseph C. Grew and the Development of the United States Diplomatic Tradition* (New York: Little, Brown, and Co., 1966).

Heinrichs, Waldo H. *Threshold of War: Franklin D. Roosevelt and American Entry into World War II* (London: Oxford University Press, 1990).

Itō, Takashi. *Jūgonen Sensō Nihon no Rekishi 30* (The 15-Year War Japanese History 30) (Tokyo: Shōgakukan, 1976).

Itō, Takashi. *Konoe Shintaisei: Taisei Yokusankai e no Michi* (The Konoe New System: The Road to the Imperial Rule Association) (Tokyo: Chūkō Shinsho, 1983).

Kiyosawa, Kiyoshi, trans. by Eugene Soviak and Kamiyama Tamie. *A Diary of Darkness: The Wartime Diary of Kiyosawa Kiyoshi* (Princeton, NJ: Princeton University Press, 2008, translation of *Ankoku Nikki*, originally published in 1948).

MacMurray, John Van Antwerp, edited by Arthur N. Waldron. *How the Peace was Lost: The 1935 Memorandum: Developments Affecting American Policy in the Far East* (Stanford: Hoover Institution Press, 1992).

Matsuura, Masataka. *Nicchū Sensōki ni Okeru Keizai to Seiji: Konoe Fumimaro to Ikeda Shigeaki* (Economy and Politics During the Sino-Japanese War: Konoe Fumimaro and Ikeda Shigeaki) (Tokyo: University of Tokyo Press, 1995).

Mikuriya, Takashi. *Seisaku no Sōgō to Kenryoku: Nihon Seiji no Senzen to Sengo* (Comprehensive Policy and Power: Prewar and Postwar Japanese Politics) (Tokyo: University of Tokyo Press, 1996).

Mikuriya, Takashi. *Baba Tsunego no Menboku: Kiki no Jidai no Riberarisuto* (Baba Tsunego's Honor: The Liberalist in the Period of Crisis) (Tokyo: Chūō Kōronsha, 1997).

Nagai, Kazu. *Nicchū Senso kara Sekai Sensō e* (From the Sino-Japanese War to the World War) (Kyoto: Shibunkaku, 2007).

Ōmae, Shinya. *Shōwasen Zenki no Yosan Hensei to Seiji* (The Formation of the Budget and Politics During the Early Showa War Period) (Tokyo: Bokutakusha, 2006).

Tobe, Ryōichi. *Piisu Fiiraa: Shina Jihen Wahei Kōsaku no Gunzō* (Peace Feeler: The Image of the Peace Efforts Following the China Incident) (Tokyo: Ronsōsha, 1991).

Tobe, Ryōichi. *Gaimushō Kakushinha: Sekai Shinchitsujo no Genei* (The Progressives of the Foreign Ministry: The Myth of the New World Order) (Tokyo: Chūkō Shinsho, 2010).

Throne, Christopher. *The Issue of War: States, Societies, and the Far Eastern Conflict of 1941–1945* (New York: Oxford University Press, 1985).

Tsutsui, Kiyotada. *Ni-Ni Roku to Sono Jidai: Shōwaki Nihon no Kōzō* (The February 26 Incident and the Era: The Structure of Shōwa Japan) (Tokyo: Chikuma Gakugei Bunko, 2006, originally published by Yūhikaku, 1984).

Tsutsui, Kiyotada. *Konoe Fumimaro: Kyōyō Shugiteki Popurisuto no Higeki* (Konoe Fumimaro: The Tragedy of Cultured Populist) (Tokyo: Iwanami Gendai Bunko, 2009).

Usui, Katsumi. *Shinpan Nicchū Sensō: Heiwa ka Sensen Kakudai ka* (New Edition the Japanese-Sino War: Peace or Expansion of the Front?) (Tokyo: Chūkō Shinsho, 2000, originally published in 1967).

Utley, Jonathan G. *Going to War with Japan, 1937–1941* (Chattanooga: University of Tennessee Press, 1985).

Chapter 13

Dower, John W. *Embracing Defeat: Japan in the Wake of World War II* (New York: W. W. Norton, 2000).

Eldridge, Robert D. *The Origins of the Bilateral Okinawa Problem: Okinawa in Postwar US-Japan Relations, 1945–1952* (London: Routledge, 2001).

Fukunaga, Fumio. *Nihon Senryōshi, 1945–1952: Tokyo, Washinton, Okinawa* (Japan Occupational History, 1945–1952: Tokyo, Washington, and Okinawa) (Tokyo: Chūkō Shinsho, 2014).

Higurashi, Yoshinobu. *Tōkyō Saiban* (Tokyo War Crimes Trial) (Tokyō: Kodansha Gendai Shinsho, 2008).

Hosoya, Chihiro. *San Furanshisuko Kōwa e no Michi* (The Road to the San Francisco Peace Conference) (Tokyo: Chūō Kōronsha, 1984).

Igarashi, Takeshi. *Sengo Nichibei Kankei no Keisei: Kōwa, Anpo to Reisengo no Shiten ni Tatte* (The Formation of Postwar Japan-U.S. Relations: The Peace Treaty and Security Treaty from the Perspective of after the Cold War) (Tokyo: Kōdansha Gakujutsu Bunko, 1995, originally published by Tokyo Daigaku Shuppankai as *Tainichi Kōwa to Reisen: Sengo Nichibei Kankei no Keisei* [The Peace Treaty and the Cold War: The Formation of Postwar U.S.-Japan Relations], 1986).

Iokibe, Makoto. *Beikoku no Senryō Seisaku: Sengo Nihon no Sekkeizu* (U.S. Occupation Policy: Plans for Postwar Japan) (Tokyo: Chūō Kōronsha, 1985).

Iokibe, Makoto. *Senryōki: Shushōtachi no Shinnihon 20 Seiki no Nihon 3* (The Occupation Period: The Prime Ministers' New Japan 20th Century Japan 3) (Tokyo: Kōdansha Gakujutsu Bunko, 2007, originally published by Yomiuri Shimbunsha, 1997).

Iokibe, Makoto. *Sensō, Senryō, Kōwa, 1941–1955 Nihon no Kindai 6* (War, Occupation, and the Peace Treaty, 1941–1955 Modern Japan 6) (Tokyo: Chūō Kōron Shinsha, 2001).

Iokibe, Makoto, ed., trans. by Robert D. Eldridge. *The Diplomatic History of Postwar Japan* (London: Routledge, 2010).

Iokibe, Makoto, Caroline Rose, Junko Tomaru, and John Weste, eds. *Japanese Diplomacy in the 1950s: From Isolation to Integration* (London: Routledge, 2008).

Kōsaka, Masataka. *Saishō Yoshida Shigeru* (Prime Minister Yoshida Shigeru) (Tokyo: Chūkō Kurashikkusu, 2006, originally published by Chūkō Gyōsho, 1968).

Kōsaka, Masataka. *Kaiyō Kokka Nihon no Kōsō* (Japan as a Sea Power) (Tokyo: Chūkō Kurashikkusu, 2008, originally published by Chūō Kōronsha, 1965).

Lee, Jong Won. *Higashi Ajia Reisen to Kanbeinichi Kankei* (The Cold War in East Asia and Korea-U.S.-Japan Relations) (Tokyo: University of Tokyo Press, 1996).

Maruyama Masao, edited by Ivan Morris. *Thought and Behavior in Modern Japanese Politics* (Acls History E-Book Project, 2006).

Masuda, Hiroshi. *Kōshoku Tsuihō Sandai Seiji Paaji no Kenkyū* (Research of Three Statesmen's Purges During the Occupation Period in Japan) (Tokyo: University of Tokyo Press, 1996).

Masuda, Hiroshi. *Makkaasaa Firipin Tōchi kara Nihon Senryō e* (MacArthur: From the Philippine Administration to the Occupation of Japan) (Tokyo: Chūkō Shinsho, 2009).

Matsuo, Takayoshi. *Kokusai Kokka e no Shuppatsu Nihon no Rekishi 21* (Becoming an International Nation Japanese History 21) (Tokyo: Shūeisha, 1993).

Shimizu, Ikutarō. *Waga Jinsei no Danpen* (A Fragment of My Life) (Tokyo: Bunshun Bunko, 1985, originally published by Bungei Shunjū, 1975).

Tsutsui, Kiyotada. *Ishibashi Tanzan: Jiyū Shugi Seiji no Kiseki* (Ishibashi Tanzan: The Path of a Liberal Politician) (Tokyo: Chūkō Gyōsho, 1986).

Watanabe, Akio, ed., trans. by Robert D. Eldridge, *The Prime Ministers of Postwar Japan, 1945–1995: Their Lives and Times* (Lanham, MD: Lexington Books, 2016).

Chapter 14

Curtis, Gerald L., with a New Preface by the Author. *Election Campaigning in Japanese Style* (New York: Columbia University Press, 2009).

Hatano, Sumio. *Rekishi to shite no Nichibei Anpo Jōyaku: Kimitsu Gaikō Kiroku o Akasu 'Mitsuyaku' no Kyojitsu* (The Japan-U.S. Security Treaty as History: Exposing the Lies of the 'Secret Agreements' Using Secret Diplomatic Records) (Tokyo: Iwanami Shoten, 2010).

Hatano, Sumio, ed. *Ikeda-Satō Seiken no Nihon Gaikō* (Japanese Diplomacy During the Ikeda and Satō Administrations) (Kyoto: Minerva Shobō, 2004).

Hara, Yoshihisa. *Kishi Nobusuke: Kensei no Seijika* (Kishi Nobusuke: The Politician Who Sought Power) (Tokyo: Iwanami Shinsho, 1995).

Inoki, Takenori. *Keizai Seichō no Kajitsu, 1955–1972* (The Fruits of Economic Growth, 1955–1972 Modern Japan 7) (Tokyo: Chūō Kōronshinsha, 2000).

Inoue, Masaya. *Nicchū Kokka Seijōka no Seijishi* (The Political History of the Restoration of Relations Between Japan and China) (Nagoya: University of Nagoya Press, 2010).

Itō, Masaya. *Ikeda Hayato to Sono Jidai: Sei to Shi no Dorama* (Ikeda Hayato: The Drama of His Life and Death) (Tokyo: Asahi Bunko, 1985, originally published by Chiseidō as *Ikeda Hayato: Sono Sei to Shi* [Ikeda Hayato: His Life and Times], 1966).

Kishi, Nobusuke, Yatsugi Kazuo, and Itō Takashi. *Kishi Nobusuke no Kaisō* (The Memoirs of Kishi Nobusuke) (Tokyo: Bungei Shunjū, 1981).

Kitaoka, Shinichi. *Jimintō: Seikentō no 38 Nen 20 Seiki no Nihon 1* (The LDP: Party in Power for 38 Years Japan in 20th Century 1) (Tokyo: Yomiuri Shimbunsha, 1995).

Kōno, Yasuko. *Okinawa Henkan o Meguru Seiji to Gaikō: Nichibei Kankeishi no Bunmyaku* (The Politics and Diplomacy Surrounding the Reversion of Okinawa in the Historical Context of Japan-U.S. Relations) (Tokyo: University of Tokyo Press, 1994).

Kuriyama, Takakazu, Nakajima Takuma, Hattori Ryūji, and Etō Naoko, ed. *Okinawa Henkan, Nicch ū Kokkō Seijōka, Nichibei "Mitsuyaku"* (The Reversion of Okinawa, Japan-China Normalization of Relations, and Japan-America "Secret Agreements") (Tokyo: Iwanami Shoten, 2010).

Murakami, Yasusuke. *Shinchūkan Taishū no Jidai: Sengo Nihon no Kaibatsugaku* (The Age of the New Middle Class: An Autopsy of Postwar Japan) (Tokyo: Chūkō Bunko, 1987, originally published by Chūō Kōronsha, 1984).

Nakashima, Takuma. *Okinawa Henkan to Nichibei Anpo Taisei* (The Reversion of Okinawa and the Japan-U.S. Alliance System) (Tokyo: Yūhikaku, 2012).

Ōtake, Hideo. *Zōho Shinpan Gendai Nihon no Seiji Kenryoku Keizai Kenryoku: Seiji ni Okeru Kigyō, Gyōkai, Zaikai* (New Enlarged Edition Political Power and Economic Power in Modern Japan: Enterprises, Industries, and Banking in Politics) (Tokyo: San-ichi Shobō, 1996, originally published in 1979).

Packard, George R. *Edwin O. Reischauer and the American Discovery of Japan* (New York: Columbia University Press, 2010).

Sakamoto, Kazuya. *Nichibei Dōmei no Kizuna: Anpo Jōyaku to Sōgosei no Mōsaku* (The Bonds of the Japan-U.S. Alliance: The Search for the Complementary Roles) (Tokyo: Yūhikaku, 2000).

Sasaki, Takuya. *Aizenhawaa Seiken no Fūjikome Seisaku: Sōren no Kyōi, Misairu-Gyapu Ronsō to Tōzai Kōryū* (The Eisenhower Administration's Containment Policy: The Soviet Threat, Debate over the Missile Gap, and East-West Exchanges) (Tokyo: Yūhikaku, 2008).

Satō, Seizaburō, and Matsuzaki, Tetsuhisa. *Jimintō Seiken* (The LDP Administration) (Tokyo: Chūō Kōronsha, 1986).

Tanaka, Akihiko. *Anzen Hoshō: Sengo 50 Nen no Mōsaku 20 Seiki no Nihon 2* (The 50-Year Search for Security 20th Century Japan 2) (Tokyo: Yomiuri Shimbunsha, 1997).

Wakaizumi, Kei, edited by John Swenson-Wright. *The Best Course Available: A Personal Account of the Secret U.S.-Japan Okinawa Reversion Negotiations* (Honolulu: University of Hawaii Press, 2002).

Yamada, Eizō. *Seiden Satō Eisaku* (The Official Biography of Satō Eaisaku) (Tokyo: Shinchōsha, 1988).

Chapter 15

Fukunaga, Fumio. *Ōhira Masayoshi: Sengo Hoshu to ha Nani ka* (Ōhira Masyoshi – Just What Is "Postwar Conservative"?) (Tokyo: Chūkō Shinsho, 2008).

Funabashi, Yoichi. *Asia-Pacific Fusion: Japan's Role in APEC* (New York: Columbia University Press, 1995).

Funabashi, Yōichi. *Managing the Dollar: From the Plaza to the Louvre* (Washington, DC: Institute for International Economics, 1989).

Funabashi, Yōichi. *Sammitokurashii* (Summitocracy) (Tokyo: Asahi Bunko, 1991, originally published by Asahi Shimbunsha as *Sammito no Shisō* [Summit Thinking], 1980).

Iio, Jun. *Nihon no Tōchi Kōzō: Kanryō Naikakusei kara Giin Naikakusei e* (Japan's Administrative Structure: From the Bureaucracy-Led Cabinet System to the Parliamentary Cabinet System) (Tokyo: Chūkō Shinsho, 2007).

Mann, James. *About Face: A History of America's Curious Relationship with China from Nixon to Clinton* (New York: Alfred Knopf, 1999).

Masuda, Hirosh, ed. *Nikuson Hōchū to Reisen Kōzō no Henyō: Beichū Sekkin no Shōgekki to Shūhen Shokoku* (Nixon's Visit to China and the Change in the Cold War Structure: The Impact of the U.S.-China Rapprochement and Neighboring Countries) (Nagoya: University of Nagoya Press, 2001).

Miyagi, Taizō, trans. by Hanabusa Midori. *Japan's Quest for Stability in Southeast Asia: Navigating the Turning Points in Postwar Asia* (London: Routledge, 2017).

Murata, Kōji. *Daitōryō no Zasetsu: Kaataa Daitōryō no Zaikan Beigun Tettai Seisaku* (A President's Frustration: President Carter's Policy to Withdraw U.S. Forces from South Korea) (Tokyo: Yūhikaku, 1998).

Nakasone, Yasuhiro, Itō Takashi, and Satō Seizaburō. *Tenchi Ujō: 50 Nen no Sengo Seiji o Kataru* (The Sentient World: Talking About the 50 Years of Postwar Politics) (Tokyo: Bungei Shunjū, 1996).

Oberdorfer, Don, and Robert, Carlin. *The Two Koreas: A Contemporary History* (New York: Basic Books, 2013).

Okada, Akira. *Mizutori Gaikō Hiwa: Aru Gaikōkan no Shōgen* (Mizutori's Secret Diplomacy: A Diplomat's Testimony) (Tokyo: Chūō Kōronsha, 1983).

Putnum, Robert D., and Nicholas, Bayne. *Hanging Together: Cooperation and Conflict in the Seven-Power Summits*, Revised and Enlarged Edition (Cambridge, MA: Harvard University Press, 1988).

Sase, Masamori, trans. by Robert D. Eldridge. *Changing Security Policies in Postwar Japan: The Political Biography of Japanese Defense Minister Sakata Michita* (Lanham, MD: Lexington Books, 2017).

Tachibana, Takashi. *Tanaka Kakuei Kenkyū Zenkiroku* (Entire Record of Research About Tanaka Kakuei) (Tokyo: Kōdansha Gakujutsu Bunko, 1982, originally published by Kōdansha, 1976).

Tanaka, Akihiko. *Nicchū Kankei* (Japan-China Relations)*, 1945–1990* (Tokyo: University of Tokyo Press, UP Sensho, 1991).

Tanaka, Kakuei. *Building a New Japan: A Plan for Remodeling the Archipelago* (Tokyo: Simul Press, 1972).

Wakatsuki, Hidekazu. *Zenhōigaikō no Jidai: Reisen Henyōki no Nihon to Ajia, 1971–1980 Nen* (The Age of "Omnidirectional Diplomacy": Japan and Asia During the Period of Change in the Cold War, 1971–1980) (Tokyo: Nihon Keizai Hyōronsha, 2006).

Watanabe, Akio. *Taikoku Nihon no Yuragi, 1972- Nihon no Kindai 8* (The Shaking of the Economic Superpower, Japan Modern Japan 8) (Tokyo: Chūō Kōronsha, 2000).

Chapter 16

Beasley, W. G. *Japanese Imperialism 1894–1945* (London: Oxford University Press, 1991).

Duus, Peter, Ramon H. Myers, and Mark R. Peattie, eds. *The Japanese Informal Empire in China, 1895–1937* (Princeton, NJ: Princeton University Press, 1989).

Duus, Peter, Ramon H. Meyers, and Mark R. Peattie, eds. *The Japanese Wartime Empire, 1931–1945* (Princeton, NJ: Princeton University Press, 1996).

Duus, Peter. *The Abacus and the Sword, The Japanese Penetration of Korea, 1895–1910* (Berkeley: University of California Press, 1998).

Kondō, Kenichi, ed. *Banzai Sōjō Jiken (San-Ichi Undō)* (Long Live the March First Movement), Vol. 1 (Tokyo: Yūhō Kyōkai Chōsen Shiryō Hensankai, 1964).

Kumagai, Naoko, trans. by David Noble. *The Comfort Women: Historical, Political, Legal and Moral Perspectives* (Tokyo: International House of Japan, 2016).

Myers, Ramon H., and Mark R., Peattie, eds. *The Japanese Colonial Empire, 1895–1945* (Princeton, NJ: Princeton University Press, 1987).

Park, Eun-sik, trans. by Gang Deok-sang. *Chōsen Dokuritsu Undō no Kesshi* (The Bloody History of the Korean Independence Movement), Vol. 1 (Tokyo: Heibonsha Tōyō Bunko, 1972).

Peattie, Mark R. *Nanyo: The Rise and Fall of the Japanese in Micronesia, 1885–1945* (Honolulu: University of Hawai'i Press, 1988).

Peattie, Mark R., trans. by Asano Toyomi. *Shokuminchi: 20 Seiki Nihon Teikoku 50 Nen no Kōbō* (Colonies: The Rise and Fall of Imperial Japan in the First 50 Years of the 20th Century) (Tokyo: Jigakusha Shuppan, 2012, originally published by Yomiuri Shimbunsha as part of its 20 *Seiki no Nihon* [Japan in the 20th Century] series, 1996).

Sōmuchō, Kanshū, Nihon Tōkei, and Kyōkai Henshū. *Nihon Chōki Tōkei Sōran (General Survey of Long Term Statistics)*, Vol. 1 (Kokudo, Gyōsei Chiiki, Jinkō, Rōdō [Territory, Jurisdictional Area, Population, and Labor]) (Tokyo: Nihon Tōkei Kyōkai, 1987).

Yamabe, Kentarō. "Nihon Teikokushugi to Shokuminchi (Japanese Imperialism and Its Colonies)," in Ienaga Saburō, et al., eds., *Iwanami Kōza Nihon Rekishi 19 Gendai 2* (Iwanami's Japan History Course, Vol. 19, Modern Day 2) (Tokyo: Iwanami Shoten, 1963).

Chronology

1792

October 18   Russian envoy Adam K. Laksman arrives in Nemuro, demands trade relations.

1804

October 10   Russian envoy Rezanov arrives in Nagasaki, demands trade relations.

1808

October 4   HMS *Phaeton*, a British warship, enters Nagasaki harbor and demands fuel and water.

1825

April 6   Shogunate issues the Edict to Repel Foreign Vessels.

1837

July 30   American merchant ship *Morrison* is fired upon by local officials after anchoring off Uraga.

1839

June 3   Lin Zexu destroys 20,291 chests of opium confiscated from British merchants.

1840

June 28   British navy blockades Guangzhou and the Pearl River (First Opium War begins and would continue until August 29, 1842).

1842

August 29   Treaty of Nanjing is signed (five treaty ports are established with British consuls, Chinese pay an indemnity, etc.).

30   Shogunate issues the Edict to Supply Fuel and Water.

1846

July 20   James Biddle, commander of the American East India Squadron, enters Uraga Bay seeking trade relations but is rejected by the shogunate.

1851

January 11   Hong Xiuquan formally declares his rebellion, and Taiping Heavenly Kingdom is established.

1853

July 8   Perry's fleet arrives in Uraga Bay and demands the opening of Japan.

14   Perry lands at Kurihama and delivers a letter from U.S. President Millard Filmore.

August 5   Rōjū Abe Masahiro requests the opinion of various *daimyō* on how to reply to the American letter.

22   A Russian fleet under Yevfimiy Putyatin arrives in Nagasaki.

1854

February 13   Seven ships under Matthew C. Perry anchor off Koshiba in Edo Bay.

March 31   Treaty of Kanagawa (U.S.-Japan Treaty of Peace and Amity) is signed.

1855

January 19   Shogunate establishes military training facilities (*kōbujō*) in six locations, including Teppōzu and Hitotsubashi in Edo.

October 5   Shogunate receives steamship *Soembing* (later renamed the *Kankō Maru*) as a gift from the Dutch king.

November 18   Shogunate appoints Hotta Masayoshi, *daimyō* of Sakura, as head *rōjū*.

1856

August 21   U.S. Consul Townsend Harris arrives in Shimoda.

October 8   In Guangzhou, Qing officials arrest crewmen from the *Arrow*, a British merchant ship. Britain demands their release and an apology (Arrow Incident).

23   British invade Guangzhou and occupy batteries in Liede (beginning of the Second Opium War).

1857

December 2   Matsudaira Yoshinaga, *daimyō* of Echizen, and others propose that Hitotsubashi Yoshinobu be named shogunal heir.

7   Harris visits Edo Castle and presents a personal letter from U.S. president.

1858

March 23	Rōjū Hotta Masayoshi visits the Imperial Palace to seek imperial consent for the Treaty of Amity and Commerce (Harris Treaty).
May 3	Hotta Masayoshi visits the Imperial Palace and receives an imperial order to solicit the opinions of the various *daimyō* and Tokugawa houses on the treaty and then to resubmit the matter for an imperial decision.
5	A confidential imperial decision on the matter of the shogunal succession that goes against the hopes of the Hitotsubashi faction is given to Hotta Masayoshi.
28	Qing sign Treaty of Aigun with Russia.
June	Qing sign Treaty of Tientsin with Russia, America, Britain, and France, granting them most favored nation status, paying an indemnity, opening more ports, allowing legations in Beijing, and so on.
4	Ii Naosuke, *daimyō* of Hikone, is appointed *tairō*.
July 29	Harris Treaty and its trade articles are signed aboard an American warship.
August 4	Shogunate announces Tokugawa Iemochi, *daimyō* of Wakayama, as the shogunal heir.
13	Orders are issued confining Tokugawa Nariaki and Matsudaira Yoshinaga to their homes and barring Hitotsubashi Yoshinobu from Edo Castle.
24	Shimazu Nariakira, *daimyō* of Shimazu, dies.
October 13	Ansei Purge begins.

1859

July 2	Ports of Yokohama and Hakodate are opened.
September 23	Shogunate orders permanent house arrest for Tokugawa Nariaki and house arrest for Hitotsubashi Yoshinobu. Shogunal officials belonging to the Hitotsubashi faction such as Iwase Tadanari, Nagai Naoyuki, and Kawaji Toshiakira are also punished.
November 1	Hashimoto Sanai is executed; Yoshida Shōin is executed on the 21st.

1860

February 4	Shogunal warship *Kanrin Maru* departs from Shinagawa.
March 24	*Ronin* from Mito Domain assassinate Tairō Ii Naosuke outside the Sakurada Gate of Edo Castle (Sakuradamon Incident).
October 2	Emperor privately gives the shogunate permission for the marriage of Princess Kazu to the shogun on the condition that either the treaty with the United States be annulled or foreigners be expelled from Japan.
17	Shogunate releases Hitotsubashi Yoshinobu, Matsudaira Yoshinaga, and Yamauchi Toyoshige from house arrest.

24	Qing sign the Convention of Beijing with Britain (Tianjin opened, Kowloon ceded to Britain, indemnity increased).
25	Qing sign the Convention of Beijing with France.
November 14	Qing sign the Convention of Beijing with Russia.

1861

January 15	Hendrick Heusken, an interpreter at the American consulate, is attacked and killed by Satsuma samurai in Azabu.
20	Qing open Tianjin. The Zongli Yamen is created.
March 13	Russian warship *Posadnik* arrives in Tsushima, seeking permission to anchor (Tsushima Incident).
June 22	Chōshū *metsuke* Nagai Uta travels to Edo to advocate for his sea voyage policy.

1862

February 13	Mito *ronin* attack *rōjū* Andō Nobumasa outside the Sakashita Gate of Edo Castle (Sakashitamon Incident).
March 11	Wedding between Shogun Iemochi and Princess Kazu is held at Edo Castle.
May 14	Shimazu Hisamitsu, father of the *hanshu* of Satsuma, leads 1,000 Satsuma samurai into Edo.
June 5	Imperial Court, in response to a proposal from Shimazu Hisamitsu, decides to dispatch imperial envoy Ōhara Shigetomi to Edo.
July 6	Imperial envoy Ōhara Shigetomi meets with Shogun Iemochi in Edo Castle. He informs him of the court's desire for Hitotsubashi Yoshinobu and Matsudaira Yoshinaga to be elevated. On July 6, Yoshinobu is named the shogun's guardian. On July 9, Yoshinaga is named supreme councilor
September 14	Satsuma samurai kill a British man in Namamugi (Namamugi Incident).
24	Shogunate appoints Matsudaira Katamori, daimyo of Aizu, as the first military commissioner of Kyōto.

1863

June 6	Shogun Iemochi tells emperor that the foreigners will be expelled on June 25.
25	Chōshū opens fire on an American merchant ship passing through the Shimonoseki Straits (Shimonoseki Incident). In the following days, it also fires upon French and Dutch ships.
July 16	USS *Wyoming* returns fire on the Chōshū batteries. Soon after, French marines occupy the batteries.
August 15	British fleet of seven ships fights with Satsuma in Kagoshima Bay (Anglo-Satsuma War).

| September 30 | *Kōbu gattai* (unity of court and shogunate) faction launches a palace coup. |

1864

January 10	Gojong becomes king in Korea with his father the Daewongun serving as regent.
February 7	Imperial Court appoints Hitotsubashi Yoshinobu, Matsudaira Yoshinaga, Matsudaira Katamori, Yamauchi Toyoshige, and Date Munenari to the imperial advisory council. Later, Shimazu Hisamitsu is also appointed.
March 27	Yamauchi Toyoshige, former *daimyō* of Tosa, resigns from the council. The others would also later resign.
April 27	French Consul Leon Roches arrives in Japan.
July 19	Tianjing falls, ending the Taiping Heavenly Kingdom.
August 19	Chōshū and shogunate forces clash (Kinmon Incident).
24	The imperial order to punish Chōshū is given to Hitotsubashi Yoshinobu (beginning of the First Chōshū Expedition).
September 5	A joint British, American, French, and Dutch fleet fight with the Chōshū batteries in the Shimonoseki Straits.
October 22	Representatives of the four countries and the shogunate reach agreement on compensation for the Shimonoseki Incident.
December 9	As a show of obedience to the shogunate, Chōshū orders those responsible for the Kinmon Incident to commit suicide.

1865

February 10	Shogunate orders its army to halt in response to an acknowledgment of guilt by the Chōshū *daimyō* and his son.
April 12	Chōshū *daimyō* Mōri Yoshichika decides domain will follow policy of "military preparation and obedience" (*bubi kyōjun*) advocated by its radical faction.
November 4	Joint British, American, French, and Dutch fleet arrives in Hyōgo Bay with representatives to negotiate with the shogunate and imperial court for the early opening of Hyōgo to foreign trade and imperial sanction for Ansei Treaties.
9	Shogun visits the Imperial Palace and receives imperial order for Second Chōshū Expedition.
22	Emperor issues an imperial rescript sanctioning the treaties but not permitting early opening of Hyōgo.

1866

| March 7 | Following the mediation of Sakamoto Ryōma, Kido Takayoshi and Saigo Takamori secretly enter into agreement on cooperation between Satsuma and Chōshū. |
| June 25 | Rōjū Mizuno Tadakiyo signs revised tariff agreement with Britain, France, America, and the Netherlands in Edo. |

July 18	Fighting begins in the Second Chōshū Expedition.
28	British Consul Harry Parkes visits Kagoshima and meets with Shimazu Mochihisa.
August 29	Shogun Iemochi dies in Osaka Castle. This is made public on September 28, and Yoshinobu is named his successor.
September 2	In Korea, American merchant ship *General Sherman* is sunk after entering the Taedong River without permission.
29	Shogunal policy to seek a ceasefire is issued; the shogunate and Chōshū agree to ceasefire on October 10.
October 1	French fleet attacks Korea, giving the oppression of Catholics as its reason.
November 20	Korea drives away the French fleet at Ganghwa Island/

1867

January 10	Tokugawa Yoshinobu is named *seii taishogun* (shogun) and *naidaijin*.
30	Emperor Kōmei dies. Prince Mutsuhito succeeds him on February 13.
March 11	Shogun Yoshinobu meets with French Consul Roches in Osaka Castle.
July 23	Gotō Shōjirō and others meet with Saigō and Ōkubo; a secret agreement is reached between Satsuma and Tosa on returning political authority to the throne.
30	Shogunate appoints ministers (*sōsai*) for domestic policy, finances, foreign policy, the army, and the navy.
October 15	Ōkubo Toshimichi meets with the Chōshū daimyo and his son; alliance is reached to raise an army to defeat the shogunate.
29	Gotō Shōjirō submits Yamauchi Toyoshige's petition, on returning authority to the emperor, to *rōjū* Itakura Katsukiyo.
November 8	Iwakura Tomomi gives Ōkubo Toshimichi an imperial rescript addressed to the daimyo of Satsuma and his father, ordering them to overthrow the shogunate.
9	Shogun Yoshinobu submits memorial to the emperor, agreeing to return political authority.
10	Imperial Court summons Yoshinobu to the Imperial Palace, and imperial sanction to the return of authority is issued.
December 8	Satsuma *daimyō* Shimazu Tadayoshi departs Kagoshima with an army, meeting with Chōshū heir Mōri Sadahiro on December 12 where they reach an agreement to dispatch troops.

1868

January 3	Imperial pronouncement is issued at the palace announcing the restoration of imperial rule. It is decided at a conference that night to order Yoshinobu to return all his ranks and lands to the throne.

19	In response to disturbances caused by Satsuma *ronin* in Edo, the former shogunate burns the Satsuma manor.
27	The forces of the former shogunate are defeated by those of Satsuma and Chōshū at the Battle of Toba-Fushimi (the Boshin War begins).
April 5	Saigō Takamori and Katsu Kaishū negotiate the surrender of Edo Castle at the Satsuma manor in Edo. An agreement is reached the next day.
6	Emperor issues the Charter Oath.
May 3	Edo Castle is surrendered. Tokugawa Yoshinobu leaves Edo for retirement in Mito.
June 17	New government issues its Document on Government Structure.
22	An alliance is formed between domains in Mutsu, Dewa, and Echigo.
July 4	Forces of the new government attack and destroy the Shōgitai at the Battle of Ueno.
September 3	Emperor issues an imperial rescript changing the name of Edo to Tokyo.
October 8	Forces of the new government surround Aizu-Wakamatsu Castle. Aizu *daimyō* Matsudaira Katamori surrenders on November 6.
23	Era name is changed to Meiji, and the practice of having one era name per emperor is adopted.
November 4	Emperor departs Kyōto to visit Tokyo, arriving on November 26, later departing Tokyo on January 20 to return to Kyōto.

1869

March 2	The *daimyō* of Satsuma, Chōshū, Tosa, and Hizen petition the emperor to accept the return of their domains.
June 27	Goryōkaku falls and Enomoto Takeaki surrenders (the Boshin War ends).
July 25	Return of domains to the emperor is approved, and governors are appointed. The peerage is established.
August 15	Government is re-formed into the Council of State (Daijōkan), Council of Divinities (Jingikan), and six ministries.
October 8	Vice-Minister of War Ōmura Masujirō attacked in Kyōto, dying on December 7.

1870

January 26	Telegraph service between Tokyo and Yokohama begins.
August 6	Ministry of Popular Affairs separated from the Ministry of Finance.
December 12	Ministry of Industry established.

1871

March 14	Postal service between Tokyo, Kyoto, and Osaka begins.
April 2	Government orders the creation of a new army composed of soldiers drawn from the forces of Satsuma, Chōshū, and Tosa.

May 22	Koseki law created.
June 10	First garrisons established and placed on the Tōsandō and Saikaidō.
10	American fleet attacks Ganghwa Island, demanding opening of the country and a resolution to the *General Sherman* Incident.
12	Korean regent Daewongun erects *cheokhwabi* across country.
27	Regulations for a new currency are enacted.
July 3	American fleet is driven away at Ganghwa Island.
August 29	Emperor gathers fifty-six domain governors in Tokyo and issues imperial rescript abolishing the domains and creating prefectures.
September 13	Friendship and Trade Treaty is signed with the Qing in Tianjin.
23	Government allows samurai to cut their topknots and go without swords.
October 4	Four garrisons are established in Tokyo, Sendai, Osaka, and Kumamoto.
7	Marriage between peers, samurai, and commoners becomes permitted.
20	Government allows the free cultivation of fields.
November 20	Iwakura Mission is dispatched to America and Europe with Foreign Minister Iwakura Tomomi as ambassador and Councilor Kido Takayoshi, Finance Minister Ōkubo Toshimichi, Vice-Minister of Industry Itō Hirobumi, and Deputy Foreign Minister Yamaguchi Masuka as vice-ambassadors.

1872

March 4	Iwakura Tomomi meets U.S. President Ulysses S. Grant.
10	Government dispatches diplomat Yanagiwara Sakimitsu to China to negotiate revisions to Friendship and Trade Treaty.
May 15	Yanagiwara's negotiates with Li Hongzhang in Tianjin breakdown.
23	Edict on the Prohibition on the Sale of Arable Lands is revoked.
April 5	Ministry of Military Affairs abolished, and the Ministry of War and Ministry of the Navy are established
July 3	Matters pertaining to Japanese trading post in Korea are transferred from the Sō clan to Foreign Ministry.
24	Ambassador Iwakura informs U.S. Secretary of State Hamilton Fish that negotiations to revise the treaties with the United States will be broken off.
September 5	New school system is promulgated across Japan.
20	Diplomat Hanabusa Yoshitada is dispatched to Korea. He takes over the Japanese trading post on October 18.
October 14	Rail service between Shimbashi and Yokohama begins.
16	Ryūkyūan King Shō Tai is made a peer as the King of Ryūkyū Domain.

30	Announcement that treaties and interactions between Ryūkyū Domain and other countries are under the jurisdiction of the Foreign Ministry.
December 5	Ambassador Iwakura meets Queen Victoria.
9	Imperial rescript issued adopting the solar calendar.
15	Regulations on a national bank are adopted, and the establishment of banks becomes permitted.
26	Ambassador Iwakura meets the president of France.
28	Imperial rescript is issued on conscription.

1873

January 9	Garrisons are placed in Nagoya and Hiroshima. Military districts for the six garrisons are established.
10	Conscription Act and its appendices are enacted.
February 28	Foreign Minister Soejima Taneomi is dispatched as an ambassador to the Qing. Instruments of ratification for the treaty are exchanged on April 30.
May 26	Vice-Ambassador Ōkubo Toshimichi of the Iwakura Mission returns to Japan.
June 21	Qing minister tells Deputy Ambassador Yanagiwara Sakimitsu that the indigenous Taiwanese population is outside the rule of the Qing emperor.
29	Ambassador Soejima Taneomi meets the Qing emperor and gives him a message from the Japanese emperor. He returns to Japan on July 27.
July 23	Vice-Ambassador Kido Takayoshi of the Iwakura Mission returns to Japan.
28	Land Tax Reform Law is promulgated.
August 3	Councilor Saigō Takamori submits opinion paper to Grand Chancelor Sanjō Sanetomi proposing that the cabinet dispatch a military expedition to Korea.
17	Cabinet decides in favor of Saigō's expedition to Korea (it is decided to postpone the announcement until Iwakura's return to Japan).
September 13	Ambassador Iwakura Tomomi returns to Japan.
October 14	Cabinet again discusses hardline policy on Korea but fails to reach a decision.
15	Discussion continues with decision to dispatch Saigō to Korea.
17	Kido, Ōkubo, Ōkuma Shigenobu, and Ōki Takatō submit their resignations from the Council of State. Iwakura also announces his resignation.
18	Grand Chancellor Sanjō suddenly falls ill. Iwakura Tomomi assumes the position of acting chancellor.

24	The emperor, accepting a proposal by Iwakura, indefinitely postpones the dispatch of an envoy to Korea. Saigō resigns from the Council of State and as commander of the imperial guard.
25	Soejima Taneoki, Gotō Shōjirō, Itagaki Taisuke, and Etō Shinpei resign from the Council of State.
November 10	Ministry of Home Affairs is established.

1874

January 12	Itagaki, Gotō, Soejima, and Etō form the Public Party of Patriots (*Aikoku Kōtō*).
17	Eight people, including Soejima, Gotō, Etō, and Itagaki, submit a petition for the creation of a popularly elected assembly to the Ministry of the Left.
February 4	Orders for mobilization are issued to the Kumamoto garrison in response to violence by Saga samurai, including Etō Shinpei.
February 6	Cabinet approves a military expedition to Taiwan.
10	Councilor and Home Minister Ōkubo Toshimichi is commissioned with suppressing the violence in Saga and ordered to the southwest.
18	Etō Shinpei and others occupy Saga Prefectural offices (Saga Rebellion).
March 1	Government forces retaking of the government offices. Etō is later arrested in Kōchi and executed on April 13.
April 4	Lieutenant General Saigō Jūdō is ordered to subjugate Taiwan.
10	Itagaki Taisuke forms the Risshisha in Kōchi.
18	Councilor and Minister of Education Kido Takayoshi submits his resignation due to his dissatisfaction with the Taiwan expedition. He is dismissed on May 13.
27	Cabinet advisor Shimazu Hisamitsu is appointed minister of the left.
May 4	Ōkubo, Ōkuma, and Saigō Jūdō meet in Nagasaki and decide to carry out the expedition to Taiwan. Saigō lands in Taiwan on May 22.
July 9	Cabinet decides it is ready to go to war with the Qing over the Taiwan issue.
August 1	Decision is made to send Councilor Ōkubo Toshimichi as an envoy to the Qing to negotiate the Taiwan issue.
6	Ōkubo leaves Tokyo, arriving in Beijing on September 10.
September 14	Ōkubo begins negotiations with Prince Gong over Taiwan.
October 31	Treaty resolving the Taiwan issue is signed in Beijing. Ōkubo returns to Japan on November 26.

1875

February 11	Kido, Ōkubo, and Itagaki meet in Osaka and reach an agreement on political reform (Osaka Conference).

22	Aikoku-sha is formed, calling upon the Risshisha and regional people's rights (*minken*) organizations.
March 8	As a result of the Osaka Conference, Kido is appointed as a councilor. Itagaki is also appointed on March 12.
April 14	Genrōin, Daishin'in, and Chihōkan Kaigi are established. An imperial rescript is issued for the gradual formation of a constitutional political system.
May 7	Treaty of St. Petersburg is signed with Russia over Sakhalin and the Kuril Islands. Instruments of ratification are exchanged on August 22.
June 20	Opening ceremony for the Chihōkan Kaigi is held (the closing ceremony is on July 17).
28	Libel Law and Press Ordinance are enacted to clamp down on antigovernment movements.
September 20	Warship *Un'yō* fights the garrison of Ganghwa Island while engaged in a show of force off the southwest coast of Korea (Ganghwa Island Incident).
October 27	Minister of the Left Shimazu Hisamitsu and Councilor Itagaki Taisuke are dismissed.
November 5	During talks with Foreign Minister Terashima Munenori, a British envoy tacitly recognizes the Ogasawara Islands as Japanese territory.
December 9	Councilor Kuroda Kiyotaka is dispatched to Korea for talks over the Ganghwa Island Incident.

1876

February 26	Kuroda Kiyotaka signs the Japan-Korea Treaty of Amity. Instruments of ratification are exchanged on March 22.
March 28	Kido Takayoshi resigns from the Council of State. He is named a cabinet advisor.
28	Bearing swords is prohibited except for court dress and military and police officials in uniform (Sword Prohibition Edict).
June 2	Emperor departs Tokyo to visit Mutsu and Dewa. He returns to the capital on July 21.
August 5	A law converting the government's stipends to the samurai into government bonds is enacted.
October 17	Government informs its officials that the Ogasawara Islands are under its jurisdiction.
24	Samurai in Kumamoto attack its garrison (Shinpūren Rebellion).
28	Yamaguchi samurai Maebara Issei attempts to lead an attack on the prefectural office, but this is suppressed (Hagi Rebellion).
December 19	Farmers in Iino County, Mie revolt against the land tax reform. They burn the court and government buildings in Yokkaichi the following day (Ise Revolt).
27	Councilor and Home Minister Ōkubo Toshimichi proposes lowering the land tax in light of the farmer revolts.

1877

January 4	Imperial rescript lowering the land tax is issued.
24	Emperor leaves Tokyo to visit western Japan.
30	Kagoshima students steal weapons and ammunition being transported to the Osaka arsenal (the Satsuma Rebellion begins).
February 15	Saigō Takamori departs Kagoshima with his troops. On February 22, they lay siege to Kumamoto Castle.
March 20	Government forces occupy Tabaruzaka after heavy fighting. On April 14, government forces, led by Kuroda Kiyotaka, enter Kumamoto Castle.
May 26	Cabinet Advisor Kido Takayoshi dies.
September 24	Saigō Takamori commits suicide at Shiroyama (Satsuma Rebellion ends).

1878

February 20	British Court for Japan finds the British merchant John Harley innocent of smuggling opium.
April 10	Second session of the Chihōkan Kaigi begins (Itō Hirobumi serves as speaker) and ends on May 3 after deliberating over three new laws.
29	Risshisha members Sugita Teiichi, Ueki Emori, and Kurihara Ryōichi depart on a tour calling for the revitalization of the Aikoku-sha.
May 14	Ōkubo Toshimichi assassinated by Shimada Ichirō and five other Ishikawa samurai in Kioi, Tokyo.
July 22	Three laws discussed at the Chihōkan Kaigi (the Law on the Organization of Districts, Wards, Towns, and Villages, the Prefectural Assembly Law, and the Local Tax Law) are enacted.
September 11	Aikoku-sha Revival Conference is held in Osaka.

1879

March 11	Ryūkyūan king informed that the domain will be abolished. He is made a peer and ordered to live in Tokyo.
27	Second Aikoku-sha Conference is held in Osaka.
April 4	It is announced that Ryūkyū domain has been abolished and made a Okinawa prefecture.
July 3	Former American president Grant arrives in Yokohama. He meets the emperor at Hamarikyū Imperial Villa on August 10.
September 10	Inoue Kaoru is appointed foreign minister.
November 7	Third Aikoku-sha Conference is held in Osaka.

1880

February 5	Third session of the Chihōkan Kaigi is held (Kōno Togama serves as speaker). It ends on February 28.
March 15	Fourth Aikoku-sha conference is held in Osaka. On March 17, the League for the Establishment of a National Assembly is formed.

April 5	Public Assembly Ordinance is enacted.
November 10	Second conference of the League for the Establishment of a National Assembly is held in Tokyo.
December 23	Public Assembly Ordinance is amended (the national police chief and governors are given the authority to dissolve political organizations and forbid individuals from making public addresses for one year).
24	Councilors Ōkuma Shigenobu, Itō Hirobumi, and Inoue Kaoru discuss the publication of a government newspaper with Fukuzawa Yukichi.

1881

March	Councilor Ōkuma Shigenobu presents an opinion paper on the establishment of a national assembly to Minister of the Left Prince Arisugawa Taruhito.
July 21	Councilor Kuroda Kiyotaka petitions for the sale of the assets of the Hokkaidō Colonization Office. After fierce debate, the cabinet decides to approve the sale.
26	Tokyo Yokohama *Mainichi Shimbun* exposes the sale of the Hokkaidō Colonization Office's assets in a series of editorials (until July 28).
October 11	At meeting in the presence of the emperor, decision is made to pursue a policy of constitutional government, cancel the sale of the office's assets, and dismiss Ōkuma (the 1881 Political Crisis).
12	Imperial rescript is issued stating that a national assembly would be created in 1890.
18	Meeting forming the Jiyūtō (Liberal Party) is held in Asakusa. Itagaki Taisuke accepts the position of party president on November 9.
21	Matsukata Masayoshi is appointed a councilor and finance minister.

1882

January 4	Imperial Rescript to Soldiers and Sailors is issued.
March 3	Itō Hirobumi is ordered to visit Europe to study the creation of a constitution.
18	Fukuchi Gen'ichirō forms the Rikken Teiseitō (Constitutional Imperial Party) and announces its platform.
April 6	Liberal Party President Itagaki Taisuke is attacked and injured while campaigning in Gifu.
16	Rikken Kaishintō (Constitutional Progressive Party) is formed with Ōkuma Shigenobu as president.
June 3	Public Assembly Ordinance is amended (the home minister is granted the authority to prohibit an organization from gathering, and political organizations are prohibited from establishing branches).
27	Bank of Japan Ordinance is enacted.

July 23	Korean soldiers in Seoul riot and attack the Japanese legation (Imo Incident).
August 30	Treaty of Chemulpo is signed (punishment of the rioters, an indemnity of 500,000 yen, and the right to station soldiers at the legation).
November 11	Itagaki Taisuke and Gotō Shōjirō depart Yokohama for Europe. They return to Japan on June 22, 1883.

1883

July 20	Iwakura Tomomi dies.
August 3	Itō Hirobumi returns from his constitutional research trip in Europe.

1884

March 17	Office for the Investigation of Institutions is established in the palace with Itō Hirobumi as its head. On March 21, he is also appointed minister of the imperial household.
May 16	Members of the Liberal Party in Gunma gather several thousand farmers and attack money lenders and police stations (Gunma Incident).
June 23	Sino-French War begins.
July 7	Peerage Law is enacted.
September 23	Members of the Liberal Party in Ibaraki and Fukushima distribute inflammatory materials at Mt. Kaba and fight with police on the 24th (Mt. Kaba Incident).
October 29	Liberal Party Congress is held in Osaka; decision is reached to dissolve the party.
31	Farmers in Chichibu, Saitama, attack district offices under the leadership of Liberal Party members (Chichibu Incident).
December 4	Pro-Japanese faction in Seoul launches a coup. On December 6, Japanese forces are driven out by the Qing army (Gapsin Coup).
6	Plot by Liberal Party members in Aichi and Nagano to raise forces against the government is discovered (Iida Incident).
17	Constitutional Progressive Party President Ōkuma Shigenobu and Vice President Kōno Togama leave the party.

1885

January 9	Treaty of Hanseong signed.
March 16	Fukuzawa Yukichi publishes "On Leaving Asia."
April 15	British fleet occupies Port Hamilton in Korea (until March 1, 1887).
18	Tientsin Convention is signed (Japan and China will simultaneously withdraw their forces from Korea and notify each other before sending troops to the country). The treaty is ratified on May 21.

June 6	It is enacted that government-issued banknotes will be convertible into silver coins from January 1886.
November 23	Plan for a coup in Korea is discovered, and Ōi Kentarō is arrested (Osaka Incident).
December 22	Council of State abolished, and the cabinet is created.
22	1st Itō Hirobumi Cabinet (until April 30, 1888) is formed.

1886

February 27	Regulations for the ministries are promulgated (the duties and authority of ministers, the presence of a vice-minister in each ministry, etc.).
April 29	Peer Succession and Assets Law is enacted.
May 1	Foreign Minister Inoue Kaoru holds the first treaty revision conference with foreign diplomats at the Foreign Ministry.
October 24	Hoshi Tōru and Nakae Chōmin host the National Gathering of Volunteers in Tokyo.
24	British ship *Normanton* sinks in the Kumano Sea and becomes a political issue.

1887

April 22	At the twenty-sixth treaty revision conference, Anglo-German proposal for judicial jurisdiction is approved after revision.
June 1	Prime Minister Itō, Itō Miyoji, and Kaneko Kentarō begin examining constitutional drafts in Kanazawa, Kanagawa.
1	Legal advisor Gustave Boissonade submits an opinion paper to the cabinet opposing the treaty revision.
July 3	Minister of Agriculture and Commerce Tani Tateki submits an opinion paper to Prime Minister Itō opposing the treaty revision
25	Regulations on the Examination, Probation, and Training of Civil Officials are issued.
29	Foreign Minister Inoue informs the foreign legations that meetings on treaty revision will be postponed until the compiling of a legal code has been completed.
September 17	Foreign Minister Inoue resigns; Prime Minister Itō takes up the portfolio.
October 3	Gotō Shōjirō's gathering is held. Grand Coalition (*Daidō Danketsu*) movement begins; Kōchi representative submits the Petition for Three Important Matters (freedom of expression, reduction of the land tax, restoration of equal diplomacy).
December 26	Peace Preservation Law is enacted.

1888

February 1	Ōkuma Shigenobu is appointed foreign minister.
April 30	Kuroda Kiyotaka Cabinet is formed (until December 24, 1889). Itō Hirobumi is named president of the Privy Council.

May 14	Ordinances for the army and navy general staffs and divisional command are issued.
June 18	Privy Council deliberates on the constitutional draft (until July 13).
November 26	Foreign Minister Ōkuma begins showing foreign diplomats his new proposal for treaty revision.
December 25	Military Officers Status Law is enacted.

1889

February 11	Meiji Constitution is promulgated.
12	Prime Minister Kuroda gives his speech on the transcendentalism.
March 22	Gotō Shōjirō enters the cabinet as communications minister.
April 19	*The Times* in London criticizes the treaty revision proposal.
December 24	1st Yamagata Aritomo Cabinet forms (until May 6, 1891).

1890

January 21	Liberal Party is established.
May 17	Mutsu Munemitsu is named minister of agriculture and commerce.
July 1	1st House of Representatives election is held (Daidō Club, 55 seats; Progressive Party, 46; Aikoku Kōtō, 35; Conservative Party, 22; Kyūshū Dōshikai, 21; Liberal Party, 17; Independents, 104—300 seats in total).
10	House of Peers holds its first election (15 counts, 70 viscounts, and 20 barons).
August 25	Liberal Party, Daidō Club, Aikoku Kōtō, Kyūshū Dōshikai, and others merge to become the Constitutional Liberal Party (Liberal Party).
November 25	1st Diet session is summoned.
December 6	Prime Minister Yamagata gives his speech on government policy ("the line of sovereignty and the line of advantage").

1891

February 24	Twenty-nine members from Tosa and others leave the Liberal Party.
March 2	Government's budget passes the House of Representatives (expenditures are cut from 7.88 million yen to 6.5 million yen).
29	Alexander III of Russia announces construction of the Trans-Siberian Railway.
May 6	1st Matsukata Masayoshi Cabinet forms (until August 8, 1892).
11	Russian crown prince is attacked and injured by Tsuda Sanzō, a policeman (Ōzu Incident).
November 21	2nd session of the Diet is convened.
December 22	Naval Minister Kabayama Sukenori gives his speech to the Diet.
25	House of Representatives passes budget after cutting it to 8.92 million yen, then dissolves.

1892

January 22   Itō Hirobumi reports to the emperor on the formation of a political party but abandons the idea after failing to receive his support.

February 15   2nd House of Representatives election is held (Liberal Party, 94 seats; Progressive Party, 38); 38 are killed and 388 injured in violence.

May 2   3rd session of the Diet convenes.

May 8   2nd Itō Hirobumi Cabinet forms (until September 18, 1896).

November 25   4th session of the Diet convenes.

1893

February 10   Imperial rescript issued in which the emperor promises to provide 300,000 yen a year from the palace budget for expansion of the military and reduces government salaries by 10 percent

22   Government budget passed by the House of Representatives.

November 25   5th session of the Diet convenes.

December 1   House of Representatives passes a motion of no confidence against Speaker Hoshi Tōru.

19   Abei Iwane submits his proposal for strict enforcement of foreign treaties.

30   Lower House is dissolved.

1894

March 1   3rd House of Representatives election is held (Liberal Party, 119 seats; Progressive Party, 48; Kokumin Kyōkai, 26).

May 12   6th Diet session convenes.

June 2   Lower House dissolved.

               Cabinet decides to dispatch one mixed brigade to Korea to oppose the introduction of Chinese troops.

16   Foreign Minister Mutsu proposes to China that the two countries jointly suppress the Donghak Rebellion and reform Korean domestic policies.

July 16   Anglo-Japanese Treaty of Commerce and Navigation signed, abolishing the rights of consular courts.

23   Japanese army occupies the Korean royal palace and disarms the Korean army.

25   Japanese fleet attacks Chinese warships at Pungdo.

August 1   War is declared on China (First Sino-Japanese War).

September 1   4th House of Representatives election is held (Liberal Party, 105 seats; Progressive Party, 45; Reform Party, 40; Kokumin Kyōkai, 30).

17   Battle of the Yellow Sea takes place.

1895

April 17   Shimonoseki Treaty is signed.

23	Triple Intervention.
June 17	Office of the Governor-General of Taiwan is established.
October 8	Japanese civilians and soldiers lead a coup in Seoul with the Dae-wongun and assassinate Empress Myeongseong.
December 25	9th Diet session convenes.

1896

February 11	Korean king and crown prince take refuge at the Russian legation.
March 1	Progressive Party (*Shimpōtō*) is formed.
April 14	Itagaki Taisuke is named home minister.
June 9	Yamagata-Lobanov Agreement is reached.
September 18	2nd Matsukata Masayoshi Cabinet forms (Foreign Minister Ōkuma Shigenobu, called the Matsuguma Cabinet, until January 12, 1898).
November 1	Progressive Party decides to cooperate with the cabinet.
December 22	10th Diet session convenes.

1897

July 10	Members of the House of Peers are elected.
October 31	Progressive Party ends its cooperation with the Matsukata government.
December 21	11th Diet session convenes.
25	Lower House dissolved following motion of nonconfidence against the cabinet.

1898

January 12	3rd Itō Hirobumi Cabinet forms (until June 30, 1898).
February 26	Kodama Gentarō appointed governor-general of Taiwan (Gotō Shimpei is made head of civilian affairs).
March 15	5th House of Representatives election is held (Liberal Party, 95 seats; Progressive Party, 91; Kokumin Kyōkai, 26).
27	Russia leases Port Arthur and Dalian from China and secures the right to build the South Manchuria Railway.
April 25	Spanish-American War begins.
May 14	12th Diet session convenes.
June 10	House of Representatives is dissolved.
11	Guangxu Emperor begins the Hundred Days' Reform.
22	Liberal and Progressive Parties merge to form Kenseitō (Constitutional Party).
30	1st Ōkuma Shigenobu Cabinet forms (Waihan Government; Ōkuma serves as foreign minister and Itagaki as home minister until November 8).
August 10	6th House of Representatives election is held (Kenseitō, 260 seats; Kokumin Kyōkai, 20).

21	Education Minister Ozaki Yukio gives his republican speech.
September 21	Wuxu Coup takes place in China.
October 27	Prime Minister Ōkuma appoints Inukai Tsuyoshi as education minister on his own initiative.
29	Former Liberal Party faction of Kenseitō dissolve party and form a new Kenseitō.
November 8	2nd Yamagata Aritomo Cabinet forms (until October 19, 1900).
30	Yamagata holds tea party for Kenseitō Diet members, announces the two would cooperate.
December 28	Liquor Tax Law is revised.
30	Land Tax Ordinance is revised (from 2.5% of land value to 3.3%).

1899

March 3	Boxer Rebellion begins.
28	Civil Service Appointment Law is revised.
September 6	Secretary of State John M. Hay announces Open Door policy.
November 20	14th Diet session convenes.
December 20	American minister proposes the Open Door policy to Foreign Minister Aoki.

1900

March 29	Election Law is revised (multimember districts introduced, number of Diet members increased, financial requirement for voting reduced, no registration necessary).
May 19	Requirement that military ministers be active duty generals and admirals introduced.
June 15	Cabinet decides to dispatch troops to the Boxer Rebellion.
August 14	Forces of the Eight-Nation Alliance enter Beijing.
September 15	*Rikken Seiyūkai* forms.
October 19	4th Itō Hirobumi Cabinet forms (until June 2, 1901).

1901

February 5	First blast furnace at the Yahata Steel Works begins operations.
June 2	1st Katsura Tarō Cabinet forms (until January 7, 1907).
21	Hoshi Tōru is assassinated (by stabbing).
December 10	Tanaka Shōzō directly appeals to the emperor concerning the Ashio Copper Mine Incident.

1902

January 30	Anglo-Japanese Alliance is signed in London.
August 10	7th House of Representatives election is held (Seiyūkai, 190; Kensei Hontō, 95; Teikokutō, 17).
December 28	House of Representatives dissolved (due to failure of a committee to approve a plan to continue collecting the increased land tax).

1903

March 1	8th House of Representatives election is held (Seiyūkai, 175; Kensei Hontō, 85; Teikokutō, 17).
June 23	Imperial Council decides to negotiate with Russia over Manchuria and Korean Peninsula problem.
July 13	Itō Hirobumi becomes the first president of the Privy Council.
14	Saionji Kinmochi becomes president of Seiyūkai.

1904

February 4	Imperial Council decides to end negotiations with Russia and begin war.
10	Declaration of war on Russia (start of Russo-Japanese War).
March 1	9th House of Representatives election is held (Seiyūkai, 133; Kensei Hontō, 90; Teikokutō, 19).
August 22	1st Japan-Korea Protocol signed.

1905

January 1	Siege of Port Arthur ends.
March 1	Battle of Mukden begins (continues until the 10th).
May 27	Battle of Tsushima begins (continues until the 28th).
June 9	U.S. President Theodore Roosevelt recommends mediation to Japan and Russia.
July 29	Taft-Katsura Agreement is signed.
August 10	Portsmouth Peace Conference begins.
12	2nd Anglo-Japanese Alliance signed in London.
14	Prime Minister Katsura and Hara Takashi meet, promises Seiyūkai's support for peace treaty if administration is turned over to Saionji.
September 5	Portsmouth Treaty is signed.
	Hibiya riots erupt.
October 12	Katsura sends American railroad magnate Edward Harriman a memorandum concerning agreement on the South Manchuria Railway (this is withdrawn on the 23rd).
November 17	Japan-Korea Treaty of 1904, or Eulsa Treaty, signed (Itō Hirobumi named first Japanese resident-general of Korea on December 21).
December 22	Japan and China sign treaty by which Japan assumes Russia's interests.

1906

January 7	1st Saionji Kinmochi Cabinet forms (until July 14, 1908).
February 1	Japan resident-general for Korea established.
February 10	HMS *Dreadnought* launched in Britain.
May 22	Conference held over the Manchurian issue.
August 1	Regulations for the Office of the Kwantung Governor-General issued (Ōshima Yoshimasa named governor-general on September 1).

September 1   Dairen made a free port.

November 26   South Manchuria Railway Company (Mantetsu) formed with Gotō Shimpei as its president (operations began on April 1, 1907).

1907

April 19   Board of Field Marshals and Fleet Admirals approves the Imperial National Defense Policy, The Military Strength Necessary for National Defense, and Strategic Summary for the Imperial Armed Forces.

June 10   Franco-Japanese Treaty of 1907 is signed.

15   The Hague Secret Emissary Affair occurs.

July 24   Japan-Korea Treaty of 1907 is signed.

30   Russo-Japanese Treaty of 1907 is signed.

November 16   1st (Japan-America) Gentlemen's Agreement (until February 18, 1908, 7th agreement).

1908

March 25   Members of the House of Peers Senge Takatomi and Hotta Masayasu named minister of justice and communications (Seiyūkai's policy toward the House of Peers).

May 15   10th House of Representatives election is held (Seiyūkai, 187; Kensei Hontō, 70; Daidō Gurakubu, 29; Yūshinkai, 29).

25   United States reduces indemnity from Boxer Rebellion, using money to encourage Chinese students to study in United States.

July 14   2nd Katsura Tarō Cabinet forms (until August 30, 1911).

October 18   U.S. Asiatic Fleet (White Fleet) arrives in Yokohama.

November 30   Root-Takahiro Agreement is signed.

1909

January 29   Prime Minister Katsura forges compromise with Seiyūkai.

February 2   Foreign Minister Komura calls for migration to Manchuria and Korea.

April 11   Japan Sugar Company bribery scandal–related arrests begin.

October 2   China signs a contract with America and Britain to build a railway between Jinzhou and Aigun (Jinai Railway).

26   Former Resident-General of Korea Itō Hirobumi is assassinated at Harbin Station by An Jung-geun.

November 6   U.S. Secretary of State Knox proposes to Britain that Manchurian Railway be made neutral (rejected by Japan and Russia on January 21, 1910).

1910

March 13   Original Constitutional Party becomes the Constitutional Nationalist Party.

July 4   Second Russo-Japanese Treaty is signed.

August 22   Japan-Korea Annexation Treaty is signed.

September 30	Office of the Resident-General of Korea becomes the Office of the Governor-General.
October 1	Terauchi Masatake appointed the first governor-general of Korea.
November 10	Four-Power Consortium (Britain, America, France, and Germany) agrees in London to invest in Chinese railways equally.

1911

January 26	Prime Minister Katsura reaches a "mutual understanding" with the Seiyūkai.
February 21	U.S.-Japan Treaty of Commerce and Navigation signed, providing Japan with sovereignty over tariffs for the first time.
June 26	Japan and Russia approach the Four-Power Consortium about loans in Manchuria.
July 13	3rd Anglo-Japanese Alliance is signed.
August 30	2nd Saionji Kinmochi Cabinet forms (until December 21, 1912).
October 10	Chinese Revolution of 1911 (Xinhai Revolution) starts.

1912

January 1	Republic of China is declared in Beijing.
February 12	Qing Dynasty ends with abdication.
March 10	Yuan Shikai becomes first president of republic.
April 5	Uehara Yūsaku becomes army minister.
May 15	11th House of Representatives election is held (Seiyūkai, 211; Kokumintō, 95; Chūō Club, 31).
June 18	Six-Power Consortium is formed.
July 6	Katsura Tarō, Gotō Shimpei, and Wakatsuki Reijirō depart for Russia.
8	3rd Russo-Japanese Treaty is signed.
30	Meiji Emperor dies; era name changes to Taishō.
November 22	War Minister Uehara proposes to cabinet that two new divisions be placed in Korea.
December 5	2nd Saionji Cabinet resigns en masse.
21	3rd Katsu Tarō Cabinet is formed (until February 20, 1913).

1913

January 20	Katsu Tarō announces formation of new political party.
February 9	Emperor speaks to Saionji about "regaining control of the situation."
11	3rd Katsu Tarō Cabinet resigns en masse.
20	1st Yamamoto Gonnohyōe Cabinet is formed (until April 16, 1914).
March 4	Woodrow Wilson becomes president of United States.
20	United States leaves six-nation China loan consortium.
April 27	Yuan Shikai signs revised loan agreement with five-party consortium.

June 13	Requirement that military ministers be active duty officers is revised.
July 12	2nd Chinese Revolution begins.
August 1	Civil Service Appointment Law is revised.
December 23	Association of Allies of the Constitution is formed with Katō Takaaki as president.

1914

January 23	Shimada Saburō attacks the government over the Siemens Scandal.
March 24	1st Yamamoto Cabinet resigns en masse.
April 16	2nd Ōkuma Shigenobu Cabinet forms (until October 9, 1916).
June 18	Hara Takashi nominated as president of Friends of Constitutional Government.
July 28	Austria declares war on Serbia (First World War starts).
August 23	Japan declares war on Germany.

1915

January 18	Twenty-One Demands are issued in five groups: (1) Shandong Province; (2) Manchuria and Mongolia (extension of the lease for the South Manchuria Railway Zone, the right to own land, etc.); (3) Hanyeping Company; (4) no further division of the Chinese coast; (5) police reforms, the introduction of Japanese advisors, the purchase of Japanese weapons.
March 25	12th House of Representatives election is held (Dōshikai, 153; Seiyūkai, 108; Chūseikai, 33; Kokumintō, 27; Ōkuma Support Organization, 12; Independent, 48).
May 7	Envoy Hioki Eki submits final note on the Twenty-One Demands, which China accepts on the 9th, becoming the Day of National Humiliation in China.
11	America informs Japan that it will not recognize violations of the Open Door and Chinese territorial sovereignty.
25	Treaty on Shandong province and Treaty Concerning Southern Manchuria and Eastern Mongolia are signed.
July 29	Home Minister Ōura Kanetake submits his resignation. Prime Minister Ōkuma and other ministers submit their resignations the following day.
August 10	Foreign Minister Katō and Finance Minister Wakatsuki resign; Prime Minister Ōkuma remains and reshuffles cabinet.
October 4	Tanaka Giichi becomes deputy army chief of staff.
December 17	Uehara Yūsaku becomes army chief of staff.
25	3rd Chinese Revolution (National Protection War) begins.

1916

March 7	Cabinet decides on anti-Yuan policy.

June 6	Yuan Shikai dies.
July 3	4th Russo-Japanese Treaty signed.
October 9	Terauchi Masatake Cabinet forms (until September 29, 1918).
10	Constitutional Association party forms.

1917

January 20	Bank of Korea, Bank of Taiwan, and the Industrial Bank of Japan grant a 5 million yen loan to the Bank of Communications (China) (the beginning of the Nishihara Loans).
25	Lower House is dissolved.
March 12	February Revolution breaks out in Russia.
April 6	United States declares war on Germany.
20	13th House of Representatives election is held (Seiyūkai, 165; Kenseikai, 121; Kokumintō, 35; Independents, 60).
June 6	Temporary Advisory Council on Foreign Relations is established.
July 20	Cabinet decides to provide financial support to Duan Qirui Cabinet in China.
August 14	Beijing government declares war on Germany and Austria.
November 2	Ishii-Lansing Agreement is signed.
7	Russian (October) Revolution breaks out.

1918

January 8	U.S. President Wilson announces 14 Points.
March 3	Treaty of Brest-Litovsk is signed between Germany and Russia.
April 23	Gotō Shimpei becomes foreign minister.
May 16	Sino-Japanese Joint Army Defense Agreement is signed (a joint naval agreement is signed on May 19).
July 8	United States proposes joint expedition to Siberia.
August 2	Siberian Expedition is announced.
August 3	Rice riots begin.
September 13	Imperial National Defense Policy is revised.
28	Industrial Bank of Japan and other banks offer the Chinese government a total of 60 million yen in loans (the last Nishihara Loans).
29	Hara Takashi Cabinet forms (until November 13, 1921).
November 11	First World War ends.

1919

January 18	Paris peace talks begin (until June 18).
February 7	Japanese representatives propose a racial equality clause at the peace talks.
March 1	March First Movement begins in Korea.
8	House of Representatives passes a revision to the Elections Law (single-member districts, 3 yen in tax paid as a qualification for voting).

April 12	Kwantung Bureau is established. Hayashi Gonsuke is appointed the first governor.
12	Nomura Ryūtarō becomes president of Mantetsu, and Nishimura Seiichi becomes vice president.
May 4	May Fourth Movement begins in China.
June 10	Crown Prince Hirohito becomes engaged to Princess Nagako.
28	Treaty of Versailles is signed.
August 12	Admiral Saitō Makoto is returned to active duty and appointed governor-general of Korea.
20	Regulations for the offices of the governor-general of Korea and Taiwan are revised.
October 29	Den Kenjirō is named governor-general of Taiwan.

1920

February 11	Demonstration for universal suffrage occur.
26	House of Representatives is dissolved.
May 10	14th Lower House election (Seiyūkai, 278; Kenseikai, 110; Kokumintō, 29; Independents, 47)
May 11	Bankers in America and Japan reach agreement over a new Four-Power Consortium (articles for the consortium are agreed to on October 15).
May 24	122 Japanese soldiers and civilians are killed in Nikolayevsk (the Nikolayevsk Incident).

1921

February 10	Imperial Household ministry announces that there is no change to the crown prince's engagement.
March 3	Crown Prince departs for Europe (returning on September 2).
November 4	Hara Takashi is assassinated (stabbed).
12	Washington Conference begins (until February 6, 1922).
13	Takahashi Korekiya Cabinet forms (until June 12, 1922).
25	Crown Prince regency begins.

1922

February 1	Yamagata Aritomo dies.
6	Washington Naval Treaty and Nine-Power Treaty on China are signed at the Washington Naval Conference.
April 28	First Zhili-Fengtian War begins.
June 6	Takahashi Korekiyo Cabinet resigns en masse.
12	Katō Tomosaburō Cabinet forms (until September 2, 1923).
July 4	Plan for the reduction of the army announced (Yamanashi Reduction).
15	Japan Communist Party formed illegally.
November 8	Inukai Tsuyoshi and others form Progressive Club.

1923

August 26	Katō Tomosaburō Cabinet resigns en masse.
September 1	Great Kantō Earthquake occurs; on 2nd, rumors of Korean riots lead to mass murder of Koreans in Japan.
2	2nd Yamamoto Gonnohyōe Cabinet forms (until January 7, 1924).
December 27	Toranomon Incident occurs; 2nd Yamamoto Cabinet resigns en masse.

1924

January 7	Kiyoura Keigo Cabinet forms (until June 11).
10	Seiyūkai, Kenseikai, and Kakushin Club begin their effort to bring down the Kiyoura government (2nd Movement to Defend the Constitution).
16	Seiyūkai splits into the Seiyūkai and the True Seiyūkai.
20	First United Front formed in China.
May 10	15th House of Representatives election is held (Kenseikai, 151; True Seiyūkai, 109; Seiyūkai, 105; Kakushin Club, 30; Independents, 69).
15	U.S. Senate passes the Immigration Act of 1924.
June 7	Kiyoura Cabinet resigns en masse.
11	1st Katō Takaaki Cabinet forms (supported by the three parties that opposed Kiyoura; lasts until August 2, 1925).
16	Sun Yat-sen appoints Chiang Kai-shek as head of the Whampoa Military Academy and Zhou Enlai as the director of its political department.
September 18	2nd Zhili-Fengtian War begins.

1925

January 20	Soviet-Japanese Basic Convention is signed.
March 29	Universal Suffrage Law is passed.
April 13	Tanaka Giichi becomes president of Friends of Constitutional Government.
22	Peace Preservation Law is promulgated.
May 10	Progressive Club and Friends of Constitutional Government decide to merge.
July 31	1st Katō Cabinet resigns en masse due to inability to agree.
August 2	2nd Katō Takaaki Cabinet forms (until January 30, 1926).
October 20	Pak Yol incident occurs.

1926

January 28	Katō Takaaki dies; cabinet resigns en masse.
30	1st Wakatsuki Reijirō Cabinet forms (until April 20, 1927).
February 28	Matsushima Prostitution Quarter corruption scandal exposed.

July 9	Chiang Kai-shek begins Northern Expedition.
December 25	Taishō Emperor dies; era name changes to Shōwa.

1927

March 15	Run on Tokyo Watanabe Bank takes place; financial panic begins.
24	Nanjing Incident.
April 3	Hankou Incident.
12	Chiang Kai-shek launches anti-Communist coup in Shanghai (Shanghai Massacre).
17	1st Wakatsuki Cabinet resigns en masse.
20	Tanaka Giichi Cabinet forms (until July 2, 1929).
22	Three-week moratorium ordered in response to the financial panic.
May 28	1st Shandong Expedition.
June 1	Kenseikai and True Seiyūkai merge to form the Rikken Minseitō; Hamaguchi Osachi becomes party president.
27	Far East Conference is held.
December 1	Comintern thesis attacking the Japan Communist Party is issued.

1928

February 20	16th House of Representatives (first general) election held (Seiyūkai, 217; Minseitō, 216; Proletariat Factions, 8; Jitsugyō Dōshikai, 4; Reform Party, 3; others, 18).
March 15	Mass arrests of Communists across the country.
April 19	Second Shandong Expedition.
May 3	Northern Expeditionary Army clashes with the Japanese army (Jinan Incident).
June 4	Zhang Zuolin assassinated.
August 27	Kellogg-Briand Pact is signed in Paris.
October 1	Soviet Union begins its first Five-Year Plan

1929

May 19	Midlevel army officers form the Issekikai.
June 3	Government recognizes the Republic of China.
15	Sino-Russian conflict breaks out over the Chinese Eastern Railway.
July 2	Tanaka Cabinet resigns en masse.
2	Hamaguchi Osachi Cabinet forms (until April 14, 1931).
October 24	New York Stock Market crashes; Great Depression begins.
November 21	Finance ministry lifts the gold embargo.

1930

January 11	Ban on the export of gold is lifted.
21	London Naval Conference opens.

February 20	17th House of Representatives election is held (Minseitō, 273; Seiyūkai, 174; Kokumin Dōshisha, 6; Proletariat Factions, 5; Reform Party, 3; Others, 5).
April 22	London Naval Treaty is signed.
25	Seiyūkai attacks the government for violating the emperor's prerogative of supreme command.
June 17	Smoot-Hawley Tariff is enacted in the United States.
October 27	Musha Incident occurs in Taiwan.
November 14	Prime Minister Hamaguchi Osachi is shot and severely wounded by Sagoya Tomeo at Tokyo Station.

1931

January 23	Matsuoka Yōsuke deploys his Manchuria and Mongolia lifeline theory in the House of Representatives.
March 20	Hashimoto Kingorō and others launch a failed coup attempt (March Incident).
April 13	Hamaguchi Cabinet resigns en masse.
14	2nd Wakatsuki Reijirō Cabinet forms (until December 13).
September 18	Liutiahu Incident (Manchurian Incident begins).
October 17	Hashimoto Kingorō and others launch a failed coup attempt (the October Incident).
December 11	2nd Wakatsuki Cabinet resigns en masse.
13	Inukai Tsuyoshi Cabinet forms (until May 26, 1932); ban on the export of gold is reestablished.

1932

January 7	Stimson Doctrine.
28	Shanghai Incident.
February 9	Former finance minister Inoue Junnosuke is assassinated by members of the League of Blood.
20	18th House of Representatives election is held (Seiyūkai, 301; Minseitō, 146; Proletariat Factions, 5).
29	Lytton Commission begins investigation.
March 1	Manchukuo is created.
5	Mitsui Holding Company Director-General Dan Takuma is assassinated by members of the League of Blood.
May 15	Prime Minister Inukai is assassinated (shot) (May 15 Incident).
26	Saitō Makoto Cabinet forms (until July 8, 1934).
August 25	Foreign Minister Uchida Kōsai gives "scorched homeland diplomacy" speech.
September 15	Government signs the Japan-Manchukuo Protocol, recognizing Manchukuo.
October 2	Foreign Ministry announces Lytton Commission report.
November 4	Soviet Union proposes nonaggression pact with Japan.
8	Franklin D. Roosevelt wins U.S. presidential election.

1933

January 30	Hitler becomes prime minister in Germany.
February 23	Operation Nekka begins.
24	League of Nations Assembly adopts Lytton Report 42–1, with 1 abstention; Matsuoka Yōsuke leaves Assembly.
March 27	Japan announces its withdrawal from the League of Nations.
May 2	Soviet Union proposes selling the Chinese Eastern Railway to Japan.
31	Tanggu Truce is signed.
September 14	Hirota Kōki becomes foreign minister.
October 3	Fiver Ministers Conference held to coordinate defense, foreign, and financial policy.

1934

January 23	Army Minister Araki Sadao resigns, replaced by Hayashi Senjūrō.
February 21	Foreign Minister Hirota sends message to Secretary of State Cordell Hull.
April 17	Amō Eiji, head of the foreign minister's information bureau, makes the Amō Statement.
July 3	Saitō Cabinet resigns en masse due to Teijin Scandal.
8	Okada Keisuke Cabinet forms (until March 9, 1936).
November 27	Finance Minister Fujii Sadanobu resigns, succeeded by Takahashi Korekiyo.
December 29	Japan informs United States of unilateral abrogation of Washington Treaty.

1935

January 21	Agreement reached between the USSR and Manchukuo over the transfer of the North Manchuria Railway.
February 18	Kikuchi Takeo criticizes Minobe Tatsukichi in the House of Peers (Organ Theory of the Emperor Incident).
May 17	Japan and China raise the status of their legations to embassies.
June 10	He-Umezu Agreement is signed.
27	Qin-Doihara Agreement is signed.
July 16	Mazaki Jinzaburō is dismissed as inspector general of military education.
August 12	Military Affairs Bureau Chief Nagata Tetsuzan is assassinated by Lieutenant Colonel Aizawa Saburō.
November 9	Foreign Ministry unofficially states that it is opposed to Chinese currency reform.
25	East Hebei Autonomous Council established as a demilitarized area south of the Great Wall (Yin Ju-keng serves as chairman).
December 18	Hebei-Chahar Political Council is established in Beijing (Song Zheyuan serves as chairman).

1936

January 13	1st Outline for Dealing with North China: policy of promoting the separation of five provinces from northern China is adopted.
21	Foreign Minister Hirota explains the three principles of China policy in the Diet (Sino-Japanese cooperation, recognition of Manchukuo, mutual defense against Communism).
February 20	19th House of Representatives election is held (Minsei, 205; Seiyūkai, 171; Shōwakai, 22; Shakai Taishūtō, 18; Kokumin Dōmei, 15; neutral and others, 35)
26	Approximately 1,500 soldiers and Kōdō-ha officers from the 1st and 3rd Infantry Regiments attack the Prime Minister's Residence, police headquarters, and the residences of ministers. Lord Keeper of the Privy Seal Saitō Makoto, Finance Minister Takahashi Korekiyo, Inspector General of Military Education Watanabe Jōtarō are killed (the February 26 Incident). Rebels surrender on February 29.
March 9	Hirota Kōki Cabinet forms (until February 2, 1937). Foreign Minister Baba Eiichi announces that he is ending the gradual reduction of government bonds.
April 2	Arita Hachirō becomes foreign minister.
May 18	Requirement that military ministers be active duty generals and admirals is restored.
June 8	Third revision of the Imperial National Defense Policy and Strategic Summary. Targeted at America and the Soviet Union, it envisions a military consisting of 50 army divisions, 142 air squadrons, 12 battleships, 12 aircraft carriers, among other units.
July 17	Civil War in Spain begins.
August 1	Berlin Olympics begins (until August 16).
7	Imperial Diplomatic Policy and The Fundamentals of National Policy are adopted at the Five-Ministers Conference (key points include strengthening of the military, expansion on the continent and to the south).
November 14	Inner Mongolian Army advances into Suiyuan with the support of the Kwantung Army but is defeated by the Chinese on November 23.
25	Anti-Comintern Pact is signed by Germany and Japan.
27	1937 budget approved by the cabinet (3.4 billion yen, of which 1.4 billion is for military expenditures).
December 12	Xian Incident.
31	Washington Naval Treaty expires.

1937

January 21	Seiyūkai Diet Member Hamada Kunimatsu has the so-called *seppuku* exchange with War Minister Terauchi Hisaichi.
23	Hirota Cabinet resigns en masse.

25	Emperor orders Ugaki Kazushige to form a government (withdrawn on January 29).
February 2	Hayashi Senjūrō Cabinet forms (until June 4).
March 3	Satō Naotake becomes foreign minister.
31	House of Representatives is dissolved immediately after passing the budget.
April 30	20th House of Representatives election is held (Minseitō, 179; Seiyūkai, 175; Shakai Taishūtō, 37; Shōwakai, 19; Kokumin Dōmei, 11; Tōhōkai, 11; Japan Proletarian Party, 1; Others 33).
May 31	Hayashi Cabinet resigns en msse.
June 4	1st Konoe Fumimaro Cabinet forms (until January 5, 1939).
July 7	Marco Polo Bridge Incident occurs (start of Sino-Japanese War).
27	Three divisions in Japan are ordered to northern China.
August 13	Cabinet decides to dispatch the army to Shanghai.
October 5	U.S. President Roosevelt gives the Quarantine Speech in Chicago.
25	Planning Board is created.
November 2	Foreign Minister Hirota tells German Ambassador to Japan von Dirksen the Japanese requirements for peace; these are conveyed to German Ambassador to China Trautmann, who informs Chiang Kai-shek on November 5. (Trautmann's efforts toward peace begin.)
3	Nine Power Treaty Conference held in Brussels (until November 15).
December 12	Navy aircraft sink USS *Panay* on the Yangtze River near Nanjing. HMS *Ladybird* comes under fire from Japanese army artillery.
13	Nanjing is occupied and Nanjing Incident occurs.

1938

January 16	1st Konoe Statement (Japan "would no longer negotiate with the Kuomintang government").
March 3	Lieutenant Colonel Satō Kenryō tells a Diet member to "Shut up!" while testifying in the Diet.
23	Nishio Suehiro expelled from the Diet.
April 1	National Mobilization Law is enacted.
6	Electricity Control Law is enacted.
May 12	Germany officially recognizes Manchukuo.
26	Reorganization of the Konoe cabinet (Ugaki becomes foreign minister, Ikeda Shigeaki becomes finance minister and minister of commerce and industry, and Araki Sadao becomes education minister).
June 3	Itagaki Seishirō becomes war minister.
July 11	Prelude to Battle of Lake Khasan begins, and hostilities break out on July 31.
26	Talks between Foreign Minister Ugaki and British Ambassador Craigie begin.

September 29	Britain, Germany, France, and Italy agree to cede the Sudetenland to Germany (the Munich Agreement).
30	Foreign Minister Ugaki resigns in opposition to the establishment of a central government organ for dealing with China (the Asian Development Board).
October 27	Japanese army takes Wuhan.
November 3	2nd Konoe Statement ("Japan's purpose for the war was the construction of a new order ensuring the eternal stability of East Asia").
December 20	Wang Jingwei escapes Chongqing and lands in Hanoi. He announces his desire for peace with the Japanese on December 30.
22	3rd Konoe Statement, in which he outlines the Three Konoe Principles for correcting Sino-Japanese relations (neighborly friendship, joint defense against Communism, economic cooperation).

1939

January 5	Hiranuma Kiichirō Cabinet forms (until August 30).
May 12	Battles of Khalkhin Gol takes place; ceasefire is agreed to on September 15.
June 14	British and French concessions in Tianjin are blockaded.
July 26	American annuls the U.S.-Japan Treaty of Commerce and Navigation (it loses effect on January 26, 1940).
August 23	Molotov-Ribbentrop Pact is signed.
28	Hiranuma Cabinet resigns en masse, with Hiranuma stating that the European situation was "complicated and puzzling."
30	Abe Nobuyuki Cabinet forms (until January 16, 1940).
September 1	Germany begins its invasion of Poland (beginning of the Second World War; Britain and France declare war on Germany on September 3; America declares neutrality on September 5; Warsaw falls on September 27).
25	Nomura Kisaburō becomes foreign minister.
November 4	Foreign Minister Nomura proposes a provisional U.S.-Japan Treaty of Commerce and Navigation; United States refuses, on December 22.
30	Winter War begins; the Soviet Union is expelled from the League of Nations on December 14.
December 26	Office of the Governor-General of Korea begins its policy of pressuring Koreans to adopt Japanese names.

1940

January 14	Abe Cabinet resigns en masse.
16	Yonai Mitsumasa Cabinet forms (until July 22).
February 2	Saitō Takao of the Minseitō gives an antimilitary speech (he is expelled from the House of Representatives on March 7).
March 30	Wang Jingwei establishes Republic of China in Nanjing.

April 9	Wehrmacht begins its invasion of Norway and Denmark.
May 10	Wehrmacht invades Belgium, the Netherlands, and northern France.
June 12	Japan-Thailand Friendship Treaty is signed.
14	Paris surrenders to the Wehrmacht without fighting.
24	Konoe Fumimaro resigns as president of the Privy Council and announces his determination to promote the New Order Movement.
July 6	Socialist Masses Party dissolves.
16	Yonai Cabinet resigns en masse due to Army Minister Hata Shunroku's resignation.
16	Friends of Constitutional Government Kuwahara Faction is dissolved.
22	2nd Konoe Fumimaro Cabinet forms (Tōjō Hideki joins as army minister and Matsuoka Yōsuke as foreign minister, until July 18, 1941).
26	Government adopts its Basic Outline of National Policy (construction of a new order in East Asia and the establishment of a national defense state).
27	Government-Imperial Headquarters Liaison Conference adopts the Principles with Regard to the Current Direction in World Affairs (management of the Sino-Japanese War, strengthening of the Axis, strengthening Japanese bases in French Indochina, securing important resources in southern Indochina, etc.). Southern expansion is adopted as national policy.
30	Friends of Constitutional Government Nakajima Faction is dissolved.
August 15	Constitutional Democratic Party is dissolved.
30	Matsuoka-Henry Agreement is reached concerning the stationing of Japanese forces in northern Indochina.
September 23	Invasion of northern French Indochina begins.
27	Tripartite Pact is signed.
28	America prohibits the export of scrap iron to Japan.
October 12	Imperial Rule Assistance Association forms.
November 5	Roosevelt is elected president of United States for third time.
December 29	Roosevelt declares that the United States would become the Arsenal of Democracy.

1941

April 13	Soviet-Japanese Neutrality Pact is signed.
16	Government decides to begin negotiations with the United States with the draft proposal for a U.S.-Japan understanding serving as its base position.
May 31	U.S. Secretary of State Hull calls for the honoring of four principles: (1) respect for territorial integrity and sovereignty of each

	and all nations; (2) support for the principle of non-interference in the internal affairs of other countries; (3) support of the principle of equality including equality of commercial opportunity; and (4) nondisturbance of the status quo in the Pacific
June 22	Wehrmacht begins its invasion of the Soviet Union.
25	Imperial General Headquarters Government Liaison Group decides on matter regarding policy to advance south, begins move to occupy Southern French Indochina on July 28.
July 2	Imperial Council approves Outline of Imperial Policy following Changes in Circumstances (preparing for war with Soviet Union, possibility of war with Britain and America); Imperial General Headquarters decides to send an additional 700,000 troops to Manchuria nominally for a special exercise.
16	2nd Konoe Cabinet resigns en masse.
18	3rd Konoe Fumimaro Cabinet forms (foreign minister changes from Matsuoka to Toyoda Sadajirō, until October 18).
25	U.S. government freezes Japanese assets in United States.
August 1	U.S. government embargoes fuel for generators and lubricants for airplanes (all U.S. petroleum exports to Japan stopped).
7	Foreign Minister Toyoda directs Ambassador Nomura to suggest to Roosevelt a meeting with Konoe.
September 6	Imperial Council decides on Guideline for the Execution of Imperial Policy (with mid-October deadline for diplomatic negotiations with the United States and date for completion of war preparations for end of October).
October 16	3rd Konoe Cabinet resigns en masse.
18	Tōjō Hideki Cabinet forms (with Tōjō serving as prime minister, army minister, and home minister, and Tōgō Shigenori as foreign minister, until July 22).
November 5	Imperial Council decides on start of use of force for beginning of December.
7	Nomura and Special Envoy Kurusu present Draft A to Secretary of State Hull.
20	Nomura and Special Envoy Kurusu present Draft B to Secretary of State Hull.
26	Hull Note is delivered, demanding Japanese military withdrawal from China.
December 1	Imperial Council decides on war with the United States, Britain, and Holland.
8	Japan invades Malay Peninsula, attacks Pearl Harbor; war is declared.

1942

January 2	Manila is occupied.
February 15	British forces in Singapore surrender.
March 9	Dutch forces in Java surrender.

April 30	21st House of Representatives election is held (Imperial Rule Assistance Political Association candidates, 381; noncandidates, 85).
May 1	Mandalay in northern Burma is occupied; first stage of southern campaign finishes.
June 5	Battle of Midway begins (until 7th).
August 8	1st Battle of Solomon Sea (Savo); 2nd begins on 24th

1943

April 18	Combined Fleet Commander-in-Chief Yamamoto Isoroku killed when his plane is attacked near Solomon Islands.
May 31	Imperial Council decides to annex Indonesia, Malay, and other areas, while granting independence to the Philippines and Burma.
September 8	Italy surrenders unconditionally.
30	Imperial Council decides on absolute defense area.
October 21	Induction Ceremony is held at Meiji Jingu Gaien Stadium for students entering military.
November 5	Greater East Asia Conference held with representatives from Japan, Manchukuo, Thailand, Philippines, Burma, and China (Wang Jingwei regime).
22	Churchill, Roosevelt, and Chiang Kai-shek meet in Cairo (until 26th, with Cairo Declaration announced on December 1).

1944

February 21	Prime Minister (and Army Minister) Tōjō becomes Chief of the Army General Staff.
June 6	Allied forces invade Normandy.
15	U.S. forces land in Saipan (until July 7, when Japanese defenders die "honorable deaths").
19	Battle of the Philippine Sea plays out.
July 1	Bretton Woods Conference begins (until July 22).
18	Tōjō Cabinet resigns en masse.
22	Koiso Kuniaki Cabinet forms (until April 7, 1945).
August 21	Dumbarton Oaks Conference begins (until October 7; United Nations Charter draft is announced on October 9).
October 24	Battle of Leyte Gulf leads to near destruction of Japanese Combined Fleet.
November 7	Roosevelt is elected for fourth term as president of the United States.
24	Approximately seventy B-29s from Marianas base begin bombing Tokyo; attacks on mainland Japan begin in earnest.

1945

February 4	Roosevelt, Churchill, and Stalin meet for Yalta Conference (until February 11).

March 9	Tokyo Fire Bombing starts and continues until the 10th; more than 80,000 are killed.
April 1	U.S. military lands on Okinawa (until June 23); Japanese military is destroyed.
5	Soviet Union informs Japan of nonextension of neutrality pact.
7	Suzuki Kantarō Cabinet forms (until August 17).
12	Roosevelt dies; Vice President Harry S. Truman succeeds him.
25	United Nations conference in San Francisco held; June 26 UN Charter is signed.
May 7	German military surrenders (surrender signed on 8th).
14	Members of Supreme Council for the Direction of the War meet and decide to seek an ending of the war.
June 8	Supreme Council for the Direction of the War decides on last stand.
July 16	United States succeeds in testing atomic bomb.
17	Truman, Churchill, and Stalin meet for Potsdam Conference (until August 2).
26	Potsdam Declaration announced (July 28, Prime Minister Suzuki ignores declaration, announces continued prosecution of war).
August 6	Atomic bomb is dropped on Hiroshima.
9	Soviet Union announces early morning declaration of war on Japan, invading Manchuria.
9	Atomic bomb is dropped on Nagasaki.
14	Sino-Soviet Treaty of Friendship and Alliance is signed.
14	Imperial Council is held and decision is made to accept terms of Potsdam Declaration (announced by radio on August 15).
17	Higashikuni Naruhiko Cabinet formed (until October 9).
28	Advance team of Occupation Forces arrive at Atsugi Air Field; Supreme Commander of the Allied Forces Douglas MacArthur arrives on August 30.
September 2	Instrument of Surrender is signed on USS *Missouri*.
11	GHQ orders arrest of thirty-nine war criminals, including Tōjō Hideki.
22	U.S. government announces Initial Post-Surrender Policy for Japan.
27	Emperor calls on MacArthur.
October 4	GHQ announces Civil Rights Directive.
4	MacArthur meets with Konoe Fumimaro (who, on 11th, becomes Imperial Appointee for Office of the Privy Seal).
5	Higashikuni Cabinet resigns en masse.
9	Shidehara Kijūrō Cabinet forms (until May 22, 1946).
11	MacArthur orders Shidehara to institute five major democratic reforms.
November 2	Japan Socialist Party is formed, Japan Liberal Party is formed on 9th, and Japan Progressive Party is formed on 16th.
6	GHQ issues order to break up business conglomerates.

20	Nuremburg Military Tribunal begins (until October 1, 1946).
December 6	GHQ issues arrest warrants for Konoe Fumimaro, Kido Kōichi, and others. Konoe commits suicide on 16th.
7	Allied Reparations Committee Pauley issues interim reparations plan.
9	Memorandum on agrarian land reform prepared (29th, first agrarian land reforms begin).
17	House of Representatives election law is revised.
18	House of Representatives is dissolved (with new election planned for January).

1946

January 1	Emperor's Declaration of Humanity is issued.
4	Purge begins of more than 1,000 officials and politicians (260 of 274 Progressive Party members, 30 of 43 Liberal Party members, 10 of 17 Socialist Party members); within cabinet, only Shidehara, Yoshida, and Ashida were untouched.
22	International Military Tribunal of the Far East (Tokyo War Crimes Trials) is announced.
24	Shidehara meets with MacArthur.
February 1	*Mainichi Shimbun* scoop comes out on Matsumoto Committee draft constitution.
3	MacArthur issues three principles on future constitution; GHQ begins preparing draft in secret, completed on 10th. Shown to Japanese on 13th.
22	Japanese government accepts GHQ draft on 22nd, completing translation on March 2. Negotiations and agreement conducted on 4th–5th.
March 5	Former British Prime Minister Winston Churchill gives Iron Curtain speech in Fulton.
6	Constitutional draft is made public as Japanese government draft.
April 10	22nd House of Representatives election is held Liberal Party; Progressive Party, 94; Japan Socialist Party (JSP), 93; Japan Cooperative Party (Coop), 14; Japan Communist Party (JCP), 5; other parties, 38; unaffiliated, 81).
22	Shidehara Cabinet resigns en masse.
May 1	May Day demonstrations for food break out.
3	Tokyo War Crimes Trials begin.
4	Hatoyama Ichirō purged from office, with Yoshida Shigeru beginning as Liberal Party president on 14th.
22	1st Yoshida Shigeru Cabinet forms (until May 24, 1947).
June 18	U.S. Prosecutor Joseph B. Keenan for Tokyo War Crimes Trials explains in Washington he will not seek prosecution of emperor.
20	Constitutional draft submitted to Imperial Diet (previously approved on 8th by Privy Council).
July 29	Ashida Revision.

August 24	House of Representatives approves constitutional draft (421 to 8).
September 24	MacArthur directs inclusion of article about civilian control.
October 1	Nuremburg International Military Tribunal reaches verdict (twelve to be hung, carried out on 16th).
6	House of Peers approves constitution with revisions (which are approved on 7th by House of Representatives).
November 3	Constitution is promulgated.

1947

January 31	MacArthur orders cancellation of February 1 Strike.
March 12	Truman Doctrine is announced.
31	Japan Democratic Party (JSP) forms, centered around Progressive Party.
April 25	23rd House of Representatives election is held (JSP, 143; Liberal Party, 131; Democratic Party, 124; National Cooperative Party (NCP), 31).
May 3	Japanese Constitution goes into effect.
20	Yoshida Cabinet resigns en masse.
24	Katayama Tetsu Cabinet forms (until March 10, 1948).
June 5	Marshall Plan is announced.
July	George Kennan's X article, "Sources of Soviet Conduct" is released (start of the Containment Doctrine).

1948

January 6	Army Secretary Royall gives speech in San Francisco, calls for Japan to be "deterrent to totalitarianism."
February 26	Kennan visits Japan, recommends change in Occupation policy to MacArthur.
March 10	Ashida Hitoshi Cabinet forms (until October 15).
June 11	U.S. Senate passes Vandenberg Resolution, with recommendations on how to participate in regional mutual security arrangements.
23	Discovery of Shōwa Denkō Scandal (Nishio Suehiro arrested in September/October).
24	Soviet Union blockades Berlin.
August 13	Republic of Korea is established.
September 9	Democratic People's Republic of Korea is established.
October 7	U.S. National Security Council approves NSC 13–2, policy for Japan.
13	Democratic Liberal Party Secretary General Yamasaki Takeshi moves to Democratic Party; rumors increase that he will be named prime minister (14th resigns parliamentary seat).
15	2nd Yoshida Shigeru Cabinet forms (until February 16).

November 12   International Military Tribunal of the Far East hands down guilty verdict on twenty-five defendants; seven (including Tōjō Hideki) are hanged on December 23.

1949

January 23   24th House of Representatives election is held (Democratic Liberal Party, 264; Democratic Party of Japan, 69; JSP, 48; JCP, 35; NCP, 14; etc.)

February 16   3rd Yoshida Shigeru Cabinet forms, including Ikeda Hayato as finance minister (until October 30, 1952).

March 7   Joseph M. Dodge emphasizes curbing inflation (Dodge Line).

October 1   People's Republic of China is founded.

December 7   Kuomintang government relocates capital city from Beijing to Taipei.

1950

January 1   In New Year's Greetings, MacArthur declares that Constitution does not forbid right to self-defense.

February 9   U.S. Senator McCarthy declares that there are Communists in State Department; era of McCarthyism begins.

14   Sino-Soviet Treaty of Friendship, Alliance, and Mutual Assistance is signed.

April 6   U.S. President Truman appoints Dulles as special advisor to State Department in charge of Allied Treaty of Peace with Japan.

June 25   Korean War breaks out.

August 10   National Police Reserves are established.

September 14   President Truman directs start of peace treaty negotiations.

15   UN forces land at Inchon.

October 25   Chinese People's Liberation Army enters war.

December 5   North Korean forces retake Pyongyang.

1951

January 25   Special Ambassador Dulles comes to Japan to discuss peace treaty.

April 11   MacArthur is dismissed.

September 4   San Francisco Peace Conference begins (until September 8).

October 24   Japan Socialist Party splits over Peace Treaty and Japan-U.S. Security Treaty.

26   House of Representatives approves peace treaty.

December 24   Prime Minister Yoshida sends Dulles letter saying that Japan would sign peace treaty with Republic of China.

1952

April 28   San Francisco Peace Treaty goes into effect, sovereignty is restored, and Japan-ROC peace treaty is signed.

August 28	Prime Minister Yoshida suddenly dissolves House of Representatives.
October 1	25th House of Representatives election is held (Japan Liberal Party (JLP), 240; Japan Reform Party (JRP), 85; JSP (Right), 57; JSP (Left), 54; etc.).
30	4th Yoshida Shigeru Cabinet forms (until May 21, 1953).
November 27	International Trade Minister Ikeda Hayato misspeaks, resigning on 29th.

1953

March 14	Prime Minister Yoshida dissolves House of Representatives after calling a parliamentarian an idiot.
April 19	26th House of Representatives election is held (JLP, 199; JRP, 76; JSP (Left), 72; JSP (Right), 66; Hatoyama LP, 35; etc.).
May 21	5th Yoshida Shigeru Cabinet forms (until December 10, 1954).
July 27	Armistice agreement signed in Korea.
October 2	Ikeda-Robertson meeting is held.

1954

April 21	Justice Minister Inukai Takeru exercises Article 14 over Public Prosecutor in order not to arrest Liberal Party Secretary General Satō Eisaku.
November 24	Japan Democratic Party is formed.
December 7	Yoshida Cabinet resigns en masse.
10	1st Hatoyama Ichirō Cabinet forms (until March 19, 1955).

1955

February 27	27th House of Representatives election is held (Japan Democratic Party (JDP), 185; JLP, 112; JSP (Left), 89; JSP (Right), 67; etc.).
March 19	2nd Hatoyama Ichirō Cabinet forms (until November 22).
August 29	Foreign Minister Shigemitsu Mamoru explores security treaty revision with Secretary of State Dulles in Washington and is rebuffed.
October 13	Socialist Party reunites.
November 15	Conservatives merge, establishing Liberal Democratic Party (LDP).
22	3rd Hatoyama Ichirō Cabinet forms (until December 23, 1956).

1956

February 24	Soviet Secretary General Nikita Khruschev criticizes Stalin in speech.
May 9	Japan-Philippines Reparations Treaty is signed.
July 26	Egyptian President Abdel Nasser nationalizes Suez Canal.
October 19	Japan and Soviet Union announce normalization of relations.
23	Hungary uprising breaks out.
December 18	Japan's joining United Nations is approved.

20 Hataoyama Cabinet resigns en masse.
23 Ishibashi Tanzan Cabinet forms (until February 25, 1957, after defeating Kishi Nobusuke in February 14 election for LDP president).

1957

January 30	Girald Incident.
February 25	1st Kishi Nobusuke Cabinet forms (until June 12, 1958).
May 20	Basic Policy on National Defense is decided.
20	Prime Minister Kishi leaves for his first trip to Asia (until June 4).
June 19	Prime Minister Kishi visits United States for summit (releases joint statement with President Dwight D. Eisenhower on June 21).
September 28	First Diplomatic Bluebook by Foreign Ministry is released.
November 18	Prime Minister Kishi leaves for second trip to Asia (until December 8).

1958

May 22	28th House of Representatives election is held (LDP, 287; JSP, 166; etc.).
June 12	2nd Kishi Nobusuke Cabinet forms (July 19, 1960).
December 27	Three cabinet members (Ikeda Hayato, Miki Bukichi, and Nadao Hirokichi) resign in protest over handling of Police Duties Bill.

1959

June 18	Kishi Cabinet is reshuffled; Ikeda Hayato rejoins cabinet.

1960

January 19	New Japan-U.S. security treaty signed in Washington, D.C.
24	Democratic Socialist Party of Japan forms.
May 19	New security treaty approved in House of Representatives by forced vote, amid boycotts and increased demonstrations.
June 16	President Eisenhower's trip to Japan postponed.
19	New security treaty approved (lack of action by House of Councilors).
23	Prime Minister Kishi resigns.
July 14	LDP presidential election, Ikeda Hayato defeats Ishii Mitsujirō and Fujiyama Aiichirō (Ōno Bamboku did not run).
19	1st Ikeda Hayato Cabinet forms (until December 8).
October 12	JSP Chairman Asanuma Inajirō is assassinated (stabbed).
November 8	John F. Kennedy is elected president in U.S. election.
20	29th House of Representatives election is held (LDP, 296; JSP, 145; Democratic Socialist Party (DSP), 17; JCP, 3; etc.).
December 8	2nd Ikeda Hayato Cabinet forms (until December 9, 1963).

27   Cabinet decides on Incoming Doubling Plan.

1961

April 19	Edwin O. Reischauer arrives as ambassador to Japan.
June 20–22	Ikeda-Kennedy meeting is held in in Washington, D.C.

1962

May 15	Revised Defense Agency Law promulgated (Defense Facilities Administration Agency created November 1).
October 22	President Kennedy announces blockade of Cuba (Cuba Missile Crisis).
November 4	Prime Minister Ikeda leaves for Europe (until 25th).
12	Foreign Minister Ōhira Masayoshi meets with Kim Jong-pil of Korean CIA.

1963

July 25	Japan provides preliminary signature to Partial Test Ban Treaty.
November 21	30th House of Representatives election is held (LDP, 283; JSP, 144; DSP, 23; JCP, 5; etc.).
December 9	3rd Ikeda Hayato Cabinet forms (until November 9, 1964).

1964

January 27	China and France establish diplomatic relations.
April 1	Japan meets Article 8 condition of International Monetary Fund.
28	Japan joins Organisation for Economic Co-Operation and Development (OECD).
July 10	Ikeda elected for third time as president of LDP.
August 2	Announcement of Tonkin Bay Incident (U.S. retaliates on 4th).
11	Cabinet decides on 1st emergency assistance to South Vietnam of $500,000.
October 15	Soviet Secretary General Khrushchev resigns.
16	China successfully tests its first atomic bomb.
November 9	LDP joint meeting of Upper and Lower House members choose Satō Eisaku as party president.
9	1st Satō Eisaku Cabinet forms (until February 17, 1967).

1965

January 13	Prime Minister Satō visits United States, issues joint statement with President Lyndon B. Johnson.
February 7	United States begins Rolling Thunder, the bombing of North Vietnam.
March 7	United States gets directly involved in Vietnam War, landing in Danang.
June 22	Treaty on Basic Relations between Japan and Republic of Korea is signed.

July 29	U.S. B-52s take off from Okinawa to bomb southeast of Saigon.
August 19	Satō becomes first prime minister to visit Okinawa.
September 30	9.30 Movement occurs in Indonesia (failed coup by Lieutenant Colonel Untung and others).

1966

February 14	Prime Minister Satō permits visit of U.S. nuclear-powered submarine, conditioned upon confirmation of its safety.
19	Government announces unified "nuclear umbrella" position in Lower House budget committee.
May 16	Cultural Revolution begins in China.
December 1	Satō wins reelection against Fujiyama Aiichirō (289–89) in LDP presidential election.

1967

January 29	31st House of Representatives election is held (LDP, 277; JSP, 140; DSP 30; Clean Government Party (CGP), 25; etc.).
February 17	2nd Satō Eisaku Cabinet forms (until January 14, 1970).
April 21	Prime Minister Sato announces three principles on weapons exports in Diet.
June 17	China successfully tests hydrogen bomb.
November 15	Prime Minister Satō meets with President Johnson, issues joint statement agreeing on reversion of Ogasawara Islands and return of Okinawa "within a few years."

1968

January 27	Prime Minister Satō officially announces in policy speech three non-nuclear principles.
March 31	President Johnson announces he will not run for reelection, that he is pausing bombing of North Vietnam, and calls for peace talks.
April 5	Japan and United States sign Ogawara Reversion Agreement (return completed on June 26).
July 1	United States, Britain, and Soviet Union sign Non-Proliferation Treaty (NPT).
August 20	Czechoslovakia Invasion
November 27	Satō wins third LDP presidential election (249 to Miki Takeo's 107, Maeo Shigesaburō, 95).

1969

January 19	Closure of Tokyo University's Yasuda Auditorium ends.
March 10	Prime Minister Satō announces Japan's negotiating stance on Okinawa reversion, "without nuclear weapons, on par with the mainland."
November 17	Prime Satō visits United States and meets with President Nixon on 19th–20th.

21	Satō-Nixon joint statement (continuation of security treaty, agreement to return of administrative rights over Okinawa).
26	Prime Minister Satō states nonacceptance of reintroduction of nuclear weapons based on three non-nuclear principles.
December 27	32nd House of Representatives are held (LDP, 288; JSP, 90; CGP, 47; DSP, 31; JCP, 14; etc.).

1970

January 14	3rd Satō Eisaku Cabinet forms (until July 7, 1972).
February 3	Japan signs NPT.
October 13	China and Canada establish diplomatic relations (followed by Italy on November 6 and Ethiopia on, December 1).
20	First Defense White Paper published.
29	Satō wins fourth term as LDP president (353 to Miki Takeo's 111).
November 25	Mishima Mikio occupies Eastern Army commanding general's office and commits *seppuku*.

1971

April 7	United States and China begin ping-pong diplomacy.
June 17	Okinawa reversion agreement signed.
July 5	3rd reshuffle of Satō Cabinet takes place, with Fukuda Takeo becoming foreign minister and Tanaka Kakuei minister of international trade and industry.
9	U.S. National Security Adviser Henry Kissinger secretly visits China, agrees to presidential visit by May of following year, announced on 15th (First Nixon Shock).
August 15	President Richard M. Nixon takes United States off gold standard, adds 10 percent surcharge on imports (Second Nixon Shock).
September 8	Lin Biao attempts failed coup, dies in airplane crash on 13th while fleeing.
22	Prime Minister Satō decides to jointly propose that both People's Republic of China (PRC) and Republic of China (ROC) represent China in the United Nations (two China policy).
27	Emperor and Empress depart for Europe (until October 14).
October 25	People's Republic of China invited to become member of United Nations, replacing Republic of China on the Security Council.
November 10	U.S. Senate ratifies Okinawa reversion agreement.
24	Lower House approves Okinawa reversion agreement and passes resolution on three non-nuclear principles and base reductions on Okinawa.
December 18	$1 is set at 308 yen (Smithsonian rate).

1972

January 3	Japan-U.S. textile agreement is signed.
February 21	Nixon visits China (until 27th).

May 15	Administrative rights over Okinawa are returned, becoming Okinawa Prefecture.
June 11	Tanaka Kakuei announces *Building a New Japan: A Plan for Remodeling the Archipelago* and publishes it on the 20th. It immediately becomes bestseller.
17	Discovery of Watergate Scandal.
July 4	South Korea and North Korea issue joint statement on peaceful reunification.
5	LDP president Tanaka Kakuei runs in presidential election (in primary contest, Tanaka receives 156 votes; Fukuda Takeo, 150; Ōhira Masayoshi, 101; Miki Takeo, 69; and in final vote, Tanaka receives 282 vs. Fukuda 190).
7	1st Tanaka Kakuei Cabinet forms (with Ōhira as foreign minister and Nakasone as minister of international trade and industry, until December 22).
August 31	Prime Minister Tanaka and President Nixon meet in Hawaii (United States expresses desire for Japan to purchase Tristar).
September 23	Philippine President Ferdinand Marcos announces martial law throughout country.
25	Prime Minister Tanaka and Foreign Minister Ōhira visit China.
29	Sino-Japanese joint statement signed; Foreign Minister Ōhira announces the expiration of the Japanese-Taiwan treaty.
October 17	South Korea President Park Chung-hee orders nationwide martial law, begins "rejuvenated order" on December 27 following passage of new constitution.
December 10	33rd House of Representatives election is held (LDP, 271; JSP, 118; JCP, 38; CGP, 29; DSP, 19; unaffiliated, 14).
22	2nd Tanaka Kakuei Cabinet forms (until December 9, 1974).

1973

January 18	Chinese Premier Zhou Enlai recognizes Japan-U.S. security treaty and U.S. nuclear umbrella over Japan.
27	Vietnam peace accords signed; Nixon announces the end of the Vietnam War on 29th.
February 10	Tokyo Foreign Exchange Market, overwhelmed with selling of dollars, closes and switches to floating exchange rate system on 14th.
August 8	Kim Dae-jung Incident.
September 21	Japan and North Vietnam (Democratic Republic of Vietnam) establish formal diplomatic relations in Paris.
26	Prime Minister Tanaka leaves for trip to Europe, and Soviet Union, holds meeting in Soviet Union for first time on October 8.
October 6	Fourth Middle East War starts.
17	OAPEC decides on reduction of oil production (First Oil Shock).
November 14	Kissinger visits Japan, discusses petroleum problem with Prime Minister Tanaka and Foreign Minister Ōhira.

22   Cabinet supports a change in Middle East policy, agreeing with demand that Israel forces leave all occupied territories.

25   Tanaka reshuffles cabinet, and Fukuda Takeo becomes finance minister.

December 10   Deputy Prime Minister Miki Takeo visits eight countries in Middle East to resolve Oil Crisis.

25   OAPEC decides Japan is a friendly nation and agrees to provide necessary amount of oil for Japan's needs.

1974

January 7   Prime Minister Tanaka travels to Southeast Asia (anti-Japanese demonstration on 9th in Bangkok and anti-Japanese riots in Jakarta on 15th).

July 7   10th House of Councilors elections are held (LDP, 62; JSP, 28; CGP, 14; JCP, 13; DSP, 5; etc.); ruling parties and opposition parties are about equal in strength.

12   Deputy Prime Minister Miki criticizes Prime Minister Tanaka and resigns, followed by Finance Minister Fukuda on 16th.

August 8   President Nixon resigns, with Gerald Ford succeeding him on the 9th.

October 10   Tachibana Takashi publishes investigative article, "Study of Tanaka Kakuei: His Money and Ties," in November issue of *Bungei Shunjū*.

November 18   President Ford visits Japan (first time for a sitting president).

26   Tanaka decides to step down as prime minister.

December 1   LDP Vice President Shiina Etsusaburō chooses Miki Takeo as party president.

9   Miki Takeo Cabinet forms (until December 24, 1976).
   (This year, the actual economic growth rate was −0.5 percent, the first time in the postwar for there to be negative growth. Consumer prices had escalated too, approximately 24.5%.)

1975

April 5   Chiang Kai-shek dies.

30   Saigon government in South Vietnam surrenders, Vietnam War ends.

July 23   Foreign Minister Miyazawa Kiichi visits South Korea, announces final resolution of Kim Dae Jung incident on 24.

August 6   Miki-Ford joint statement (includes reference to importance of Korean security).

September 30   Emperor and empress leave for first trip to United States (until October 14).

November 15   First summit of leaders of developed nations held in Rambouillet, France.

1976

January 8	Zhou Enlai dies.
February 4	U.S. Senate Subcommittee on Multinational Corporations, under the Foreign Relations Committee, discusses Lockheed Company's bribery of foreign officials (Lockheed Scandal).
March 1	Kim Dae Jung calls for national salvation of South Korea, arrested on 10th.
April 13	Pol Pot regime established in Cambodia, genocide begins.
June 25	New Liberal Club (NLC) is formed.
July 2	Socialist Republic of Vietnam proclaimed, following merger of North and South Vietnam.
27	Former Prime Minister Tanaka arrested for Lockheed Affair.
August 2	Japan establishes diplomatic relations with Cambodia.
September 9	Mao Zedong dies, Hua Guofeng becomes Chinese Communist Party Chairman on October 7, and the Gang of Four are arrested on October 12.
October 21	Coordination Council to Support the Party Structure forms within LDP, promoting Deputy Prime Minister Fukuda to succeed Miki.
29	National Defense Program Outline decided.
November 5	Government decides to keep defense budget within 1 percent of GNP.
December 5	34th House of Representatives election is held (LDP, 249; JSP, 123; CGP, 55; DSP, 29; JCP, 17; NLC, 17; etc.).
24	Fukuda Takeo Cabinet forms (until December 7, 1978).

1977

January 20	Jimmy Carter becomes U.S. president.
May 7	Prime Minister Fukuda promises at London Summit that Japan's actual economic growth will reach 6.7 percent.
August	Border conflict breaks out between Cambodia and Vietnam.
6	Prime Minister Fukuda leaves for six countries in Southeast Asia, announcing Fukuda Doctrine in Manila on 18th.
12	Four modernizations (industry, agriculture, national defense, and science and technology) announced at 11th Central Committee of Chinese Communist Party.
November 19	Egyptian President Sadat visits Israel (until November 21).

1978

April 12	Chinese fishing boats assemble in large numbers near Senkaku Islands.
May 11	Defense Agency Director General Kanemaru Shin announces assumption of part of costs of stationing U.S. forces in Japan (so-called sympathy budget).

July 16	At Bonn Summit, Japan announces it will achieve 7 percent economic growth.
August 12	Sino-Japanese Treaty of Peace and Friendship signed.
October 22	Vice Premier of China Deng Xioaping visits Japan, stating on 23rd that "it is understandable if Japan maintains the bilateral alliance with the United States and increases the strength of its Self-Defense Forces."
November 3	Soviet Union and Vietnam sign friendship and cooperation agreement.
26	Prime Minister Fukuda loses to LDP Secretary General Ōhira in party presidential primaries and chooses not to run in final contest on 27th.
December 7	1st Ōhira Masayoshi Cabinet forms (until November 9, 1979).
15	United States and China announce normalization of relations from January 1, 1979.
25	Vietnam invades Cambodia.

1979

January 1	United States and China restore diplomatic relations.
7	Pol Pot regime in Cambodia collapses; Vietnam-supported regime of Heng Samrin is established.
17	Major international oil companies announce reductions on oil exports to Japan (Second Oil Shock).
February 1	Iranian Revolution takes place under direction of Ayatollah Khomeini.
17	China invades Vietnam, and Sino-Vietnamese War begins (until March 16).
April 3	China announces to Soviet Union its abrogation of Sino-Soviet Treaty of Friendship and Alliance.
June 28	5th Summit held in Tokyo. On 29th, countries decide on individual import reduction targets.
October 7	35th House of Representatives election is held (LDP, 248; JSP, 107; CGP, 57; JCP, 39; DSP, 35; NLC, 4; etc.).
26	South Korean President Park Chung-hee is assassinated.
November 4	Iranian students occupy U.S. Embassy in Teheran.
9	2nd Ōhira Masayoshi Cabinet forms (until July 17, 1980).
December 12	Chief of South Korean Defense Security Command Chun Doo-hwan leads coup.
27	Soviet Union military invades Afghanistan.

1980

February 29	Hu Yaobang becomes General Secretary of the Chinese Communist Party; Former Chairman of the People's Republic Liu Shaoqi is rehabilitated.

April 25	U.S. military fails in operation to rescue hostages from embassy in Teheran.
May 16	Socialist Party submits motion of nonconfidence in the Lower House against cabinet; passes due to absence of antimainstream factions of LDP. Lower House is dissolved on 19th.
18	South Korea issues martial law order throughout country. On 21st, students and police clash in what becomes known as the Gwangju Uprising, suppressed by the 27th.
June 12	Prime Minister Ōhira dies suddenly.
22	36th House of Representatives election is held (LDP, 284; JSP, 107; CGP, 33; DSP, 32; JCP, 29; NLC, 12; etc.; independents, 7; etc.). 12th House of Councilors election is held (LDP, 69; JSP, 22; CGP, 12; JCP, 7; DSP, 5; etc.; various factions, 2; independents, 8). LDP wins big in first-ever double elections for Upper and Lower houses.
22	Venice Summit.
July 17	Suzuki Zenkō Cabinet forms (until November 27, 1982).
19	Moscow Olympics begin (Japan, United States, West Germany, China, and others boycott).
September 1	Chun Doo-hwan becomes president of South Korea.
9	Iran-Iraq War begins.
November 4	Ronald W. Reagan wins presidential election in United States.

1981

May 4	Prime Minister Suzuki visits United States (announces Japan-U.S. alliance joint statement on May 8).
16	Foreign Minister Itō Masayoshi resigns over statement controversy.
17	Former American Ambassador Edwin O. Reischer says that nuclear weapons had been on U.S. vessels making port calls.
October 2	U.S. President Reagan announces Strategic Weapons Program.

1982

June 22	Three anti-Vietnam factions sign statement forming Coalition Government of Democratic Kampuchea.
July 11	Internationally recognized exile government for Cambodia is established.
Summer	School textbook problem in Japan (regarding Second World War history).
November 27	1st Nakasone Yasuhiro Cabinet forms (until December 27, 1983).

1983

January 11	Prime Minister Nakasone visits South Korea, meets with President Chun Doo-hwan, agrees to extend $4 billion in economic assistance to South Korea.

19	Prime Minister Nakasone's description of Japan as an "unsinkable aircraft carrier" reported in U.S. press.
March 23	U.S. President Reagan announces Strategic Defense Initiative (SDI).
May 28	Williamsburg Summit begins (until 30th).
August 21	Anti-Marcos Regime politician Benigno Aquino Jr is assassinated.
September 1	Soviet jet shoots down KAL 007 flight near Sakhalin.
December 18	37th House of Representatives election is held (LDP, 250; JSP, 112; CGP, 58; DSP, 38; JCP, 26; NLC, 8; etc.)
December 27	2nd Nakasone Yasuhiro Cabinet forms (until July 22, 1986).

1984

September 6	South Korean President Chun Doo-hwan visits Japan, Emperor states his regret at state dinner about the unfortunate history between the two countries.
November 6	President Reagan reelected with large majority.

1985

January 2	Prime Minister Nakasone visits United States, expresses support for SDI.
31	Prime Minister Nakasone states that it is unlikely that defense budget can remain within 1 percent of GNP.
March 11	Mikhail Gorbachev becomes general secretary of the Soviet Union Communist Party.
August 15	Prime Minister Nakasone officially visits Yasukuni Shrine.
September 22	Finance ministers and Central Bank governors from five developed countries agree on economic policy (Plaza Agreement).
October 15	Secretary General Gorbachev announces Perestroika.
December 12	North Korea joins Non-Proliferation Treaty.

1986

February 25	Corazon Aquino becomes president of the Philippines.
May 4	Tokyo Summit begins (until 6th).
July 6	In double election, 38th House of Representatives election is held (LDP, 300; JSP, 85; CGP, 56; DSP, 26; JCP, 26; NLC, 6; etc.), and 14th House of Councilors election is held (LDP, 72; JSP, 20; CGP, 10; JCP, 9; DSP, 5; etc.).
July 22	3rd Nakasone Yasuhiro Cabinet forms (until November 6, 1987).
28	Gorbachev gives speech in Vladivostok (announces partial withdrawal of forces from Afghanistan and improvement in relations with China).
September 15	Cabinet-level GATT meeting is held (Uruguay Round).
December 30	Draft defense budget goes above 1 percent of GNP.

1987

January 30	Japan and United States sign agreement to increase cost sharing for U.S. Forces Japan (USFJ) by partial assumption of labor costs for Japanese workers employed by USFJ.
June 29	South Korean presidential candidate Roh Tae-woo announces wide-ranging reforms if elected as part of June Democracy Movement.
July 14	Taiwan ends martial law, in place for thirty-eight years since May 1949 (next day, National Security Law goes into effect).
October 2	Japan and United States agree to joint development of New generation jet fighter (FSX).
November 6	Takeshita Noboru Cabinet forms (until June 3, 1989).
29	North Korean terrorists cause KAL Flight 858 to explode in midair.
December 16	Roh Tae-woo elected president of South Korea.

1988

January 13	Taiwan President Chiang Ching-kuo dies, succeeded by then Vice President Lee Teng-hui.
July 5	Recruit Scandal emerges.
23	Maritime Self-Defense Force submarine *Nadashio* crashes into recreational fishing boat.
September 18	Defense Minister and Chief of Staff Saw Maung leads a coup in Burma, starting a military junta.
December 24	Bill proposing consumption tax passes, effective April 1, 1989.

1989

January 7	Shōwa Emperor dies; era name changes to Heisei.
April 5	Vietnam announces unconditional withdrawal from Cambodia.
June 3	Uno Sōsuke Cabinet forms (until August 10).
4	Tiananmen Square incident occurs, with violent repression of protests by students and citizens.
July 23	15th House of Councilors election is held (JSP, 46; LDP, 36; Rengo Party, 11; CGP, 10; JCP, 5; DSP, 3; etc.).
August 10	1st Kaifu Toshiki Cabinet forms (until February 28, 1990).
September 4	Japan-U.S. Structural Impediments Talks begin (interim report announced April 6, 1990).
November 6	1st APEC Cabinet Members meeting held (until 7th); APEC is established.
9	Border between East Germany and West Germany opens (Berlin Wall begins to fall).
December 2	U.S. President Bush and Secretary General Gorbachev meet on Malta, declaring end to Cold War the next day (3rd).

Sources

Iwanami, Shoten Henshūbuhen. *Kindai Nihon Sōgō Nenpyō* (Comprehensive Chronology of Modern Japan), 4th ed. (Tokyo: Iwanami Shoten, 2001).

Katō Yūkō, Seno Seiichirō, Toriumi Yasushi, and Maruyama Yōsei, eds. *Nihonshi Sōgō Nenpyō* (Comprehensive Chronology on Japanese History) (Tokyo: Yoshikawa Kōbunkan, 2001).

Gaimushō Gaikō Shiryōkan, and Gaikōshi Jiten Hensan Iinkaihen. *Shinpan Nihon Gaikōshi Jiten* (New Japanese Diplomatic History Dictionary) (Tokyo: Yamakawa Shuppansha, 1992).

Index

Note: Page numbers for figures are in *italics*, and page numbers for tables are in **bold**.